AF725575

JUSTICE, MERCY, AND CAPRICE

CLARENDON STUDIES IN CRIMINOLOGY

Published under the auspices of the Institute of Criminology, University of Cambridge; the Mannheim Centre, London School of Economics; and the Centre for Criminology, University of Oxford.

General Editors: Loraine Gelsthorpe and Kyle Treiber
(University of Cambridge)

Editors: Alison Liebling
(University of Cambridge)

Tim Newburn, Jill Peay, Coretta Phillips, and Robert Reiner
(London School of Economics)

Mary Bosworth, Carolyn Hoyle, Ian Loader, and Lucia Zedner
(University of Oxford)

RECENT TITLES IN THIS SERIES:

Young Criminal Lives: Life Courses and Life Chances from 1850
Godfrey, Cox, Shore, and Alker

The Chinese Mafia: Organized Crime, Corruption, and Extra-Legal Protection
Wang

Dirty Money: On Financial Delinquency
Ruggiero

Reinventing Punishment: A Comparative History of Criminology and Penology in the Nineteenth and Twentieth Centuries
Pifferi

Taking Care of Business: Police Detectives, Drug Law Enforcement and Proactive Investigation
Bacon

The Politics of Police Detention in Japan: Consensus of Convenience
Croydon

Justice, Mercy, and Caprice

Clemency and the Death Penalty in Ireland

IAN O'DONNELL

OXFORD
UNIVERSITY PRESS

OXFORD
UNIVERSITY PRESS

Great Clarendon Street, Oxford, OX2 6DP,
United Kingdom

Oxford University Press is a department of the University of Oxford. It furthers the University's objective of excellence in research, scholarship, and education by publishing worldwide. Oxford is a registered trade mark of Oxford University Press in the UK and in certain other countries

© Ian O'Donnell 2017

The moral rights of the author have been asserted

First Edition published in 2017

All rights reserved. No part of this publication may be reproduced, stored in a retrieval system, or transmitted, in any form or by any means, without the prior permission in writing of Oxford University Press, or as expressly permitted by law, by licence or under terms agreed with the appropriate reprographics rights organization. Enquiries concerning reproduction outside the scope of the above should be sent to the Rights Department, Oxford University Press, at the address above

You must not circulate this work in any other form
and you must impose this same condition on any acquirer

Crown copyright material is reproduced under Class Licence Number C01P0000148 with the permission of OPSI and the Queen's Printer for Scotland

Published in the United States of America by Oxford University Press
198 Madison Avenue, New York, NY 10016, United States of America

British Library Cataloguing in Publication Data
Data available

Library of Congress Control Number: 2017950104

ISBN 978–0–19–879847–7

Links to third party websites are provided by Oxford in good faith and for information only. Oxford disclaims any responsibility for the materials contained in any third party website referenced in this work.

... the gallows is not merely a machine of death, but the oldest and most obscene symbol of that tendency in mankind which drives it towards moral self-destruction.

Arthur Koestler, *Reflections on Hanging,* 1956

General Editors' Introduction

The Clarendon Studies in Criminology series aims to provide a forum for outstanding theoretical and empirical work in all aspects of criminology and criminal justice, broadly understood. The Editors welcome submissions from established scholars, as well as excellent PhD work. The Series was inaugurated in 1994, with Roger Hood as its first General Editor, following discussions between Oxford University Press and three criminology centres. It is edited under the auspices of these three centres: the Institute of Criminology at the University of Cambridge, the Mannheim Centre for Criminology at the London School of Economics, and the Centre for Criminological Research at the University of Oxford. Each supplies members of the Editorial Board and, in turn, the Series Editor or Editors.

Ian O'Donnell offers a close examination of the decision to grant clemency to men and women sentenced to death during the almost seven decades between the end of the civil war in 1923 and the abolition of capital punishment in 1990. Notwithstanding an important referendum in 2001 with overwhelming public approval to the Constitutions that removed all references to capital punishment, the final link with the practice was not severed until December 2015 when the last men sentenced to death were released from prison, having served thirty years of their commuted life sentences. This book reflects painstaking and sensitive exploration of closed prisoner files that were made available (on request) by the Department of Justice and Equality as well as documents held by the Department of the Taoiseach (Prime Minister), the Office of the Attorney General, and the Office of the Secretary to the President. Court of Criminal Appeal and Supreme Court judgments are also considered where the imposition of the death penalty triggered legal challenges. Leaving no stone unturned, Ian O'Donnell also examined a small number of relevant files held by the Department of Foreign Affairs, as well as reading the record books of the Central Criminal Court, the venue for all murder trials and contemporaneous newspaper reports and other miscellaneous archival material. He also interviewed a small number of people, including two men sentenced to death, but spared.

The book offers an incisive and compelling account of the exercise of discretion. The ninety-eight men and women sentenced to death during the period of 1923–1990, whose convictions were all upheld on appeal, faced uncertain justice. The government was faced with a stark choice, whether or not to allow the law to take its course or to exercise mercy. In thirty-five cases the ultimate penalty was exacted and in sixty-three cases the Governor General (and later the President) was advised by the government of the day to commute the sentence to penal servitude for life. The latter group forms the substance of this book.

What we are offered is a richly-textured empirical account of an aspect of discretion that has hitherto escaped attention. But *Justice, Mercy, and Caprice* is so much more than an empirical study of an aspect of criminal justice system decision-making. The book addresses important issues of law and penology and in this sense the book is of huge relevance for countries which continue to employ capital punishment. Indeed, while the primary focus here is on Ireland, there is little doubt that the matters under consideration will be of relevance to academics and researchers across the common law world where the processes under consideration share many similarities. The book reveals the inevitable tensions between justice and mercy, fairness and harsh justice, discretion and desert.

Close scrutiny of cases reveals how the state chose to spare some men—and nearly all the women—from the noose or the firing party, but how and why some of those convicted were spared and others were not defies uniform explanation. O'Donnell surgically examines different cases to illuminate the extent to which the clemency process can be understood as an attempt to achieve justice in a criminal justice process that allowed only one penalty—death—to be imposed on convicted murderers. He also examines the contributions of jury, judge and cabinet to the decision-making process and how the latter responded to lobbying.

In some instances the decision-making appears to have been capricious, government having been swayed by entreaties of a local or national respected figure, in other cases the result of political machinations. That so many women were spared the gallows in seeming acts of chivalry does not indicate always particular mercy, especially as some of those women lived out their days coercively confined in religious houses. Decision-making in regard to mental abnormality or instability seemed tied to interpretations of complex family configurations and dynamics, decision-makers being swayed by family histories of 'mental defection' but in other cases not. That someone's fate could depend on such imprecise interpretation, subjective judgement and other vicissitudes of criminal justice processes is telling of the making and unmaking of justice.

This is a fine and impressive book in which O'Donnell gives us a colourful and gripping sense of the life and death manoeuvres of those in power in the courts, in government, and in the community. As General Editors, we think that Ian O'Donnell's book makes very significant contribution to criminal justice history and to our understanding of the gradual emergence of a more humane Irish state. We warmly welcome *Justice, Mercy, and Caprice: Clemency and the Death Penalty in Ireland* to the *Clarendon Studies in Criminology* Series. This is a unique and valuable resource for legal scholars, historians, sociologists, and criminologists alike.

Loraine Gelsthorpe and Kyle Treiber
Institute of Criminology, University of Cambridge
August, 2017

Preface

This is a book about a decision that was of direct relevance to a small number of convicted criminals—ninety-eight by my reckoning—but that had profound consequences in each case (lethally profound in thirty-five of them). It is a treatise on the exercise of clemency by successive Irish governments from the post-civil war period until the abolition of capital punishment in 1990, a span of almost seventy years. It examines the reasons behind the commutation of death sentences and traces the custodial careers of the beneficiaries of these decisions. It argues that, in most cases, sparing a life served the interests of justice, not of mercy. At several junctures the decision to deflect the law from its course was capricious, an apparently resolute government being swayed by the entreaties of a respected episcopal or judicial figure, or finding itself outmanoeuvred by one of its own members.

As a subject of academic study the death penalty has proved fruitful for scholars and a great deal is known about executions and executioners. Indeed, it might be said that there is an inverse relationship between the use of the sanction and the volume of interest it has attracted; the further it has gone into decline the greater the proliferation of books and articles. But little is known about the men and women whose appointment with the executioner was cancelled by the state. There is no historiography of this fortunate group.

My interest in this area was piqued during the summer of 2007 when, in the National Archives of Ireland, I came across a letter from Thomas Pierrepoint to the authorities of the Irish Free State regarding the tardy reimbursement of expenses incurred for what proved to be a wasted journey from Yorkshire to Dublin. Unbeknownst to Pierrepoint before he set off, the man he thought was to be hanged (Patrick Aylward) had in fact been spared. That someone who had broken so many necks could be troubled about small quantities of pounds, shillings, and pence seemed peculiarly mundane.

So too was the nature of other letters on the file. On one occasion Pierrepoint apologized for not responding to a communication by return of post, explaining that the envelope had become stuck in the letter box and his wife had not noticed it there. On another he recounted how, travelling back to England on the mail boat, he heard passengers talking about the execution he had officiated at and wondering who among them might be the hangman, but he was not singled out for attention. The other passengers may have been looking for a man with a bag containing a rope and various pieces of pinioning equipment. But Pierrepoint always travelled light, carrying no luggage. The tools of his trade—a ruler, a measuring tape, and a pair of pliers—were small enough to conceal in a pocket. These missives, in turn obsequious and disgruntled, planted the seed for an inquiry that would bear fruit, a decade later, in the form of this book.

I was also intrigued by the fact that when Irish criminals were to be hanged, the services of an English hangman—usually Thomas Pierrepoint or his nephew Albert—were always called upon. The best efforts of the authorities to recruit locally came to naught, suggesting a national ambivalence towards capital punishment that is interesting to ponder.

As my examination of the archival sources broadened and deepened I became struck by the extent to which women who were sentenced to death but spared tended to be viewed sympathetically. This seemed to redound to their advantage in that they spent a relatively short time in prison. But this benevolence had a dark side; many were discharged to the care of religious congregations where they were coercively confined for extended periods and, on occasion, for life. To understand executive clemency necessitates a focus beyond the criminal justice system.

This book is about the conflict that sometimes arose between the imperative to do justice and the desire to show mercy, and the challenges posed by its resolution. Why were some of the condemned spared while others paid the ultimate price? If mercy intrudes must the law be wrong? If it is not, then to show mercy is to allow injustice. Matters were further complicated by cases where a decision had been made but it was suddenly and surprisingly reversed.

In an essay published in 1995, Nigel Walker (whose occasional seminars on punishment I was fortunate to attend as a graduate student at Cambridge) observed that: 'Anatomists of criminal justice systems usually ignore the tiny organ called "mercy" or "clemency".' One of my aims in this book is to take a scalpel to this concept to see what is revealed by repeated incisions. While I do not pretend to anything like the same analytical skills—or, indeed, limpidity of prose—that characterized the late Professor Walker's endeavours, I hope that when I wield the knife it is not too crudely or too ineffectively.

The matters under consideration in the chapters that follow were scoured from primary materials such as government memoranda, police and prison records, trial transcripts, and the voluminous correspondence that emanated from concerned citizens and public servants. They are the product of years of determined sleuthing. The archive is the repository of national memory and it was thrilling to excavate it with a view to bringing the clemency process to the surface. But there were contemporary resonances also. In the closing weeks of 2015, while I was in the early stages of writing this book, the last men sentenced to death (Noel Callan and Michael McHugh) were released from prison having each served thirty years for the murder of Garda Sergeant Patrick Morrissey. When they regained their liberty, Ireland's final link with the death penalty was severed.

Reading about the desperate acts of desperate people and the callousness of the state's response exacts a cumulative emotional toll. The plaintive pleas for mercy from citizens who resignedly accepted their fate are reminders of a more subservient time. Several years of immersion in stories of violence and human suffering, and the legally and morally complex questions that they raise, do not leave the reader's equilibrium undisturbed.

I had an opportunity to present some of the emerging themes of the book as the thirty-second Hugh M. Fitzpatrick Lecture in Legal Bibliography on 1 December 2015 (coincidentally, the day that Michael McHugh was released from prison). This long-standing lecture series provides a valuable opportunity for scholars to expose their thoughts to a large and well-informed audience of lawyers, judges, historians, and diverse members of the public, and I was delighted to be part of it. Mr Justice Seán Ryan, President of the Court of Appeal, was kind enough to introduce and chair my lecture which was hosted by the Bar Council of Ireland.

As in any project of this nature there are debts to be acknowledged. I am grateful to the Irish Prison Service and the Information Unit of the Department of Justice and Equality for granting permission to view the closed prisoner files which added heft to my analysis, and to the National Archives of Ireland (NAI) for providing a facility in which to study their contents. I am obliged to the staff of the reading room in the NAI for producing so many files on so many days and to the Department of the Taoiseach for allowing me to inspect materials that had been withheld from the NAI and remained in its own archives. In particular I would like to record my thanks to Aisling Brennan, Joe Goode, Frank Hanlon, Helen Hewson, Jim Mitchell, and Seán Reynolds. When my data collection began in earnest I was fortunate to be able to avail of the assistance of David Doyle who worked for me as a post-doctoral research fellow. For his diligence, hard work, and good humour I extend my sincere thanks.

Two men sentenced to death but spared granted me interviews as did two of the three surviving Ministers for Justice who were in office when confronted with this life and death decision. Their perspectives were invaluable and, while they remain anonymous, their insights have informed my writing.

Roger Hood read several draft chapters and commented on them in detail. In addition to being an international authority on the death penalty he is a consummate stylist and has been a steady mentor since I worked under his direction at the Oxford University Centre for Criminological Research (as it then was) twenty-five years ago. I appreciate his support and friendship. I have had a long and happy association with Linacre College, Oxford as a Junior Research Fellow and then a Senior Research Fellow in the mid-1990s, and as an Adjunct Fellow ever since. Regular visits to Linacre and the Bodleian Library were important, not so much for the materials they yielded, but for the comfortable and congenial surroundings that they offer, which are ideal for sustained engagement with complex data.

For nigh on two decades my academic home has been the School of Law at University College Dublin, a place where criminology and legal history thrive and where Lynsey Black, Mark Coen, Kevin Costello, Niamh Howlin, Thomas Mohr, and Nial Osborough lent me the benefit of their expertise. Chris Cowley from the UCD School of Philosophy also found time to read and comment upon a chapter. Colleagues in other institutions were generous with their time and their observations. I would like to pay particular thanks to Cormac Behan, Tim Carey, Fergal Davis, Mark Finnane, Conor Hanly, John Jackson, Shane

Kilcommins, Seán McConville, Tom O'Malley, Eoin O'Sullivan, Julian Roberts, and Carolyn Strange.

When this book went to press, Ireland's 'decade of centenaries', initiated in 2012 to mark the foundational events leading to independence, was gathering pace. It is to be hoped that the analyses presented in the pages that follow will bring out of the shadows an aspect of criminal justice history that has previously escaped attention.

My last book—*Prisoners, Solitude, and Time*—which also appeared as part of the Clarendon Studies in Criminology series was dedicated to my wife, Kirsty Kirkwood. This one is for my parents, Eddie and Frances, during whose childhoods the executioner became redundant and my children, Caoilfhionn and Tadhg, for whom the notion of hanging convicted criminals by the neck is a grotesque reminder of a barbarous (and not too distant) past.

Ian O'Donnell
Dublin
March 2017

Contents

List of Tables xxi

1. Introduction **1**
The Revolutionary Period 2
Parameters of Inquiry 12
Avoiding Death-eligibility 20

2. Classifying Clemency **30**
Who, Where, How? 30
A Tripartite Scheme 39
The 'Prerogative' 49

3. For and Against Clemency **54**
Discretion and Desert 56
Cons 63
Pros 71
Justice, Mercy, Caprice 77

4. Juries and Judges **85**
Weighing the Evidence 85
Composition 91
Softening the Verdict 95
Donning the Black Cap 102
A Singular Case 110

5. Extraordinary Courts **115**
Special Powers Tribunal 117
The 'Terror Court' 120
Astounding Legal Manoeuvres 125
Capital Murder 132

6. Governments **142**
Limits to Discretion 143
Public Opinion 147
Groupthink 150
Arbitrary or Principled Decisions? 155

7. Blurring the Separation of Powers **159**
Interfering Judges 160
A Belt of the Crozier 172
Entreaties from His Excellency 177
Judges Again, Now Expediting Release 180

8. Undoing Death I **182**
A Cruel Lottery? 182
The Burden of an Unwanted Child 185
Sex and Jealousy 196

9. Undoing Death II **204**
Dreadful Deeds Done in Turbulent Times 204
Legally Sane but Strikingly Odd 209
Chivalry 213
Caprice 221

10. Release **224**
Procedures 226
When? 229
Whither? 234
Why? 243

Postscript **252**
Executioner Wanted—in 1976 256
Posthumous Pardon 259

Appendices 263
I. Convicted of Murder after Trial by Jury, and Spared 263
II. Convicted of Murder after Trial by Jury, and Hanged 267
III. Sentenced to Death by a Non-jury Court 269

Bibliography 271
I. Primary Sources 271
II. Secondary Sources 282
Index 291

List of Tables

1.1 Victims of lethal violence (average annual rates) 6
1.2 Recorded murder 6
1.3 A century (and more) of commutations 8
1.4 Attrition in murder trials 22
2.1 Gender 31
2.2 Geography 33
2.3 Murder methods 34
2.4 Varieties of clemency 44
4.1 Speed of jury deliberations 87
4.2 Recommendations to mercy 98
4.3 Disquiet in the jury room 100
4.4 Hanging judges? 104
4.5 Clemency by mode of conviction 113
4.6 Clemency to men after trial by jury 113
5.1 Persons convicted by non-jury courts (all crimes) 130
6.1 Merciful ministers? 146
8.1 Avoiding a date with the hangman 185
10.1 Months in prison 231
10.2 Post-prison destinations 235
10.3 Months in coercive confinement 237

1

Introduction

Mirroring renewed international interest in the 'killing state', the history of the death penalty in twentieth-century Ireland has received a significant level of critical attention in recent years. The politics of abolition have been sketched out (O'Brien 2006), the life histories and criminal exploits of the hanged have been described (Carey 2013), the machinations of the criminal justice system have been analysed and the secular trend explored (Doyle and O'Donnell 2012), the protective effect of gender has been outlined (Black 2016), and the role and identities of the executioners—all English—have been revealed (O'Donnell and Doyle 2014).[1]

But there remains one significant gap in our understanding. We know little about those who were spared, why they escaped the hangman or firing party, and what became of them. By examining the use of what is loosely (and, in the wake of the 1937 Constitution, inaccurately) described as the 'prerogative' of mercy we can learn something about the emergence of a legal order which sometimes struggled to reconcile the competing demands of justice and mercy in death penalty cases. This was a gradual transition over seven decades from independence in 1922 to the abolition of capital punishment in 1990. The *coup de grâce* was delivered in 2001 when the public voted in a referendum to remove all references to capital punishment from Bunreacht na hÉireann [the Irish Constitution] and to prohibit its reintroduction.[2] By the

[1] The English hangmen seemed to enjoy their visits to Ireland. After dispatching John Cox, Thomas Pierrepoint remarked that: 'There is very little trouble with Irish prisoners. I admire their fortitude and resignation, and, I may add, their spirituality. They generally go quietly. But I have extreme bother with condemned Englishmen. There is always trouble at the last moment.' (*Irish Independent*, 26 April 1929)

[2] The turnout was 35 per cent with almost two-thirds (62 per cent) voting in favour of the twenty-first amendment to the Constitution.

Justice, Mercy, and Caprice: Clemency and the Death Penalty in Ireland. First Edition. Ian O'Donnell. © Ian O'Donnell 2017. Published 2017 by Oxford University Press.

beginning of the twenty-first century the Irish people had made a decision their leaders felt they would have made in the 1920s had they been given the option (Doyle and O'Donnell 2012: 65–6). The final link with this grisly practice was broken on 1 December 2015 when Michael McHugh was released from prison having served thirty years of his commuted death sentence.[3]

The Revolutionary Period

There is an extensive literature on the relationship between political violence and capital punishment in Ireland; while not a central concern of this book, some of the pertinent material is adverted to in Chapter 5. It is sufficient for present purposes to note that the response to the struggle for Irish independence was characterized by waves of repression in which state-sanctioned killings played a pivotal role. Fifteen republican insurgents were executed after the rebellion that took place during Easter 1916 (fourteen in Dublin and one in Cork); all were shot during the first two weeks of May. Roger Casement, executed three months later in Pentonville Prison in London, was hanged. Twenty-four men were executed during the War of Independence which began in January 1919; ten were hanged and fourteen were shot.[4] All of the foregoing executions were carried out by the British.

The War of Independence was brought to an end by a truce that began on 11 July 1921. This was followed by a period of bilateral negotiations culminating in the Anglo-Irish Treaty, signed in London on 6 December 1921, which created Saorstát Éireann [the Irish Free State], an entity comprising twenty-six of the thirty-two counties on the island of Ireland. The six counties that did not join the Free State remained part of the United Kingdom as Northern Ireland. The treaty did not win universal acceptance and precipitated a bitter civil war that, after some initial skirmishes, began in earnest on 28 June 1922 with the bombardment of the Four Courts in Dublin where anti-treaty forces were garrisoned.

[3] Noel Callan, who had been sentenced to death for the same offence—the murder of a police officer who gave chase after an armed robbery in Ardee, County Louth—was released the previous day.

[4] Kevin Barry was first, on 1 November 1920. Patrick Maher was last, on 7 June 1921. Both were hanged.

The advent of civil war led to the introduction of the Army Emergency Powers Resolution.[5] Military courts and committees were created and given wide-ranging powers to secure public safety. Eighty-one prisoners were executed by firing party between November 1922 and the end of hostilities in May 1923, a group eulogized, erroneously, as 'the seventy-seven'.[6] This policy was pursued ruthlessly with a view to bringing the conflict to an end that favoured the Free State forces. Garvin (1996: 163) cited a chilling observation made by W.T. Cosgrave, speaking in February 1923 in his capacity as President of the Executive Council of the Free State, to the effect that: 'The executions have had a remarkable effect. It is a sad thing to say, but it is nevertheless the case ... if the country is to live and we have to exterminate ten thousand Republicans, the three millions of our people are bigger than this ten thousand.'[7]

Kevin O'Higgins (Vice President of the Executive Council and Minister for Home Affairs—later Justice—of the first and second Executive Councils of the Free State) and Richard Mulcahy (Minister for Defence in both administrations) were zealous proponents of this ferocious approach to the restoration of order. At a stormy election rally in 1925, O'Higgins declared that: 'I stand over those seventy-seven executions, and seven hundred and seventy-seven more if they be necessary' (*Irish Times*, 19 January 1925). While this policy may have been instrumental in crushing the spirit of the opponents of the new state, O'Higgins paid with his life two years later, assassinated by the Irish Republican Army (IRA) as he walked to Sunday Mass. Mulcahy, by contrast, was at the cabinet table when decisions were made about whether to allow the law take its course for men and women sentenced to death during more ordinary times.[8]

[5] Dáil Debates, 28 September 1922, vol. 1, cols 927–30.

[6] Macardle (1937: 983–5) chronicled seventy-seven civil war executions but omitted from her list Luke Burke and Michael Greery who were executed in Mullingar on 13 March 1923, and Michael Murphy and Joseph O'Rourke who were executed in Tuam on 30 May 1923.

[7] An Executive Council headed by a president met between 1922 and 1937 and a government headed by a Taoiseach thereafter. The Ministers and Secretaries Act, 1924 created the Department of Justice.

[8] As Minister for Education, Mulcahy was present at the government meeting that decided to recommend commutation in Mary Cadden's case in 1957, thirty years after Kevin O'Higgins was assassinated. This brief meeting took place in

In addition to state-sanctioned killings there were numerous murders of collaborators and informers and spates of reprisal attacks. Some saw the turbulent times as an opportunity to settle personal scores in the name of the Republic. It was difficult, O'Brien (2006: 226) observed, to distinguish between 'civilian' and political offences. One startling conclusion is unavoidable: the emerging Irish state was not reluctant to execute its citizens, showing a degree of promiscuity in this regard that distinguished it from the situation under British rule. The authorities of the Free State executed twice as many Irishmen during the civil war as the British had after the Easter Rising of 1916 and throughout the War of Independence, combined. This added an interesting psychological twist: a practice that was abhorred as marking an unbalanced relationship with an overbearing neighbour was taken to with alacrity by the architects of independence.

The executions that took place during the revolutionary era—which have excited a high level of interest—are beyond the scope of this book. The focus here is on the period after armed resistance to the Free State subsided in May 1923, when the criminal justice system began to deal with peace-time killings. While outside the temporal parameters of my inquiry, the ready resort to execution during the civil war, and an accompanying lack of emphasis on due process values, shows how the country was brutalized at this time. Human life had been devalued by the First World War. The demobilization of many battle-hardened men, together with the country's collective experience of large numbers of deaths and injuries on foreign fields, reduced levels of sensitivity to violence. In tandem, these factors were conducive to some of the brutality that occurred on the home front between 1919 and 1923, and to the willingness to resort to judicial execution in the years that followed. The preparedness to use the death penalty during the civil war led to a hardening of attitude that took some years to soften.

A decline in violence

There were only two periods after the civil war when there was more than one execution each year; these were 1923 to 1926

the Taoiseach's room in government buildings between 1 p.m. and 1:15 p.m. Cadden's death sentence was the only item on the agenda.

when eleven men were hanged, along with Annie Walsh, the only woman to be executed post-independence, and 1940 to 1943 when five men were hanged and five were shot.[9] Most of the post-independence executions occurred during these two four-year periods. Each was followed by a tailing off in numbers, the latter of which was not reversed. These were temporary, and short-lived, reversals to a pattern of long-term decline, a gradual elevation of what Elias called 'thresholds of repugnance' (cited in Smith 1996: 23).[10]

The decline in the use of capital punishment reflected the emergence of a more pacific society. Table 1.1 shows that the homicide rate declined from the 1920s—continuing a well-established downward trend—and that the killing of infants had almost disappeared by the time infanticide legislation was belatedly introduced in 1949. When the focus is limited to murder, and the timescale is truncated, the same pattern of declining violence until the 1960s is apparent (Table 1.2). By the 1950s, when the level of lethal violence had dwindled dramatically, the death penalty was, to all intents and purposes, a dead letter, as it had been in the 1910s. In the 1970s the homicide rate began to increase (O'Donnell 2005a) but by then the scope of the death penalty had been dramatically curtailed and, although (small, shallow) pockets of support for capital punishment existed (see Postscript), no Irish government was prepared to countenance the exaction of the ultimate penalty. There was a flurry of capital convictions in the first half of the 1980s; commutation was automatic in each case.

It would be simplistic to attribute the high number of executions in the mid-1920s to the number of homicides taking place at the time. This is because the level of lethal violence was higher in the first decade of the twentieth century but executions had almost ceased by this stage. There was a single execution between 1911 and 1919 (excluding those associated with the 1916 Easter Rising). Vaughan (2009: 11) noted that: 'The last hanging before

[9] Annie Walsh was convicted of murdering her husband, Edward, with a hatchet. So too was her husband's nephew, Michael Talbot. The pair were hanged by Thomas Pierrepoint in Mountjoy Prison on 5 August 1925. She was the first woman to be executed since Mary Daly in 1903. Daly too had murdered her husband with a male accomplice and both paid with their lives.

[10] Executions moved behind the scenes, they took place less frequently, and the public appetite for violent death (whether lawful or unlawful) waned.

Table 1.1 Victims of lethal violence (average annual rates)

	Infants	Aged over one year	All
1850–9	18.3	19.9	38.2
1860–9	9.1	15.4	24.5
1870–9	6.0	18.6	24.6
1880–9	5.7	19.9	25.6
1890–9	4.5	18.8	23.3
1900–9	3.2	12.8	16.0
1910–19	3.1	11.9	15.0
1925–9	4.7	5.8	10.5
1930–9	2.4	4.3	6.7
1940–9	1.7	3.6	5.3
1950–9	1.2	2.6	3.8
1960–4	0.8	2.7	3.5
1965–90	0.3	7.2	7.5

Note: Based on O'Donnell (2005b: 677, Table 1). Data are unavailable between 1920 and 1924. Figures prior to 1919 relate to the island of Ireland; afterwards to the twenty-six counties that became the Irish Free State (and, in 1949, the Republic of Ireland). Rates are expressed per million population. All varieties of homicide (murder, manslaughter, and infanticide) are included. The death penalty was restricted in 1964 and abolished in 1990.

Table 1.2 Recorded murder

	All	Annual average	Proceedings taken	Annual average
1927–9	71	23.7	66	22.0
1930–9	141	14.1	114	11.4
1940–9	90	9.0	71	7.1
1950–9	61	6.1	39	3.9
1960–4	26	5.2	19	3.8
1965–90	463	17.8	357 [11]	13.7 [0.4]

Note: Based on O'Donnell et al. (2005: Tables 1.1 and 1.2). Data on proceedings taken are unavailable prior to 1927. Between 1927 and 1946 the number of persons proceeded against was recorded; thereafter it was the number of offences in which proceedings were taken. The thirty-three persons killed in bombings in Dublin and Monaghan in May 1974 are omitted. Persons proceeded against for 'capital murder', as defined by the Criminal Justice Act, 1964 are shown in brackets; before this date the death penalty was mandatory for all murders. Three capital murder convictions were quashed on appeal.

the first world war was in 1911, and by 1914 it could have been said that capital punishment was practically obsolete in Ireland.' The fact that executions were resorted to with such enthusiasm in the 1920s, when the homicide rate was lower than in the preceding decades, suggests that the horrors of the prevailing circumstances played a role in making judicial execution acceptable again. Governments had become accustomed to widespread loss of life and this made the trip to the scaffold a less weighty matter.[11] Had Annie Walsh's case come up for deliberation a few years later—or earlier—it is arguable that she would have been spared.

During the 1940s, when the number of executions spiked, the homicide rate was heading towards an all-time low. Table 1.3 shows the proportion of death sentences that were carried out between the 1850s and 1990, when capital punishment was abolished for all crimes. The commutation rate, which had been 90 per cent between 1910 and 1919, fell to 57 per cent between 1923 and 1929. Again this shows that there was no straightforward correlation between the number of murders and the execution rate; more important was the government's willingness to allow the law take its course. Post-independence, the commutation rate was lowest (50 per cent) during the 1940s. This is explained by political determination to respond to a renewed subversive threat with unwavering resolve.

There are two points to tease out from Table 1.3. First of all, there were more death sentences imposed, and executions carried out, in the latter half of the nineteenth century (255 and 107 respectively between 1852 and 1899) than the first half of the twentieth century (128 and 51 between 1900 and 1949) and this was the continuation of an established trend. Linebaugh (2003: 50) adopted the term 'thanatocracy' to 'characterize a government that ruled by the frequent exercise of

[11] A large number of Irish soldiers died fighting for the Crown during the First World War, probably around 35,000 (O'Donnell 2005b: 685). There were far fewer deaths on home soil during the conflicts that began during, and continued after, the war in Europe. O'Halpin (2012: 150–3) enumerated 2,141 deaths from political violence between January 1917 and December 1921, comprising 898 civilians, 467 IRA members, 514 police officers, and 262 British military personnel; another 482 fatalities were attributed to the Easter Rising that took place between 24 and 29 April 1916, and its aftermath. There are no reliable figures for the death toll during the civil war, with estimates ranging from under 1,000 to over 3,000 (Whelehan 2014: 633).

Table 1.3 A century (and more) of commutations

	Sentenced to death	Executed		Commuted	
		No.	(per cent)	No.	(per cent)
1852–9	79	25	(32)	54	(68)
1860–9	42	18	(43)	24	(57)
1870–9	30	16	(53)	14	(47)
1880–9	73	33	(45)	40	(55)
1890–9	31	15	(48)	16	(52)
1900–9	28	15	(54)	13	(46)
1910–19	20	2	(10)	18	(90)
1923–9	35	15	(43)	20	(57)
1930–9	17	5	(29)	12	(71)
1940–9	28	14	(50)	14	(50)
1950–9	7	1	(14)	6	(86)
1960–4	3	0	(0)	3	(100)
1965–90	8	0	(0)	8	(100)
All	401	159	(40)	242	(60)

Note: Figures for 1852 to 1919 are from the General Prisons Board's *Death Book*, and relate to the island of Ireland. Executions carried out after the Easter Rising (1916), during the War of Independence (1919–21), and during the civil war (1922–3) are omitted. From 1923 the focus is on the twenty-six counties that became the Irish Free State (and, in 1949, the Republic of Ireland).

the death penalty'. In the period prior to the First World War, Ireland was a long way from being such a place. Secondly, although hanging had virtually disappeared by the end of the first decade of the twentieth century, it came back with a vengeance thereafter.

The fact that the downward trend in hangings for murders with no political aspect was bucked in the 1940s is probably accounted for by the desensitizing effect of the executions carried out after decisions made by non-jury courts presided over by army officers and again, perhaps, by the numbing effect of another world war. It seems reasonable to argue that the coarsening effects of conflict, and the destruction of much of Europe, would have made the prospect of judicial execution less shocking. (The period between 1939 and 1945 was known in Ireland—which remained neutral during the Second World War—as 'the Emergency'.) This desensitization was on the part of the government members who considered how to proceed in these cases rather than the military men or judges who had no choice but to impose the prescribed penalties on those found guilty, or the public, whose knowledge of such matters may not have been all that profound given wartime censorship.

Capital punishment was touted by politicians as a vital safeguard against subversion. The rationale for its retention was that politically motivated crimes resulted from a careful calculation of costs and benefits that was likely to accord significant weight to the threat of death; this set them apart from the wider class of killings which were impulsive, emotional, and fueled by alcohol. But, in a cruel irony, most executions involved killings that had no conceivable political dimension. The rising number of executions at a time of declining homicide, and the changing balance between executions and grants of clemency during the Emergency, are not fully explained by the use of capital punishment to deal with the threat to the Free State posed by the IRA. Most of those executed during this period (seven out of thirteen) were ordinary citizens whose displays of interpersonal violence had no political roots or wider ramifications. The severity of the response to the IRA contributed to callousness insofar as other killers were concerned.

There was another legacy of the civil war execution policy: governments learned that killing the state's enemies could have a real effect, however awful the cost. The Provisional Government found capital punishment to be a useful tool and did not want to deplete its arsenal of sanctions for fear of being found wanting on a future occasion. De Valera remembered this as Taoiseach [prime minister] in the 1940s when there were fewer opponents to kill but the rationale remained the same: subversives responded best to crushing force (see Chapter 5).

Bloody biographies

As noted above, the first Free State Minister for Justice, Kevin O'Higgins, was assassinated during his term of office. This was an opportunistic killing for which no one was ever convicted, a group of armed IRA men chancing upon the minister as he walked to Mass on 10 July 1927. O'Higgins had been instrumental in the executions of eighty-one prisoners during the civil war (one of whom, Rory O'Connor, had been best man at his wedding) and his murder was a retaliatory strike. His father had been murdered for the same reason. As Minister for Home Affairs (later Justice) he oversaw the hanging of a dozen civilian offenders during the early years of independence, including the only woman to enter—but not exit—a hang house. His willingness to allow common criminals to hang cannot be unrelated to his callous treatment of former friends and allies. He was in office during a violent decade but one wonders whether he was somewhat insulated from the effects of his actions given the horrors to which he had borne personal witness. He was a young man whose character had been forged in a violent context and who did not have the benefit of the distance or maturity that might have moderated his views.[12] Either O'Higgins or Gerald Boland, another man bruised by conflict, was in charge of the justice department for the majority of capital cases between 1923 and 1990 (Table 6.1). Neither lacked firmness of purpose.

O'Higgins' immediate successor, W.T. Cosgrave, who was in post for three months following his colleague's assassination, had been sentenced to death following the Easter Rising. His cell in Kilmainham Gaol was next to that of Major John MacBride whom he heard taken away and shot at daybreak on 5 May 1916, fearing that he would be next.[13] He learned that afternoon that his sentence had been commuted to penal servitude for life.[14] While Cosgrave did not preside over any executions this was simply a question of timing. He had been prepared to execute many of his former colleagues summarily during the civil war despite his stated opposition to capital punishment. In a debate about the establishment of military courts he observed that, 'although I have always objected to a death penalty, there is no other way I know of in which ordered conditions can be restored in this country'.[15]

[12] O'Higgins was 35 years of age when he was assassinated.

[13] Major MacBride's son, Seán, shared a cell with Rory O'Connor until the latter was executed (MacBride 2005: 66–7). Seán MacBride was a leading member of the IRA, and subsequently a barrister who acted in many capital cases, before turning his attention to politics and becoming a government minister. His name appears regularly in the pages that follow.

[14] Bureau of Military History, witness statement 268, Liam T. Cosgrave, at pp. 18–19.

[15] Dáil Debates, 27 September 1922, W.T. Cosgrave, vol. 1, col. 877.

James FitzGerald-Kenney and James Geoghegan, the next justice ministers, were successful lawyers who had not been combatants during the War of Independence or civil war. P.J. Ruttledge, Minister for Justice in the 1930s, was imprisoned during the War of Independence and seriously injured during the civil war. Gerald Boland served time in prison and his brother Harry was killed during the civil war. Seán MacEoin had been sentenced to death during the War of Independence for the murder of a Royal Irish Constabulary inspector. (Having shot the inspector, MacEoin whispered an act of contrition in his ear, before effecting his escape.)[16] Daniel Morrissey, who served as justice minister for three months in 1951, was a former trade unionist and successful businessman without a military pedigree. James Everett was a trade unionist and Labour Party TD [Teachta Dála; Member of Parliament] who lacked a military background. Oscar Traynor fought in the Easter Rising, the War of Independence, and the civil war. Charles Haughey, the last justice minister when murder attracted a mandatory death penalty, was too young to have played a role in the state's turbulent gestation, having been born in 1925.

Clearly, then, a number of the men who held the justice portfolio had been close to death. Some had killed, others had lost family members and close friends to violence. Several had been interned or imprisoned. A couple had themselves been sentenced to death. This may go some way to explaining why they did not place a high price on human life. The same was true of their government colleagues, also members of a revolutionary generation. In other words, when the decision about whether or not to spare a convicted murderer was brought forward for their consideration, one cannot imagine that they were all that squeamish about allowing the law to take its course. (This is not the full story, of course, as capital punishment was popular at the time in other countries where politicians' hands were less bloody. But there is one vital difference: in Ireland the ultimate sanction was used in the context of a fledgling state that faced an existential threat.)

Heads of government also had violent pasts. W.T. Cosgrave (President of the Executive Council, 1922 to 1932) was not the

[16] Bureau of Military History, witness statement 1716, General Seán MacEoin, at p. 97.

only one to have been sentenced to death in 1916. So too was Éamon de Valera (President of the Executive Council and then Taoiseach, 1932 to 1948, 1951 to 1954, and 1957 to 1959).[17] Seán Lemass (Taoiseach, 1959 to 1966) had not been sentenced to death but had shot dead his younger brother (accidentally) and been involved in numerous armed actions against the British, some of which resulted in loss of life; his brother Noel was abducted and murdered during the civil war (allegedly by James Murray, the army captain whose death sentence for the murder of Joseph Bergin was commuted in 1925). John A. Costello (Taoiseach, 1948 to 1951 and 1954 to 1957) was the only head of government when capital punishment was mandatory for murder who had not taken up arms. He was a reluctant Taoiseach, in post because the leader of Fine Gael, General Richard Mulcahy, proved unacceptable to coalition partners. This was on account of his brutality during the civil war, especially his lack of restraint when it came to executing opponents.

Parameters of Inquiry

Before advancing any further it is necessary to state what this book is not about. First of all, it is not an attempt to chart the path to the abolition of capital punishment. This is an interesting story but it is for another to tell. Langhamer (2012: 420) described the death penalty debate in the United Kingdom in the 1940s and 1950s as the defining moral issue of the times, 'a boundary marker within political culture'. It never had the same prominence in Irish intellectual or political life. While there was no great appetite among the public for capital punishment, nor was the

[17] As President of Ireland between 1959 and 1973, de Valera was required to commute death sentences on three occasions. When it comes to matters of state-sanctioned death there can have been few politicians of any hue in any country, whose experience ranged as widely. His successor as president was another major public figure whose life had been directly touched by capital punishment. Erskine Childers' father (also Erskine) was executed during the civil war; he stood before a firing party on 24 November 1922 at Beggar's Bush barracks in Dublin. His crime was the possession of a pistol which he was said to have received as a gift from Michael Collins (commander-in-chief of the National Army, killed in an ambush in August 1922) when the two men were on the same side.

same public sufficiently troubled about the occasional use of the ultimate sanction to agitate for its abolition.[18]

Writing about nineteenth-century Ireland, Vaughan (2009: 317) opined that: 'When abolitionists did appear they were not only small in numbers, but diffident.' The same applied one hundred years later. On 30 October 1935, a Society for the Abolition of the Death Penalty was established at a meeting in Dublin (*Irish Times*, 31 October 1935). The Irish Pacifist Movement was created a few years later, in 1938, but seems to have kept a low profile. The movement's honorary secretary wrote to the Minister for Justice, Charles Haughey, congratulating him on the introduction of legislation to abolish the death penalty in all but a small number of cases, and exhorting him to move towards complete abolition 'when you consider the time ripe and the country prepared for it'.[19] The letter suggests an organization that was reluctant even to use forceful language to achieve the ends to which it had committed itself. The difference between pacifism and timidity was lost here.

It was a curious situation whereby the drafters of the Free State Constitution debated abolition against a background of a decline in civilian executions (Table 1.3), and the public did not evince any great support for the continuation of a practice long tainted by association with the colonial power, but there was no enduring abolition movement. The executions of IRA members during the Emergency attracted significant attention, although wartime censorship probably blunted the associated protests. Some other death sentences resulted in large petitions, but these were based on special pleading in individual cases rather than principled opposition to the practice of capital punishment. There was a staccato feel to proceedings, a pattern of ambivalence punctuated

[18] Superstitious attitudes persisted. The governor of Mountjoy Prison during the 'hanging years' recalled how a woman had written to him requesting a piece of the rope that had been used in an execution and enclosing payment in anticipation of a favourable response. Her son had epilepsy and she believed that a touch of the rope would cure him (Memories of Mountjoy jail as told by former governor Sean Kavanagh to Liam MacGabhann, Mountjoy Prison Museum). A plaque in the prison's boardroom shows that Kavanagh was in charge between 12 February 1928 and 24 February 1933 and again between 21 November 1933 and 20 February 1962.

[19] Letter from Brenda Yassin to Charles Haughey, 24 March 1964, National Archives of Ireland (NAI) JUS/2004/32/20.

by occasional bursts of activity, but without sustained lobbying between times.

Nor is this book a descriptive history of capital punishment, setting out the stories behind the executions. I am not writing what Linebaugh (2003: xxiii) characterized as 'history by the neck'. Indeed, it is the necks that were not stretched and snapped that are central to my purpose. I am not concerned to present a catalogue of individual cases. Paraphrasing what the files have to say might result in an interesting string of anecdotes, or bring to light some long-forgotten facts, but at the expense of analytical torque. The book does not attempt to give a voice to the marginalized men and women who found themselves, however briefly, the focus of national attention as they stood in the dock and heard the sentence of death pronounced. While their stories underpin the text, and are organized around several key themes in Chapters 8 and 9, the primary purpose is not to excavate them and to offer them as a series of disjointed accounts of tough justice in rough times. There may be a place for such an exercise but it is not here.

The seduction of the archive is the specific. Its logic is to pull one towards the particular with the resultant danger of remaining at the level of case description rather than thinking inductively. Thorough description is important but it is only the first stage in a more rigorous (and, dare I say, imaginative) approach. There is also a risk of imposing coherence where it does not exist, of creating a mosaic that is altogether too beguiling. I have been alive to the twin dangers of reciting cases without illuminating trends and of revealing patterns that further investigation might prove illusory. While I may not have avoided these pitfalls entirely, I hope that I have managed to strike an appropriate scholarly balance. There are fewer excerpts from the files than one might expect to find in a work of social or legal history, and less theorizing than one might expect to find in a criminological study, but I hope that I have identified a middle ground that allows an interesting narrative to unfold against a background that is reasonably well illuminated. Historical research is painstakingly incremental and it would be enough if my examination of the archival materials acted as a midwife for more empirically or theoretically elaborate work.[20]

[20] This blended approach is paralleled in the system of referencing used throughout. For secondary material the Harvard style is adopted while primary sources are dealt with in footnotes.

In a magisterial survey of capital punishment in Germany over 400 years, Evans (1996: xiii) warned that: 'Not a few histories of capital punishment have been written with sensational or titillating intent. Many authors have traded in the pornography of suffering and death by producing books which appeal mainly to the reader with sadistic inclinations.' This is not such a volume and nothing prurient is to be found in what follows. There are no elaborate descriptions of execution scenes accompanied by a tone of high moral indignation. There is no gore. Nor is the book about the petitions submitted on behalf of condemned men and women although these may repay scrutiny in terms of content (often formulaic) and signatories (number and nature; sometimes they are signed by uneasy jurors). Nor is it about developments in Northern Ireland, which are fascinating in their own right and await their narrator.[21]

Focus

My purpose is to account for what happened in a single jurisdiction (what became the Republic of Ireland) during a defined historical period (1923 to 1990); it is for others to tease out the comparative dimension in so far as such an exercise may be warranted and proves sufficiently alluring. This singularity of focus is for two reasons. First, there is a need to complete the remedial work required to describe the national situation before it can be juxtaposed against developments elsewhere. Secondly, the Irish case stands on its own merits and its elucidation does not require constant cross-referencing to neighbouring jurisdictions. This should not be taken to mean that the findings are of purely parochial relevance as the issues examined in the context of Ireland are pertinent wherever the penalty of death was imposed but not carried out. By keeping the focus sharp I hope to place under the scholarly microscope issues that are of broader significance and that would repay closer examination elsewhere.

In essence my project is an examination of the law and politics of clemency. The former is documented and easy to state, the latter is unexplored and enigmatic. My primary concern is whether the

[21] Robert McGladdery was the last person hanged in Northern Ireland. The executioner was Harry Allen. The pair met, briefly, in Belfast's Crumlin Road Gaol on 20 December 1961 (*Donegal News*, 30 December 1961).

decision to allow the law to take its course, or to divert it to a less than lethal outcome, was a cruel lottery, or if there are patterns to be discerned. My work starts in earnest when a finding of guilt has been made and upheld on appeal; it was only at this point that the issue of clemency came under consideration. My approach is to probe the primary sources for meanings that have remained hidden and that may point to themes of wider concern; to relate judicial, administrative, and political deliberations to the dwindling number of death penalty cases. Many students of punishment have concentrated on the application of the law; few have devoted themselves to exploring the occasions when it was deflected from its course. This book places me in the latter camp. My aim is to uncover the factors that inspired restraint in punishment.

The decision of the jury and the passing of the sentence of death were announced in public, with dreary ceremony. There was a ritual aspect to the proceedings and what followed: the donning of a black cap and the intoning of an archaic form of words by the judge; the sheriff (later, prison governor) writing to the executioner; the latter's weighing and measuring and pinioning and masking; the bells tolling; the inquest; the interment; and the notice posted on the prison gate.[22] The rituals emphasized the long-established nature of the practice and, by extension, its inviolability and legitimacy. The clemency decision was an altogether quieter affair, arrived at behind closed doors for reasons that were never divulged. If the Executive Council (later, government) did not advise the governor general (later, president) to commute the sentence, the wheels of justice ground towards the gallows (or firing party).

The drama of an execution resulted in comprehensive record keeping, public debate, reportage, and, on occasion, robust parliamentary exchanges. The archival materials are extensive and come readily to hand. When clemency was granted, sometimes all that was available was the date that the decision had been made; it required persistent sleuthing to unravel its rationale. This book opens the door as far as the extant records allow to reveal how and why this important decision was made. It offers not a theory of clemency but an examination of the practice and an attempt to make sense of the factors that animated it. It also examines

[22] The sheriff's office was abolished by s. 53 of the Court Officers Act, 1926 and this role was taken on by the prison governor thereafter.

the consequences of clemency by tracing the custodial careers of those to whom it was shown.

Wider concerns

Writing about punishment, Garland (1990: 19) observed that as well as having an instrumental purpose it has 'a cultural style and an historical tradition'. Following this lead, what follows is about the cultural style and historical tradition of clemency in post-independence Ireland. Clemency is incomprehensible without understanding the legal, political, and societal settings in which it occurred. The colonial hangover is clear in Ireland (especially, perhaps, in the continued use of English hangmen), yet the glacial pace of law reform, the role of the Catholic Church, the style of government decision-making, and the ferocity of the response to subversion, all have a distinctive Hibernian tinge.

The point is that the timbre of clemency will differ according to the context in which it is expressed. If we get a measure of a country by how it treats its lowest citizens, the exercise of executive clemency offers a portal into an important set of connections between law, politics, and culture. Specifically, the exercise of clemency provides a window onto political imperatives and the values they reflect. Restraint in punishment may feel the same to each of its beneficiaries but its mode of expression says a lot about priorities and preferences; the government chose whom to spare and my goal is to scrutinize this choice. What results is the first attempt to chart the contours of clemency in Ireland.

The clemency decision spoke to social and political preferences as well as to the internal workings of the criminal justice system. Its ramifications extended beyond the legal sphere, highlighting the paramountcy of certain social mores. Some aspects of the cultural style of clemency in Ireland, which are dealt with in the chapters that follow, include breath-taking censoriousness towards unmarried mothers, extending to victim blame in some cases; a more free-floating anxiety about extramarital sex; a low value placed on infant life; a bifurcatory response to political offenders (prior to the 1980s), who were killed hastily or spared and then released quickly and unconditionally; the dominance of Catholicism shown, for example, by the release of convicted murderers to mark a major religious celebration; administrative failures such as premature and unplanned releases on licence; and a willingness to be swayed by authority figures, to the extent that the separation of powers was occasionally breached. The study of clemency tells us a great deal about these other matters which reflect in turn the priorities set—and challenges faced—by an emergent state.

The execution of a death sentence was a powerful statement of sovereign power; by breaking necks (literally) the state was flexing its muscles (figuratively). It is no coincidence that the peaks in execution in Ireland coincided with times when the state was under severe pressure in the 1920s (as the fledgling entity struggled for survival) and the 1940s (when the subversive threat loomed again). As noted above, not only were more people sentenced to death during these testing times but they were more likely to be executed. The state was under duress again in the 1970s and early 1980s as a result of the Troubles in Northern Ireland but at this stage the tide had turned against capital punishment. Ireland was part of the European Economic Community, it was growing in prosperity and confidence, and there was no realistic possibility that it would revert to being a killing state, however great the provocation.

Attitudes to capital punishment must be seen in the context of attitudes to death more generally; these were undoubtedly destabilized by the experience of war across Europe and the accompanying carnage. When life is degraded during conflict the prospect of hanging an occasional murderer excites less concern. Large numbers of combat casualties during war drive homicide rates upwards in the post-conflict period and it would not be surprising if there was a similar effect on the number of executions; both trajectories are explained by diminished regard for human life. When innocent heroes are dying in their thousands in far-away theatres of war, who cares about the fate of a few vicious criminals at home? Death sentences seemed less extreme against a background of massive loss of life across Europe. The civilian murderers executed in the 1940s were collateral damage from a coarsening of attitudes caused by the wider European conflict and a harsh response at home to the threat posed by the IRA.

The slaughter of infants occurred even when it was seen as a crime that merited a harsh penalty (although, as we shall see, the courts were generally lenient) and when there was a widespread fear about the consequences for a baby that had been denied baptism and, as a result, was believed to be consigned to an afterlife in Limbo. That it was regularly recorded nonetheless says a great deal about the pressures faced by unmarried mothers. It was more than economic duress and the burden of shame that led them to kill their offspring. There was also a prevailing attitude that infant life was of little value. Unwanted babies were choked, drowned, or buried alive.

Increasing prosperity was accompanied by increasing concern for children. In addition, improvements in hygiene and medicine shifted an entrenched attitude about the inevitability of death and meant that all newborns came to be seen as individuals who could—and should—survive the transition to childhood and beyond. When survival is more predictable the loss of life comes as a greater shock. In an environment where death was omnipresent, arguments for the sanctity of human life carried little weight. This growing respect for newborns can be seen in improved life expectancy. The infant mortality rate in Ireland fell from 99 to 6 per 1,000 live births between 1900 and 1995 (Kennedy 2001: 35). When high, a critical risk factor was whether the child had been born out of wedlock. According to Kennedy: 'In 1930 one out of every four illegitimate children died in the first year of life; their mortality rate was four times greater than that of children of married parents' (p. 37). By the time that contraceptives were legalized in 1979 and became widely available (having been banned by s. 17 of the Criminal Law Amendment Act, 1935), the destruction of unwanted children was virtually unheard of and would have been considered unconscionable.

Sources

The parameters of any piece of historical research are determined by the available primary materials. In this case they were copious. In addition to the publicly available records held by the Department of the Taoiseach, Department of Justice, Governor General's Office, Attorney General's Office, Department of Foreign Affairs, Bureau of Military History, and Office of the Secretary to the President, I was granted permission to view the closed prisoner files, which were available for all but one of the jury trials; William Wall's file could not be located despite strenuous and wide-ranging searches.[23] Additionally,

[23] In order not to risk breaching the requirements of data protection and confidentiality set by the Department of Justice and Equality as conditions of access to the closed prisoner files, I have been parsimonious in the extent to which I quote from them. On rare occasions this has disallowed me from publishing

I examined the Trials Records Books of the Central Criminal Court, the General Prisons Board Death Book, judgments of the Court of Criminal Appeal and Supreme Court, transcripts of trials (where available), and minutes of meetings of the Executive Council (1923 to 1937) and the government (1937 to 1986). Finally, I was granted access to the contents of the Mountjoy Prison Museum, including its records of death sentences and commutations and its collection of capital punishment-related paraphernalia.

In short, the archival materials were detailed and the availability of multiple sources allowed adequate cross-checking and data verification. Gaps were filled with contemporaneous newspaper reports and a review of proceedings in the Houses of the Oireachtas [parliament].[24] The range and depth of the available material did not mean I could answer every question posed by the research—sometimes a relevant document was missing or had never been generated—but I am confident that I had access to sufficient data to formulate robust conclusions.[25]

Avoiding Death-eligibility

Table 1.2 shows the number of murders recorded by An Garda Síochána [national police force] that led to proceedings. A conviction for murder resulted in a mandatory death sentence until 1964 but, even if proceedings were initiated, a conviction did not necessarily follow and, if it did, it may have been for something

snippets of information that might cause distress to the living even long after the events in question. Sometimes this stipulation has prevented me from being as precise as I would have wished with a citation but, on balance, it was felt that a little unavoidable vagueness was a price worth paying for access to such a rich data source. When I use the material culled from the closed prisoner files it is usually paraphrased or aggregated. Direct quotations are given only if this is essential for context. A comprehensive listing of the case files included in the analysis is given in the bibliography.

[24] The bibliography does not constitute an exhaustive list of primary materials consulted; if a record contained nothing of relevance it is not listed. Similarly, the secondary sources are limited to the subset of the examined literature that has been drawn upon directly in the text.

[25] Victims' voices were conspicuously absent from the files. Occasionally their families petitioned for leniency. More often they played no role. They certainly did not bay for blood or protest when clemency was shown. They had no advocates.

other than murder.[26] This gives a sense of the maximum number of death-eligible cases. What is considered next is how the pool of killers was reduced to those who received the mandatory death penalty.[27] Where a charge of murder was brought, a conviction for murder was a relatively uncommon outcome.

The killer can cheat the noose through suicide and this is not unknown when victim and perpetrator are intimates. Table 1.4 shows that, between 1946 and 1961, more accused persons took their own lives than were acquitted.[28] The police can decline to make an arrest but murder allegations are so serious that such an option was not open in any meaningful sense. The prosecuting authority can divert accused persons from a possible death sentence by deciding to take no further action or in the choice of charge.[29] The role for prosecutorial discretion in charge selection was substantial (e.g. preferring concealment of birth to murder) and prosecutors were involved in many more cases of unnatural death (whatever legal designation they finally attracted) than judges, juries, and governments. Juries can convict of manslaughter rather than murder and thereby remove the death penalty from consideration. They can nullify the effect of the law through acquittal, should they realize that they possess this power, or give the accused person a second chance by failing to agree; a hung jury may prevent a hanged prisoner. Acquittals were relatively common between 1928 and 1955, accounting for around one in five court outcomes, but seem to have fallen off thereafter.

[26] The Criminal Justice Act, 1964 limited the death penalty to what became known as capital murder. This was defined, at s. 1 of the legislation, as the deliberate killing of on-duty members of An Garda Síochána or the prison service as well as treasonable offences and the politically motivated murder, on Irish soil, of foreign heads of state, diplomats, or government members. The death penalty was abolished for all crimes by the Criminal Justice Act, 1990.

[27] Just as not all killers were sentenced to death so too not all of those sentenced to death were killers (see Appendix III). Furthermore, to be convicted of murder did not require that the individual fired the fatal shot or struck the lethal blow (or, indeed, that they caused any direct harm to the deceased); it was enough for them to be part of a joint enterprise that resulted in death.

[28] Suicide was a crime until the passage of the Criminal Law (Suicide) Act, 1993 and an unsuccessful attempt could result in criminal proceedings.

[29] Prosecutions were taken in the name of the People and at the suit of the attorney general until the Office of the Director of Public Prosecutions was created in 1974.

Table 1.4 Attrition in murder trials

	1928–55	1946–61
Acquitted	41	4
Unfit to plead	39	19
Guilty but insane	16	7
Convicted	102	18
Suicide	—	7
Died awaiting trial	—	1
Committed to mental hospital without arraignment	—	15
All	198	71

Note: Based on figures in *Murder Trials 1928–1955*, Mountjoy Prison Museum (excluding cases dealt with by Special Powers Tribunal or military courts, and crimes that would be considered infanticide; convictions can be subdivided into 67 for manslaughter and 35 for murder); and *Murders 1946–1961*, NAI, JUS/2004/32/20 (excluding one case where information was refused and another of justifiable homicide).

Jury nullification is a way of frustrating the law's intent when its application would lead to manifest injustice. It is a check on overbroad or excessively harsh laws. Juries are not required to explain their actions and the prohibition on double jeopardy prevents a retrial on the same charge. Given that a modest proportion of cases resulted in acquittals, and accepting that in some of these cases there must have been genuine doubts about the accused person's culpability, it is clear that this power was either not well understood or that juries were not moved to exercise it. Juries could also make recommendations to mercy in the hope of tempering the inevitable consequence of their decision and they routinely availed themselves of the opportunity to add a rider to their verdict (see Chapter 4).

The data shown in the two columns in Table 1.4 relate to different but overlapping time periods, were compiled to answer different questions, and are not easy to reconcile with other available statistics (such as those shown in Table 1.2). Nevertheless, they are of some value, indicating that murder trials led to a variety of outcomes and that it was not uncommon for an accused person to be diverted to a mental hospital, either for a period prior to arraignment in court, or after formal proceedings had commenced; more than twice as many accused murderers were found unfit to plead as guilty but insane after trial.

Madness

The defence could argue that their client was unfit to plead or had been insane at the time of their act. The issue of unfitness to plead was decided by a jury on the balance of probabilities. Gibbons et al. (1999) examined the characteristics of almost 500 persons found unfit to plead in Ireland between 1850 and 1995. All were sent to the Central Criminal Lunatic Asylum (later, Central Mental Hospital (CMH)) where they stayed for an average of 14.3 years (range: less than one year to 65 years), with 46 per cent remaining in custody until they died. For those charged with violent crimes the average length of stay was 15.9 years. Only 4 per cent were ultimately returned for trial having spent an average of four years in detention. Those found unfit to plead spent longer incarcerated than convicted murderers whose death sentences were commuted to penal servitude for life (Table 10.1).

Section 2 of the Trial of Lunatics Act, 1883 specified the circumstances under which the jury could return a special verdict of guilty but insane. The relevant test of responsibility was set out in the McNaghten Rules which required that to establish a defence on the ground of insanity it must be proved that, at the time the act was committed, the accused person was labouring under such a defect of reason, from disease of the mind, as not to know the nature and quality of the act he was doing, or, if he did know it, that he did not know what he was doing was wrong. It was necessary for the defence to prove insanity, although the civil standard applied (i.e. on the balance of probabilities rather than beyond reasonable doubt). Progressively, from the 1930s onwards, it was accepted that these rules might not cover all the circumstances in which a person could successfully plead the insanity defence and in 1974—ten years after the mandatory death sentence for murder was abolished—the Supreme Court accepted that the defence was also available to a person who acted on an irresistible impulse resulting from a defect of reason owing to mental illness.[30]

[30] *Doyle v Wicklow County Council* [1974] IR 55. This had already been accepted at trial court level in *People (AG) v Hayes* (Central Criminal Court, unreported, 30 November 1967). The issue of irresistible impulse was raised, unsuccessfully, by a number of the murderers whose crimes feature in this book, namely Leo O'Brien, Patrick Boylan, Michael Manning, and Vincent McGrath.

Gibbons et al. (1997) examined the case files relating to admissions to the CMH between 1850 and 1995 after a finding of guilty but insane. Around half had been convicted of lethal violence. They found that for persons admitted before 1950, more than four out of ten died in custody after an average stay of almost twenty years. The remainder were discharged, either to the community or to the care of their district asylum, after eleven years on average, with men being held significantly longer than women. Most of the thirty-eight patients admitted after 1950 were still in the CMH when Gibbons et al. completed their analysis; four had died there after an average stay of 9.3 years and nine had been discharged after an average of 8.8 years.

These figures cannot be disaggregated by crime type, but assuming insane killers were not too dissimilar from insane arsonists, thieves, sex offenders, assaulters, and attempted suicides (the other categories studied) in terms of prognosis, a finding of guilty but insane meant a long stay behind high walls. Men charged with murder who were found guilty but insane spent a lot longer coercively confined than other alleged murderers who went to trial, were convicted, and had their sentences commuted to penal servitude for life.[31] The picture was less clear-cut for women; those who were sent to the CMH spent longer there than they would have in prison, but it is not clear where they went afterwards. Some were transferred to a district asylum, but the duration of stay was not reported.[32]

[31] 'Coercive confinement' is a term coined by O'Sullivan and O'Donnell (2007) to capture the range of institutions in which men, women, and children were involuntarily detained, including psychiatric hospitals, reformatory and industrial schools, mother and baby homes, prisons, and Magdalen asylums. The conditions in these institutions were austere and, while some of them were ostensibly directed at the welfare of their inhabitants, they were experienced as degrading, stigmatizing, and punitive places. (For a range of contemporaneous inmate accounts, see O'Sullivan and O'Donnell 2012.)

[32] The insanity defence was used less often when murder ceased to attract the mandatory death penalty. In a study of 610 homicides between 1972 and 1991, Dooley (1995: 20) found that thirty-one (5.1 per cent) resulted in a finding that the defendant was unfit to plead or guilty but insane. A follow-up study of 205 homicides between 1992 and 1996 found that only four (2 per cent) resulted in such a disposal (Dooley 2001: 20). The dwindling numbers suggest that what was at issue in at least some of these cases was the avoidance of a possible date with the hangman rather than the desire to receive treatment for an underlying illness.

Infanticide

It was very unusual for a woman who killed her child to end up on trial for her life. According to Brennan (2013: 7) almost three-quarters of 160 women who found themselves in this situation between 1922 (the foundation of the Free State) and 1949 (the enactment of infanticide legislation) pleaded guilty to a lesser offence such as manslaughter or concealment of birth. When a trial did proceed, around half were acquitted and most of those convicted were found guilty of manslaughter or concealment of birth. Custodial sentences were imposed on around half of the convicted women and they tended to be short. Most of these sentences were suspended, usually on condition that the woman resided at a religious institution. So too, when women were conditionally discharged under s. 1 of the Probation of Offenders Act, 1907 a condition of residence at a convent was regularly attached. Occasionally, a prison sentence was not imposed on condition that the woman got married.[33] This was an exercise in crime prevention: the sacrament of matrimony precluded the future arrival of more 'illegitimate' children whose lives would be at elevated risk.

A letter from the Chief State Solicitor described the high rate of attrition over the previous three years in prosecutions of women who killed their children. Of thirty-six charges of murder, there were two convictions for murder and one for concealment of birth, one acquittal, twenty-eight pleas of manslaughter, and three pleas of concealment of birth. There was a single finding of guilty but insane.[34] It is surprising how few mothers who killed their babies were deemed to satisfy the legal definition of insanity given the degree of psychological upheaval associated with parturition recognized by the infanticide legislation introduced in England and, eventually, in Ireland.[35]

[33] Mary Hanley was charged with the murder of her unnamed son on 27 April 1931. She was convicted of concealment of birth on 18 June 1931. James McEvoy, the sole witness at the trial, undertook to marry Miss Hanley immediately. She was released from custody on her own recognizance to allow the marriage proceed without delay. NAI, Trials Record Book, Change of Venue Cases, Nov. 1927–June 1933.

[34] Letter from chief state solicitor to ard-aighne [attorney general], 1 August 1944, NAI, AG/2000/10/2922.

[35] The Infanticide Act, 1949 allowed infanticide as an alternative charge or conviction to murder in circumstances where a mother killed her child aged under twelve months and, 'at the time of the act or omission the balance of her mind

The mothers who were competent to stand trial but who did not benefit from the preferment of an alternative charge to murder, or the offering to the jury of the possibility of manslaughter, and who were duly convicted, constituted a very small proportion of the total number of child killers, numbering just ten out of 160. It is not possible to say for certain if they differed as a group from the others without examining the circumstances of the cases that led to more lenient outcomes but my analysis of the archival materials suggests some points of contrast.

It is arguable that they were older (none was aged under 21), and that the children had survived longer before death indicating greater deliberation and effort (especially in those cases where the birth took place in an institution and the child may have been given a name, thereby further humanizing them). There is quite a difference between a distressed teenager destroying an unwanted child immediately after an unassisted labour in a field, and a woman in her twenties killing a healthy infant after leaving the county home (former workhouse). They may also have differed in that they had a previous conviction for a similar offence or had other illegitimate children so could not plausibly claim to have been shamed into action by their predicament (see Chapter 8). The fact that in all but one case they were not married to the child's father no doubt counted against them; a married woman in similar circumstances may have found it easier to argue that the child had been stillborn.

Age

Extreme youth provided a final way to avoid becoming death-eligible. Mary Cole, a domestic servant from County Laois, was tried in March 1928 for killing two of her employers' children. Each was drowned in what were initially believed to be accidents. Cole was fourteen when she committed the murders and fifteen

was disturbed by reason of her not having fully recovered from the effect of giving birth to the child or by reason of the effect of lactation consequent upon the birth of the child' (s. 1.3.c). In a study of 191 'infanticide' cases dealt with by the Central Criminal Court between 1922 and 1950, Rattigan (2010: 184) found that only three resulted in verdicts of guilty but insane and that just one woman attempted suicide (which, because it was a crime, led to additional criminal proceedings).

when tried. The judge told the jury during his summing up that, whatever their verdict, they would have the consolation of knowing that a capital sentence would not be imposed and he told the prisoner when passing sentence that, had she been a few months older, he would have had no option but to sentence her to death (*Irish Times*, 24 March 1928).[36] The jury took forty minutes to convict Cole of the double murder. Her appeal failed and she was committed to Mountjoy Female Prison to be detained at the pleasure of the governor general. Less than six months after her conviction the minister issued a licence under s. 105 of the Children Act, 1908 permitting her to be discharged from prison to the authority of the 'sister superior' at Our Lady's Home for Discharged Female Prisoners in Dublin.[37]

Gerard Noone, aged fifteen, was convicted of murder in 1959 and sentenced to be detained at the government's pleasure. He had beaten Margaret Anne Finn, a 61-year-old widow and neighbour, over the head with a copper pipe during an attempted burglary. The jury added a strong recommendation to mercy but were reassured by Mr Justice Dixon that there was no need to do so. According to a report in the *Cork Examiner* on 9 July 1959, the judge told them that: 'As far as the boy was concerned, there would be a question of Borstal treatment, or something like that'.[38] (The jury in Mary Cole's case added no such rider. This may have been because the judge explained before they commenced their deliberations that the death penalty would not apply, or because they were appalled by her conduct and desired the court to be unsparing in its response.)

[36] The death penalty for those aged under sixteen was abolished by s. 103 of the Children Act, 1908 and the minimum age at which a person could be executed was raised from sixteen to seventeen by the Children Act, 1941. The youngest person executed in post-independence Ireland was 19-year-old William O'Neill.

[37] It seemed a neat solution as: 'She will be under proper reformative influences and at the same time the community will be protected from a person of the gravest criminal tendencies. If she, after a space of years, appears to be completely reformed the question of allowing her at large can be considered. If the Nuns fail to keep control over her we can always send her back to Prison.' Memorandum from secretary, Department of Justice to President of Executive Council, 28 August 1928, NAI, TSCH/3/S5744.

[38] Between 1940 and 1963, one other under 17-year-old was convicted of murder. Note for minister's information, October 1963, NAI, JUS/2004/32/20.

Final tally

My sample comprises everyone sentenced to death whose conviction was not overturned on appeal. (Cases that were successfully appealed resulted in either an acquittal or a conviction for a non-capital crime so the question of clemency did not arise.) By my estimation there were ninety-eight such persons, of whom thirty-five were executed (see Appendices I to III).[39] Several had more than one trial with the original conviction upheld on a subsequent occasion. Twenty were convicted before non-jury courts which had been established to deal with the subversive threat (see Chapter 5).

Appeals were generally heard swiftly but there were some exceptions. Peter Pringle was sentenced to death by the Special Criminal Court on 27 November 1980 along with Patrick McCann and Colm O'Shea. His conviction was quashed by the Court of Criminal Appeal on 16 May 1995 and a retrial was ordered but the Director of Public Prosecutions subsequently entered a nolle prosequi. There was a long time lag between Pringle's conviction and its quashing but it seems logical to omit him on the basis that I do not include convictions that were overturned or downgraded on appeal; the interval is of secondary importance.

I do not omit Henry Gleeson from consideration; he received a posthumous pardon in 2015, but this does not alter the fact that he was hanged for what he was believed to have done. The sentence stood for long enough to be carried out and this is worth memorializing.

Judges and governments were key players in the clemency process, the former setting out their views in confidential letters to the Minister for Justice after the sentence had been confirmed, and the latter advising the governor general (later, president) to grant clemency, advice he was bound to accept. Juries often, but not always, played a role, being replaced in political cases by a panel of judges. Before examining their relative contributions (Chapters 4 to 7), it is necessary to devote some time to setting out, in broad terms, the characteristics of death-eligible crimes and offering a schema for their classification, based on the underlying rationale. This is the purpose of Chapters 2 and 3. Once

[39] In the interests of clarity and brevity, when I mention specific cases I try not to clutter the text with details that are reported in the appendices.

this framework has been articulated, and the key elements of the clemency decision have been unpacked, attention shifts to the types of murderer who escaped the noose (Chapters 8 and 9), and how long they spent in custody prior to release (Chapter 10). The book concludes with a Postscript describing how the death penalty continued to resonate as recently as December 2015 with the release of Michael McHugh, the final death-sentence prisoner, and the posthumous pardon granted the same month to Henry Gleeson.

2

Classifying Clemency

It is possible to learn a considerable amount from the primary sources about the attributes of those to whom clemency was shown and how they differed from those who were executed. Scrutiny of the files suggests that there were three possible routes to clemency—justice, mercy, and caprice—and these are set out below after the pertinent case characteristics have been reviewed and the various stages between the imposition of a death sentence and its implementation have been outlined. The chapter concludes with a consideration of the most appropriate terminology to capture the deliberative processes that are at the heart of the analysis presented in this book.

Who, Where, How?

Annie Walsh was the only woman sentenced to death who actually went to the gallows. Another twenty-one, including her namesake (who similarly joined forces with her lover to kill her husband), heard the solemn pronouncement that they would be hanged by the neck until dead in the prison from whence they came, but they were spared. Sometimes this was an attempt by the government to temper the ferocity of the law with compassion for the distressed mother who destroyed her infant child. But, leaving baby-killing aside, the gender difference in execution remained pronounced: half of male murderers were executed after trial by jury, compared with one in ten females.

In the four years between the convictions of Annie Walsh (9 July 1925) and Annie Walsh (21 June 1929), the prospects for female killers improved markedly. Both of these crimes involved older women and younger men and the latter case was, if anything, more shocking as there had been previous attempts on the husband's life and the wife was rumoured to have brought

Justice, Mercy, and Caprice: Clemency and the Death Penalty in Ireland. First Edition. Ian O'Donnell. © Ian O'Donnell 2017. Published 2017 by Oxford University Press.

Table 2.1 Gender

		Victim	
		Male	Female
Perpetrator (commuted)	Male	17	11
	Female	12	9
Perpetrator (executed)	Male	16	12
	Female	1	0

Note: Cases dealt with by non-jury courts—in which all of the protagonists were male—are omitted from this table. Twelve of the female perpetrators whose sentences were commuted murdered a new-born child (seven boys and four girls); there are fewer victims than perpetrators because Elizabeth Edwards and Rose Edwards were both convicted of murdering the former's two-week-old daughter, Mary Teresa.

about her first husband's death in the United States. A confidential Garda report described her as a 'wicked criminal' to whom the Executive Council should be slow to show clemency.[1] It is also noteworthy that the jury recommended mercy for the Annie Walsh who was executed but not for the Annie Walsh who was spared. In one case both parties were hanged. In the other, neither was. After Annie Walsh's execution on 5 August 1925, a prisoner's gender sufficed to cancel an appointment with the hangman.

Table 2.1 shows the relationship between perpetrator gender and victim gender. While males predominated, especially among those who were executed, there were more female perpetrators than is usually found in studies of lethal violence. This is on account of the inclusion of ten mothers, a grandmother, and an aunt who murdered newborn babies. For cases involving non-infant victims that led to murder convictions after trial by jury, the following was the gender breakdown:

52 per cent of men who murdered women were executed
48 per cent of men who murdered men were executed

In other words, victim gender does not appear to have impacted significantly on the likelihood of execution.

[1] Letter from [name illegible] to secretary, Department of Justice, 4 July 1929, NAI, JUS/H234/2599.

As well as being predominantly male, the protagonists in these cases tended to be young. The median age at death for those executed was 31 years (range: 19 to 48). Those who were spared were a little younger on average—28—and the range was wider (19 to 63). Omitting the babies who were murdered, and looking at cases where clemency was shown, the median victim age was 34 years (range: 18 months to 83 years).[2] The victims of those executed were aged 36 on average (range: 18 years to 84 years).

The offender's motivation was another key consideration. The likelihood of execution in a politically motivated case was less than one in three (Table 4.5), whereas for other men it was exactly fifty-fifty (Table 4.6). In other words, despite all of the fierce rhetoric about crushing the IRA, the chaotic domestic killer was more likely to be executed than the armed and organized insurgent.

Table 2.2 shows the distribution of capital sentences by the county where the incident attracting the sentence occurred. Unsurprisingly, the top position, in terms of numbers, is occupied by Dublin (which includes the capital city and its surrounds), where nineteen people—one in five of the total—were sentenced to death. No crimes that resulted in the imposition of the death penalty took place in Leitrim, the least populous county, or in Cavan. Given the span of almost seventy years encompassed by the table (1923 to 1990), most counties were exposed to the kinds of events that culminated in capital punishment no more than once every couple of decades.

The most popular methods used to cause death were, in descending order of significance: shooting, beating, choking, stabbing or hacking, drowning, and poisoning (Table 2.3). There was a single case of burning (Patrick Aylward threw an 18-month-old child onto a fire) and one case of a newborn being buried alive (Elizabeth Hannon's unnamed son). There was one case (involving two perpetrators, Elizabeth Edwards and Rose Edwards) where a body was never recovered so the cause of death could not be established and there was one case of a botched abortion (Mary Cadden) where death resulted from heart failure. A torso was discovered in Bernard Kirwan's case but it was

[2] While prosecutions were taken in a single name, on occasion there was more than one victim (see Appendices).

Table 2.2 Geography

	Executed	Commuted	All
Carlow	0	1	1
Cavan	0	0	0
Clare	0	3	3
Cork	2	6	8
Donegal	1	0	1
Dublin	9	10	19
Galway	0	4	4
Kerry	1	3	4
Kildare	0	1	1
Kilkenny	0	2	2
Laois	1	1	2
Leitrim	0	0	0
Limerick	4	3	7
Longford	1	0	1
Louth	2	2	4
Mayo	0	1	1
Meath	2	3	5
Monaghan	0	2	2
Offaly	2	2	4
Roscommon	2	6	8
Sligo	1	0	1
Tipperary	2	3	5
Waterford	1	2	3
Westmeath	0	3	3
Wexford	2	3	5
Wicklow	2	1	3
Various	0	1	1
All	35	63	98

Note: Based on county where crime occurred. 'Various' refers to the kidnapping of Stephen Hayes for which Seán McCaughey was sentenced to death. Hayes was held captive at locations in Dublin, Louth, and Wicklow before he made good his escape.

Table 2.3 Murder methods

	Executed	Commuted	All
Shooting	10	12	22
Beating	10	6	16
Choking	3	9	12
Stabbing / hacking	3	7	10
Drowning	1	8	9
Poisoning	1	2	3
Burning	0	1	1
Burying alive	0	1	1
Botched abortion	0	1	1
Not known	1	2	3
All	29	49	78

Note: Two death sentences were imposed in a case where a victim's body was not recovered (the Edwards sisters). One was imposed where a torso was found and a cause of death could not be established (Bernard Kirwan). The twenty cases dealt with by non-jury courts are excluded; all involved firearms with the exception of Seán McCaughey who was convicted of assault and false imprisonment.

decomposed to such a degree that the reason for his demise could not be ascertained.

Murderers who used weapons were not treated more harshly than their unarmed counterparts. Table 2.3 shows that most of those sentenced to death for shooting or stabbing/hacking were not executed. Poisoning also requires deliberation and, while there were only three cases involving poisoners, two of them were spared. The batterers' discount that others have reported was not evident in the post-independence period as the majority of those who beat their victims to death were executed.[3] Newborn babies were usually choked or drowned.

[3] In his study of murder trials in the nineteenth and early twentieth century Vaughan (2009: 321) reported that: 'The use of firearms, knives, and poison, which suggested deliberation, were almost certain to lead to hanging.' It must be acknowledged that many unarmed killers will have been convicted of manslaughter so the capital cases are the most serious among their number. See O'Donnell (2010: 67–71) for an account of the sliding scale of culpability and punishment in homicide cases.

Rapidity

In countries where capital punishment has not been abolished, arguments aimed at getting prisoners off death row alive often centre on the degree to which they have been transformed in the interval between the crime and the eventual determination of a date for the sentence to be carried out. As a result of maturation and reflection they are no longer the same person who was convicted. Their peer group has changed, they are free of drugs and alcohol, the risk they pose is greatly reduced, they may have found God. Over time a persuasive case can be made for deep and enduring remorse, and evidence of repentance can be compiled. A compelling redemption narrative may emerge. Also, the emotion that surrounded the events may have dissipated, with the person whose fate hangs in the balance occupying a less prominent place in the lives of those who were harmed by his or her actions. If a prisoner does not waive their right to appeal, this interval can be very lengthy indeed.[4] In Ireland during the period under examination the speed at which the process moved meant that the murderer was a figure very close to public and political awareness.

The time intervals between crime and conviction, and between conviction and execution, repay scrutiny on account of their brevity and the almost unseemly haste with which prisoners were put to death. For the twenty-nine non-political offenders who were executed, the average time between the commission of the offence and the sentence of the court was a little over four months. There was a wide range, from ten days for William Downes to more than two years for James Myles. Things happened quickly thereafter with executions taking place around one month later. Into this brief period of time were compressed petitions on behalf of the condemned person; the appeals process; the preparation of a memorandum for government; the government's review of the sentence, judicial observations, and the jury's recommendation (if any); confirmation of the execution and the practical arrangements for securing the services of an English hangman. William Gambon was one of a small number of 'volunteers': he did not

[4] An extreme example is Brandon Jones, executed in the United States on 3 February 2016, thirty-six years after he was convicted of murder.

appeal and, three weeks after his conviction, his neck was broken in Mountjoy Prison.

For IRA members facing execution, matters progressed with even greater rapidity once an arrest was made. For example, Patrick McGrath and Thomas Green were convicted four days after the murder of Richard Hyland, and after another seventeen days they were executed. This was strikingly fast considering that the executions were delayed by unsuccessful applications to the High Court and to the Supreme Court. George Plant and Maurice O'Neill were executed seven days post-conviction. As these cases had been dealt with by non-jury courts with a limited (or non-existent) right of appeal in a context where the government was resolute and the execution was carried out by local soldiers, there were few potential obstacles to overcome.

Deterrence theorists write of the importance of certainty (likelihood of apprehension), celerity (speed of case processing), and severity (onerousness of sanction) if punishment is to be effective in terms of reducing crime. Certainty is the most important and severity the least important of the three factors. These conditions are seldom met today with many serious crimes going undetected, and those which do lead to arrest taking a considerable amount of time to prosecute to a conclusion. During the early decades of Irish independence all three criteria were met. Murders invariably led to an arrest. The time to conviction was brief. The sanction was undeniably severe.

There is another element to speed. This is the alacrity with which the hanging was carried out and the associated formalities completed. There were ten distinct steps to be taken. *First* of all the condemned person had to be readied for execution and escorted to the gallows. This was a short walk, only fifteen paces according to one newspaper's account of the execution of John Cox (*Irish Independent*, 26 April 1929). On reaching the final destination, the prisoner was placed on heavy oak trapdoors directly beneath a beam from which hung a three-quarter inch Italian hemp rope. Before the noose was put in place and tightened, the condemned person's legs were strapped and a white linen cap was placed over his (or, on one occasion, her) head. The trap doors were then thrown open.

The nooses used in Mountjoy Prison had a wash-leather covering so that the soon-to-be-dead person's neck would not suffer chafing; there was to be no unnecessary discomfort in the seconds before the drop. If the preparations had been sufficiently thorough, and the metal eyelet on the rope was correctly positioned to the left of the jaw, the neck was broken (usually around the third cervical vertebra) and death was immediate. Otherwise strangulation ensued with prisoners remaining suspended until the life was choked out of them. Albert Pierrepoint estimated that, if everything went smoothly, 'between nine and twelve seconds' elapsed from his entering the condemned cell to extinguishing its occupant's life.[5]

Secondly, the priest in attendance went down the steps into the pit to anoint the corpse (all but one of those hanged were Catholics).[6] *Thirdly*, there was an inspection by the doctor to confirm death, after which the body was left hanging for one hour.[7] *Fourthly*, a notice was pinned to the outside of the prison gate confirming that the sentence of the court had been carried out.

Fifthly, the body was taken down. The rope, white linen cap, and pinioning straps were removed, and it was prepared for viewing by the inquest jury. This was a process that involved some delicacy as the involuntary bowel movements that could accompany hanging meant that there were certain sanitary tasks to be performed before the corpse, with its elongated neck, could be displayed. (For women there was the additional horrific prospect that their 'insides' may have fallen out.[8]) A piece of wood

[5] Minutes of Evidence Taken before the Royal Commission on Capital Punishment, 2 November 1950, para. 8452.

[6] Memories of Mountjoy jail as told by former governor Sean Kavanagh to Liam MacGabhann, Mountjoy Prison Museum.

[7] Memorandum of instructions for carrying out the details of an execution, Mountjoy Prison Museum.

[8] This was believed to have happened when Edith Thompson was hanged in England in 1923, 'suggesting that she was pregnant and miscarried on the gallows' in full view of the witnesses (Kennedy 2007: 41). The hangman, John Ellis, was said to have been visibly distressed and he attempted suicide not long afterwards. A new rule was introduced after this event stipulating that women would be provided with canvass undergarments so that witnesses would not be exposed to the sight of blood or excrement (Kennedy 2007: 47). The chaplain in attendance at Thompson's execution was so disturbed by what he witnessed that he had a nervous breakdown and was required to resign the service (Potter 1993: 132, 189). The Home Secretary who refused to grant her clemency was said to have never fully recovered from the experience and the governor's anguish apparently caused a change in his physical appearance (Langhamer 2012: 431, 437). In his autobiography, Albert Pierrepoint (1974: 57, 207) disputed

was placed under the head to raise it by three inches for the inquest.[9]

Twice there was a double hanging. Thomas Delaney and Thomas McDonagh perished simultaneously at 8 a.m. on 12 December 1923. The executions of Michael Talbot and Annie Walsh two years later took place separately, with the latter getting the courtesy of an extra three-quarters of an hour of life. The files and newspaper reports are silent as to whether Walsh was hanged in the women's prison but, as it had its own hang house, it is almost certain that she was dispatched there while Talbot was dangling in the adjacent men's prison. A short interval would have been required for Thomas Pierrepoint and his entourage to cover the distance between the two killing sites. There were gates to open and close and formalities to be observed which meant that a sombre procession like this could not be rushed. An internal gate allowed access between the men's and women's prisons. The alternative would have been to escort Mrs Walsh from one prison to the other, a distance that was far too great given the potential for distress and disruption; a long walk to the gallows would have constituted a cruel protraction of an already gruesome procedure.[10]

Sixthly, the body was transported from the hang house to the mortuary, probably in a handcart. *Seventhly*, the inquest was conducted before a jury.[11] *Eighthly*, the jury returned its verdict having heard evidence from the prison governor and medical officer, and the coroner formally recorded same.[12] *Ninthly*, the coroner issued the order for burial. *Tenthly*, and finally, the criminal's remains were brought to the burial ground and interred in

that the execution had been as awful as reported and denied that the timing of his own resignation had been influenced by his role in the hanging of another woman, Ruth Ellis.

[9] Memorandum of instructions for carrying out the details of an execution, Mountjoy Prison Museum.

[10] Fielding (2008: 107) agrees that two gallows were in operation that day, one each in the men's and women's prisons.

[11] There were no inquests into executions by firing party. For an account of how these events were choreographed see Doyle and O'Donnell (2012: 81–3).

[12] A typical example is the finding that James McHugh died from: 'Fracture of the 3rd cervical vertebra following hanging. Said act being carried out in the interests of justice'. Abstract of Verdict, 24 November 1926, NAI, JUS/H234/1490.

the chaplain's presence. This was a short distance but would have involved the handcart again no doubt. In Mountjoy Prison these graves were not marked and were somewhat scattered, making the precise location of remains impossible; to add a further complication, buildings have been constructed atop some of them.

In Annie Walsh's case all ten steps were accomplished within four hours: she was hanged at 8:45 a.m. and her grave was closed at 12:45 p.m. the same day. This was not unusually quick. Hangings were normally scheduled for 8 a.m., inquests took place at 11 a.m., and bodies were in the ground an hour or so later. The choreography of the final act of this drama was as noteworthy for its speed as the opening act, when the trial jury wasted no time in arriving at its decision (see Chapter 4).[13]

But most of those sentenced to death (sixty-three out of ninety-eight) did not have to take any of these ten steps, benefiting from the state's decision to exercise clemency in their favour.

A Tripartite Scheme

'Clemency' refers to a reduction, by politicians, in the severity of punishments lawfully imposed by judges. It is a recognition of law's inherent limitations. It is contemptuous of legal rules and emerges from a deliberative process that is not open to scrutiny.[14] It involves the government drawing on a range of factors within and without the law. It is distinct from forgiveness which is a matter for individual aggrieved parties and in which the state can play no role.[15] It may result from a search for justice, it may

[13] There was some variation in practice in the early days. For example, William Downes was identified by his brother, the chief state solicitor was present at the inquest, and family members were permitted to enter the prison to view his remains and say some prayers over them before they were buried. Delaney and McDonagh were executed a fortnight later and, while the chief state solicitor attended the inquest, evidence of identification was provided by the principal prison warder, and the family was not allowed sight of the corpse.

[14] According to Weihofen (1939–40: 114): 'Historically, pardon has always been the broadest and least limited of powers. By its very nature, it could not be subjected to rules or restrictions. Its function was rather to break rules, wherever in the opinion of the pardoning authority mercy, clemency, justice or merely personal whim dictated.'

[15] Clemency is a public act that results from a political process while forgiveness is a private response, perhaps with religious roots. Anyone who has been injured can forgive but not anyone can extend clemency. It is not necessarily the

be motivated by mercy, or it may be capricious in its operation. Clemency is lenient treatment, however it comes about; it is not synonymous with mercy. Its pros and cons are reviewed in the following chapter; here the focus is on its diverse manifestations.

Clemency can appear in a variety of guises, each of which eases the weight of the imposed punishment. These include *reprieve* (a pause before the sentence is carried out, for example to allow an appeal; routinely granted if requested); *commutation* (the substitution of a less severe punishment; granted in two-thirds of death penalty cases in Ireland during the period under consideration); *remission* (the penalty is reduced in whole or in part; inevitable unless the individual dies in confinement); and *pardon* (punishment and guilt are invalidated and the individual is absolved from the legal consequences of their conviction; a single case—the aforementioned Henry Gleeson).

Clemency also embraces *amnesties* which differ from pardons in that they are usually addressed to a category of offender rather than specific individuals, are often limited to political offences, and are generally a matter for the legislature rather than the executive or head of state.[16] They have the effect of remitting the punishment, without reconsideration of guilt or innocence; they entail forgetting without forgiving.

All of the foregoing find shelter under the conceptual umbrella provided by 'clemency'. For present purposes the focus is on clemency as commutation, of which there are three variants. These I define as justice, mercy, and caprice and they are dealt with next in descending order of importance.[17]

case that forgiveness will be accompanied by mitigation of punishment. Nor does it have to be complete; it is a shift in attitude that can take place gradually or not at all. It is particularly problematic when the victim is dead; under these circumstances, it is far from obvious who has standing to forgive.

[16] For example, the accelerated releases of qualifying prisoners under s. 3 of the Criminal Justice (Release of Prisoners) Act, 1998 which gave effect to the terms of the Good Friday Agreement, copper-fastening the peace process in Northern Ireland. Previous IRA releases, involving much smaller numbers, were decided upon by the executive without the need for new legislation. Sometimes amnesties were granted to mark an occasion of national celebration and they were not limited to political prisoners.

[17] The rationale for each case in which clemency was shown is specified in Appendices I and III.

Justice

Justice was about tailoring the punishment to the individual's circumstances so that variations in culpability and harm were taken fully into account. Sometimes the decision to commute a death sentence was a response to factors that could not be considered by the court because the sentence was a mandatory one, but that under any other circumstances would have acted in mitigation. Mothers who killed their children before the introduction of the Infanticide Act, 1949 and were spared, experienced justice. Their treatment prefigured the legislation and the reason they were spared bore directly on the conduct for which they were convicted; the state had a legal but not a moral right to take their lives. Nobody believed they deserved to die. There was one exception to this rule. Kate Owens was a multiple murderer who killed four of her babies. While the jury recommended mercy in her case the judge—exceptionally—did not support this call.

There were several cases where concerns about the safety of the conviction led to its categorization as an example of justice rather than mercy. These cases were not successfully appealed and the jury and judge were not necessarily sympathetic but the judge expressed reservations about aspects of the evidence (e.g. the convictions of Annie Walsh and Martin Joyce were based on the uncorroborated testimony of two children; Thomas Kelly may have had an alibi; James Fennell's sanity was in question and so too, by implication, was his responsibility for his actions).[18]

Mercy

Mercy was when deserved punishment was softened out of compassion for the offender's plight; what was due was not awarded. Mercy was about undoing justice. It was prompted by factors that were not relevant to the ascertainment of a proportionate penalty. For my purposes mercy was always supererogatory. It fell into the class of actions that were morally good although not strictly required, that went above and beyond the call of duty.

[18] For those who were executed, the outcome was just, apart from the solitary case (John Fleming) where a judge's preference for commutation was ignored (see Chapter 4). Scruples aside, as long as the penalty existed on the statute book those to whom it was applied must be considered to have 'deserved' it, at least in a formal legal sense.

These were valuable acts that were morally optional. They were gifts from one to another.[19] It is illogical to think of an act that one is obliged to perform as merciful. This is why mercy is begged for rather than claimed. Lord Diplock put it pithily thus: 'Mercy is not the subject of legal rights. It begins where legal rights end'.[20] Failing to perform a supererogatory act is never wrong; no blame can be attached to non-performance. A government could not properly be criticized for allowing the law to take its course but might be praised for deflecting it from a lethal outcome. The executive was entitled to treat the criminal harshly but could waive this right by advising the president to spare his or her life.

Considered in these terms, mercy is morally gratuitous. Those who get what they deserve are cheated of mercy. Those who are spared are treated unjustly but mercifully. It is an act of mercy to allow someone to live when there are no obstacles to prevent justice taking its course and the weight of opinion is that it should. Mercy is a step beyond justice; it is where compassion trumps justice. There is another step beyond justice, when act and motive are rendered out of kilter; this is caprice (see below). Caprice is not mercy because it does not result from an intentional, rational action, as mercy must. As Brien (1995: 496; emphasis in original) expressed it: 'One cannot act mercifully *by accident*.'

As there is no obligation to be merciful, those to whom mercy is not granted have no legitimate cause of complaint, however drastic the consequences. One begs for mercy after justice has been done and, if granted, whoever bestows it rises in our estimation.[21] Mercy is when deserved suffering is relieved. It operates independently of justice. Where severe treatment is deserved and expected, but not exacted, this is mercy. Failing to show mercy on occasion does not imply that the individual is merciless. Indeed, if granted on every occasion it loses its gift-like character, becomes

19 According to Rainbolt (1997: 226), mercy has three key characteristics: it is morally good, modifies the demands of justice, and has a gift-like quality.

20 In the decision of the Privy Council in *de Freitas v Benny* [1976] AC 239, at p. 247.

21 As Portia remarked in an oft-quoted passage from *The Merchant of Venice*: 'The quality of mercy is not strain'd; / It droppeth as the gentle rain from heaven / Upon the place beneath. It is twice blest; / It blesseth him that gives and him that takes.' Such sentiments chime less loudly in secular environments where divine forms of authority have been consigned to history.

viewed as an entitlement and can no longer be properly categorized as mercy.

Caprice

Caprice was when an unexpected turn of events altered what appeared to have been a foregone conclusion. It involved a sudden and unpredictable change of direction. This differed from mercy because it was not undergirded by sympathy; it did not spring from benevolent intent. Caprice describes the scenario where the executive would have preferred to allow the law take its course but was persuaded to reverse a decision to which it had been committed. This volte-face was explained by respect for the person who requested the change of direction rather than sympathy for the prisoner who benefited. In several cases where the government reversed its decision this was on account of 'tributes' being paid to a judge or a bishop rather than indicating a shift in the executive's attitude to capital punishment (see Chapter 7). This was less a change of heart than an acknowledgement of, and genuflection to, the status of the petitioner. In these cases the outcome depended on luck rather than a benign frame of mind on the part of those charged with the clemency decision.

Thus, a gesture of clemency could be stimulated not by pity but by deference. To deny a bishop or a senior judge a view was to question several of the fundamentals upon which independent Ireland had been founded, including obedience, subordination, and the rule of law. There was a difference between local clergymen signing a petition, which was common, and a direct intervention from the bishop's palace. Well-meaning curates and parish priests lacked the power that went with the mitre. Absent these unexpected interventions the condemned man would have been hanged; on more than one occasion the executioner had been summoned and was in the prison waiting to earn his fee. Caprice leads to clemency in the absence of compassion. Like mercy, it is at loggerheads with justice.

Categorization

The allocation of cases to the categories in my tripartite scheme was based on an assessment made in the round. There were some occasions where a bishop intervened that I did not

Table 2.4 Varieties of clemency

	Justice	Mercy	Caprice
1923–9	17	2	1
1930–9	7	4	1
1940–9	9	4	1
1950–9	1	2	3
1960–4	1	2	0
1965–90	8	0	0
All	43	14	6

consider to be examples of caprice as, even without such input, there was little likelihood that the execution would have proceeded.[22] When influential figures played a decisive role they did not intervene on behalf of the well-connected or popular prisoner, except perhaps in the case of Tomás MacCurtain (see Chapter 7). Indeed, condemned persons did not know what actions were being taken on their behalf. It was not the case that authority figures saved their peers; some of the cabinet ministers who allowed the law to take its course, or introduced legislation to make conviction more likely and execution more timeous, had been comrades of those whose lives they terminated. On the contrary, people in high places occasionally took actions that led to life-saving decisions, or reversals of decisions, for poor and marginalized criminals who had no obvious allies.

While clemency could be prompted by justice, mercy, or caprice, considerations of justice were paramount, accounting for two-thirds of all cases (Table 2.4). In a review of the prerogative of mercy and the pardoning power in England and Wales, Smith (1983: 398–9) observed that: 'When the death sentence for murder was commuted, it was usually an exercise of mercy … rather than strict legal justice.' This was not the case in Ireland where the defining feature of most clemency decisions was a desire to achieve a closer approximation to a just outcome. In purely numerical terms, justice was three times more

[22] For example, Patrick Davern and Michael Walsh (see Chapter 5).

significant than mercy, and mercy was twice as significant as caprice.[23]

Motivation

There is a debate about whether mercy is a quality of an act or, whether to qualify as merciful, an act must spring from a benign motivation. Muller (1993: 307) took an uncompromising line, writing that 'it is at best fruitless, and at worst quite dangerous, to see mercy as an action. Mercy is not an action at all; rather, it is an attitude that influences and guides the action that the sentencer ultimately takes.' He further stated that: 'mercy is a frame of mind induced by the imaginative effort to see both the impact of the possible sentences and the nature of the criminal conduct from the defendant's perspective' (p. 329). Seen in this way, mercy is akin to legal empathy and any consideration about whether or not an act was merciful must ignore its appearance and seek out the underlying motivation. Muller was concerned that to focus solely on the action 'might blind us to darker purposes that seek to masquerade as mercy' (p. 312). He argued that it was necessary to apprehend the mental attitude that engendered the action in order to determine whether there was a moral difference between cases that appeared similar on the surface.[24]

If we confine our attention to the action we risk mistaking caprice for mercy. To avoid such confounding what I shall do is label as 'mercy' cases where the evidence suggests that the act and its motivation were compassionately inclined, and label as 'caprice' those where the desire was to allow the law to take its course but events conspired to dictate otherwise. In the latter case, act and motivation are out of alignment. (For the condemned

[23] For women, it was more often justice that prevailed (seventeen for justice and four for mercy). For men, justice also predominated but caprice intruded on occasion (twenty-six for justice of whom eleven were political; ten for mercy of whom two were political; and six for caprice, of whom one was political). The overall pattern is shown in Table 2.4.

[24] Statman (1994: 341; emphasis in original) concluded that 'as a distinct moral quality, mercy, or merciful, is a feature of *persons*, not of *acts*.' He saw it as synonymous with compassion and preferred the latter term believing that it would be no great loss to the moral lexicon to remove the word 'mercy'; 'far from enriching our vocabulary' he argued 'it serves to confuse and confound' (p. 349).

person such niceties are irrelevant: the act without the attitude is preferable to the attitude without the act.)

This distinction allows one to differentiate among cases that have similar outcomes but that spring from qualitatively different sources. It allows one to show how the decision to spare a pathetic murderer whose conduct merited the ultimate sanction but who evoked universal pity differs from the decision to spare a dangerous terrorist who could draw upon expert legal and political support. It also allows one to acknowledge that there is a distinction between the moral status of acts and the underlying motivations. It is reasonable to think of cases as being capricious because the intention was to allow the person die but there was a late change of mind, if not of heart. But these clement acts do not display the virtue of mercy; they are morally inferior to acts that have the same effect but that are benevolently inspired.

There were no cases where the desire existed to spare an individual but this did not happen. Where the motivation was merciful, there were no legal impediments to granting clemency. Merciful motivation had just one outcome—leniency. An absence of merciful motivation could have either of two results—the law took its course or the individual was spared. Motives matter because they distinguish mercy from caprice. By allowing for motivation in my scheme I maintain the important analytical distinction between mercy and caprice, as the latter is not based on compassion or pity. Capricious actions are not virtuous because they do not emerge from a deliberative process that is oriented towards mercy.

Secular trend

Over time, there was a decline in the number of commutations grounded in considerations of justice (the law caught up to deal with infanticide), or characterized by caprice (the space for arbitrariness shrank as bureaucratic systems developed and the separation of powers doctrine became more deeply embedded). Mercy—while never common—became relatively more significant. After 1964, when the death penalty was limited in scope, it was justice alone at work.

The governments of the 1980s, when there was a spate of death-eligible cases, did not think that even the most heinous capital murderers deserved to die, so sparing them was not merciful. There was no sympathy for men who killed members of An Garda Síochána but as one Minister for Justice who dealt with cases of capital murder expressed it, governments were not 'bloodthirsty'; they contained no hawks clamouring for death.[25] Mercy is a combination of a compassionate mind set and a decision to thwart justice from its course, so if the former was missing this is an inaccurate characterization. These governments were also unprecedentedly resolute—there was no question of the men being released early (by mistake or intention) as had happened in the past (see Chapter 10).

The post-1964 cases were instances of justice but of an unprecedentedly harsh kind in terms of time served in lieu of execution. No distinction was made among the condemned men according to degrees of culpability. Patrick Davern and Michael Walsh did not kill Michael Devereux in 1940 and in the interests of justice were released, unconditionally, after less than four years. Patrick McPhillips, Brian McShane, and Thomas Eccles did not fire the shot that killed Garda Frank Hand in 1984 but it required the peace process in Northern Ireland, and new legislation, to precipitate their releases on licence almost fourteen years later. (Neither of the two IRA gunmen involved in this attack was apprehended.) Noel Callan did not shoot Garda Sergeant Patrick Morrissey in 1985 but it required persistent litigation to secure his release after thirty years in custody. (Michael McHugh, who shot Morrissey dead, walked free the day after Callan.) After 1964, the death penalty was very narrowly applied with the result that the small number duly convicted were deemed to deserve extreme punishment. The forty-year sentences that were imposed declared the state's determination to take firm action, as did the lack of differentiation among cases. This was unmitigated law enforcement, reserved for the 'worst of the worst' murderers.

The release decision presented a second opportunity to soften the imposed punishment. Sometimes a renewed search for proportionality was involved, an attempt to reward good conduct in prison and to recognize a low risk of reoffending. Sometimes caprice was evident in a thwarted desire to ensure that a specified

[25] Interview with author, 15 May 2016.

minimum time was served before any consideration would be given to discharge from prison. Sometimes matters of mercy were foregrounded and the decision sprang from sympathy for the prisoner's plight (the release process is explored in Chapter 10). Those who were executed may have been treated justly by the standards of the day but, by definition, mercy was not extended to them. Those who were spared may have received justice but not mercy (e.g. if coercively confined until they died), or a combination of justice and mercy (e.g. if released especially early), or mercy and mercy (e.g. political prisoners who were shown clemency and then released swiftly). In other words, for remission as well as commutation the stimulus could be justice, mercy, or caprice.

The sixty-three men and women whose death sentences were commuted to penal servitude, and whose treatment is at the heart of this book, all benefited from acts of clemency. Sometimes this involved no more than a recalibration of the scales of justice, bringing the punishment into line with what they deserved. Some were undergirded by pity, and mercy shone through as an autonomous virtue. Some were prompted by unacceptable biases and the privileging of illegitimate interests. Lenient actions were not an accurate guide to merciful motivations. The tripartite classification outlined above provides a backbone for what follows; it allows for justice, mercy, and caprice each to lead to a benign outcome, often, but not always, one that was morally deserved.

There is a further wrinkle here. For women post-1925, governments, all of whose members were male, inclined towards leniency no matter how horrific the case and even in the absence of recommendations to mercy from (all male) judges and (all male) juries (see Chapter 4).

Summary

Each of those sentenced to death but spared fits into one of three groups: *justice* (it would be morally wrong for them to pay the ultimate price); *mercy* (they deserve to die but evoke pity and so are spared); or *caprice* (they deserve to die and there is a desire for them to die but the decision to allow the law take its course is reversed for reasons that are not grounded in compassion). A similar allocation is possible around the release decision although, as we shall see in Chapter 10, at this stage the trajectories are very different for the three groups.

Just as the reasons for clemency were variegated so too were its effects. Sometimes the outcomes were persistently painful. Those who experienced justice (e.g. mothers who killed their infant children) found that it had a hard edge and could spend longer incarcerated than those whose initial treatment was deliberately less lenient. The women who spent many years coercively confined in convents after their release from prison may have been surprised to think of this as constituting compassionate treatment; for them, clemency came at a price. A few, who were institutionalized and had nowhere else to go, may have been grateful, choosing the penitential life over membership of a potentially hostile community.

Palacios (1996: 331–2) noted that the clemency power 'operates in derogation of the law. It is the antithesis of the rule of law because it is called upon when legal rules have failed to do justice. It is inherently paradoxical because it enhances justice in general by overriding the justice system in a specific case.' This allows the system to adjust penalties where their imposition would be unjustly harsh and might cause the public to question the legitimacy of the laws that govern their behaviour. The appropriate place for clemency (if any) in criminal justice is reviewed in Chapter 3. Bresler (1965: 59) described clemency as 'a power exercised in secrecy and shadowed in obscurity'. In Chapters 4 to 7, I hope to throw some light on this important decision-making process. But, before proceeding, a word on terminology is required.

The 'Prerogative'

The Enlightenment philosopher, John Locke, defined the prerogative as 'the power to act according to discretion, for the public good, without the prescription of the Law, and sometimes even against it' (cited in Hussain and Sarat 2007: 6). This idea of doing good without a rule epitomizes the prerogative power. By definition it is discretionary; its efficacy depends upon it being unmoored from the law. It constitutes, in Hussain and Sarat's words (2007: 6), an instance of 'legally sanctioned alegality'. (This captures the situation in Ireland where, after 1937, the Constitution allowed the executive to determine whether clemency would be shown in capital cases.[26]) But this is precisely why it is controversial: no person should be able to trump the rule of law for determinedly arbitrary reasons. (It could be argued that its exercise is not completely unaccountable when vested in a government rather than, for example, a hereditary monarch or a dictator, as the people can decide not to return that government to office should they have concerns about how the power is being used.)

In capital cases, commutation was a matter for the governor general (later, president), following the advice of the Executive Council (later, government). On a small number of occasions, the Executive Council made the decision itself, either because the emergency legislation under which the conviction was secured permitted it to do so, or because the decision was made in the interval between the last governor general leaving his post and the first president taking up his. The primary constraints on the cabinet in terms of executive clemency were its members' consciences and sense of public duty (although, as we shall see in Chapter 6, group dynamics may also have exerted an influence). It was the government that acted justly, mercifully, or capriciously, not the governor general or president whose role was too tightly circumscribed to allow for any independent decision-making. While he did more than simply convey the government's decision, he did less than contribute to the outcome in any meaningful way. His personal proclivities were of no relevance and on the rare occasions when he attempted to express a view it was disregarded (see Chapter 7).

The governor general's involvement diminished over time. On 20 May 1935 it was decided that he should no longer be sent the file on the case, as had previously been the practice. This was because he was not entitled to know the reasoning behind the decision and was bound to act in accordance with the direction of the Executive Council. It was also decided that the communication with him would consist solely of a brief formal note, in

[26] According to Bunreacht na hÉireann the president could commute or remit punishment in capital cases or grant a pardon (Article 13.6) but only on the advice of the government (Article 13.9). The Criminal Justice Act, 1951 empowered the Minister for Justice to commute or remit any penalty with the exception of a capital one (s. 23).

the Irish language, sent by the Department of Justice.[27] The governor general of the day, Domhnall ua Buachalla, was unlikely to have been troubled by these developments. He was an Irish-language activist and former militant republican, whose entry in the *Dictionary of Irish Biography* notes that he killed three British soldiers during the 1916 Rebellion. He shared de Valera's view that his office was a vestigial one that would be abolished when a suitable opportunity arose. (The procedure followed by the governor general when he was being sent the file was to signify his assent to the Executive Council's recommendation either by endorsing the file or issuing a special warrant.[28])

Between 11 December 1936 (when the office of governor general was abolished)[29] and 25 June 1938 (when the first president of Ireland was installed; the new Constitution having entered into force on 29 December 1937) there was no governor general to exercise the prerogative on the king's behalf and no president to exercise an analogous function on behalf of the people. During this eighteen-month period the decision-making authority resided entirely with the executive. Thereafter it became a matter for the president, acting on the government's advice.[30]

A prerogative is an ancient customary right. It is not conferred or defined by statute and is subject to no restriction or interference. It constitutes an act of grace by, or on behalf of, a king or queen who, as the source of justice, is also the fount of mercy. It involves the Crown waiving its rights over a subject. Bresler (1965: 28) noted that, even in England, it was not accurate to

[27] Death sentences, procedure file, 20 May 1935, NAI, TSCH/3/S7788A.

[28] Letter from T.A. Finlay to attorney general, 22 March 1926, NAI, TSCH/3/S9485A.

[29] The Constitution (Amendment No. 27) Act, 1936 was intended to abolish the office of governor general but further legislation—the Executive Powers (Consequential Provisions) Act, 1937—was required to address some residual issues relating to the office and its final occupant, and to complete the transfer of functions.

[30] According to Article 49.1 of the Constitution: 'All powers, functions, rights and prerogatives whatsoever exercisable in or in respect of Saorstát Éireann immediately before the 11th day of December, 1936, whether in virtue of the Constitution then in force or otherwise, by the authority in which the executive power of Saorstát Éireann was then vested are hereby declared to belong to the people.'

refer to the clemency decision as involving a royal prerogative because in 1535 a law was introduced to bestow the pardoning power on the monarch.[31] Having noted that it was a misnomer to describe what the monarch did as the exercise of a 'prerogative' Bresler followed the established practice by so describing it; to do otherwise would have involved cumbersome and confusing language, but not to acknowledge the imprecision of the term would have offended against his lawyerly instinct for exactitude.[32]

The term 'prerogative' was often used to describe the practice that is central to this book. But it is not a term of art I favour as it should have been removed from the lexicon of capital punishment when the office of governor general was abolished. It is anachronistic and inaccurate to describe executive clemency in a republic as involving the operation of a prerogative. The fact that those involved in the process continued to describe it thus is telling: it shows that they saw what they were doing as an act of grace, a gesture that came *de haut en bas*, rather than an exchange between citizens of equal worth, however they might differ in terms of their criminal status.

It is appropriate to talk about the prerogative before the enactment of the new Constitution in 1937 but not thereafter, even though it continued to be used as a shorthand for the commutation process. A republic cannot have a prerogative with its connotations of monarchical grace but perhaps a Free State can have it, albeit in a diluted form, as long as the decision is formally made by the monarch's representative (i.e. the governor general between 1922 and 1936).[33]

[31] Jurisdiction in Liberties Act, 27 Henry VIII c. 24.

[32] Rolph (1978: 20) disagreed with Bresler: 'The Act of 1535 merely ratified and preserved the royal power, while extinguishing that of bishops and priors and other bigwigs to order executions of their own choosing.' It may indeed have been a tidying up exercise but I am inclined to side with Bresler; once a customary right is given statutory expression it ceases to be a true prerogative.

[33] The Free State Constitution of 1922 was silent on the question of the prerogative; it remained vested in the king and was exercised through his representative, the governor general. Kelly (1988) reviewed the debate about whether the prerogative was ever expelled from Irish law. The Supreme Court held in *Byrne v Ireland* [1972] IR 241 and in *Webb v Ireland* [1988] IR 353 that it did not survive the creation of the Free State but this seems implausible when it comes to capital punishment where everyone acted as if the power had been transferred and the language of the prerogative remained in use.

While the term 'prerogative' tended to be used loosely to describe the mechanism by which capital penalties were converted to penal servitude, there was an awareness in the Department of Justice that such usage sacrificed accuracy to convenience. A note dated 13 March 1951 regarding whether it was correct for the government to talk in terms of a 'prerogative' concluded that it was not and that the president had no prerogative powers as all of his powers were conferred on him either by the Constitution or by law.[34] Practice was slow to change, however, and as late as 1960 the judge who sentenced Vincent McGrath to death wrote to the government to recommend that it exercise the 'prerogative of mercy'.[35]

[34] Department of the Taoiseach, Note, 13 March 1951, NAI, TSCH/3/S7788B.

[35] Letter from F.G.O. Budd to Minister for Justice, 14 March 1960, NAI, JUS/2005/171/4697.

3

For and Against Clemency

A legal decision that was made in the absence of discretion (i.e. the imposition of a death sentence by a judge after a conviction for murder) was preceded and succeeded by legal decisions that involved the secretly exercised, unexplained, and unreviewable use of discretion (i.e. the jury's decision whether to convict and the government's decision whether to recommend clemency). Depending on the outcome of the government's deliberations a final legal decision may have been required, again one where there was no space for discretion (i.e. the governor general's (later, president's) commutation of the sentence). The rules were clear in the second and fourth decisions and one of the goals of this book is to illuminate them for the third decision. What transpired in jury rooms will remain unknowable.[1] This was an unusual sequence of decisions: potentially unfettered discretion alternating with its polar opposite.

Strange (1996: 130) noted with regard to the long-standing tension between discretion and bureaucracy that: 'Whenever critics discover pools of discretion they demand that administrators mop them up, either by restricting the scope of discretion or by reducing the number of discretionary actors.' As Weber (1922/1968: 975) put it in a classic formulation: 'Bureaucracy develops the more perfectly, the more it is "dehumanized", the more completely it succeeds in eliminating from official business love, hatred, and all purely personal, irrational, and emotional elements which escape calculation.' Advanced bureaucracies squeeze out the room for discretion.

In Ireland there were clear rules regarding payment rates for executioners, foodstuffs allowed to occupants of condemned

[1] On some occasions jurors added their names to petitions for mercy indicating the tone and intent, if not the content, of their deliberations.

Justice, Mercy, and Caprice: Clemency and the Death Penalty in Ireland. First Edition. Ian O'Donnell. © Ian O'Donnell 2017. Published 2017 by Oxford University Press.

cells, and permitted visitors. If a prisoner wished to purchase a daily newspaper or to have additional cigarettes instead of a bottle of stout, the rules were consulted, paperwork ensued, authorizing signatures were collected, and instructions issued. For the decision about whether or not his or her life should be spared there were no formal restrictions on the government's behaviour and there was no way it could be reviewed. As noted in Chapter 1, by scrutinizing the pattern of decision-making in capital cases and attempting to identify inhibiting forces, we can learn something about underlying political and social values.

While the decision regarding clemency was not bound by legal rules it was not anarchic. There were established ways of proceeding in terms of the gathering and presentation of evidence. Precedent was followed, moral evaluations were made, observations were sought from the judge, petitions were considered and, over time, working rules emerged. Sometimes these considerations were trumped by the desire to advance a policy objective that had become pressing, such as national security. Under these circumstances, laws and procedures could be radically altered to facilitate convictions. On occasion this became vengeance, barely concealed by a veneer of due process (see Chapter 5).

Deflecting the law from its course was based on more than the application of abstract legal principles. It included an assessment of the condemned person in the round, sometimes drawing on first-hand knowledge. When the relational distance grew, such assessments could no longer be conducted with confidence. This may go some way towards explaining the uniformly harsh treatment meted out in capital cases in the 1980s when the empathy gap between politicians and condemned men was too wide to be bridged.

As signalled in the previous chapter, clemency could appear in one of three guises. Sometimes it injected mercy where there were no doubts that the punishment was deserved. Sometimes it involved a post-hoc recalibration of the scales of justice, where a lethal outcome would have been patently unfair; if there was a gap between legal and moral justice, the clemency process could close it. Sometimes it was capricious. The aim of this chapter is to examine the arguments for and against executive clemency with a view to specifying their relevance to the Irish context. Unlike the rest of the book, what follows has no particular jurisdictional anchor. Like the rest of the book, the issues of concern are apposite beyond the context in which they are raised. Having reviewed the competing claims as to the desirability and necessity of clemency, the tripartite scheme set out in Chapter 2 will be recapitulated and its suitability to the task at hand will be clarified. Before reviewing them a comment is required on the prevailing sentencing framework given its obvious impact on the nature of the clemency regime.

Discretion and Desert

A mandatory sentencing scheme may generate outcomes where judge or jury (or both) believe that the punishment does not fit the crime and call for the executive to tailor it according to the individual's culpability so that what is imposed is deserved rather than blindly prescribed. Alternatively, they may believe that the punishment does indeed fit the crime but call for mercy nonetheless. When the court has no discretion, mercy cannot intrude as an autonomous virtue at sentencing; indeed, justice often proves elusive. Juries sometimes make their views known by convicting of a lesser charge, acquitting, failing to agree, or finding the defendant unfit to plead, or guilty but insane. But, once a guilty verdict was returned on a murder charge in Ireland prior to the Criminal Justice Act, 1964 which abolished the mandatory death penalty for murder, the judge's hands were tied. Even if he was minded to be lenient, his capacity to act accordingly had been eliminated. His only decision was whether to don the black cap when announcing that the prisoner was to forfeit his or her life.

Judges are precluded from showing mercy in their official capacity, whatever they may feel as private citizens. Their job is simply to follow correct procedure and apply the law, without fear or favour, without being compromised by pity or compassion. When there was a mandatory sentence to apply, any room for manoeuvre in court evaporated. They were not free to choose an alternative disposal because they were moved by an offender's plight. Had judges been allowed to pass sentences other than death they would often have done so, as they made clear in their confidential letters to the Minister for Justice (see Chapter 4). These letters gave judges an opportunity to comment on what would have been a just sentence had they been given a freer hand,

and what would be a merciful way to deal with the case even if the person had got what he or she deserved.

Given that the sentence was a mandatory one, the judge could not consider, or even learn about, mitigating factors if they did not arise during the trial. These factors could be relevant with regard to culpability. Those subject to the mandatory sentence had passed through a series of filters where discretion was repeatedly used in favour of the more deserving cases, beginning with the selection of an appropriate charge. Thus it might be argued that the sample of death-eligible cases consisted of a group of men and women who had got their just deserts.

But, in many of them judge or jury (or both) felt that although they had followed the law, the result was too severe all things considered, and they made a recommendation to mercy (see Chapter 4). In a system where the mandatory sentence for murder was death, if juries believed that the sentence would inevitably be carried into effect no matter how pitiable the prisoner's circumstances, there was a possibility that to avoid this undesirable outcome they would fail to convict. Jury nullification would remove the possibility of injustice at the clemency stage by introducing injustice at an earlier stage in the proceedings.

The absence of judicial discretion at sentencing meant that the locus of discretion moved to the executive and it is to the clemency decision that we must direct our attention. Mandatory sentencing laws shifted life and death decisions from the public arena of the courtroom to the privacy of the cabinet room. It was up to the executive to ensure that punishments were appropriately tailored to individual cases. Quite often, what was described as the exercise of mercy is better understood as the punishment being made to fit the crime in a different forum.

The mandatory death penalty for murder was a relic of a more punitive and less accommodating time. It sat uncomfortably with the desire to individualize punishment. It meant that courts could not take account of any particular mitigating or aggravating factors. It meant that justice was deaf and dumb as well as blind. James Chuter-Ede, the longest-serving British Home Secretary of the twentieth century, described the clemency power as 'a civilizing restraint on the survival of a harsh aspect of the law' (foreword to Bresler, 1965). This was equally true in Ireland during the period when a conviction for murder resulted in an automatic penalty of death.

Clemency tends to make philosophers of punishment uncomfortable, whatever their stripe.[2] For retributivists it is problematic because it threatens equality of treatment and introduces disproportionality. For utilitarians it is problematic because it involves a departure from what would best serve society. While legally permissible, it stands outside the law. It defies the law's demands for transparency and review. It is unpredictable.

When mercy tempers justice it leads to a different outcome. But is this not an injustice? When mercy refers to individualization of punishment then is it not simply an aspect of justice? Murphy (1988: 169) captured this dilemma well in his comment that: 'In short, mercy is either a vice (injustice) or redundant (a part of justice)'; either way, it has little to commend itself. The judge who acts mercifully cannot do justice.[3] If mercy is an autonomous virtue it cannot be reconciled with justice; the two are at loggerheads. If mercy must not be random then it must be patterned somehow and these patterns will operate within a framework of rules, however loose and non-prescriptive. When this framework is too rigid or too encompassing we are out of the realms of mercy, but it will not always be obvious when we have arrived at this point.

The retributive dilemma

For those who equate punishment with retribution, a tension arises between mercy and justice whenever a convicted person comes to be sentenced. To impose less than the individual deserves is an affront to the principles underlying punishment as well as an insult to the integrity of the person in the dock who is not held morally accountable for his or her acts. Mercy requires the sentencing judge to allow idiosyncratic factors to impede the progress of justice. To treat someone with mercy may mean that they get less than their just deserts. Mercy, therefore, requires injustice. If we believe in equality of outcome we must oppose mercy.

[2] Some penologists use the terms 'clemency' and 'mercy' interchangeably. As explained in Chapter 2, I do not, preferring to view the latter as a species of the former. I believe that such a refinement is analytically fecund.

[3] Digeser (2003: 172) turned this argument on its head: 'defenders of genuine mercy can also play this rhetorical game ... If being merciful is equivalent to being unjust, then always being just is the same as being unmerciful'.

Statman (1994: 339; emphasis in original) endorsed a hard form of retributivism, which allowed no space for mercy, holding that: 'A court that lets its feelings of sorrow and compassion determine its sentence betrays its role as a court of *justice*.' Mercy, in other words, should not be equated with judicial action. But a government that is moved by a condemned person's plight, and stands between him or her and the gallows, is not constrained in its actions by the same legal considerations that pertain in a courtroom.

The hard retributivist takes the line that it is unjust to deviate from the deserved punishment, that its imposition is required. In Walker's (1995: 28) words: 'Inconsistency always worries retributivists.' Under a truly proportionate sentencing scheme there would be little room for clemency, save as a fail-safe to remedy miscarriages of justice. Hurd (2007: 390–1) argued that 'there is no moral basis for mercy, properly described, by officials within a justice system that is devoted to achieving retributive justice ... one cannot adhere to retributivism and defend the occasional, partial, or complete suspension of an individual's just punishment without contradiction'. Retributivists have qualms about the moral status of mercy as it involves softening what is deserved; once an offender has been awarded the punishment he or she deserves, tampering with the sentence is illegitimate.

Hestevold (1987) attempted to reconcile mercy and desert by arguing that for any offence there existed a range of penalties, of varying severity, each of which could suffice as an appropriate punishment. 'To show mercy', he argued, 'is to levy one of the less severe penalties' (p. 250). By so doing, one retained 'the supererogatoriness of mercy and the obligatoriness of punishment' (p. 257). While such an approach acknowledges that there is no single, easy to identify, deserved punishment in a given case, it also loosens the idea of desert to such an extent that it begins to lose analytical precision. It means that like cases might not be treated alike. Not all retributivists are prepared to tolerate such a potential diversity of outcomes.

Sometimes a penalty is adjusted to bring it into closer alignment with desert. Card (1972: 194) called such realignment 'pseudo mercy' and argued that it is 'intended to correct injustice in the rules' (p. 195). This is not mercy in my tripartite scheme; rather it is justice making an appearance at a slightly later than usual point in the proceedings. This is part of the choreography of justice rather than the appearance of mercy. To push the theatrical analogy a little further, when mercy appears it is always a cameo performance that divides the critics. (Caprice remains behind the scenes.)

The kind of formal equality before the law envisaged by Immanuel Kant excluded mercy. It was (unbendingly) firm and (irretrievably) just.[4] The implications for murderers were clear:

> If, however, he has committed a murder, he must die. In this case, there is no substitute that will satisfy the requirements of legal justice ... Even if a civil society were to dissolve itself by common agreement of all its members (for example, if the people inhabiting an island decided to separate and disperse themselves around the world), the last murderer remaining in prison must first be executed, so that everyone will duly receive what his actions are worth and so that the bloodguilt thereof will not be fixed on the people because they failed to insist on carrying out the punishment; for if they fail to do so, they may be regarded as accomplices in this public violation of legal justice. (Kant 1797/1965: 102)

But even Kant made an exception for infanticide, seeing this as a type of crime for which lenient treatment might be justified as the state that prosecutes it fosters the conditions that promote it:[5]

> A child born into the world outside marriage is outside the law ... and consequently it is also outside the protection of the law. The child has crept surreptitiously into the commonwealth (much like prohibited wares), so that its existence as well as its destruction can be ignored (because by right it ought not to have come into existence in this way); and the mother's disgrace if the illegitimate birth becomes known cannot be wiped out by any official decree. (p. 106)

Moore (1989: 164) presented Kant's argument as follows: 'If the state fosters the prejudice that an illegitimate child is a disgrace and is outside the law, then the state is being hypocritically

[4] According to Kant (1797/1965: 100): 'The law concerning punishment is a categorical imperative, and woe to him who rummages around in the winding paths of a theory of happiness looking for some advantage to be gained by releasing the criminal from punishment or by reducing the amount of it.' By this analysis, condign punishment was a necessity; society demands nothing less.

[5] Another exception, for the same reason (i.e. it was unlawful but not blameworthy), was duelling. Duelling was against the law but soldiers and university students were honour-bound to accept a challenge. If they were victorious, the state that valorized courage and honour could not then punish a man whose actions exemplified the values it nurtured.

self-righteous when it punishes a mother for killing her illegitimate child.' Even in Ireland, where hypocritical self-righteousness was not unknown among politicians, the mother who killed her newborn child, often in circumstances of abject poverty and in a futile attempt at maintaining—or claiming—a reputation for decency, was the object of clemency as a matter of routine (all of these children had been conceived out of wedlock; see Chapter 8). It was unfair to punish a mother for behaving in a way that accorded with society's demand for celibacy before—and fidelity during—marriage.

The utilitarian dilemma

For utilitarians the goal is for punishment to fit the needs of society rather than having to fit the crime or the criminal. The calculus is not desert-based and inconsistency is not a problem as different sentences might be required to maximize utility in similar cases. In Smart's (1968: 356) words:

> The utilitarian has no choice; he must recommend the course of action that produces most good, and if this means imposing a certain penalty he cannot act mercifully and impose less than that penalty. Real mercy is never a possibility for him because he must always impose what is, according to his ethic, the fully justifiable penalty.

For a strict utilitarian then, any departure from the penalty that would best serve society is wrong. As Markel (2004: 1431) expressed it, 'one need not be a retributivist to be allergic to mercy'. Muller (1993: 339) captured the nub of the problem in his comment that:

> ... if we were analyzing mercy from a strict utilitarian perspective, it would surely emerge a vice. A moral virtue to a utilitarian is something that facilitates the realization of the greatest good for the greatest number. Mercy ... is a moment in the sentencer's deliberative process when the sentencer focusses upon the greatest good for only one person—the defendant.

While it is an important moral virtue, mercy, as commonly understood, poses problems for systems of criminal justice; it involves a divergence from justice.

Utilitarian decision-makers would object to leniency that went beyond Jeremy Bentham's principle of frugality which holds that punishment should be no more severe than is necessary to achieve its purpose. As Bentham put it: 'Under a government which has, for its actual end, the greatest happiness of the greatest number, thus it is that mercy is unknown' (cited in Brien 1995: 493). For the utilitarian there is no room for leniency, whether on moral or logical grounds. Bonaparte (1910: 604) captured this sentiment when he wrote that the power to pardon (another expression of clemency; see Chapter 2), 'can be rightfully exercised only for the public benefit; the wishes and interest of the culprit or of his family or of his friends are altogether immaterial, except in so far as these individuals constitute an infinitesimal fraction of the public affected'. For Bonaparte, himself a former United States attorney general, a state governor who acted out of personal sympathy for the criminal did not differ in kind from one who accepted a bribe to issue a pardon.

Cesare Beccaria was unsettled by pardons as he believed them to weaken the deterrent power of the law. His view was that certainty was more important than severity and that a mild system could be effective as long as penalties were consistently applied. He accepted that there were so many preposterous and harsh laws in existence during the eighteenth century that clemency powers remained an unfortunate necessity (see Sebba 1977: 225). Beccaria's view was that as a legal system approached perfection the scope for executive interference would dwindle to a point of irrelevance:

> Clemency ... should be redundant in a perfect administration where punishments are mild and the methods of judgement are regular and expeditious. This truth will seem hard to one who lives amid the chaos of a criminal system in which amnesties and pardons are called for in proportion to the absurdity of the laws and the awful severity of the sentences. (cited in Barkow 2008: 1360)

As noted in Chapter 2, utilitarians believe that the certainty, severity, and celerity of punishment are essential to its effectiveness. Clemency undermines the first and second of these core principles and this is why they tend to be uneasy with the practice.

Clemency requires bespoke treatment, a preparedness to allow that there are more suitable and less suitable candidates, even if they are guilty of intending and causing comparable harms. A desire to treat each case on its merits shines through an examination of the archival records in Ireland. There was an abiding commitment to the individualization of punishment. This was true both for the clemency assessment and the decision about early release. At issue was less the precise nature of the harm caused—which was of the utmost gravity in all of these cases—and more the individual's motivations and the likelihood of a recurrence. The victim was almost completely absent from these deliberations although the view of the local community was taken into account, through petitions and the confidential police report on the case.

Clemency will always occupy an awkward position in a legal system, regardless of its underlying rationale. It would not be fruitful for me to attempt to craft a place for it that causes less friction at a conceptual level (many better scholars have attempted this task) because the likelihood is that it will always be problematic at the level of application. However, there is some value in laying bare the arguments for and against the practice and this is attempted next.

The pros and cons that are identified are set out in broad brushstrokes and, for reasons of economy and clarity, are not weighed down with too many caveats and qualifications. Generally speaking, they are relevant not just to capital punishment in Ireland but to clemency regimes more generally, wherever located, whenever politicians are the final arbiters of life or death, and particularly when the process lacks clear and principled foundations. However, given that the focus of the book is Ireland, examples from this jurisdiction are sometimes given to illustrate the point in question.

Cons

A useful way to unpack the argument against executive clemency in capital cases is as follows.

Inequitable

Clemency is inequitable because it does not treat like cases alike. It tampers. Similar cases end up with different outcomes; sometimes the difference is a matter of life and death. Unduly lenient treatment is inherently problematic because it violates the notion of equality before the law and fails to maximize utility. (It may also have the undesirable effect of nourishing impunity by showing that crimes do not always meet with consequences.) It does not matter what motivates clemency for it to be problematic in this respect. It might be compassion. It might be favouritism. It might be public opinion. It might be venality. It might be an attempt to recalibrate the scales of justice. It might be happenstance. When mercy and caprice redound to the obvious advantage of the condemned man or woman this is clearly at odds with the imperative to treat similar cases in a similar fashion.

During the early years of the Free State not every woman convicted of murder was treated leniently; Annie Walsh was hanged on 5 August 1925. Sparing one female murderer while allowing another go to the gallows may have been arbitrary, but it was not unfair, in that there was no obligation to spare either. However, an unbroken sequence of commutations stretching over several decades meant that a stage was reached when a female execution became almost inconceivable. Against such a background, to single out any particular woman for execution would have been unfair; the practice of clemency had become systematized, it was no longer arbitrary. The squeamishness shown by the men who sat around cabinet tables reflected their shared belief in the necessity of female virtue for the success of the national project. As for men, there continued to be an element of arbitrariness in that the odds of execution after jury trial were even. The pattern was one of unfair discrimination against male murderers.

Private

While it is a private virtue to be cherished, clemency has no role in public institutions of criminal justice. Judges are obliged to act justly but not mercifully. Criminals are entitled to justice but not to mercy. Murphy (1988: 174) subscribed to this position: 'There thus simply is no room for mercy as an autonomous virtue with which … justice should be tempered'. He recommended—provocatively—that if actors in the criminal justice system, including judges, prosecutors, and parole board members, wished to be merciful: 'Let them keep their sentimentality to themselves for use in their private lives with their families and pets' (p. 174).

Duff (2007: 361) described mercy as an 'intrusion' into the realm of criminal justice of values and concerns that came from outside its domain, for which he saw a 'proper but limited role' (p. 387). Repeated intrusions may bring the system into disrepute. Hurd (2007: 398) believed that while the cultivation of mercy was important for mature human relationships, there was no place for institutional acts of mercy which, she suggested, 'are morally (and therefore legally) indefensible, at least on grounds consistent with a retributive theory of punishment'. By her account mercy was misplaced if it was exercised by actors within a criminal justice system.

Irrational

Clemency is irrational and this is an affront to reasonable people. Life and death decisions should not be whimsical. The public on whose behalf they are made should be confident that they are based on valid criteria that are carefully considered and consistently applied; opacity is the enemy of good government. The difficulty is that we cannot make a judgement about the propriety of the decision unless we have access to its rationale, and we do not—a grant (or not) of clemency requires no stated reasoning or written opinion. The logical extension of the view that mercy conflicts with rationality and consistency, as expressed by Harrison (1992: 108), is that a properly run state 'cannot be merciful'. He was offended by the notion that like cases might be treated differently without the need to provide valid reasons: 'Only by forgoing mercy can we enable the state (or other authority) to behave like a fully rational entity, accountable for all its actions to the people over whom it has power. Otherwise we have mere power without accountability' (p. 118).

The clemency decision is made in secret and is unamenable to review.[6] If the power of states over citizens should be reviewable, and if meaningful review requires access to the reasons behind actions, then there can be no place for clemency. Unchecked discretion is anomalous in the law and viewed with suspicion by lawyers. Modern democratic institutions strive to snuff out arbitrariness.

Undemocratic

Clemency is undemocratic because it ignores the will of the people as expressed through the legislature in the criminal law. If

[6] On the justiciability—or otherwise—of the prerogative of mercy, see Harris (2003).

the law's outcomes are perceived as undesirable the correct approach is to draft new laws rather than to nullify the effects of the existing ones. If the law's outcomes unfold as intended, the government's role is to accept them rather than to frustrate their implementation through executive action. Every time the law is deflected from its course—and those who have come into conflict with it are prioritized over those who have lived by it—the criminal justice system is held up as a failure. Markel (2004: 1456) was against mercy because it 'stands at odds with the nature of the modern liberal democratic regime under rule of law'. For Markel, clemency was pernicious, even if it sprang from virtuous motivations. (The involvement of a jury might be perceived as allowing scope for community sentiment to intrude but, as we shall see in Chapter 4, juries were far from representative of society and their recommendations carried little weight unless endorsed by the trial judge.)

Unfettered

Clemency is unfettered and unchecked. There should always be restraints on decisions that can have irreversible consequences for life and liberty. Bedau (1990–1: 257) observed that: 'Clemency decisions—even in death penalty cases—are standardless in procedure, discretionary in exercise, and unreviewable in result.' He went on to describe the clemency hearing in a capital case as 'a terminal stage of lawlessness in criminal justice decision making' (p. 257). Advanced legal systems are embarrassed by rulelessness.

Potentially corrupt

Clemency is open to political meddling and favouritism. It has long been recognized that, like any power, the power to be clement can corrupt. Favours can be bought. In Bentham's words: 'From pardon power unrestricted, comes impunity to delinquency in all shapes: from impunity to delinquency in all shapes, impunity to maleficence in all shapes; from impunity to maleficence in all shapes, dissolution of government: from dissolution of government, dissolution of political society' (cited in Barnett 1927: 490). This is the apocalyptic view of clemency's impact when it is given free rein. Society pays a heavy price for easing the criminal's burden and public confidence can be dented if executive clemency is used to mitigate punishments that are perceived as proportionate and legitimate.

Bonaparte (1910: 603) gave the example of a close friend of the governor of Tennessee who was sentenced to a long term of imprisonment for his role in the killing of a newspaper editor, and whose conviction was upheld on appeal. Within a few minutes of the appeal the governor issued a pardon on the basis that he believed his friend to be innocent and disagreed with the courts' rulings. Palacios (1996: 351–3) cites instances of commutations being sold. Such blatantly corrupt uses of executive clemency are rare. More recently, Love (2003: 185) described the tumult that followed the pardons granted by Bill Clinton on his last day in office as president of the United States, which were 'almost universally condemned as an abuse of executive power'.[7] Inegalitarianism of this kind is offensive to right-minded people.

Promotes inertia

Clemency facilitates legislative inertia. The existence of mandatory capital punishment for murder rendered the legal system in Ireland incapable of achieving one of the key ends for which it was established, namely to make the punishment fit the crime. This threatened to call its legitimacy into question. Had the government not possessed a clemency power, the pressure to reform the law would have been impossible to resist for so long. It was unimaginable that mothers who killed newborn children would have been hanged; the infanticide legislation would have been introduced much earlier if this was the only way to prevent such an eventuality. The existence of an executive clemency power allowed for the persistence of harshness. Instead of amending the law so that it did not result in death sentences being imposed on women who killed their infants, the clemency process provided a safety valve. Additionally, as described in Chapter 1, the fact that the death penalty remained on the statute book meant that when the state took firm action against its political enemies, attitudes hardened and other criminals who paid the ultimate price became collateral damage, caught up on a wave of repression.

[7] Love (2015: 102), who had been US Pardon Attorney for seven years, elsewhere described the granting of these pardons as 'the most egregious misuse of the power in the history of the American presidency'.

Violates separation of powers doctrine

The autonomy of the judiciary is compromised when the executive interferes in its sentencing function, through commutation or remission of a sentence, even if this interference is constitutionally permissible and welcomed by judges who find that they are required to impose punishments that do not fit the crimes. Clemency provides a mechanism whereby the executive can frustrate the enforcement of laws introduced by the legislature. The danger is that justice in sentencing is trumped by mercy or caprice at the clemency stage.

This danger might be less acute in Ireland because the body of law was inherited from the colonial power so Dáil Éireann [lower house of national parliament] may not have had the same degree of fidelity towards it as it would have to laws introduced under its own authority. Also, it took some time for laws to be abolished and amended and, as a result, the statute book was not in synchrony with legislative sensibilities; this allowed the executive to arrive at a position that would have been welcomed by the legislature (e.g. sparing mothers who had murdered their newborn infants) and that was given legislative effect in due course. But the point remains that the existence of a mechanism for executive clemency pits the executive against the legislature (which is responsible for creating an appropriate legal framework) as well as the judiciary (which is responsible for putting the laws into practice). Each time clemency was exercised the executive branch indicted the legislative branch for allowing an untenable situation to persist.

Involves non-judicial actors

Unreviewable discretion epitomizes lawlessness, especially when it is in the hands of non-judicial actors. This causes anxiety among those who subscribe to the view that it is for the courts alone to prevent unfair applications of the law. Barkow (2008: 1336) argued that the development of the administrative state explained this court-centred focus, bringing in its wake, 'a new emphasis in the law on the importance of predictable processes, reasoned decisionmaking, and judicial review'. These principles—predictability, reason, and review—are entrenched in contemporary legal culture. Clemency is problematic because it violates all three of them. It is also problematic because 'our legal culture looks to judges as uniquely qualified to solve inequities in a law's application' (Barkow 2008: 157); it seems incongruous, at the very least, for politicians to play such a role.

Lacks standing

If clemency involves the relinquishing of a right owed by one individual to another, can the state do this on behalf of the wronged individual who, in capital cases, is precluded—by reason of death—from contributing to this debate? If the punishment constitutes the debt owed to society, then how can any executive body have the right to commute or remit it? When the body making this decision comprises elected representatives this criticism carries less force as it could be argued that they are speaking on behalf of the people they represent. This could not be said of a judiciary, or parole board, or clemency authority that was unelected. (In earlier times, it might have been possible to argue that the life of the condemned subject belonged to the king or queen who had the right to waive their claim to it.) In Ireland, victims' families were notable by their absence from the debate about the merits, or otherwise, of clemency and their views were not canvassed. The argument that to show leniency to offenders is to disrespect, or even denigrate, victims has gathered momentum over the years.

Compromises the jury

Not only does clemency interfere with the separation of powers, it also intrudes on the sanctity of the jury room and the decisions made therein. It usurps the jury. Marshall (1948) identified as a criticism of the prerogative of mercy as it operated in England and Wales that it was 'inconsistent with the constitutionality of juries' (p. 111). He dismissed this argument as 'ingenious but unsound' (p. 112) on the basis that the prerogative had existed for at least as long as the jury system and their parallel existence over the centuries was 'certainly not proof of the illegality of the one and the constitutionality of the other' (p. 112). Also, he argued that the Home Secretary did not reverse the jury's finding of guilt but simply mitigated its effects.

Unduly burdensome

The task of deciding whether or not to recommend commutation is too great to be shouldered by one person no matter how capable or distinguished, especially if they have moral qualms about the ramifications of the decision and the law that gave rise to it. In Ireland responsibility was taken collectively by the government rather than individually by the Minister for Justice so the burden was shared. Nonetheless the existence of a clemency process placed the decision about whether a human life should be ended in the hands of a group of politicians who lacked any particular expertise or insight into matters of such gravity; it was not reasonable to expect them to shoulder such a load.

Condescending

Clemency comes from above, the gift of a patronizing state. The criminal begs for his or her life, and tries to sway the state with petitions that accept the validity of the criminal process but wish to find a special reason for deflecting it from its grisly end. They do not query the propriety of the verdict and its consequence as to do so would be to question the integrity of the state upon which they are calling to act in their interests. Instead they appeal to the latent virtue of their superiors; their plea for justice is couched in terms of mercy. The government accedes to this request or allows the law to take its course.

A hierarchical arrangement along such lines is not appropriate in a republic where the people are sovereign rather than subjects of a monarch who holds the power of life and death, and where rights should be asserted rather than exceptional treatment pleaded. Clemency is condescending because it does not see law-breakers as responsible agents; citizens become supplicants. Criminals have a right to be punished; this is a way of taking them seriously, respecting their choices, and communicating society's displeasure at their conduct. To spare them the consequences of their actions is to treat them as less than fully autonomous and morally accountable actors (Morris 1981). By treating them as objects of pity criminals are further diminished.

Routine

When most death sentences are commuted to penal servitude the currency of executive clemency is devalued. Rather than being an exceptional measure it becomes the norm; the exception becomes the rule. The solemn nature of the pronouncement of death is reduced to an empty formula. If the law does not do what it says, its majesty is tarnished.[8]

Pros

If executive clemency is incompatible with the rule of law, an affront to democratic principles, and an exercise in arbitrariness, how can it be justified? The arguments in its favour are put next.

Flexible

Clemency allows flexibility. It was a necessary anomaly at a time when murder attracted a mandatory death sentence and it allowed the executive to show favour to a class of killers who were disadvantaged by this arrangement (e.g. mothers who destroyed their children prior to the introduction of the Infanticide Act, 1949). These were cases where the lawful outcome was not morally deserved. The exercise of clemency was an attempt to deal with the rigidity of a sentencing framework that allowed only one option, death, for convicted murderers. By being clement the government was aligning the penalty with the prisoner's level of culpability and popular conceptions of the harm caused. It was balancing the scales of justice, distinguishing between the robber or rapist who was reckless as to his victim's survival and the single mother who destroyed her newborn child out of a toxic mixture of grief and shame.

Chadwick (1992: 288) observed that:

> The concept of mitigation which traditionally underlay the Prerogative of Mercy was one of compromise. It was a compromise which allowed the Common Law to preserve simple, broadly defined and absolute definitions of felony while at the same time recognizing both degrees and shifts in the community's perception of guilt and blameworthiness.

Laws are necessarily framed at a high level of generality—clarity is essential if they are to govern human conduct effectively. When

[8] If there had been no room for clemency and the sentence of the court had been carried out in every case, the number of executions in Ireland would have been almost three times greater between 1923 and 1990.

individual cases fit uneasily within their parameters some fine-tuning is required. For those facing execution this fine-tuning could not be more important.

Precursor to law reform

When the pace of legislative reform is slow, politicians can respond to the public's desire for the law to be changed by mitigating its consequences. It is not that they are usurping the public's will by deflecting the law from its course, more that in the (unconscionably) long time it takes to do what they have been elected to do as legislators, this is one way that they can realize the intent of the legislation to which they are committed in the years prior to its enactment.[9] Such a perspective deals with the objection that by interfering with lawful outcomes, politicians are usurping the democratic function.[10]

Reflecting on the implications for clemency of law reform, Sebba (1977: 234) commented that: 'In terms of the clemency power, the effect of this should be the ever-narrowing scope of its ambit, as problems of substance in the penal system are solved by alternate means, and the laws, if not perfected, are at least improved.' As legal systems evolve, the clemency power withers. When legislators chose not to reform the law they were indelibly tainted by association with a sordid and dismal practice. Unlike the operators of the gallows or the members of a firing party they could not

[9] It was not just legislators who moved slowly. A committee of judges established in April 1939 to consider aspects of capital punishment submitted its brief (four typed pages) and cautious report at the end of July 1941, just before the courts rose for their summer vacation. The secretary of the Department of Justice greeted this paltry submission with the sardonic comment to a colleague in the attorney general's office that: 'I think it is true to say that the judicial mind is usually a conservative mind and that when reform of the present kind is under discussion it would be a mistake to regard the judicial view as settling finally the bounds beyond which it is unsafe to go'. Memorandum from S.A. Roche to P.P. O'Donoghue, 25 August 1941, NAI, TSCH/3/S7788A.

[10] In a historical overview of statutory encroachments on the monarch's freedom to exercise the prerogative, Grupp (1963: 60) observed that: 'The pardon seems to have been the vehicle for extending mercy to include those individuals who at a later time would not have incurred criminal responsibility.' It had an anticipatory aspect.

claim to be exercising a quasi-religious duty (like Pierrepoint) or just following orders (like soldiers).[11]

Promotes public confidence

The exercise of clemency maintains public confidence in the political process, if not the law, by allowing space for the expression of community sentiment. Where the criminal law is uncompromising, if it is to remain legitimate it must leave room for executive clemency. Bonaparte (1910: 604) noted that: 'In the public interest, therefore, there must be some means of meeting exceptional cases, adapting the situation to changed circumstances, and sacrificing minor to attain greater results, when the attainment of both may be impracticable.' When the law is too cruel it risks losing popular support; the threat of a broken neck coarsens public sentiment rather than civilizing it.

Clemency is about compassion tinged with prudence. This was perhaps especially true in Ireland given the longstanding public antipathy towards capital punishment; as a sanction that was treated with ambivalence or disdain by the public, it had to be used sparingly and in a targeted way in order not to generate an unmanageable level of dissatisfaction. Its discretionary nature was precisely why executive clemency worked without causing too many ripples of disquiet in Ireland's criminal justice system during the period under examination, when the retributive roots were shallow, the number of criminals was few, and public confidence in the institutions of the state was high.

Corrects error

Clemency allows room for manoeuvre in a system that might otherwise have been uniformly lethal. Even a criminal justice system replete with checks and balances and opportunities for appeal can never be perfect. Its operatives are fallible so the argument for clemency is strong, especially when the penalty it is mitigating is so severe (to say nothing of being irreversible). Mistakes are bound to be made in an adversarial process, particularly where there is an inequality of arms between prosecution and defence. Clemency

[11] In his evidence to the Royal Commission on Capital Punishment, Albert Pierrepoint spoke of the 'sacred' nature of his calling. Minutes of Evidence, 2 November 1950, para. 8468.

acts as a remedial mechanism when doubts remain about an individual's guilt or sanity, or the propriety of the verdict.

It is prudent to have a fail-safe given what we know about the unreliability of human decision-making and the profound consequences of getting it wrong when lives are at stake. The more exacting the demands of procedural justice become, the less the need for later executive intervention. Nevertheless, the administration of justice, as a flesh and blood enterprise, is inevitably imperfect. Innocent people will occasionally be punished and guilty people will sometimes be punished too much. Clemency is necessary to correct such errors.

Tempers excessive harshness

If one accepts that the law can be too severe on occasion—even if correctly applied—then executive clemency is an elegant way to mitigate its effects, without the need for creating additional administrative structures. (We are all potential beneficiaries of such arrangements.) The murder trial is about the pursuit of legal and moral certainty. When the former is satisfied but there remain quibbles about the latter, either jury or judge is in a position to draw attention to these, so that the executive may consider taking appropriate action.

It is rarely the case that there are concerns about factual guilt; a conviction is unlikely if these persist during trial. More often there are concerns about the verdict returned (e.g. the judge feels that it should have been manslaughter rather than murder or that the jury was perverse in not finding the accused person insane), or its implications (e.g. the jury feels that the conviction was correct, and appreciates that the death penalty is the only option available to the judge, but believes that it would be unjust for the sentence to be carried into effect). Markel (2004: 1464) concluded that 'a nation confident in its laws and secure in its institutions should be ashamed of the practice of mercy in its criminal justice system'. But experience suggests that the degree of confidence required can never be reached and a 'shameful' practice can provide a vital safeguard, albeit in a dwindling number of cases.

Keeps things personal

There are arguments in favour of allowing the personal to intrude, even if this introduces a risk of capriciousness. The alternative is predictability and procedural justice but with clemency squeezed out. The clemency decision necessitates the insertion of the personal; sometimes this is about justice (sparing those whose are legally but not morally deserving of the ultimate sanction), sometimes it is about mercy (sparing the undeserving).

In Ireland the justice minister of the day conducted an extensive review of the case, taking soundings from the police, judge, and departmental officials, and considering petitions submitted by and on behalf of the condemned person. The proposal he brought to government was based on deep deliberation but it was vulnerable to the peculiarities of context. According to Barkow (2008: 1364):

> ... review requires that there be some specified standard to allow good reasons for leniency to be sifted from bad ones. But ex ante specification of when mercy is appropriate contradicts the reason for having mercy in the first place: it is because not all factors can be anticipated in advance that the discretionary check is important.

In other words, if clemency is to play an effective role it must not be hemmed in too closely by rules and laws. If we believe in clemency we must accept that there will have to be a lawless space in which it operates. There is an inherent tension between justice, which is rules-based, and mercy, which is discretionary and unruly.[12]

Maintains standards

Describing bureaucratic mercy in Victorian Britain, Chadwick (1992: 381) opined that:

> Nowhere were the expressive functions of the law more important than in the highly visible decisions of the Prerogative of Mercy. In determining the limits of criminal responsibility, in the most odious of crimes, the secretary of state and his advisors were protecting standards in the field of criminal justice as a whole.

On the neighbouring island during the following century, the treatment of capital cases continued to serve an important 'expressive function'. The decision to spare a life sent a strong

[12] I share the view expressed by Tasioulas (2003: 130) that 'even if procedural fairness is violated ... it is but one value among others, and it may be judged worth the cost of introducing an element of inconstancy into the penal system if it is thereby rendered more humane'.

message about what the state considered to be the parameters of acceptable conduct and in what limited circumstances stepping beyond them might not have lethal consequences.

Leaves space for intervening factors

The existence of a clemency power allows the criminal justice system to respond to circumstances that developed since trial, such as persuasive rehabilitative efforts on the part of the condemned person. It acknowledges the redemptive possibilities of criminal justice. Sometimes such issues were raised by petitioners, but given the brief time between sentencing and death (see Chapter 2), this was seldom of any great significance during the period under examination in this book.

Differentiates

Clemency facilitates the differentiation of levels of culpability. If several parties were involved in the same crime it is likely that, while equally guilty in the eyes of the law, they will have played different roles in the killing that led to their conviction. Clemency allows a sense of proportionality to be restored. It is a final opportunity to consider the moral as well as legal propriety of the penalty so that the more deserving are spared the ultimate sanction. (It also allows the state to reward a guilty party who has opted to give evidence against his peers.)

Looks forward

Sometimes a murder arises in circumstances that will never be repeated and that may have greatly diminished the life chances of the perpetrator; such as the killing of a spouse after a long marriage. To allow an execution in such cases seems unnecessarily cruel. Clemency allows the system to respond to a low predicted risk of future dangerousness.

Enables supererogation

The existence of a clemency process allows for the injection of mercy, independent of any other consideration. It creates space for actions that are morally good although not strictly required, that go above and beyond the call of duty. Mercy must be particular; this is a key element of its quiddity. If it could be codified it would be justice. Failing to perform a supererogatory act is never wrong; no blame can be attached to non-performance. A government could not be criticized for allowing the law to take its course but might be praised for diverting it away from a lethal outcome. The Irish government was entitled to treat the criminal harshly but could waive this right by advising the president to spare his or her life.

Disguises leniency as firmness of purpose

Grants of clemency can make more political sense than decisions to drop charges or not to prosecute. The latter courses of action may appear weak and indecisive; the former has the additional advantage of holding a punishment over the accused person if the sentence is commuted and release is conditional.

Allows celebration

Clemency can also play a role in marking events of national importance and promoting social solidarity. Barnett (1927: 492) noted that 'it has very generally been the custom of pardoning authorities to grant the "gracious gift" on holidays and the like—the Passover, Christmas Day, Thanksgiving Day'. It is not unusual for the power of executive clemency to be exercised in recognition of what Sebba (1977: 232) described as public events 'giving rise to national jubilation'. He gave as illustrations the general pardons issued in Belgium in 1951 and 1960 to celebrate King Baudouin's coronation and marriage respectively.[13] An example taken from Ireland is the releases of convicted murders in honour of the Eucharistic Congress in 1932 (see Chapter 10).

Justice, Mercy, Caprice

Clemency allowed the government to do justice, show mercy, or behave capriciously. Whether on balance this was a good thing

[13] This practice continues. Hood and Hoyle (2015: 317–18) reported that King Mohammed of Morocco commuted eleven death sentences in 2007 to mark the birth of his daughter, and the President of Zambia commuted 113 death sentences in 2013 to mark Africa Freedom Day.

is to some extent in the eye of the beholder (condemned persons whose death sentences were commuted to penal servitude are likely to have shared a benign view). Its alternative—rigid and unconditional application of the law—has the virtues of consistency and rationality, but they come at a significant human cost.

While the law may be about treating like cases alike, politics is not, and clemency—as exercised in Ireland during the post-independence period—was a political process. As long as the decision remained one for elected officials it was vulnerable to political considerations. These were not cases of judges allowing the rule of law to be contaminated by their own feelings of compassion, but rather politicians, who did not owe the same duty to the justice system, exercising their lawful power in another arena. They were required to take account of community sentiment as well as legal rules. The common good might necessitate some tampering with justice; mercy could be allowed for its leavening effect.

Where there is discretion, there may also be mercy or caprice. Once this is accepted, however grudgingly, the clemency issue becomes less controversial. If clemency is abolished, a measure of humanity is stripped from the system, and this might be considered too great a price to pay for greater consistency. Its continued existence can be viewed as a necessary anathema.

The clemency decision may be, but is not always, rooted in mercy. It is necessary to distinguish merciful considerations from those that are more appropriately ascribed to justice. For example, if the judge thinks that a manslaughter conviction would have been the correct one and that the jury's determination of murder is perverse, then commuting the penalty is about imposing what is deserved rather than exercising mercy. These are two very distinct matters. Mercy can intrude into the clemency process but it is seldom the only, or determinative, factor.

Walker (1995: 28) credited Alwynne Smart with stimulating interest among penologists in the concept of mercy, its inherent contradictions, and its place in schemes of punishment.[14] Smart (1968: 345) opened her argument with the observation that: 'A theory of punishment should give some account of mercy and

[14] So too did Brien (1995: 493), commenting that Smart 'resurrected the contemporary debate about mercy'. Earlier efforts, such as Barnett (1927), did not gain traction.

yet it is true to say that very little has been said about it at all'. The approach taken in this book shares much with Smart's. She argued that, in many cases, 'showing mercy often turns out to be merely fitting the punishment to the crime where the law is too inflexible and unsophisticated to do so' (p. 349). What masqueraded as mercy, in other words, was often justice in disguise. If this is the case, the conflict between the two dissolves. Any clash between mercy and justice is illusory if showing mercy equates with equitable treatment. It is only mercy when the penalty finally imposed is a downward departure from what is deserved.

Laws are couched in general terms; to deal appropriately with exceptions requires the kinds of adjustments that are sometimes misnamed as mercy. What is really at issue here is avoiding an unduly harsh penalty and arriving at a just and fitting one, taking account of all the circumstances to ensure the criminal gets no more than his or her conduct merits. For Smart, real mercy comes into play, 'when the judge benevolently decides to impose less than the just penalty' (p. 355). I am broadly in sympathy with this approach and in many cases of executive clemency in Ireland what was at issue was justice being determined by the executive when the judiciary was precluded from so doing. These were not examples of mercy intruding as an autonomous virtue but of remedial justice.[15]

However, the analysis in this book differs from that of Smart and others in that what is under consideration are not sentences passed in a court where the judge is bound by law and precedent, but decisions made by a non-judicial body (the Irish government) subject to no such constraints and whose decisions were not reviewable. Judicial discretion and executive clemency are quite different matters and when considering justice, mercy, and caprice it is necessary to be alive to this difference.

When the range of behaviours attracting a mandatory death sentence was wide—from the anxious mother killing her newborn child to the lethal attack with arms in pursuit of financial gain—a single sentencing option failed to distinguish between degrees of culpability and so an adjustment by the executive restored a

[15] I do not concur with Smart (1968: 359) that thinking of mercy in this way 'only makes strict logical sense in a retributivist view of punishment'. As argued above, mercy can also be defined as a downward departure from a punishment that has been selected to maximize utility.

sense of proportionality. Without doubt, this amounted to (constitutionally permissible) interference with justice but it did so in the interest of making the sentence fit the crime in a framework where the trial process did not permit such an alignment. Had the judge or jury been able to do so, many of these individuals would not have been sentenced to death. Different rules would have resulted in qualitatively different outcomes. Juries made this clear when they recommended 'mercy' and so did judges when they committed their thoughts in writing to the minister of the day; the argument may have been couched in terms of 'mercy' but it was really an argument for justice.

What was happening here was a post-hoc alignment of the penalty with what was deserved, an action that was made necessary by the rigidity of the legal arrangements. To grant clemency to a mother who killed her baby in a moment of derangement, or an impetuous and jealous lover who lashed out to his eternal regret, was not, strictly speaking, an exercise in mercy, but rather in justice. This was simply an attempt to ensure that the more responsible were punished more, and the less responsible, less.

It was only when there was no just reason to interfere with the decision of the court that mercy intruded. Justice had been served and now mercy could be considered. The essence of mercy was that it relieved deserved suffering. The letter from John Kelly, a young legal academic in Oxford, arguing for clemency in Mary Cadden's case (see Chapter 9) is an example of this. He acknowledged that Cadden had no doubt exhausted public sympathy, given her previous convictions and continued defiance of the law, before stating, 'mercy to those who deserve it is not really mercy, but only justice; to be merciful is to spare those who do not deserve it'.[16] The essence of mercy is that it gives criminals what they have no right to claim and are not seen to deserve; it is unmerited leniency. As Roberts (1971: 353) put it: 'A genuine act of mercy is always unjustified.'

Mercy is an independent virtue that conflicts with and, on occasion, trumps justice. The paradoxes of mercy are that if people deserve their punishment how can it be just to relieve them of it, and why should some be spared and not others? The problem

[16] Letter from John Kelly to Minister for Justice James Everett, 16 November 1956, NAI, JUS/18/3562A & B.

with the moral status of mercy can be stated simply. Mercy is a virtue. But since it is granted to undeserving people its exercise is unjust. This makes it a vice. Solving this puzzle has been a challenge for philosophers since St Anselm of Canterbury identified it in the eleventh century (Steiker 2007: 20–1). Caution is required to avoid becoming immured in an argument, the parameters of which are clear, but which remains an aporia in the law. I am not attempting to offer a solution but, while difficulties remain, I believe that I have come up with an approach that is coherent when applied to the problem of executive clemency in capital cases during a defined period of history (1923 to 1990) in a single jurisdiction (the Republic of Ireland).

It is reasonable to argue that discriminatory and capricious decisions are an abuse of the clemency power, that just ones are not, and that when it comes to the exercise of mercy this is where the answer is uncertain. As outlined above, it is possible to justify mercy even when it will disadvantage some (terminally), when the reasoning behind the decision is opaque, and when a number of the original arguments in favour of the practice are discredited and anachronistic. Despite these formidable objections, there was a place for mercy when sentencing frameworks were unbendingly harsh and, although the law is less 'sanguinary' (to quote the framers of the constitution of the United States) today, and there is a greater guarantee of justice, for a system to disallow an infusion of mercy as an independent virtue on occasions that might not be imaginable presently would not be an unambiguously positive development.[17]

Beyond setting out some general principles, it is a fool's errand to attempt to bureaucratize clemency if it is seen as an antidote to error or a way of dealing with extraordinary cases. No matter how comprehensive the rule book, there will always be exceptions and it is more parsimonious to leave some residual capacity for clemency than to attempt to regulate every conceivable (and inconceivable) potential problem out of existence. Clemency can play a role when rules are followed or when they are flouted.

Bresler (1965: 308) captured this sentiment well when he wrote that 'the infinite variety of human life could not be caught

[17] Hamilton (1788) believed that without the possibility of executive clemency, 'justice would wear a countenance too sanguinary and cruel.'

upon the hooks of precise formulae, that inevitably justice must be pragmatic'. The law must reflect life in all of its messy uncertainty and it is chimerical to think that a workable scheme could be devised to embrace every possible exception.[18] It is important to accept complexity, ambiguity, opacity, imprecision, and occasional incoherence if space is to be left for clemency. When legislators and courts fail to prevent injustice it is acceptable for the executive to act on behalf of the people. Justice without discretion is impoverished.

There is, of course, an argument that no criminal deserves to die, however appalling their conduct. This argument gathered momentum throughout the latter half of the twentieth century and the mandatory death penalty for murder began to appear conspicuously unjust when applied to particular cases. It had always been a blunt instrument but now it was too unwieldy altogether. Shifting public attitudes meant that what might once have been seen as merciful came to be seen as just. When capital cases appeared before the courts in the 1980s, no government of Ireland, regardless of political hue, had the stomach to allow an execution go ahead; complete abolition was only a question of time.

Conclusion

It might be that the conflict between justice and mercy can never be resolved. Duff (1990: 63) seemed to arrive at such a conclusion, commenting on the tension between the competing demands of mercy and retributive justice thus: 'we should resist the temptation to suppose that life cannot confront us (cannot be allowed to confront us) with such irresoluble conflicts between incommensurable values'. There is no need to be embarrassed by clemency in general or by mercy in particular. But there are dangers that should not be downplayed or forgotten. Discretion, which is necessary for mercy, can be obscure in its operation and objectionable in its outcomes, it can slide into favouritism, or worse. The flip side of mercy is unpredictable unfairness. The clemency process is open to abuse.

Despite the attendant risks, namely that mercy leads to undeserved leniency (is unjust), unequal treatment (is undemocratic), and

[18] Recalling Kant's well-known aphorism: 'Out of the crooked timber of humanity, no straight thing was ever made.'

condescension (treats criminals as less than fully accountable) it offers some broad societal benefits. Kobil (2007) saw these benefits as threefold. First, and particularly in capital cases, as 'an eloquent statement that our society is a strong and confident one' (p. 52), in other words that it was robust enough to absorb the harms of crime without exacting the ultimate penalty. Secondly, that showing clemency was an acknowledgement of the fallibility of law and the frailty of humankind; it was a demonstration of humility. Thirdly, it was a statement that however appallingly someone had behaved they still mattered because of our shared humanity. These benefits mean that, on balance, a problematic clemency process is preferable to rigid, relentless lawfulness.

Clemency is an acknowledgement of human weakness on two levels—that the condemned person may deserve compassion, and that those who make life and death decisions are prone to error. As long as some people make decisions that bring other people's lives to premature and violent ends, whether lawfully or unlawfully, clemency will be a necessary adjunct to a criminal justice system. To retain a place for clemency is to acknowledge human frailty no matter how close the system approaches legal perfection.[19]

Over time, the legal environment has softened considerably. Few developed countries retain capital punishment. In those that do, few crimes attract the ultimate penalty and, even if imposed, it is seldom carried out. Furthermore, the range of options open to judges is wider and the law has evolved to take account of how culpability can be affected by factors such as insanity, self-defence, and provocation. There is greater clarity around the exercise of discretion in sentencing and appellate review is well established. As a result of the foregoing the demands for a clemency power have reduced in number and intensity.

Given that the practical problems clemency addressed are now non-existent or less pressing as a result of criminal law reform, and noting the strength of the arguments against the practice from retributivists and utilitarians, it is surprising at first glance that support for its continued existence has not dwindled away entirely. But there will always be hard cases and wrong decisions

[19] I am favourably disposed towards Duff's (2007: 387) conclusion that: 'Justice is not served by mercy; but sometimes it is properly defeated by mercy'.

that require rectification outside the courtroom. For these reasons it lives on.

Walker (1995: 27) described mercy as a device that 'allows benign interference when the programming of the system seems to be having unacceptable effects in special cases'. He continued: 'As the other organs of the system evolve they tend to take over this function: appellate courts are an example. Like the human appendix, mercy may become vestigial. Some penologists and philosophers have welcomed that; but it is open to question whether it is an altogether healthy development.' Walker saw clemency and mercy as synonyms. As explained above I prefer to see the former as an umbrella term under which shelter the analytically distinct concepts of justice, mercy, and caprice.

As will become clear in subsequent chapters, in the cases that I am examining, where a sentence of death has been mandatorily imposed, clemency was more often a post-hoc attempt at justice than an expression of mercy. Occasionally, it can only be understood as an instance of caprice. The first parties with an opportunity to call for a penalty of death to be modified were the jury (who made the finding of guilt) and the judge (who imposed the mandatory sentence). Their respective contributions are addressed in the following chapter.

4

Juries and Judges

Murder trials were major public events. Courtrooms were packed with curious spectators and newspaper coverage of proceedings was extensive. Speculation was rife about the likely motivation behind the act of extreme violence that was under consideration. The possibility that a killer could in turn be killed added a morbid frisson of excitement to discussions. But the public role was not an entirely passive one. There was an opportunity for community sentiment to intrude via the jury of laymen who determined whether the prosecution had made its case beyond a reasonable doubt.

The purpose of this chapter is to explore the role of the jury, including the time it took to arrive at a decision that could result in the imposition of a death sentence, and any subsequent actions that attempted to soften the impact of this decision, such as the addition of a rider that recommended mercy. The judge could steer the jury in a particular direction through his conduct of the trial, his attitude to counsel, the tenor and frequency of his interventions, and his summing up. But, once a verdict of guilty to murder was returned he had no option but to impose a sentence of death. Judges had an opportunity to influence the government's decision by communicating a written view, in confidence, when invited to do so. They were invariably invited to submit such a letter and the contents of these missives, supplemented with contemporary newspaper accounts, inform the analysis that follows.

Weighing the Evidence

Capital cases were dealt with speedily, trials generally concluding within a matter of days. When James Murray was convicted in 1925 his four-day hearing was the longest on record.[1] There is

[1] Key dates are given in the appendices. The crimes committed by the individuals named in this chapter to whom clemency was shown are described in Chapters 8 and 9.

Justice, Mercy, and Caprice: Clemency and the Death Penalty in Ireland. First Edition. Ian O'Donnell. © Ian O'Donnell 2017. Published 2017 by Oxford University Press.

another aspect to speed. This is the time taken by juries to arrive at their verdict. Given that the charge in every case was murder and that the penalty of death was mandatory upon conviction, one might imagine that deliberations were agonizingly protracted. Nothing could be further from the truth. Notwithstanding the life and death implications of their decision, juries did not tarry in making it.

Thomas Delaney, a former Irish Guardsman and injured veteran of the First World War, beat Patrick Horan, a wealthy shopkeeper, to death with a slasher and a tongs. He was apprehended at the scene where he removed his boots and declared that he was mad. Having heard the case against him, and knowing that a guilty verdict would result in the imposition of the death penalty, the jury began its deliberations. Three minutes later it returned its guilty verdict. It is not clear from the extant material if the jury actually left the box and, if it did, it is difficult to imagine that there was more than a single show of hands before it hurried back to report its finding.[2]

The media coverage of the trial does not suggest that the judge or condemned man were perturbed by how quickly the verdict was made available. Indeed, it was reported that the Lord Chief Justice, Thomas Molony, who tried the case, commented that the jury had arrived at its decision after 'the most careful consideration', that it could have come to no other conclusion, and that Delaney could hold out no hope of mercy and so should use the brief amount of time left to him to make 'peace with God' (*Irish Times*, 17 November 1923). Delaney was hanged the following month.

The three minutes that the newspapers report it took the jury to arrive at a verdict in Delaney's case is not a complete outlier; the jury took just ten minutes to convict Patrick Aylward for roasting a child on a fire. Less than ten minutes was required to dispense with Michael Talbot's case, a fact to which his barrister drew attention in his letter to the Minister for Justice, arguing—unsuccessfully as it transpired—that consideration be given to setting aside the death sentence.[3]

[2] In his book on criminal procedure in Ireland, Thompson (1899: 89) noted that the jury retired to their room to consider the verdict only 'if necessary'.

[3] Letter from Michael Lennon to Kevin O'Higgins, 11 July 1925, NAI, JUS/H234/831.

Table 4.1 Speed of jury deliberations

	Executed		Commuted	
	No.	(per cent)	No.	(per cent)
Thirty minutes or less	5	(17)	6	(13)
Between thirty minutes and one hour	9	(31)	14	(30)
More than one and less than three hours	10	(34)	23	(49)
Three hours or more	5	(17)	4	(8)
All	29	(99)	47	(100)

Note: In two cases that ultimately led to commutation, the length of the jury's deliberations could not be ascertained from archival sources or newspaper reports. Rounding explains why column per cent (executed) does not equal 100.

Looking at the overall pattern, almost half of the deliberations in death penalty cases concluded within the hour (Table 4.1). Fewer than one in eight took three hours or more and the longest time spent deliberating was four hours and fifty minutes for Joseph McManus, who was hanged despite the jury's protracted absence and its attachment to the verdict of a recommendation to mercy. The average (median) deliberation time was shorter when the jury made a recommendation to mercy than when it returned a verdict unadorned by any rider (sixty minutes versus eighty minutes), perhaps indicating that when the need to temper a harsh legal outcome was evident it was patently so. More complex or ambiguous cases may have taken longer to resolve because the jury did not want the mandatory penalty to follow. Such speedy decisions are extraordinary by today's standards. Yesterday's maximum is today's minimum.[4]

[4] In 2016, a verdict in a bank fraud case was returned after sixty-one hours and forty-six minutes of deliberations spread over fourteen days. This was reported to have been the longest jury absence in Irish legal history (*Irish Times*, 10 June 2016). While fraud trials may be particularly prone to protracted deliberations, it would be exceptional for a jury in a twenty-first century murder trial to return its verdict in less than an hour, as commonly happened when capital punishment was mandatory for murder. Swiftly concluded jury deliberations have a long history in England (e.g. King 2000: 239, Langbein 2003: 16–17).

One of the factors that may have encouraged juries to come to swift decisions was that, in murder trials, they could not separate until a verdict was returned.[5] This meant that there was some urgency about bringing proceedings to a conclusion.[6] However, the speed at which they arrived at decisions suggests that the lack of separation was hardly a significant issue. Other reasons for their promptitude might include a high level of trust in the police and justice system, especially during the early years of state formation when the turbulence associated with the independence struggle had begun to subside, and among the Dublin property owners who made up jury panels. This was translated into confidence that if a prosecution had been initiated there must have been a good reason for so doing. (Politically motivated crimes were an entirely different matter and, as we shall see in Chapter 5, juries were dispensed with in these cases for fear that they would be hostile to the state or intimidated by its enemies.) In addition, most of the cases where there was a significant doubt about sanity or culpability were filtered out either with a finding of guilty but insane, or unfitness to plead, or a conviction for a lesser offence (Table 1.4). This meant that when a charge of murder was preferred, and proven, the case was unambiguously heinous.

It is possible that jurors moved swiftly to convict because they felt that by adding a rider they could ameliorate the outcome. But if they had paid attention to newspaper reports of previous capital cases they would have learned that the jury's recommendation did not always have the desired effect. (If juries had been aware that their recommendation to mercy would be of little value in the absence of a judicial endorsement they may have used acquittal as an alternative route to the nullification of overly harsh legal consequences.) Finally, it is possible that the male ratepayers who sat on juries bore no principled objection to capital punishment, or believed in its deterrent value, and that they were content for the ultimate sanction to be exacted on occasion.

Despite the weighty matters under consideration, jurors were prone to distraction. During the trial of Vincent McGrath in 1960 the jury expressed dissatisfaction about the length of time proceedings were taking. They wanted matters expedited so that

[5] The Juries Act, 1927, s. 63.

[6] The Juries Act, 1976 changed this, allowing separation in all cases at the judge's discretion (s. 25).

they would be finished in time for a rugby international that several among them desired to watch. They apologized for this crassness the following day and the trial proceeded to a conclusion with typical timeliness; having opened on Tuesday, it concluded on Saturday with the jury returning a not guilty verdict at 8:45 p.m., after four hours and forty minutes deliberating.[7]

Procedures

Felix McMullen's case came before the first sitting of the Central Criminal Court that had been established by the Courts of Justice Act, 1924. The jury could not agree on the murder charge and, through their foreman, intimated to the judge (Thomas O'Shaughnessy) that they would agree to a verdict of manslaughter.[8] The judge refused to accept this verdict, the jurors resumed their deliberations, but inconclusively, and they were discharged. A few days later a new jury, sitting with the same judge, convicted McMullen of murder but with a strong recommendation to mercy. Each jury submitted a unanimous petition calling for clemency to be shown. The original jury's petition noted that, as the first person to be put on trial for his life under the new legal dispensation, it would not be good for public confidence in the criminal justice system if McMullen was executed despite the first jury's thwarted desire to convict him of manslaughter and the second jury's strong recommendation to mercy. The second jury came to its conclusion 'with deep regret' and feeling that it had been 'coerced' by the judge on points of law.[9]

These petitions arrived after the memorandum for government had been typed, one on the day of the Executive Council meeting about the case (via McMullen's solicitor) and one the day

[7] By the time they emerged from court Wales had achieved a narrow victory over the home side at Lansdowne Road.

[8] Petition from jurors to Minister for Justice, 28 July 1924, NAI, JUS/H234/209. The judge did not have to accept the first verdict offered by the jury and he was free to direct them to reconsider it. However, if they insisted on their initial verdict being recorded, either at once or after reconsideration, he was bound to accept it (Thompson 1899: 91). In other words, had the first jury held firm, the judge would have been obliged to accept their verdict of guilty to manslaughter and McMullen would not have been hanged.

[9] Petition from jurors to governor general, 26 July 1924, NAI, JUS/H234/209.

before (forwarded by the governor general). As a result, they were not mentioned in the memorandum which simply stated that the jury recommended mercy but gave no grounds for doing so. This meant that if the Minister for Justice did not specifically draw the Executive Council's attention to these matters in his oral submission it may have allowed the law to take its course without reflecting on the extremely important issues raised. Kevin O'Higgins was minister at the time and it is not going too far to state that he was coarsened by his experience of executions and, accordingly, may have been inured to legal niceties, such as the jury's doubt about whether McMullen should have been found guilty of murder.

McMullen also had the dubious distinction of being the first person to be sentenced to death who took an appeal to the Court of Criminal Appeal that had been set up under the 1924 statute. Hitherto, prisoners had no right to lay their case before an appellate tribunal, and their options were to submit to their fate or to petition the authorities, hoping that they would be shown clemency.[10] Apart from Michael Talbot, Annie Walsh, and William Gambon, everyone who was eventually executed after July 1924 exercised their right of appeal. There was a more mixed picture for those who were spared as most who killed their newborn children did not appeal.

As McMullen's case was the first to be dealt with under the new legislation, the secretary of the Department of Justice wrote to the clerk of the crown and peace at the Central Criminal Court setting out the practice to be followed henceforth in the event of a conviction for murder.[11] There were to be two formal communications. Immediately after the close of proceedings the judge would write to the Minister for Justice stating that a death sentence had been imposed and noting if the jury had made any

[10] Their only other hope was that if a point of law arose the judge would respite the judgment and submit a written case to the Court for Crown Cases Reserved (CCCR). Whether to reserve a point of law for the CCCR to decide was entirely at the judge's discretion. This court was used sparingly, hearing just one or two Irish cases each year in the closing decades of the nineteenth century and seldom sitting after 1900 (Greer 2006: 195, 201). It could quash a conviction but otherwise its powers were limited; it could not order a retrial. The Criminal Appeal Act, 1907 was not extended to Ireland.

[11] Letter from H.J. O'Friel to George Fottrell, 11 July 1924, NAI, JUS/H234/209.

recommendation but without providing additional commentary. A view would be solicited from the judge on a later occasion when the appeals process, if initiated, had run its course and petitions for mercy were being considered. It was noted, in deference to the judiciary, that there was no impediment to such a view being submitted unprompted, but the intention was that the Minister for Justice would control this process.[12] Once the government had made its decision, a letter was generally sent to the judge informing him of this fact. This procedure was followed until 1964 after which time juries no longer played a role in death penalty cases.

Composition

Lavinsky (1965: 38) described executive clemency as 'a vehicle for the expression of society's compassion, as an outlet from the rigorous inflexibility of a judicial system'. I would agree with the second part of this statement but not the first given how often the government ignored the jury's call for mercy to be shown (see the next section, 'Softening the Verdict'). Granted, juries were not all that representative of society at large (being male property owners aged between 21 and 65).[13] Prior to 1927, women were occasionally called for jury service in criminal trials but the practice was for them not to be sworn.[14] After 1927, even the small number of

[12] Very occasionally a judge seized the initiative and submitted his view on clemency while an appeal was pending. While there was nothing to prevent such action its impact would be deferred.

[13] Hanly (2016) estimated that the property requirement rendered 95 per cent of men in Dublin city in 1926 ineligible for jury service. The Sex Disqualification (Removal) Act, 1919 placed men and women on an equal footing and juries began to include women for the first time from 1921. Matters changed in 1924 when legislation was introduced to allow women seek an exemption from jury service; almost 80 per cent did so immediately. Further restrictions were introduced in 1927 when women were automatically excluded but could apply to have their names added to the jurors' list. This law had a dramatic effect. Hanly showed that just one woman was available to serve as a juror in Tipperary and Limerick in 1927, compared with over 1,000 four years previously. Gender equality was not restored until the Juries Act, 1976, which also abolished the property requirement (s. 6).

[14] When Thomas Clune appeared before the Dublin City Commission on a murder charge it was reported that: 'As in previous murder trials at this Commission, all women jurors were ordered by the prosecution to stand by' (*Irish Independent*, 2 November 1923). He was found not guilty of murder but guilty of manslaughter.

women who satisfied the property owning requirement set out in the legislation were not liable for jury service unless they made an application to serve.[15] Few of those who were eligible took the trouble to do so (see Beatrice Dixon's account of her efforts to serve on a jury in *Irish Times*, 9 January 1959). A petition in Jane O'Brien's case in 1932 drew attention to the fact that an absence of female representation meant that she was not tried by a jury of her peers and that this was an affront to justice.[16]

The first woman juror in Dublin's Central Criminal Court was Kathleen Swanton, a member of Dublin Corporation who was empanelled for the trial of a homeless man charged with larceny (*Irish Times*, 11 July 1959). Three death sentences were imposed in jury trials after this date (Vincent McGrath, David Galvin, and James Kelly) and, while highly unlikely, it is possible that a woman served on one of them.[17] The least that can be said with confidence therefore is that no woman ever served on a jury that returned a death sentence that was carried out.

In a letter prompted by the decision to commute the death sentences imposed on the Edwards sisters, Elizabeth and Rose, Hanna Sheehy-Skeffington called for the juries in these cases to include mothers, reasoning that 'men cannot be trusted because of lack of experience of conditions that affect maternity' (*Irish Times*, 24 May 1935). She felt that the existence of all-male juries 'deprives unhappy girls of any chance of justice'. While no doubt well intentioned, Sheehy-Skeffington's concerns were wide of the mark. The high attrition rate in prosecutions of mothers who killed their children shows that the men who dealt with their cases treated them leniently. Only a small fraction resulted in a murder conviction and in these cases the juries (always) and the judges (in all but one case) called for mercy, a request to which the government invariably acceded.

Just as the jurors were men, so were the members of An Garda Síochána who carried out the investigations,[18] the attorneys

[15] The Juries Act, 1927 allowed men who were not themselves property owners but whose wives satisfied the rateable criteria, to serve (s. 3).

[16] Petition to Minister for Justice, undated, NAI, JUS/18/2737A & B.

[17] The remoteness of this possibility is indicated by the fact that only two women served on juries in the ten years leading up to 1973 (*de Burca and Anderson v Attorney General* [1976] 1 IR 38).

[18] The Garda Síochána Act, 1958 allowed women to become members of the force (s. 1) and the first female recruits entered training the following year.

general who determined the charge,[19] the senior counsel involved in prosecuting and defending these cases,[20] and the presiding judges.[21] If the execution went ahead the executioners were men and so were the prison governors and custodial staff; wardresses were not allowed to enter the hang house.[22]

Women were scarcely represented among the legislators who were slow to reform the law, particularly in infanticide cases; only a handful of women was elected to Dáil Éireann or Seanad Éireann [upper house of national parliament] in the first half-century after independence.[23] Also, the governments that decided whether the law should be deflected from its course after the jury returned a guilty verdict were exclusively male.[24] All of the justice ministers who dealt with death penalty cases were male. So too were all of the secretaries to the Department of Justice. All of the governors general and presidents were men too.[25]

In other words, women charged with murder found themselves in an environment where all of the key personnel were male. The only male absentee, for those charged with killing an infant, was he who had contributed to their predicament, who was nowhere to be seen (save on those rare occasions where marriage was substituted for a prison term).[26] For those charged with killing an

[19] The first female attorney general was Máire Whelan, who was appointed in 2011.

[20] In 1977, Mella Carroll was the second woman to take silk but the first to practice as a senior counsel.

[21] Eileen Kennedy was the first female judge in Ireland. She was appointed as a Justice of the District Court (court of summary jurisdiction) in 1964. In 1980, Mella Carroll was the first woman appointed to the High Court.

[22] Albert Pierrepoint explained to the Royal Commission on Capital Punishment that: 'The women do not see the execution. The men take over out of the cell just before the execution.' Minutes of Evidence, 2 November 1950, para. 8498.

[23] In general elections between 1923 and 1964, there were never more than five women returned to Dáil Éireann.

[24] In 1979, as Minister for the Gaeltacht [Irish-speaking regions], Máire Geoghegan Quinn was the first woman to be appointed to the cabinet. She became the first female Minister for Justice in 1993. Constance Markievicz was Minister for Labour between 1919 and 1922, before the Free State was established.

[25] In 1990, shortly after capital punishment was abolished for all crimes, Mary Robinson became the first female President of Ireland.

[26] When the pregnancy resulted from a crime, legal action could follow. For example, the father of Mary Anne Somerville's child was prosecuted, unsuccessfully, for unlawful carnal knowledge; both parties were aged 16 at the time.

adult, the victim was more often a man than a woman. So, the men who were wrapped up in the conduct that had led to their indictment for murder were invisible while their fate during the trial was determined, exclusively, by other men. This was an odd set of gender arrangements.

Female murderers benefited from a mixture of squeamishness, chivalry, paternalism, and precedent. They could not have fared better if their peers were involved and it is quite possible that they would have been worse off. This is particularly true of the unmarried mothers among them whose fates may have been adversely affected by the bitter censoriousness of those who had been tempted but not fallen (or, even worse, those who had never been tempted or for whom prudishness and celibacy were integral to their characters as well as cherished values). Indeed, it was when they were under the care of members of their own sex in the religious institutions to which many were sent from prison (Table 10.2) that the screw of coercion was tightened and that their moral failings were accentuated. The prisoner had clarity about the conditions and duration of her confinement; the penitent did not.

The language used when pronouncing the sentence of death was antiquated. The ready availability of a formula of words relieved some of the emotional pressure on judges and its archaic syntax must have added to the distance between themselves, their utterance, and its intended effect. The entire process from conviction through to the coroner's inquest (and in the early part of the twentieth century the raising of a black flag above the prison and the tolling of a church bell) was rooted in tradition. This made participation easier as each player understood his role.

As well as being antiquated the language was inaccurate, suggesting judicial unawareness of how hangings were actually carried out. Condemned persons were told that they would be taken to the 'common place of execution in the prison' where they would be 'hanged by the neck until ... dead'.[27] However, the

[27] The full pronouncement was as follows: 'The Sentence and Judgment of the Court are and it is ordered and adjudged that you [name] be taken from the bar of the Court where you now stand to the prison from whence you last came and that on [date] you be taken to the common place of execution in the prison in which you shall be then confined and that you be then and there hanged by the neck until you be dead and that your body be buried within the walls of the prison in which the aforesaid Judgment of Death shall be executed upon

days of hanging criminals by the neck until the life was choked out of them were long gone by the time the Free State came into existence. Disturbed by the cruelty and inhumanity of allowing a convulsing criminal to dangle at the end of a rope for between five and forty-five minutes until he died, Haughton (1866) advocated that a longer drop be used so that the neck was broken, resulting in instantaneous death.[28] The 'table of drops' based on Haughton's work was used by the English executioners who travelled to Ireland.[29]

It seems anomalous (but perhaps indicative of the reluctance of the legal profession to change; the motto of the King's Inns in Dublin, adopted in 1792, is *Nolumus mutari*) that the innovation of a Dublin professor (Haughton was a fellow of Trinity College), while dramatically altering the conduct of executions, had not affected the language of the city's judges.

Softening the Verdict

Prior to 1964 a verdict of guilty of murder resulted in the imposition of a mandatory death sentence. But juries had an opportunity to soften the impact of their decision by adding a rider that exhorted the government to exercise its discretion in favour of the condemned person.[30]

When the jury made a recommendation to mercy it was usually a strong one. Occasionally a few words of justification were included in the rider such as references to the prisoner's 'low mentality' (Hannah Flynn), 'the unsettled state of the country at the time' (Charles Molloy), 'the exceptional circumstances under

you. And may the Lord have mercy upon your soul.' The final sentence was not always included.

[28] Haughton (1866: 30) noted that, in England, the original purpose of hanging a person sentenced to death for treason was not to extinguish life but to anaesthetize him prior to the disembowelling ('drawing') and quartering that would follow. The practice of allowing other criminals to hang by the neck until they expired followed despite the fact that it was not intended to facilitate a speedy death.

[29] All but two of the executions were carried out by a Pierrepoint. The exceptions were James Myles who was hanged by William Willis and John Fleming who was dispatched by Robert Baxter (see Appendix II).

[30] The twenty cases dealt with by non-jury courts are treated elsewhere (see Chapter 5).

which the act was committed' (Deborah Sullivan), or the age of the perpetrator (if especially young or old). Perhaps the most emphatic statement by the jury was disregarded by the government. This was in the case of John Cox whom the jury found guilty but added 'the strongest possible recommendation to mercy as Jacob Kunz's death might not have ensued had his skull not been thinner than usual'.[31] On two occasions where clemency was shown (Patrick Aylward and Hannah O'Leary), the jury was unanimously in favour of conviction but divided as to mercy, and the rider was supported by a majority.[32]

With just one exception—John Fleming (see later under 'A Singular Case')—if the judge expressed a view in favour of mercy the government moved to commute the sentence. When judge and jury both expressed a view in favour of mercy this recommendation was invariably accepted. But it was not uncommon for governments to recommend commutation when the trial judge had not advised it; this happened ten times. In other words, politicians accepted the judge's call for mercy on all but one occasion, but were not inhibited about recommending commutation even if the judge had not advocated such a course of action. The jury's recommendation carried little weight unless it was endorsed by the judge. On three occasions (Frances Cox, Robert Stevenson, and Mary Cadden) both judge and jury said no to mercy but the government begged to differ. Looking at the overall pattern, the gradient is clear: governments were more lenient than juries, and juries were more lenient than judges.[33]

There was a gender bias in jury recommendations to mercy. For women, a rider was attached in nineteen out of twenty-two cases (85 per cent) compared with thirty out of fifty-six for men (54 per cent). While the attachment of a rider may have settled uneasy

[31] Central Criminal Court, 1929 sittings, NAI, Trials Record Book, Change of Venue Cases, Nov. 1927—June 1933. Seán MacBride had been in Mountjoy Prison at the same time as Cox and the pair exercised together in a yard beside the hang house. There was a workshop in this yard where they could see Cox's coffin being made; this deepened MacBride's opposition to capital punishment (MacBride 2005: 108).

[32] Thomas McDonagh's jury was also divided on whether a recommendation to mercy should attach to the verdict; this equivocal support did not prevent his execution.

[33] Judges recommended mercy in thirty-six cases, juries in forty-five, and forty-nine were spared.

minds, it did not do a great deal, independently, to influence the outcome. The jury's recommendation was not generally persuasive in the absence of judicial approval. In nine cases where the jury, but not the judge, called for mercy the individual was executed. In seven where the same call issued, he or she was spared. It is difficult to avoid agreeing with the former British Home Secretary who told the Royal Commission on Capital Punishment that the recommendation to mercy was a 'frill' (cited in Bresler 1965: 113). With the notable exception of Fleming, governments were reluctant to 'retry' cases and to allow someone to die unless they were confident that this was a course of action to which the judge had not objected. They showed little compunction when it came to ignoring the jury's recommendation.

There is a problem with the government disregarding the jury's recommendation to mercy, because who is to know in how many cases an alternative verdict would have been returned or the jury would have hung or acquitted had they known their recommendation would have had no effect? Why allow such a system to persist if the recommendations, stated in open court, reported in the press, and conveyed to the minister by the trial judge (who informed the jury that he would so do), were not adhered to? If the recommendation to mercy was a compromise to allow unanimity, or was intended to draw attention to factors that were legally irrelevant but elicited sympathy, and it was ignored, this is intensely problematic.[34] It would have been more honest to discourage or even prohibit this practice rather than allowing it to continue as a false balm to troubled consciences. (Although, it might be argued that the rider system had some value nevertheless as it allowed jurors to balance legal duty with conscience.

[34] A letter to the *Irish Times* on 13 March 1953, regarding the case of William Hopkins, whose sentence the government declined to advise the president to commute despite the jury's recommendation, asked rhetorically: 'If a recommendation to mercy brought in by jurors in exceptional cases is to be flouted, is there not grave danger that juries in the future will bring in verdicts not strictly based on conscience, but designed to avoid inflicting the supreme penalty?' Hopkins was retried and found unfit to plead. The judge in Martin Griffin's case could not understand why the jury added a recommendation to mercy and suggested that perhaps 'they needed to attach such a rider to achieve unanimity'. Letter from A.K. Overend to Minister for Justice, 9 June 1943, NAI, JUS/18/6470A & B.

Table 4.2 Recommendations to mercy

	Jury only	Judge only	Both	Neither	Not known
Executed	9	1	0	16	3
Commuted	7	6	29	3	4

Note: Based on rider, if any, attached to jury verdict, letter from trial judge to Minister for Justice expressing a view on whether the law should take its course, and judge's comments when passing sentence. (Seven cases are categorized 'not known' because the judicial view could not be established; juries made a recommendation to mercy in four of these cases, two of which resulted in commutation.)

Without this device they may have had more difficulty applying the law which would have undermined the jury system itself.)

Where judge and jury made a recommendation to mercy this was often because they believed that while it may have been legally correct to impose the sentence, it would not have been morally acceptable to carry it out. The rider specified 'mercy' and judges wrote in favour of the government exercising its 'prerogative of mercy', but what was at issue was a plea for justice, an attempt to mitigate the consequences of a lawful decision when the mandatory sentence meant that legal and moral imperatives were out of kilter, as discussed in Chapter 3.

The jury recommended mercy in eleven out of twenty-nine cases (38 per cent) where an execution ensued and thirty-eight out of forty-nine (78 per cent) where it did not (Table 4.2; including cases where the jury's view was known but the judge's was not). For judges the respective figures were one (3 per cent) and thirty-five (71 per cent). The degree of overlap was substantial in that for most cases that proceeded to execution neither judge nor jury called for mercy (sixteen out of twenty-nine; 55 per cent) and in most of those that were commuted, both parties did (twenty-nine out of forty-nine; 59 per cent).

There were no cases where judge *and* jury recommended mercy but the government allowed the law to take its course.[35] There were sixteen executions where neither judge nor jury called for mercy (Table 4.2). Adding in the three commuted cases where

[35] It looked like this was going to happen in Patrick Boylan's case but the judge intervened. In Patrick Heffernan's case the trial judge recommended mercy, but the government appeared resolute until an intervention from a judge who had been part of the appeal court that had considered the case (see Chapter 7).

neither judge nor jury called for mercy, this gives a total of nineteen cases where an execution was not deemed to be unjust by the courtroom actors. These were the occasions where mercy could have been introduced as an autonomous virtue but this seldom happened. The government was merciful only in one in six of these cases. What the government was doing was finessing justice (something at which it was accomplished) rather than finding room for mercy (which it refrained from doing). When it came to considering the execution of death sentences, the government was just but merciless. On those rare occasions (Cox, Cadden, and Stevenson) when it showed mercy it was driven by a combination of precedent (it would be grotesque to hang a woman when so many had previously been spared) and paternalism (by virtue of her gender she could not be held fully accountable for her actions), or the intervention of the Holy See (see Chapter 9).

There were seven cases where the judge recommended mercy but the jury did not. For Martin Joyce and Annie Walsh there was a concern about the children's evidence which led to their convictions. For Patrick Heffernan the judge felt a proper verdict would have been manslaughter. For William Wall the judicial misgivings probably related to his doubtful sanity. For David Galvin, it is not clear but seems to have been related to a lack of premeditation. For Fleming, it was the absence of direct evidence of guilt. William Devereux was different in that there were no qualms regarding the nature of the verdict or the safety of the conviction. The judge was at a loss to find a legally valid rationale for clemency and made a plea *ad misericordiam.*[36]

Trends

Juries became quieter over time. The likelihood that they would make a recommendation to mercy was lower in the 1950s and 1960s than in earlier decades (Table 4.3). There was a corresponding increase in the time taken to arrive at a verdict. This is

[36] He wrote that while he felt the verdict was fully justified by the evidence: 'I feel a sympathy for this poor man ... and I would be quite satisfied if the prerogative of mercy was exercised in his favour, although I must confess I find it impossible to suggest a logical ground for the exercise of such prerogative'. Letter from T.F. Molony to Minister for Home Affairs, 12 December 1923, NAI, JUS/H234/3507A.

Table 4.3 Disquiet in the jury room

	Recommendations to mercy		Deliberations exceeding one hour	
	No.	(per cent)	No.	(per cent)
1923–9	24	(69)	8	(24)
1930–9	12	(75)	11	(69)
1940–9	10	(59)	14	(82)
1950–9	2	(29)	7	(100)
1960–4	1	(33)	2	(66)
All	49	(63)	42	(55)

Note: In two cases during the 1920s the deliberation time was unknown. After 1964 capital cases did not involve juries.

partly explained by the disappearance of cases involving women and other close family members who killed newborn infants, which were easy to decide and where mercy was invariably recommended.[37] But this does not tell the full story as such cases had all but disappeared from the criminal calendar by the 1940s. Perhaps juries saw less need to recommend mercy as it became increasingly unlikely that the law would be allowed to take its course? Or perhaps they struggled with the decision given its enormity but felt they were duty bound, despite their scruples, to return a proper verdict regardless of the consequences?

Table 4.3 shows that the deliberation time exceeded an hour for 24 per cent of cases in the 1920s, rising to 69 per cent in the 1930s, and 100 per cent in the 1940s, before falling back to 66 per cent in the 1960s (although by then the number of trials was very small). All of the deliberations resulting in execution that took thirty minutes or less occurred in the 1920s. So did almost all of the next category (thirty to sixty minutes).

It is possible that juries were less likely to be merciful as time passed because the murder cases that remained death-eligible were at the extreme end of the spectrum and seemed even more

[37] The only case of child murder where the deliberation time exceeded an hour involved the Edwards sisters where matters were complicated by the absence of a body (the jury required sixty-three minutes to find both guilty), and Deborah Sullivan where the jury was concerned about the prisoner's state of mind and returned after one hour to receive further direction from the judge.

transgressive when viewed against a downward trend in lethal violence (Tables 1.1 and 1.2). Maybe the proportion of murders attracting recommendations to mercy was lower in the 1950s and 1960s than in the 1920s and 1930s because during the later period only the most flagrantly brutal and unambiguously deliberate offences resulted in murder convictions; in the earlier period, murder cases were more heterogeneous.

Juries in the Central Criminal Court in Dublin, where all murder trials took place, may have had little direct experience of the conditions of life in rural Ireland where murders occurred (Table 2.2 shows the geography of capital punishment).[38] Sometimes the fact that Dublin jurors would not have been capable of understanding rural life was referred to in court and, on rare occasions, such as during the trials of Annie Walsh (commuted) and James Kelly, evidence was given in Irish by native speakers of the language and translated, thereby furthering the distance between the accused man or woman and the twelve men determining their guilt or innocence. The non-availability of a transcript in Irish became one of the grounds of appeal in Walsh's case. These jurors could not be said to represent the local community's sense of what justice demanded.

There was an urban/rural divide in the likelihood that the jury would make a recommendation to mercy. There were fourteen guilty verdicts relating to murders that took place in Dublin; in seven (50 per cent) the jury recommended mercy. There were sixty-four guilty verdicts relating to murders that occurred outside Dublin; the jury recommended mercy in forty-two (66 per cent). Omitting the killings of infants, all but two of which took place outside Dublin and all of which attracted a recommendation to mercy, the difference was less pronounced but still evident. The Dublin jurors added recommendations to mercy in five of the twelve Dublin cases (42 per cent) but in thirty-one of the fifty-three that took place outside the capital's boundaries (58 per cent). Rural life was supposed to be innocent and idyllic, the repository of the true and

[38] The relocation of murder trials to Dublin was a departure from the common law tradition that trials be held in the locality where the alleged crime occurred, thereby allowing for the ventilation of community sentiment. Had judges considered distance to be an impediment to effective fact-finding there was legislative provision for the jury to view the crime scene or any other place the judge deemed it expedient for them to see (Juries Act, 1927, s. 60).

virtuous Ireland and when this fiction was exposed it was all the more shocking. Nevertheless, an inability to comprehend their lives did not act to the disadvantage of rural dwellers.

Majority verdicts were introduced by s. 5 of the Juries (Protection) Act, 1929 in response to the murder of a witness in a criminal trial and the attempted murder of a juryman (O'Sullivan 1940: 255–8).[39] In capital cases the judge was obliged to ascertain from the foreman the number of dissentients. Patrick McDermott was the only person to be executed following a jury verdict that was not unanimous. He was convicted by a nine to three majority, the legal minimum required for a valid finding of guilt. The legislation contained a sunset clause to the effect that it would expire on 30 September 1931, unless renewed. It was renewed for another two years in 1931, the year before McDermott killed his brother. Had this provision not been temporarily extended, McDermott would not have been convicted of the crime, let alone executed.[40]

Donning the Black Cap

It took longer to sentence a person for larceny than for murder. In the former scenario the judge was required to consider the individual's previous convictions (if any), to listen to pleas in mitigation (if offered), to reflect on the response to previous sanctions (if relevant), and to identify an appropriate rationale for the punishment. In the latter, the only decision was whether to place a piece of black cloth on his head before uttering the prescribed form of words about being taken from the dock to the prison where the gallows would be made ready. He did not even have to cogitate about setting a date as the procedure in this regard was clear.[41]

[39] The new legislation also prohibited the publication of jurors' names and introduced penalties for juror intimidation. Reflecting on its passage and aftermath, O'Sullivan (1940: 240) opined that, 'the time was approaching when trial by jury for cases of alleged political crime would have to be abolished altogether'.

[40] The unanimity requirement was removed by the Criminal Justice Act, 1984 which permitted a conviction if at least ten jurors agreed (s. 25).

[41] The rule for regulating the execution of capital sentences introduced by George Wyndham, on 23 August 1902, in his capacity as Chief Secretary for Ireland, stated that: 'For the sake of uniformity it is recommended that Executions should take place in the week following the third Sunday after the

There was just one black cap in Ireland—'a clumsy piece of cloth roughly-fashioned into the shape of a cap'—kept by the County Registrar in Dublin's Four Courts, and brought into court whenever a death sentence was to be passed (*Irish Times*, 31 January 1963).[42] George Gavan Duffy broke with tradition in Thomas Kelly's retrial in November 1937, leaving his head uncovered, reputedly the first judge to do so (Deale 2007: 87; *Irish Times*, 25 November 1937). Thereafter, whether judges donned the black cap was largely a matter of personal preference. George Murnaghan put the cap on his head when sentencing Michael Manning (*Irish Times*, 18 February 1954) but Cahir Davitt did not do so when sentencing Thomas O'Rourke (*Irish Times*, 2 May 1959).

Henry Hanna wrote to the *Irish Times* on 30 April 1943 to draw attention to the fact that two of his judicial colleagues had opted for a bare pate when passing death sentences. He felt that this was arbitrary and that a consistent practice should be adopted given the longevity and 'deep significance' of the tradition.[43] There was a pseudonymous letter in reply pointing out that nowhere in the rules of court were judges required to wear a black cap as part of their costume (*Irish Times*, 4 May 1943). Having recently retired after a legal career spanning forty-six years, Hanna must have been quite agitated by matters sartorial if one of his first acts was to pen such a missive. Given how often he presided over murder trials, and how seldom he inclined towards leniency (Table 4.4), perhaps his attachment to macabre headgear is not all that surprising.

day on which sentence is passed, on any week-day but Monday, and at 8 a.m.' Rules made by the Chief Secretary to the Lord Lieutenant of Ireland, pursuant to the provisions of the Capital Punishment Amendment Act, 1868 for regulating the execution of capital sentences in Ireland, NAI, GPB CN5 Death Book, Home Circuit-Dublin Commission.

[42] The custodian of this garment seems to have changed over time. Henry Hanna stated that the black cap 'was always in the custody of the President of the High Court and was handed to the tipstaff of the judge going to the Central Criminal Court to be used, when necessary' (*Irish Times*, 8 May 1943).

[43] The Royal Commission on Capital Punishment (1949–53) noted that the use of the cap—'a square of black silk' in England (para. 684) and a tricorn in Scotland (para. 691)—was not governed by any statutory provision and that it was not always worn.

Table 4.4 Hanging judges?

	Recommendations to mercy		
	Yes	No	Not known
Thomas Molony	2	5	0
Jonathan Pim	1	3	0
William Johnston	2	3	0
James Creed Meredith	1	0	0
Thomas O'Shaughnessy	1	1	0
Timothy Sullivan	2	0	1
Henry Hanna	1	5	5
John O'Byrne	12	5	0
Conor Maguire	1	0	0
George Gavan Duffy	3	0	0
William Black	1	0	0
Martin Maguire	0	3	0
Kevin Haugh	0	1	0
Andrew Overend	1	4	0
Cahir Davitt	4	1	0
Kevin Dixon	0	2	0
Theodore Kingsmill Moore	1	0	0
Gardner Budd	1	0	0
Richard McLoughlin	0	1	1
Thomas Teevan	1	0	0
George Murnaghan	1	1	0
All	35	36	7

Note: Listed by year of appointment to the High Court. Thomas Molony (last Lord Chief Justice of Ireland) and Jonathan Pim had been High Court judges prior to the Courts of Justice Act, 1924. Thomas O'Shaughnessy was the last Recorder of Dublin. Based on contents of letter from trial judge to Minister for Justice, and judge's comments when imposing sentence.

The practice of wearing a black cap when imposing a death sentence had ended by the time Patrick McCann and Colm O'Shea came up for sentence before the Special Criminal Court.[44] Given that, after 1964, the courts imposing death penalties were

[44] 'Mr Justice Hamilton was not wearing a black cap when he pronounced the death sentences, as that custom has been discontinued' (*Irish Times*, 28

three-judge panels, the symbolism was somewhat different. There was no jury to impress with the majesty of the law and three older men placing clumsy pieces of cloth on their heads—when there was no realistic prospect of execution—risked looking farcical rather than awesome, with the result that the power of the gesture would be diluted. It would have looked even odder if some chose to wear the garment and others did not; this may have been interpreted as an indication that the non-wearers wished to distance themselves from the judgment.

Judicial recommendations

To classify the judge as having recommended clemency there must have been a positive expression to that effect in his correspondence with the minister or an explicit endorsement of the jury's decision if it called for mercy. Sometimes, judges were clear that they approved of the verdict and identified no impediment to the law taking its course. Sometimes they retained a studied neutrality, not taking a view one way or the other, and simply outlining the facts of the case. For the purposes of the analysis that follows, these 'neutral' observations were coded 'No' because there was no indication that they thought the 'prerogative' should be exercised in favour of the condemned person. It is only where I could find what appeared to be a clear statement of the desirability of leniency that I counted this as a 'Yes' on the judge's part.

In seven of the twenty-nine jury trials that led to an execution (24 per cent) the extant archival materials did not yield an indication of the view expressed by the sentencing judge to the minister regarding commutation. In six of these, the Department of Justice could find no record of any judicial observations, suggesting that nothing had been placed on the file.[45] Where a confidential letter from the judge was not available, his view was sometimes apparent from comments made when imposing sentence.

In James McHugh's case, the judge stated that he 'entirely agreed' with the jury's verdict (*Irish Times*, 28 October 1926). In Henry

November 1980). The Special Criminal Court had been disestablished at the time of the 1964 legislation so synchronized hat wearing might not have been a consideration.

[45] Return of Persons Sentenced to Death from 1 April 1922 to 31 January 1932, NAI, TSCH/3/S7788A.

McCabe's case, Mr Justice O'Byrne addressed the condemned man in the following terms:

> ... after a long and patient trial you have been found guilty of the terrible crime of murder. It is only right and proper that I should say that in that verdict I entirely concur. I can hold out to you no hope of mercy in this world, and I can only advise you to spend the remainder of the time allotted to you in this world in preparing to appear before your Maker. (*Irish Times*, 20 November 1926)

There were no comments from the judge noted on the transcript prepared for the Court of Criminal Appeal in Gerard Toal's case other than his advice, when asked by the jury, that there was nothing in the evidence that would justify returning a verdict of manslaughter.[46] The newspapers reported his agreement with the jury's verdict (*Irish Times*, 4 August 1928). In none of these cases did the jury attach a rider. All three are classified as 'No' to mercy on the judge's part.

In Michael Manning's case the jury added no rider and the judge endorsed its decision, stating: 'If it is any consolation to you to know, gentlemen, I agree with your verdict'.[47] Newspaper reports indicated that Mr Justice Murnaghan 'thoroughly agreed' with the verdict (*Irish Times*, 18 February 1954). It is possible that a judge might feel that the jury had arrived at the correct verdict legally speaking, but that he would still find reason to recommend a commutation—in confidence—to the minister. However, the fact that the judge made a point of stating his agreement with the verdict in open court adds weight to the notion that the absence of any correspondence on file reflects a lack of any desire to deflect the law from its grisly course. I class this as 'No' to mercy on the judge's part.

As regards Con O'Leary, Michael Talbot, and Annie Walsh, the jury were sympathetic towards O'Leary and Walsh but not Talbot; the archives and press are silent as to the judge's view. As a result, these three cases cannot be classified from a judicial perspective; they remain 'Not Known'.

It was less common not to find a letter on file for cases that led to commutation. In seven of the forty-nine jury trials that had this outcome (14 per cent), a letter from the judge stating his view

[46] Transcript of trial, p. 270, 26 July 1928, NAI, CCA 20/28.

[47] Charge to jury, p. 22, 17 February 1954, NAI, TSCH/3/S15641.

was not available. In other words, if the judge felt that the law should be deflected from its course he was more likely to convey this sentiment in writing. If he saw no reason that a lawful sentence should not be executed, no action was required on his part and he may have felt that by declining an invitation to provide a view he was making his position clear.

In Jane O'Brien's case the newspapers reported that the judge 'entirely concurred' with the verdict of guilty with a strong recommendation to mercy and stated that he would pass it on to the proper quarter (*Irish Independent*, 9 June 1932). In Denis Foy's case the judge declared himself in agreement with the jury's strong recommendation to mercy (*Irish Times*, 20 February 1959). I class both of these cases as 'Yes' to mercy.

As for Hannah O'Leary and Patrick Fagan there was no indication of the judge's view on the transcripts prepared for the Court of Criminal Appeal or in contemporaneous newspaper accounts. In James Murray's case, the judge made no comment on the jury's verdict, which came without a rider (*Irish Times*, 13 June 1925). For James Kelly, whose finding of guilt was similarly unaccompanied by a rider, Mr Justice McLoughlin told the jury that 'they were perfectly in order in returning the verdict' (*Irish Times*, 25 June 1962) which is some distance from a ringing endorsement. All four remain 'Not Known'.

The final case was that of William Wall where the jury was not inclined to be merciful but the judge (Cahir Davitt) attended the government meeting when the death sentence was considered (see Chapter 7). Given that Davitt had previously intervened to save Patrick Heffernan's life it is reasonable to assume that he took a similar line on this occasion. If the government was minded to spare Wall it would hardly have invited the judge along. If it was minded to hang him and the judge agreed, surely he would have been hanged? The most plausible interpretation is that Davitt persuaded a wavering executive to advise the president to commute the sentence to penal servitude for life. For this reason I have taken the view that Davitt was inclined to be merciful.

Table 4.4 shows judges and their recommendations to the government.[48] If anyone deserved the mantle of 'hanging judge'

[48] If there was more than one trial the judge in the final trial is counted as it was only he who would have been invited to submit comments to the government. There were judges who passed death sentences that were overturned

it was Henry Hanna; only Elizabeth Doran was known to have elicited his sympathy. Hers was the only case where he expressed in writing his view that the sentence he imposed should not be carried out (ever a stickler for protocol he donned the black cap even in this case). In all of the others—including Annie Walsh, the sole woman to be executed—he recommended that the law should take its course or he remained silent. Of the other judges who sentenced murderers on multiple occasions, Thomas Molony, Jonathan Pim, Andrew Overend, and Martin Maguire were also inclined to be severe.[49] John O'Byrne, on the other hand, who dealt with the greatest number of capital cases post-independence, was the most lenient. (This is largely explained by his mix of cases, which included eight child murders.)

While Hanna did not sentence the greatest number of people to death (this dubious honour fell to O'Byrne) his career in capital cases exceeded that of any of his judicial colleagues, extending from the conviction of James Murray on 12 June 1925 to that of Patrick Kelly on 23 October 1941. Also, more of the cases that he dealt with proceeded to a lethal outcome (eight were executed compared with four each for Molony and O'Byrne).[50]

on appeal or replaced with an alternative sentence. They are not included in Table 4.4 which, like the rest of the analysis in this book, is based on those cases where a recommendation regarding clemency was made to the governor general, through whom the king acted (1922 to 1936) or to the president, who embodied the people (1937 to 1990).

[49] In 1925, Oliver Wendell Holmes wrote about the duty to punish in the following terms: 'If I were having a philosophical talk with a man I was going to have hanged (or electrocuted) I should say, I don't doubt that your act was inevitable for you but to make it more avoidable by others we propose to sacrifice you to the common good. You may regard yourself as a soldier dying for your country if you like. But the law must keep its promises' (cited in Moore 1989: 39). Molony and Hanna—the judges least likely to make a positive intervention in the condemned person's favour—seem to have been determined that the law 'must keep its promises'.

[50] Mr Justice Richard McLoughlin, who had sentenced Mary Cadden and James Kelly to death, also dealt with one of the first murder cases where the death penalty was not mandatory. He questioned the wisdom of the new legislation, believing it to be contrary to the interests of public protection (*Irish Times*, 10 November 1964). It is not known whether James Ennis, the man in the dock before him, who went on to spend more than half a century in custody, shared this view. Francis Murtagh, the first murderer to avoid the mandatory death penalty, was convicted on 20 July 1964.

Bresler (1965: 114) wrote that when judges in the United Kingdom discussed capital cases with Home Secretaries they tended not to offer advice on what course of action should be taken, confining themselves to the provision of background information on the crime and giving a view as to the quality and attentiveness of the jury and what they thought of the accused person and the witnesses. Their Irish counterparts were not as circumspect, regularly taking the opportunity to indicate whether and why it would, or would not, be appropriate to be clement.

It would be reasonable to adopt the position that judicial involvement should end with the finding of guilt and that it is for the executive to determine how the sentence ought to be administered. Further judicial involvement, if required to clarify proceedings or expand on a point of law, should not trespass on the question of whether a lawful sentence should be carried out. Irish judges were uninhibited when it came to advising the executive how they might like to proceed. Given that it was routine for them to be invited to express a view to the Minister for Justice it is perhaps unsurprising that some of them took a further step and addressed a meeting of the government (see Chapter 7).

In all but Fleming's case, when the government deviated from the judicial view it was in the direction of leniency.[51] Fleming was the only person to be executed where the judge positively recommended mercy, and his case is dealt with in the next section. Sometimes the judge did not recommend mercy, but the condemned person was spared nonetheless. In all but three of these cases the jury recommended mercy. The exceptions, where neither judge nor jury asked for mercy, were Frances Cox, the poisoner, and Mary Cadden, the abortionist—who, as women, were unlikely to die however aggravating the circumstances—and Robert Stevenson, a merchant seaman who killed a prostitute and had the benefit of papal intervention (see Chapter 9). It was a violation of the principle that like cases should be treated alike to see these heinous offenders spared when others, who were no more culpable, and whose crimes were no more vicious, went to the gallows.

[51] Boylan, Heffernan, and Wall would have been similar departures had they not benefited from judicial intervention.

A Singular Case

John Fleming was found guilty of bludgeoning his wife to death with a hammer (after an unsuccessful attempt to poison her with strychnine). The motive was to put himself in a position to marry Rita Murtagh, a young woman whom he had impregnated and promised to marry and who was unaware that her lover lived with his wife in another part of Dublin. His trial attracted huge public attention, containing an intoxicatingly prurient mixture of sex, violence, deceit, and denial. A lack of direct evidence meant that questions could be raised about Fleming's innocence, however unlikely this might have been in the circumstances. The letter to the judge from the secretary to the Department of Justice was clear that the Minister for Justice was minded to advise the Executive Council to allow the law take its course, but invited the judge to make observations if he cared to do so.[52]

While agreeing that the jury had returned a correct verdict based on the evidence, and noting that he was not in favour of the complete abolition of capital punishment, Mr Justice Meredith stated that the ultimate sanction should be reserved for exceptional cases, and not ones, like Fleming's, that relied on circumstantial evidence alone. It is clear from his letter that Meredith felt the Executive Council should spare Fleming: 'I would be much gratified to see the sentence commuted'.[53] The Executive Council did not agree on the basis that if a killer was spared because the conviction depended on circumstantial evidence, this would mean an automatic commutation in almost every case, as few murderers perpetrated their crimes in front of witnesses.[54] (There was also a view that if Fleming was spared, public opinion would be outraged.[55]) This was the only occasion in Meredith's judicial career when he was required to impose a death sentence.

[52] Letter from Domhnall de Brún [Daniel Browne] to Mr Justice Meredith, 28 December 1933, NAI, JUS/H234/6221B.

[53] Letter from James C. Meredith to Minister for Justice, 30 December 1933, NAI, JUS/234/6221B.

[54] Letter from Domhnall de Brún to Minister for Justice, 1 January 1934, NAI, JUS/H234/6221B.

[55] Letter from Domhnall de Brún to Minister for Justice, 1 January 1934, NAI, JUS/H234/6221B.

Fleming also had the benefit of a personal intervention by the governor general (see Chapter 7). He was uniquely unfortunate in that the trial judge and governor general would have been pleased to see a commutation, but he was executed nonetheless. The jury had not made a recommendation to mercy in his case. A letter to 'My dear Judge' from the Minister for Justice written on the day that the government decided not to accept the judge's invitation to commute the sentence, informed Meredith that his views 'received the most earnest consideration' but that after a full review the Executive Council decided not to grant clemency. Perhaps surprisingly, given the nature of the decision, the letter lacked a personal touch; it was not signed by the minister but stamped with his name.[56]

For the government to dismiss a judge's plea for mercy was unprecedented and never repeated. It might be thought that this betrayed a lack of political capital on Meredith's part. But this is unlikely to have been the case. He was a man of enormous accomplishment and was at the peak of his powers in 1933 when he sentenced Fleming to death. Born in 1875, he was a champion athlete (the best quarter miler of his day in the British Isles) and a highly regarded scholar—his translation of Kant's *Critique of Aesthetic Judgement* was published by Oxford University Press in 1911[57]—as well as an eminent jurist. He wrote novels and plays and was president of the Statistical and Social Inquiry Society of Ireland between 1926 and 1929. He was a Quaker; his letter to the Minister for Justice indicated he was not a complete abolitionist, but presumably his inclinations would have been against the death penalty.[58] As a renowned Kantian scholar, Meredith must have had an intellectual appreciation of the dangers inherent in the exercise of executive clemency. This made his appeal all the more significant.

[56] Letter from P.J. Ruttledge to Mr Justice Meredith, 2 January 1934, NAI, JUS/H234/6221B.

[57] Reissued in 2008 as an Oxford World Classic, the publisher described Meredith's text, which had been 'lightly revised and updated' as 'classic and elegant'. The later work incorporated his translation of the *Critique of Teleological Judgement*, which had appeared in 1928.

[58] The judge in Gaffney's case, also a Quaker, was emphatic in his rejection of the jury's recommendation to mercy: 'all I have to say is that the murder was as premeditated, cold-blooded and horrible a crime as has ever been committed. I can conceive of no reason whatever why any mercy should be extended to the prisoner.' Letter from Jonathan Pim, 4 March 1924, NAI, JUS/H8/1085.

In Chapter 7, I discuss how governments sometimes deferred to a recognized authority figure when it came to commutation, and that they did so as a gesture of respect rather than because the decision resonated with their view. Fleming's case was exceptional in this regard. One wonders what would have happened had Meredith insisted on addressing the government in person, as his colleague John O'Byrne would do a couple of years later? Could they have resisted a direct appeal from such a substantial legal figure? Was Meredith more keenly aware of the separation of powers and more circumspect about trespassing upon them than O'Byrne? Meredith did not win the day in Fleming's case, but if he had insisted on an audience with the government things might have turned out differently.

As discussed in Chapter 3, a common criticism of clemency is that its exercise is unchecked. This was not true in cases where the judge was invited to express a view to the minister (a routine occurrence) or to address the government directly (a rare but impactful event). There was no restriction on what the government could consider when coming to a decision about clemency. There was no right to clemency so there was no appeal against the Executive Council's (later, government's) decision not to recommend commutation to the governor general (later, president). The individual whose life was in jeopardy had no right of audience or representation. He could petition and the petition could raise legal issues but he would not know what weight these were given. His legal representatives were kept at arm's length. He did not learn the reason for the government's decision, so could not challenge it.

Table 4.5 shows the likelihood of clemency according to the court of conviction. There was a clear dip in the 1940s, indicating that the fierce response to the IRA during the Emergency spilled over into a much stricter than usual reaction to other killers. Prior to 1964, the overall chances of commutation were higher for those convicted before a judge and jury. When the focus is narrowed to men, as seems appropriate given that all of those dealt with by special courts whose convictions were upheld on appeal were male, and a significant number of those dealt with before judge and jury were female, for whom commutation was automatic after 1925, the pattern is different. Table 4.6 shows

Table 4.5 Clemency by mode of conviction

	Jury trial				Non-jury trial			
	Executed		Commuted		Executed		Commuted	
	No.	(per cent)	No.	(per cent)	No.	(per cent)	No.	(per cent)
1923–9	15	(43)	20	(57)	0	(0)	0	(0)
1930–9	5	(31)	11	(69)	0	(0)	1	(100)
1940–9	8	(47)	9	(53)	6	(55)	5	(45)
1950–9	1	(14)	6	(86)	0	(0)	0	(0)
1960–4	0	(0)	3	(100)	0	(0)	0	(0)
1965–90	—	—	—	—	0	(0)	8	(100)
All	29	(37)	49	(63)	6	(30)	14	(70)

Note: The Criminal Justice Act, 1964 restricted the application of the death penalty and subsequent cases were dealt with by non-jury courts. The Criminal Justice Act, 1990 abolished capital punishment. All of those sentenced to death by non-jury courts were male.

Table 4.6 Clemency to men after trial by jury

	Executed		Commuted	
	No.	(per cent)	No.	(per cent)
1923–9	14	(58)	10	(42)
1930–9	5	(50)	5	(50)
1940–9	8	(62)	5	(38)
1950–9	1	(17)	5	(83)
1960–4	0	(0)	3	(100)
All	28	(50)	28	(50)

that 50 per cent of men convicted after a jury trial had their death sentences commuted. This compares with 70 per cent overall for those dealt with by non-jury courts (50 per cent before 1964; Table 4.5).

The decision whether or not to spare a political prisoner was complicated because its likely ramifications extended beyond the individual case. Typically they involved subversive activity that was intended to shake the foundations of the state. They were unambiguously serious. This makes it all the more noteworthy that they were less likely to be executed than the common or garden murderers who appeared before judges and juries in the ordinary courts. In the next chapter we turn our attention to cases where juries had no role to play and where panels of army officers were the arbiters of guilt or innocence. As will become clear, when it came to political offenders, little was left to chance.

5

Extraordinary Courts

In a small country riven by political strife, the protagonists in the national struggle were well-known to each other. As a result, justice was often thought of in relational terms rather than simply as the application of abstract legal principles to strangers. Clemency was always political in the sense that the decision whether to show it was based, not on a set of written guidelines, but on the viewpoints of a group of public representatives who sat around the cabinet table. When personal factors intruded—as often happened when IRA members turned their guns against the state during the first decades of independence—matters were intensely problematic; punishment, politics, and the personal became lethally intertwined.

These tangled connections were made explicit when the state dispensed with judges and juries and set up special tribunals, staffed by army officers, to ensure that prosecutions were secured, and enemies dispatched. While governments attributed the retention of capital punishment to the risk posed by the IRA, simultaneously they railed at the ineffectiveness of the ordinary courts. The jury had long been vulnerable to outside influences, whether this involved its packing with members supportive of the authorities or its intimidation by subversive elements.[1] A complicating factor, especially in political or agrarian crimes, was sympathy for perpetrators which translated into a reluctance to convict. Johnson (1996: 270) described the Irish jury as, 'always a tender plant, requiring much nurture to sustain it and the continual removal of weeds which threatened to choke it'. When the political threat loomed large, the prospect of failed prosecutions

[1] During the 1920s, Cumann na mBan, a paramilitary women's organization, sent anonymous leaflets to jurors' homes, signed 'Ghosts', threatening them with dire consequences if they convicted republicans (see, for example, *Evening Herald*, 9 December 1926).

Justice, Mercy, and Caprice: Clemency and the Death Penalty in Ireland. First Edition. Ian O'Donnell. © Ian O'Donnell 2017. Published 2017 by Oxford University Press.

took on additional significance and—pursuing the horticultural analogy—rather than attempting to clear the ground around it, the jury itself was uprooted.

Once the extraordinary courts had done their work the decision about whether an execution would proceed was reserved to the government. This was a blatant demonstration of the death penalty serving as an instrument of state power. Capital punishment showed that the government would not falter in its determination to crush subversion. If the normal courts were not fit for purpose they would be replaced. This was an iron fist in an iron glove. The fact that most of the condemned men were allowed a 'soldier's death'—shooting rather than hanging—also indicated that these 'criminals' were viewed differently and that their elimination was seen as a regrettable necessity if a thorny political problem was to be seized and resolved. Death by shooting was believed to allow for a more dignified exit; in the popular mind, hanging carried with it an enduring stigma—it was the common criminal's fate.[2]

Not all of the twenty men sentenced to death by non-jury courts were charged with murder. Seán McCaughey was convicted of assault and false imprisonment and condemned to die by shooting. His sentence was commuted, and he perished on hunger and thirst strike. Richard Goss and Maurice O'Neill (both executed) were convicted of shooting with intent to resist arrest. While their actions were reviled by the authorities, these men were understood by government members who once stood where they stood and aimed where they aimed (this capacity for empathic understanding had evaporated by the time the last swathe of death-eligible political murderers came before the courts in the first half of the 1980s).

With one exception (Michael Conway), non-jury capital cases were dealt with in two phases: 1940 to 1944 and 1980 to 1985. The treatment of the earlier cases—all of which involved IRA activities—was characterized by a measure of steely resolve and

[2] One of the petitioners in Tomás MacCurtain's case implored the Taoiseach to spare his life but 'in God's Holy name please don't hang Thomas MacCurtain, if die he must let him die facing a firing squad'; a soldier's death would spare the young man the final indignity of the noose. Letter from E.H. Steele to Éamon de Valera, 2 July 1940, NAI, TSCH/3/S11974. Charles Kerins was the only IRA man to be hanged post-independence.

leniency; executions took place soon after arrest and those who did not die spent relatively brief periods incarcerated before being released unconditionally (Table 10.1); the threat they posed was seen as context-dependent. The later cases—half of which involved the IRA—invariably resulted in clemency (despite, as we shall see, intermittent pressure for executions to be carried out).[3] But the commuted prison sentences were enormously long—averaging twenty-three years and eleven months—and would have been longer again had it not been for a successful Supreme Court challenge taken by Noel Callan and the legislative initiatives that accompanied the peace process in Northern Ireland. When released, conditions applied. The elongation in time served reflected a similar trend for homicide offences in general (O'Donnell 2010: 67–9) but was more pronounced.

Special Powers Tribunal

Michael Conway was convicted of the murder of John Egan in Dungarvan, County Waterford in April 1936. Conway arrived in the town late at night with several other IRA activists, the party travelling in a car that had been stolen from a local District Justice. When they called to Egan's home he was not there but they located him on the street nearby, summoned him by name and shot him dead. The incident was witnessed by Egan's mother. The victim was a former IRA member who was believed to have given information to the police that had led to a number of arrests.[4]

This killing took on additional significance because a few weeks earlier the IRA had committed what Nic Dháibhéid (2011: 123) described as 'one of the most reviled murders in its catalogue of horror'. This was the shooting dead in Cork of retired Vice Admiral Henry Boyle Townshend Somerville who had been advising local men about how to pursue a career in the Royal Navy. A card was left beside his corpse stating he was a recruiting agent for the British. Egan's murder was followed

[3] Patrick McCann, Colm O'Shea, Michael McHugh, and Noel Callan were not members of the IRA.

[4] The Minister for Justice stated some years after the event that Egan 'never gave one tittle of information' (Dáil Debates, 29 May 1946, Gerald Boland, vol. 101, col. 1125).

by the government's decision to proscribe the IRA. Large-scale arrests of the organization's members ensued.

The evidence linking Conway to the crime was slight. There was nothing to suggest that he had fired the fatal shot, but his fingerprint was found on the car door and he was a known subversive who had been imprisoned for three months the previous year for unauthorized possession of ammunition. Conway refused to recognize the court, stating that he would only offer a defence if tried by a jury of his peers. There was huge controversy about the use of a military tribunal to convict him. The legitimacy of a trial process that proceeded without any lay involvement meant that the public felt unrepresented. While juries were far from a representative cross-section of the population they had the virtue of allowing community sentiment to intrude both during the trial (via acquittal or conviction on a less serious charge) and afterwards (via the attachment of a recommendation to mercy). The month before Conway's trial got underway the Minister for Finance, Seán McEntee, told a crowd of republican hecklers that the government knew who had shot Egan and that 'it will be a sorry day for those responsible for the crime. It will be their last shooting.'[5] Conway told the tribunal that such public utterances were proof that he would not receive fair treatment.[6]

Conway was dealt with under the Constitution (Special Powers) Tribunal created by the Constitution (Amendment No. 17) Act, 1931 which inserted Article 2A into the 1922 Constitution.[7] The tribunal comprised five army officers not below the rank of commandant, who sat in panels of three. Its powers were wide and it could impose any punishment it saw fit, even if greater than allowed in the criminal law for the same offence. There was to be no right of appeal and no inquests were to be held after executions. Sentences were to be carried out by the civil authorities and the Executive Council had absolute discretion regarding commutation, remission, and pardon without reference to the governor general.

These arrangements allowed the tribunal to operate freely, without the risk of any 'interference' from the courts, or those

[5] *Irish Press*, 22 June 1936.

[6] *Irish Times*, 22 July 1936.

[7] During the lifetime of the Free State (1922 to 1937) the Constitution could be amended by ordinary legislation; a referendum was not required.

who felt that the rule of law should not be trumped by a perceived emergency. Little stood in the way of convictions and it is hardly surprising that over 90 per cent of IRA members were found guilty by what Ó Longaigh (2006: 277) described as 'a statutory, almost parallel legal system'.[8] The military tribunal continued in existence until the new Constitution came into force on 29 December 1937, although it was seldom being used by this stage.[9]

Conway was duly sentenced to death by hanging but the Executive Council commuted the penalty to one of penal servitude for life. Released unconditionally after twenty-one months he reimmersed himself in militant republicanism. With Patrick McGrath (executed in 1940), Conway trained IRA volunteers for the 1939–40 bombing campaign in Britain, known as the Sabotage Campaign (or 'S Plan'). Appearing before the Special Criminal Court on 29 July 1940 for possession of incriminating documents and ammunition, membership of an unlawful organization, and assault with intent to resist arrest, he received a sentence of two years penal servitude. He was back before the Special Criminal Court on 4 April 1946 when he was imprisoned for four months for failing to account for his movements. Once again after his release he re-engaged with the IRA but only until 1950 when, believing the movement for national reunification was back on its feet, he entered a monastery.[10]

All of the other political offenders or killers of on-duty police officers were dealt with after the introduction of the 1937 Constitution, either by the Special Criminal Court or the military court that came into existence because the Special Criminal Court was considered inadequate to the task.[11] The two bodies

[8] It is not known what representations, if any, members of non-jury courts made to the Executive Council regarding their decisions.

[9] In 1931, thirty-five persons were tried by the tribunal, of whom four were acquitted. These numbers rose to 494 and forty-eight respectively by 1934 before dwindling to thirteen and one in 1937 (Dáil Debates, 11 July 1946, Gerald Boland, vol. 102, col. 609). The attempt to limit the right of appeal to the courts was, ultimately, unsuccessful (Davis 2007: 45).

[10] In 1950 he joined the Cistercian Order and, as Brother Maolmhuire, lived in its monastery in Collon, County Louth. He died, aged 87, after forty-seven years a monk. One of his siblings, Fr Colmcille, was a member of the same Order but lived at a different monastery (Obituary, *Saoirse—Irish Freedom*, January 1998).

[11] Part V of the Offences Against the State Act, 1939, relating to the Special Criminal Court, came into force on 22 August 1939. The military court was introduced by the Emergency Powers (No. 41) Order, 1940 on 16 August

shared the same personnel but the military court was not bound by the criminal law and persons convicted before it had no right of appeal. The Special Criminal Court differed in that there was a right of appeal and it was required to follow the practice and procedure of the Central Criminal Court in the trial of accused persons; it was bound by the normal rules of evidence and operated within the parameters of the criminal law. Furthermore, the Special Criminal Court lacked the enhanced sentencing powers of the military court which could impose the death penalty for any matter that came before it if this was deemed expedient.

The first person to be sentenced to death by the Special Criminal Court was Tomás MacCurtain whose date with the hangman in July 1940 was cancelled on account of some scheming on the part of his legal team which benefited from leaks at the highest level of government (see Chapter 7).

The 'Terror Court'

Hunger strikes and shootings at members of An Garda Síochána coalesced with a wider deterioration in the security situation to ensure that the clemency afforded to MacCurtain would not be extended to others. On 7 May 1940, the Taoiseach, concerned by Ireland's precarious situation as a small and poorly defended neutral country during a time when Europe was at war, declared that:

> Our policy of patience has failed and is over ... I warn those now planning new crimes against the nation that they will not be allowed to continue their policy of sabotage ... The law will be enforced against them. If the present law is not sufficient it will be strengthened; and in the last resort, if no other law will suffice, then the Government will invoke the ultimate law—the safety of the people. (Cited in Moynihan 1980: 433–4)

Despite this stark pronouncement, the summer of 1940 saw an escalation in the number of encounters between An Garda Síochána and the IRA in what Bowyer Bell (1997: 183) described as a 'pattern of provocation, retaliation and vengeance'. When a team of Garda detectives was searching a building in Dublin on 16

1940. Both forms of non-jury court were permitted under Article 38 of the Constitution.

August 1940, they were shot at from within. Two of them died as a consequence and Patrick McGrath, Thomas Green (aka Francis Harte or Tom Harte), and Thomas Hunt fled the scene under fire from the remaining detectives. Green was wounded, and when McGrath retreated to assist him, both men were apprehended. Hunt managed to escape, only to be arrested five days later.

The military court was established by the Emergency Powers (No. 41) Order, 1940 the same day as the killings perpetrated by McGrath, Green, and Hunt and in response to this atrocity. It comprised 'any three persons, being commissioned officers of the Defence Forces, who are for the time being members of any Special Criminal Court'. The court was to determine its own procedures, and every question arising before it was to be decided by majority vote. Where the military court found a person guilty of an offence specified in the schedule to the Order,[12] it was required to sentence them to 'suffer death by shooting'; this was the sole available sanction.[13] The legislation stipulated that 'no appeal shall lie in respect of such conviction or sentence'[14] but every death sentence imposed by the court would be brought to the attention of the government which could commute it, without reference to the president. If it declined to reduce the sentence the adjutant general was required to carry it out within forty-eight hours.

According to the Department of Justice, 'the normal method of executing the death sentence, viz, with the interval of several weeks after judgement—longer in cases of appeal—and then by a process (hanging) which requires the attendance of a skilled executioner, whose attendance might be prevented by accident or design is not suitable for cases in which the speed and certainty of punishment are essential considerations' (cited in Ó Longaigh 2006: 249). There was to be no coroner's inquest after the execution (presumably to deny supporters of the dead man a public opportunity to galvanize support). The court was intended

[12] Numerous offences were listed in the schedule including: treason; possession of documents prejudicial to public safety or the integrity the state; damage to equipment belonging to the Defence Forces; murder; resisting arrest; unlawful imprisonment; causing explosions; possessing explosive substances, firearms or ammunition; and attempting or conspiring to commit any of the foregoing.

[13] Emergency Powers (No. 41) Order, 1940, Statutory Rules and Orders, 1940, No. 237.

[14] Emergency Powers (Amendment) (No. 2) Act, 1940, s. 3.

to constitute the ultimate deterrent and legal niceties would not be allowed to temper the state's response to subversion; terrorists would be dealt with in kind.

A death sentence handed down by the military court did not always result in an execution. It merely transferred the case to the government, and replaced the question of culpability with the question of clemency. Indeed, there appeared to be no anticipation that all of the convicted persons would be executed. The list of scheduled offences had been accepted by the government on the basis that there would be an opportunity in every case to substitute penal servitude for death (Ó Longaigh 2006: 252). This would suggest that the government was making its decisions on an individualized basis; having created a context where a court could return a swift and terminal decision it reserved the right not to follow through.

McGrath and Green were tried by the military court. They were convicted and sentenced to death by shooting after twenty-four minutes deliberation on 20 August 1940.[15] The following day the government decided not to commute their sentences. On 6 September 1940, the day after the Supreme Court unanimously upheld the validity of their convictions, they became the first persons to be executed by firing party since the civil war.[16] The swiftness with which these men were dispatched, and the associated legal manoeuverings, were an affront to fundamental democratic and legal principles. This was uncompromisingly swift and superlatively severe justice. Hunt came up for separate consideration. At its meeting on 25 September 1940 the government decided to commute his sentence to penal servitude for life. Because the death penalty had been imposed by the military court there was no role for the president in its commutation.

There was a concern at the time that it was contrary to the principles of natural justice to try three men, and execute two of

[15] Shooting at 98A Rathgar Road, resume of case and of court proceedings, 20 August 1940, NAI, TSCH/3/S12048A.

[16] There was no entry in Mountjoy Prison's 'Registry of Deaths' for the IRA members who were shot there in the early 1940s (McGrath, Green, and O'Neill). However, they were buried beside their comrade, Charles Kerins, and the governor added a diagram to Kerins' entry to show the location of the graves. It was no doubt felt that at some future point they would be moved home, as indeed they were. In 1948 the bodies of all four were exhumed and given to their families for reinterment.

them, using a procedure that had not been brought into existence until a few hours after they committed their crimes. McGrath and Green could have been convicted without resort to the Emergency Powers (No. 41) Order, 1940, the differences being that they would have been dealt with by the Special Criminal Court and within the ambit of the criminal law and, if their convictions were upheld on appeal, they would have been hanged rather than shot. Given the volatility of the times, and the fact that previous warnings from the government about the consequences of subversion had not been heeded by those at whom they were directed, 'the Government felt it was desirable to use the simplest and sternest weapon at their disposal'.[17]

Thirteen men were tried before the military court, of whom nine were convicted (five executed, four commuted) and three acquitted. An order was made by the court in favour of one person who was released from custody. The last person to appear before the military court was Michael Quille who was acquitted on 20 January 1943 of the murder of detective sergeant Denis O'Brien. Charles Kerins appeared before the Special Criminal Court the following year on the same charge, was convicted, sentenced to death, and hanged. Several decades were to elapse before the Special Criminal Court handed down another death sentence.[18]

The Department of Justice took a firm line against 'political murder' which was defined by its long-serving secretary, Stephen Roche, as 'the assassination of Ministers, the shooting of police officers, and generally the use of the gun as a political argument'. Roche compared such killings to 'a deadly and highly infectious disease' which required radical treatment: 'It is too dangerous to be tolerated at all. The appropriate penalty is death, inflicted with as little delay as possible. Such cases should not go before the ordinary Courts at all, because of the factors of delay, intimidation and prejudice.'[19]

[17] Emergency Powers Order No. 41 (1940), setting-up of the military court, undated, NAI, TSCH/3/S11905A.

[18] The Special Criminal Court was not intended to be a permanent court. It was disestablished in 1946 and re-established in 1961, remaining in existence for almost a year before being disestablished. Again, it was staffed by army officers. It did not sit for a decade and was reactivated in 1972 since when it has been continuously in existence and staffed exclusively by civilian judges.

[19] Trials for Murder, 25 August 1941, NAI, TSCH/3/S7788A.

Like those dealt with by juries, the cases handled by special courts were conducted at speed. The court was at pains to convey the impression that the principles of natural justice had been observed and sometimes there was an adjournment of several hours or a day to allow a defendant reconsider his refusal to recognize the court. When the proceedings resumed and it was evident that the defendant had not changed his stance, the sentence was duly passed.

There was no lay involvement, decisions on questions of law and fact being made by a panel of judges—army officers in the early days—and it might have been thought that some time would be required for them to exchange views and arrive at a consensus. Not so. Even when multiple defendants were involved, deliberations did not take long. The three majors who decided Thomas Hunt's case took only thirty minutes to do so. When the court convened seventeen months later to deal with Patrick Davern and Michael Walsh it took less than three quarters of an hour to decide that they should be put to death along with George Plant but that Joseph O'Connor should be acquitted. (The tribunal in Michael Conway's case had taken longer to make up its mind, retiring for two-and-a-half hours before sentencing him to death by hanging.)

Spared, but dies on hunger strike

Seán McCaughey did not commit murder. But, as noted above, neither did Richard Goss or Maurice O'Neill, both of whom were executed. The difference was that McCaughey's actions did not threaten the lives of servants of the state. He had been involved in the kidnap and brutal interrogation of a suspected informer, IRA Chief of Staff Stephen Hayes, who had ordered the abduction and killing of Michael Devereux, for which Plant, Davern, and Walsh were sentenced to death. Coogan (2002: 155) claimed that: 'During the time Hayes was being held, McCaughey was approached to say that the life of Richard Goss … might be saved if Hayes were set free. McCaughey refused this plea.' By the time Hayes escaped his captors in September 1941 Goss had already been executed, shot at dawn (5:30 a.m.) on 9 August 1941, in Portlaoise Prison, by a firing party from the army's Curragh Command.

According to MacEoin (1997: 536) the decision to spare McCaughey was based on a political calculation: 'It is safe to say that following the sentence McCaughey was within an ace of a Free State firing squad, now becoming quite used to execution; but wiser and more influential voices prevailed.' He continued, rhetorically: 'Could the Belfast man be executed following conviction on a mere charge of assault and unlawful detention?' Seán McCaughey's case was considered by the government on 25 September 1941 and it was decided to commute his sentence to penal servitude for life.

McCaughey was militantly unrepentant and although his death sentence was overturned, he died in custody while on hunger and thirst strike, having spent a prolonged period in solitary confinement, without visits or outside exercise, and naked apart from prison-issue blankets. This self-imposed hardship, which emanated from his refusal to wear a prison uniform, exacted a significant psychological toll. McConville (2014: 629–30) concluded that McCaughey became mentally unstable as a result. According to a republican pamphlet he began his hunger strike on 19 April 1946, abstained from water also from 24 April and died in the early hours of 11 May: 'From the day he entered Portlaoighise prison until his wasted body was covered by a Franciscan habit on his death, he was naked except for his prison blankets' (O'Reilly 1947: 15).

The emaciated martyr lying beneath a shroud resonated powerfully with republican sympathizers. It exemplified heroic suffering in the face of overwhelming odds; giving one's life for an ideal which has not proved possible to attain through force of arms; victory, or at least legitimation, through endurance. The inquest was controversial and, under cross-examination by Seán MacBride, the prison doctor admitted that he would not have treated his dog the way McCaughey had been treated.[20]

Astounding Legal Manoeuvres

George Plant's conviction for the murder of Michael Devereux was legally novel in that he was first brought before the Special

[20] According to his entry in the *Dictionary of Irish Biography*, Gerald Boland, the justice minister during McCaughey's imprisonment, knew what it felt like to go without food, having taken part in a forty-day hunger strike by republican prisoners in 1923. He claimed in later years that his practice of yoga had sustained him throughout the fast.

Criminal Court but discharged when a nolle prosequi was entered and then rearraigned before a military court where he was convicted and sentenced to death on the basis of the unsworn statements of his co-accused (Patrick Davern and Michael Walsh).[21] In a submission to the government his lawyers argued that Plant's treatment, while it may have been legal, had no parallel in Ireland, Britain, or the US; that the stress of such a double trial should make the government sympathetic to the possibility of a commutation; and that the changes made to the law in order to effect his conviction may have strained the public's belief that justice was blind in its administration.

The submission was carefully worded so that it did not openly criticize the government but the force of its argument was unblunted, in particular the assertion that: 'the State could, now that his life has been forfeited, forgo its right to take it, partly because of the factors that have led to his present position and partly in return for his services during the struggle which brought about the establishment of this State'. It concluded by observing that: 'The State has vindicated the legality of its action; it can now freely exercise its prerogative of mercy'.[22]

The argument was two-pronged. First, that it was unreasonable to expect men whose characters were formed in a violent milieu where they were obliged to follow orders, however distasteful, to change completely when circumstances changed. Secondly, that there should be some recognition of services rendered to the fledgling state: had Plant—and others like him—not been prepared to risk everything in combat twenty years earlier, the state that now had the power to take their lives may not have come into existence. The government held firm and Plant's execution went ahead.

There had not been any intention to charge Davern or Walsh with a capital offence. From the outset, the goal of the prosecution was to convict Plant, who had carried out the actual

[21] The Emergency Powers (No. 41F) Order, 1941 allowed the men to be brought before the military court. Moroney (1989: 6) argued that the Devereux and Hayes cases were linked in that the latter ordered the execution of the former in order to divert attention from his own traitorous activities.

[22] Considerations submitted to the government as to why the sentence of death passed on George Plant by a military court sitting at Collins Barracks in the City of Dublin on the 26th day of February 1942 should not be carried out, 27 February 1942, NAI, TSCH/3/S12682.

shooting, and a fourth man, Joseph O'Connor (who was acquitted). The admissions made by Davern and Walsh, who had guarded Devereux and supported the operation, would have assisted in this regard but they refused to give evidence in the Special Criminal Court confirming their earlier statements. Their reticence was understandable as, before the trial opened, the IRA circulated pamphlets stating that anyone who testified would be shot. The state case broke down and, due to their change of heart, they were charged with murder along with the other two men, who were believed to be more culpable. The government used emergency powers legislation to ensure that all four appeared before the military court and that voluntary statements previously made would be admissible, even if their authors refused to speak, and that the usual rules of evidence would not apply.[23]

The reason for de Valera's (belated) ferocity when it came to dealing with political prisoners was articulated in a speech he made to the Dáil on 1 December 1944, the day that Charles Kerins was hanged. The Taoiseach recounted that, having been moved to release a man (Patrick McGrath) who was on hunger strike, and at the point of death, he had on his conscience a total of six fatalities rather than one. McGrath had fought in the Easter Rising and the War of Independence and a British bullet was lodged in his chest; the idea that such an eminent republican could be allowed to die on hunger strike caused much public concern and de Valera transferred him from prison to hospital as a prelude to dropping all of the charges against him (Nic Dháibhéid 2011: 137–8).

When de Valera decided to vacate the proceedings against McGrath, the IRA was not a potent threat to the state, so there was space for magnanimity. This soon disappeared. As described above, when McGrath recovered his health he reprised the armed struggle, with lethal consequences for two Garda detectives. In the intervening period the government's resolve had stiffened. A hunger strike by IRA prisoners was met with intransigence and two of the strikers, Tony Darcy and Jack McNeela, died before the action was called off in April 1940. (Tomás MacCurtain also

[23] For an account of the finagling involved, see Memorandum for government in connection with petition for the release of Michael Walsh and Patrick Davern, 7 November 1945, NAI, TSCH/3/S12741.

participated in this hunger strike.) De Valera rued the day when he allowed sentiment to win out over national security:

> I was taught a lesson then and ... I will never forget it. I was taught the lesson that, in giving way and being clement in the case of one man [Patrick McGrath], I was responsible for six deaths. We will never do that again. This man [Charles Kerins] was found guilty of murder and, if we let him go, we would have other cases of murder.[24]

This was an issue that de Valera had spoken about on other occasions. In a speech the previous year he referred to McGrath's release in December 1939 as 'one of the great regrets of my whole life ... one of the biggest mistakes that I have made in my life'.[25]

O'Brien (2006: 239) described the executions of IRA members during the Emergency as taking place 'against a background of near-deafening public protest'. But the government did not waver in its efforts to shore up its position. Speaking in the Dáil after the cessation of hostilities the Minister for Justice was unambivalent:

> This court has been described outside as a terror court. I have no objection to its so being described. That is exactly what it was. It was a terror court—a court set up to meet terror in a drastic and summary manner in order to save this nation from perils which threatened it at the time.[26]

It was no coincidence that the use of capital punishment escalated when the state felt most acutely the need to fortify its position in the eyes of those it governed as well as to outside observers. Clemency is a sign of confident government, of a state with a stable core and an optimistic view of the future. During the Emergency the Irish state was still recovering from a difficult birth and its institutions had yet to achieve universal acceptance. It had reason to worry, especially after the Sabotage Campaign in Britain during the early years of the Second World War, that a feeble response to the IRA at home could threaten its continued

[24] Dáil Debates, 1 December 1944, Éamon de Valera, vol. 95, col. 1459. Kant (1797/1965: 107–8) wrote that: 'The right to pardon a criminal (*jus aggratiandi*), either by mitigating or by entirely remitting the punishment, is certainly the most slippery of all the rights of the sovereign. By exercising it he can demonstrate the splendor of his majesty and yet thereby wreak injustice to a high degree.' De Valera found himself slipping along this path to injustice when, out of compassion, he spared Patrick McGrath, only to then have multiple (preventable) deaths on his conscience.

[25] Dáil Debates, 9 July 1943, Éamon de Valera, vol. 91, col. 604.

[26] Dáil Debates, 29 May 1946, Gerald Boland, vol. 101, col. 1116.

existence. A government under siege appreciates the communicative power of capital punishment.

A less apprehensive state can afford to temper firmness of purpose with a degree of leniency. When its enemies are fewer, and the threat they pose is not an existential one, a more muted response can be presented as proportionate. Clemency betokens a government that desires to be perceived as legitimate in the eyes of those it governs rather than wishing to terrorize its opponents into submission.

Political prisoners were treated differently, even after death. Their bodies were removed from prison burial grounds and reinterred, sometimes amid considerable fanfare. The remains of George Plant, a member of the Church of Ireland, were removed from Portlaoise Prison on 20 September 1948 and conveyed to Christ Church Cathedral in Dublin for a funeral service before continuing to Fethard, County Tipperary for burial. A notice giving the full itinerary, including the times at which the cortege would pass through some of the main towns en route from Dublin was published in the *Irish Independent* on 16 September. There were certain conditions attached to the reburial of Plant and the five other IRA men who had been executed during the Emergency, namely that the bishop of the diocese in which the prison was located gave his assent, that no expenditure from public funds was entailed, and that no demonstrations apart from religious services would accompany these events.[27] This was the sesquicentenary of the United Irishmen rebellion, adding another dimension to the reburials.

The crackdown on the IRA during the early 1940s contravened what many observers regarded as vital legal safeguards, but it was effective. According to Nic Dháibhéid (2011: 211): 'By the end of 1942, the IRA was entirely broken as a revolutionary force in the southern state; such residual cases as did occur were no more than the last gasps of a dying organisation.' The number of men prepared to make the ultimate sacrifice depended, to however limited a degree, on the likelihood that their actions would someday achieve the desired result. The potential martyr saw his death as a means to an end. When the achievement of the end

[27] Application for removal of remains of persons buried in prisons, 10 August 1948, NAI, TSCH/3/S12682.

Table 5.1 Persons convicted by non-jury courts (all crimes)

	Special Criminal Court	Military court
1939	33	—
1940	257	3
1941	184	2
1942	128	4
1943	97	—
1944	85	—
1945	78	—

Note: Based on data presented by Minister for Justice, Gerald Boland, Dáil Debates, 6 June 1946, vol. 101, col. 1460.

became a vanishingly remote possibility, its pursuit was an exercise in bitter futility.

Table 5.1 shows that non-jury courts took on a significant burden during the Emergency. In 1940, 331 persons were convicted on indictment at the Circuit Court and Central Criminal Court. A further 257 were convicted at the Special Criminal Court and three at the military court. The Special Criminal Court was not exclusively used to deal with subversives. Over the course of the Emergency the balance between political and non-political cases shifted significantly towards the latter (e.g. charges relating to black market offences such as the distribution of tea and flour). Of the 257 persons convicted by the Special Criminal Court in 1940, 255 involved cases where there was a charge, background or allegation of violence or the threat of violence or intimidation, or membership of, or association with, an unlawful organization. In 1945 the respective figures were seventy-eight and twenty-one; the military courts had ceased to operate by this time and the ordinary courts dealt with another 560 persons.[28]

Three men (Plant, Davern, and Walsh) were sentenced to death for killing Michael Devereux and another (McCaughey) was sentenced to death for the false imprisonment of the man (Hayes) who had ordered this act. There were two further casualties. According to Moroney (1989: 7), Denis O'Brien was the

[28] The Emergency Powers (No. 41) Order, 1940 was revoked with effect from 11 May 1945.

detective who solved the mystery of who had killed Devereux and he was shot dead outside his home in Dublin in September 1942. (O'Brien had also led the Special Branch raid that resulted in the deaths of two detectives and the capture of McGrath and Green.[29]) Charles Kerins was executed for his part in the murder of O'Brien. Another of the men involved in this killing, Archie Doyle, was one of the gunmen who had murdered Kevin O'Higgins in 1927 (see Chapter 1).[30] This captures the small-scale, brutality, and tangled relationships that characterized Irish militant republicanism; it is a constant that its internecine struggles exacted a terrible toll.

The execution of Kerins for O'Brien's murder was a hammer blow to the IRA, an organization that was already on its knees (some elements no doubt in prayer but most having buckled under the ferocity of state repression). According to Bowyer Bell (1997: 234):

> For the first time in generations the line had been broken. There no longer was a Chief of Staff or a GHQ or an Army Council or even an IRA ... The Irish Minister of Justice, Gerald Boland, announced in pride that the IRA was dead and that he had killed it. He had been helped by the RUC, the British police, the Irish Army, and of course by the IRA itself, but to all intents and purposes he spoke the truth. Once committed to a campaign of terror after 1938, the IRA was on a one-way road to victory or defeat, life or death. In 1945 the IRA had apparently died, defeated, another romantic cord in the pattern of Irish history frayed and broken.

The determination shown by de Valera's government during the Emergency did much to crush the capacity of the IRA to resist and to deter others from taking up arms. Capital punishment, corporal punishment, internment, and the associated hardships eventually took their toll on even the most committed republicans and their families. Add to the mix a lack of public support,

[29] According to Brady (1974: 237): 'There was little grieving even in the Special Branch for Dennis O'Brien, for he was over-zealous even in the eyes of his own colleagues.'

[30] Doyle made a gift of the gun he used to shoot O'Higgins to Harry White, who was himself sentenced to death a few years later, but whose murder conviction was quashed on appeal and replaced with a conviction for manslaughter. On his deathbed in 1980, Doyle summoned White and asked for the gun to be returned to him but White no longer possessed it (MacEoin 1985: 106).

and continuing the struggle became a Sisyphean task. The Irish government's efforts in this regard were no doubt bolstered by a nagging fear that if IRA provocation of the United Kingdom went too far, through a sustained bombing campaign on the British mainland or repeated overtures to Germany, an Allied intervention in Ireland might result (McConville 2014: 613).

The non-political murderers who were more likely to be sentenced to death and executed when the extraordinary courts were in operation were collateral damage (Table 4.5). When Patrick Kelly's case came up for consideration in 1941 the secretary of the Department of Justice, Stephen Roche, argued that in normal times he would have been spared but that given the circumstances—there had been three executions already that year—to allow him to live would signal weakness to a public that wished to see retribution. Roche seemed pained by the implications of his own logic, namely that clemency should be denied, not because there was a good reason for so doing but because to do otherwise might be misinterpreted.[31] Patrick Kelly was a victim of poor timing. As Roche's note showed, the decision about whether he should live or die was based on the wider political context rather than the exigencies of his case; compassion was trumped by external circumstances.[32]

Capital Murder

As will be discussed in Chapter 7, execution remained a real possibility for William Wall in 1959 and for David Galvin in 1962, but after the introduction of the Criminal Justice Act, 1964—when the death penalty was limited to capital murder (see Chapter 1)—the chances that anyone would be executed, however heinous the crime, were practically non-existent. Peter

[31] Memorandum from S.A. Roche to Minister for Justice, 12 December 1941, NAI, JUS/18/4780A & B.

[32] Roche had previously argued that: 'My own view is that the infliction of the death penalty is largely a survival from a rougher and more callous period, that it is in itself highly objectionable on broad grounds of civilisation and humanity, and that it should be adopted only under pressure of stern necessity, when no lesser punishment will serve the public interest. As a working rule, I am inclined, therefore, to look around for any reasonable excuse for not carrying out the death sentence.' Memorandum from secretary to Minister for Justice, 17 December 1937, NAI, JUS/18/1767A & B.

Pringle (2012: 7) claimed in the opening pages of his autobiography (subtitled 'surviving Ireland's death row') that he thought he was going to be hanged, having been sentenced to death by the Special Criminal Court in 1980, and that he overheard prison officers making observations to this effect. This account is not convincing given the lack of any political support for the death penalty at the time, the fact that it had been completely abolished in Britain and Northern Ireland, that the European tide had turned strongly towards abolition, and that the last execution (that of Michael Manning) had taken place twenty-six years previously.

Every (upheld) conviction for capital murder was recorded between 1980 and 1985. The crimes in question usually involved more than one perpetrator (and sometimes more than one victim). Patrick McCann and Colm O'Shea were convicted with Pringle of murdering two members of An Garda Síochána, Henry Byrne and John Morley, although each was convicted on a single count of capital murder relating to Garda Byrne. Patrick McPhillips, Brian McShane, and Thomas Eccles murdered Detective Garda Frank Hand and injured his colleague Michael Dowd. Michael McHugh and Noel Callan murdered Garda Sergeant Patrick Morrissey. Only Peter Rogers acted alone. When his van was stopped and searched by armed police near Ballyconnick, County Wexford, he ran for cover, there was an exchange of shots, and Detective Garda James Quaid died. When judgment was passed in Rogers' case the presiding judge of the Special Criminal Court was quite clear that he was to be hanged; no more the soldier's death for the IRA volunteer.[33]

The capital killers of the 1980s were all dealt with by the Special Criminal Court and their sentences were commuted to forty years penal servitude rather than life (see Chapter 10). A justice minister who had been involved in a number of these cases recalled that there was no appetite for carrying out the sentences but at the same time, given the context of the late 1970s and early 1980s—hunger strikes, armed robberies, the Troubles in Northern Ireland—neither was there any great appetite for abolition.[34] The death penalty was considered anomalous at this

[33] Summation and judgment of the President of the Special Criminal Court, 11 March 1981, NAI, TSCH/3/2011/127/839.

[34] Interview with author, 15 May 2016.

point but the febrile state of the country meant that there was no political desire to remove it from the statute book.[35] The anger that a Garda could be killed on duty was not translated into a desire that his killer should, in turn, be killed. By the 1980s, the notion of execution clashed with political principles and public sensibilities. There were some pockets of support for the death penalty but they were small and shallow and their demonstration did not progress beyond empty rhetorical flourishes.

Another former justice minister who had been involved in these commutations stated that: 'I don't remember there being any sympathy for the condemned person but there was revulsion at the idea of taking a life.'[36] Horror at the barbarity of the death penalty coexisted with a desire to punish these men in an unambiguously severe fashion. There was no dissent at government level nor was there any real debate. There was no direct communication with the judges of the Special Criminal Court. Whatever Pringle may have thought, there was no prospect that his sentence would be carried out.

A member of the IRA who was sentenced to death in the 1980s stated that he never believed he would be put to death, that the government did not have the courage to do so, and that they would have faced serious repercussions from the IRA had they attempted to hang its volunteers. He added that had he been on active service he might have been killed so he was not unduly perturbed by a sentence which he did not think would be implemented. Nor did he believe that he would serve the full forty years. He had set his mind for a twenty-year term which, as matters transpired, was a significant overestimate.[37]

Capital murderers were convicted of dreadful crimes—killing police officers in the course of their duty—but none of them was executed. This shows how much things had changed, given that in previous decades around half of men convicted of murder were hanged, even though by the standards of more callous and less

[35] A justice minister during the Troubles recalled being informed that the gallows in Mountjoy Prison was in a state of disrepair and ordering that it be fixed and readied for action. The purpose of this instruction was not with a view to actually using the apparatus but in the knowledge that details of the project would leak, the IRA would learn of it, and this might indicate the government's resolve and have some deterrent value. Interview with author, 15 May 2016.

[36] Interview with author, 8 June 2016.

[37] Interview with author, 1 June 2016.

forgiving times, they were pathetic individuals whose acts were impulsive and did not threaten the state or its agents.

The last six men to have their sentences commuted were dealt with by Fine Gael justice ministers. As the party was opposed to capital punishment in principle, and had introduced legislation to abolish it in 1981 which failed to complete its legislative journey because the government fell, there was no realistic prospect that these sentences would be carried out. Fine Gael was in coalition with the Labour Party, which also opposed capital punishment. Although Fianna Fáil objected to the total abolition of capital punishment neither was the party prepared to countenance an execution. Charles Haughey was Taoiseach when the government considered Pringle, McCann, and O'Shea. Given his long-standing opposition to capital punishment he was unlikely to have brooked much discussion of the options. By this time the notion that a judge might address the government was a foreign one. As the government of the day did not believe that these men deserved to die, the commutations of their death sentences must be characterized as instances of justice rather than mercy, because the latter refers to the imposition of a punishment more lenient than is thought to be deserved (see Chapter 2).

In the 1940s, IRA men who were sentenced to death were believed to deserve their fate, but were sometimes spared. The political culture of the country, including its narrative of origin, meant that their motivation was accepted, even if the methods were rejected. In the 1980s, not even the most abhorrent killer was believed to deserve capital punishment, but they were seen to deserve extended prison terms instead. That the sanction remained on the statute books was an anachronism.[38] There was no sympathy for the men involved and, while their actions were met with universal clemency, it was of an unprecedentedly severe kind. Variation and individualization were replaced with categorically harsh treatment. There was no compassion for their plight, but their lives were spared because not to do so would have caused international outrage and because the notion of

[38] This pattern of gradual abolition by stages was common across Europe, 'first the reduction of the number of crimes legally punishable by death until only murder and (sometimes) treason are left, then systematic use of commutation, leading to *de facto* abolition, and eventually abolition *de jure*' (Ancel 1962: 3).

judicial execution was anathema to governments in the 1980s. Forbearance came with a hard edge, namely decades of confinement without any realistic prospect of unprompted early release.

The IRA men of the 1940s benefited from justice, mercy, and caprice when the clemency decision was being made (see Appendix III) and from mercy when their release was considered. The capital murderers of the 1980s, half of whom were in the IRA, were treated in accordance with a new, and more severe, conception of justice when the clemency decision was being made and received no mercy when the release decision came up for consideration.

A change in political conditions has long been a cue for clemency. If the conflict is over and the danger has passed, the continued detention of political prisoners is seen as unnecessary, inhumane, and possibly counterproductive. But when the conflict is intense, severity is possible. The state was confident enough in the 1980s not to impose the death penalty and confident enough in the 1990s to allow the early release of political prisoners, despite the attendant controversy. The releases of IRA men took place in the context of an amnesty related to the peace process in Northern Ireland; this differed from mercy in that it was not motivated by a desire to ease the prisoner's suffering but rather to advance larger goals of peace and security. Those who were released under the terms of the Criminal Justice (Release of Prisoners) Act, 1998 which followed the Good Friday Agreement, served less than half of the forty-year terms to which their death sentences were commuted (much less for Patrick McPhillips, Brian McShane, and Thomas Eccles who each served thirteen years and nine months). The peace process propelled the government towards decisions that would otherwise have been avoided (see Chapter 10).

The contrast with capital murderers who were not IRA members was striking.[39] They had to fight long and hard in the courts

[39] When Noel Callan and Michael McHugh were sent to Portlaoise Prison they were assigned to a wing that housed members of the Irish National Liberation Army (INLA), a republican socialist paramilitary group, but whether their crime had been committed to further the interests of militant republicanism was not clear. When sentenced to death McHugh gave a clenched fist salute and shouted 'Victory to the INLA' although a detective had told the court that he was not a member of the organization and that the robbery that preceded the murder had not been carried out on its behalf (*Irish Times*, 4 December 1985).

to force the state to grant them any kind of early release. The government's response to their plight ranged from indifference to hostility and their releases were determined by judicial action, namely a successful Supreme Court challenge taken by Noel Callan, in the absence of which the prisoners in question were destined to serve forty years without reduction. The Supreme Court found that Callan was serving a sentence (as opposed to a 'commutation') and that this meant he was entitled to standard remission (one quarter) and eligible to apply for enhanced remission (one third).[40] This decision also applied to other men serving forty years even if, unlike Callan, their sentences had been imposed by a government determined that they would serve them in full.

Noel Callan and Michael McHugh, the last men to whom clemency was shown, were released on 30 November and 1 December 2015 respectively, thirty years after their convictions, and ten years sooner than had been expected. As the nation looked forward to the centenary of the 1916 rebellion, the last link was severed with a practice that had convulsed the country then and that set the tone for the independence struggle that followed. These men emerged from prison quietly, several days earlier than expected, and returned to their communities. There was little media interest.

Politicians in the 1980s, who were the readers rather than the authors of the history of the national project, lacked both the implacable resolve and the capacity for mercy exhibited by their forebears. The men who sat around cabinet tables in the 1940s had been directly touched by violence—and had inflicted it, some of them in person. They made decisions in rougher times with different values. They knew that IRA men planned their offensives carefully, were ideologically driven,

Patrick McCann claimed in an interview on 6 March 2011 that Colm O'Shea and he were not members of the INLA as had been reported at the time of their arrests, but rather were operating on behalf of Saor Éire, a small radical group generally believed to have been disbanded several years prior to the bank robbery and double murder that they committed (https://cedarlounge.wordpress.com/; site accessed 5 February 2015).

[40] Mr Justice Hardiman dismissed the state's contention that Callan was serving a 'commutation' as 'in terms of logic, law and language ... a nonsense'. *Callan v Ireland* [2013] IESC 35.

and difficult to deter. But equally they knew from their own experience that political offenders no longer posed a threat when the context changed and that it was preferable to release them than to allow their continued incarceration to act as a vehicle for dissatisfaction. Many of them had taken up arms against the British and then the Free State forces so they knew first-hand the routes into, and out of, militancy. Government members in the 1980s were a long way removed from the violence of the independence struggle and its aftermath. Things were less personal by then.

The governments in the 1940s that advised the president to commute a death sentence (or made the decision themselves) could understand the IRA men, with whom they may have had shared objectives in the past, and whose motivation was clear even if impugned. They vehemently disagreed with them but appreciated what lay behind their violence. They were a world away from the typical murderer whose limited intelligence, sordid lifestyle, and brutal actions were difficult to fathom. Where the empathy gap was wider, clemency was less likely. This theory is supported by the fact that when non-politically motivated offenders petitioned for mercy they drew attention to their revolutionary pedigree, if such existed, in order to demonstrate common cause with the men who would decide their fate.[41] Just as unmarried mothers were products of a social culture that promoted infanticide and then punished them for destroying their children, so too could the IRA men who found themselves facing execution 'not unreasonably claim to be the logical products of the political culture which now sought to suppress them' (Lee 1989: 224).

[41] One of the grounds stated by John Hogan's solicitor in his appeal to the Minister for Home Affairs to have the death sentence commuted to penal servitude for life was that 'there was nothing political or agrarian in connection with the crime'. Petition from T.J. Hunt to Kevin O'Higgins, 6 November 1923, NAI, JUS/H234/2024A. However, when Hogan's early release from prison was under consideration he was described as a 'prisoner of war' (by his mother; letter from Mrs P. Hogan to Mr Fitzgerald Kenny [sic], 5 June 1931, NAI, JUS/H234/2024A) and a man whose acts must be understood as 'political or semi-political' (by Clare County Council, which passed a unanimous motion calling for his release; letter from secretary, Clare County Council to secretary, Department of Justice, 16 March 1928, NAI, JUS/H234/2024A).

Avoiding state-sanctioned death

Political offenders were always deemed to be rational, insanity was never an issue (with the possible exception of McCaughey as he deteriorated in prison), and the death penalty was retained on the basis that they might make different choices if the costs outweighed the benefits. But this was to ignore the history of blood sacrifice and martyrology that was intertwined with militant republicanism. When those convicted prior to 1944 were spared they were viewed as different and tended to serve short terms followed by unconditional release. Some resumed their subversive activities when they regained their liberty, betraying the trust shown in them. (No doubt they would not have seen this as betrayal given that they did not recognize the authority of the state that tried them.)

Government confidence was misplaced twice. First, to think that men who were prepared to die for their cause, and who were part of a movement that revered its dead, would be deterred by the prospect of death ordered by the enemy. Secondly, that they would change with the times and like those who now held their fates in their hands, they would bend to a new dispensation and relinquish any claim to political (if not popular) legitimacy. Both of these calculations were too optimistic.

The crimes committed by prisoners who appeared before non-jury courts had little in common in terms of motivation and impact with the murderers whose cases are categorized in Chapters 8 and 9. Why were their sentences not executed? For Conway, it seems that his connection to Egan's killing—a fingerprint found on the stolen car used in the murder—while enough to convict him, was insufficient to show that he had played a direct role. This, in combination with the controversy surrounding his trial, saved him. For MacCurtain it was caprice. Pierrepoint had arrived at Mountjoy by the time the government reversed its decision to allow him hang. His life was spared as a result of political intrigue, orchestrated delay, and episcopal intervention (see Chapter 7).[42]

[42] The length of time MacCurtain served prior to release is another indicator of how his crime was viewed; at ninety-three months he spent twice as long in prison as the other IRA men whose death sentences were commuted in the 1940s. As noted above, those who followed in his footsteps in the 1980s served much longer again.

Insofar as other IRA men were concerned, proportionality was a key consideration. Where several were convicted and there had already been an execution it could be argued that the demand for retribution had been satisfied. In the case of Thomas Hunt, McGrath and Green had been executed by firing party more than a fortnight before his case was considered by the Executive Council. The Minister for Justice later divulged that he had deemed Hunt 'the sort of young fellow who got landed in it more by accident than anything else', preceding this remark with the comment that: 'I felt that that boy was more a tool than anything else'.[43] This, along with the fact that he had not fired any shots, distinguished him from his two comrades who were executed. Hunt's sentence was commuted two days after his conviction.

Patrick Davern and Michael Walsh were spared because Plant had been executed. The petition submitted on Walsh's behalf drew attention to the fact that while correctly convicted of murder he was not the triggerman and for this reason should be spared; some relevant English case law was offered in support of this assertion.[44] A petition submitted on behalf of Davern, an illiterate farm labourer of low intelligence, stated:

> ... now that The People have a right to demand his life in atonement for his offence The People could relinquish that right to take his life in consideration of the fact that it was in the past freely offered by Davern himself for the benefit of The People.[45]

Similarly, it would have been disproportionate to kill Seán McCaughey who had been convicted not of murder but of assault and false imprisonment.

There were no qualms about incarcerating the men sentenced to death by the Special Criminal Court in the first half of the 1980s for stretches of time that would have been unimaginable for their counterparts during the Emergency. It is difficult to imagine Alan Dukes or Michael Noonan, the last justice ministers to deal with

[43] Dáil Debates, Gerald Boland, 29 May 1946, vol. 101, col. 1132.

[44] Memorandum from Patrick J. Roe to Maurice Moynihan, 27 February 1942, NAI, TSCH/3/S12682.

[45] Considerations submitted to the government as to why the sentence of death passed on Patrick Davern by a military court sitting at Collins Barracks in the City of Dublin on the 26th day of February 1942 should not be carried out, undated, NAI, TSCH/3/S12682.

condemned men, using the kind of language that Gerald Boland (a man who had been close to violence himself during the revolutionary period) used in the 1940s in Hunt's case. Even if such words were thought it would have required huge courage to utter them, especially in the heat of a parliamentary debate. These matters are not unrelated. The career politician of the 1980s was much further removed from the violent origins of the state he served than his counterpart in the 1940s. It is arguable that men who had not been directly affected by political violence were likely to have held less ambivalent views about the motivations behind its expression.

Several of those convicted in the 1980s, and sentenced to forty years penal servitude, were known not to have been the gunmen in the murders that led to their convictions, but no attempt was made to differentiate them from those who played a more direct role in the events for which they were condemned. For the capital murderers of the 1980s who were believed to deserve the full weight of the law, but where there was no realistic chance of execution, the state did not recognize degrees of culpability.

Participation in the armed struggle was not a point in the individual's favour in the 1980s, either at the time of conviction or when the release decision was being made. When former men of violence were considering the treatment of current men of violence during the 1940s they were more lenient than their successors in the 1980s, who had not directly experienced the brutalizing effects of the revolutionary period. It could be argued that this distancing widened the empathy gap with the result that they served much, much longer inside. When eventually released it was on a convict's licence rather than being unconditional like their predecessors. We will return to the question of release in Chapter 10, having considered a typology of clemency cases in Chapters 8 and 9. But before addressing these issues it is necessary to scrutinize the pattern of government decision-making and the factors that animated it. This is the focus of the next two chapters.

6

Governments

A highly discretionary system, where the decision-makers shared important characteristics (all men, virtually all steeped in the Catholic faith tradition, all marked by the struggle for national independence, all conscious of the need to affirm the strength and value of the fledgling state) meant that a quick consensus could usually be reached regarding cases where an execution would be unjust and cases where it would not be, but the argument for mercy won out. Even when it was decided to allow the law take its course, a decision could be reversed, with surprising rapidity and life-sparing consequences.

Much time and energy was expended in advance of government meetings when a death penalty case was on the agenda. Reports were requested from the police and the judge; their contents were collated and summarized; the arguments for and against clemency were set out; the Minister for Justice was briefed by his officials; petitions from the condemned person, his or her legal team, and the public were considered; the government was appraised of the case and made a determination. These decisions required considerable effort, albeit against a tightly compressed time scale.

Ireland departed from the United Kingdom in that the decision whether or not to recommend commutation was made by the government collectively rather than by one of its members acting independently.[1] The virtue of the Irish arrangement—from the condemned person's perspective at any rate—was that there existed multiple potential points of influence; pressure could be exerted more widely than on the Minister for Justice. Such efforts

[1] The only occasion in the twentieth century when the UK cabinet as a whole became involved in the decision about whether a condemned person should live or die was when Roger Casement, British diplomat and Irish revolutionary, came up for consideration in 1916 (Bresler 1965: 119). This hugely controversial case aside, the Home Secretary's burden was never shared.

Justice, Mercy, and Caprice: Clemency and the Death Penalty in Ireland. First Edition. Ian O'Donnell. © Ian O'Donnell 2017. Published 2017 by Oxford University Press.

would have been futile in the United Kingdom where the Home Secretary was not troubled by cabinet colleagues in arriving at this decision; it was for him alone, having considered the advice of his civil servants, reflected on any representations received, and discussed background issues with the trial judge.

By deciding who to execute and who to spare, the fledgling state was asserting its sovereignty. It was flagrantly displaying its power to deflect the law from the lethal outcome it was otherwise bound to reach. A legally valid decision was set aside for reasons that remained opaque and were not subject to the rules and safeguards, checks and balances, that usually accompanied important decisions. The unregulated nature of executive clemency stood out against a background of bureaucratic decision-making which strove to be open, consistent, and dispassionate. As discussed in Chapter 3, because it must be unregulated and discretionary, retaining space for clemency has always raised concerns; it was a necessary ambiguity—something that was required in an imperfect world. Sarat and Hussain (2006: 179) described this as 'the conundrum of clemency's lawful lawlessness'.

Limits to Discretion

Governments were not limited to the consideration of legal doctrine. Rather, they were free to consider any factor they deemed relevant and to accord it whatever weight they deemed appropriate. Political musings can range more widely than judicial ones; there is room for the application of community standards. Having said this, it is clear that the decision was not free-flowing; similar matters were considered in each case and outcomes were patterned rather than random. The clemency decision was not as unconstrained as might appear at first glance. Following Hawkins (1992: 38):

> ... it does not make sense from a social scientific point of view to speak of 'absolute' or 'unfettered' discretion, since to do so is to imply that discretion in the real world may be constrained only by legal rules, and to overlook the fact that it is also shaped by political, economic, social, and organizational forces outside the legal structure. It is important not to strip away these contexts since they exert considerable influence.

This is an important qualification. While not bound by legal rules, the clemency decision was not anarchic. It allowed extra-legal factors to play a role. Precedent, tradition, working rules and administrative techniques, repeated case handling (especially by the three secretaries to the Department of Justice who oversaw the preparation of briefing memoranda in all but four of the death-eligible cases dealt with when capital punishment was mandatory for murder; see later in this section), and moral evaluation served to structure the process and to render outcomes predictable (or, at least, less mysterious). The proof of this is to be found in how few cases were truly capricious (Table 2.4).

There are two aspects to moral evaluation. The first relates to an assessment of the disreputability (or otherwise) of the prisoner. The second relates to the credibility (or otherwise) of any contrary voices. On occasions where the government was redirected by a personal intervention, the individual in question was always of impeccable moral character, high social standing, and superior educational attainment. Their sincerity, competence, and trustworthiness were beyond reproach. They had no personal agenda to advance and nothing to gain, regardless of the decision ultimately made. This is why they were effective at disrupting a process that was thought to have been brought to a conclusion.

The President of the Executive Council (1922–37) or the Taoiseach of the government (from 1937) chose the members of his cabinet taking account of their characters and abilities. This allowed him to put the justice portfolio in the hands of someone who could make hard decisions and follow through on them. If the incumbent proved reluctant he could always be replaced. So, the way that discretion is exercised depends upon the personalities of the individuals who are appointed to exercise it. The next pertinent factor is how the decision-makers are socialized, the norms that they share, and the goals they strive towards.

Government ministers in the first decades of independence shared values that had been inculcated by their experience of war, first against the British and then against former comrades in arms. They were a largely homogeneous group in terms of age, gender, and formal religious observance. These common experiences, demographic characteristics, and political priorities meant that that they were likely to share a perspective on capital cases and to find particular kinds of reasoning persuasive.

Officials in the Department of Justice also constrained discretion, for example in the way the argument was structured in the memorandum prepared for the Executive Council or government regarding the clemency decision or, when it came to considering release, by providing a summary of the time served by other murderers whose sentences were commuted in Ireland as well as in neighbouring jurisdictions. Clear procedures were followed by departmental officials when preparing briefing documentation. The data were collected from the same sources in the same way on each occasion and this bureaucratization reduced the government's room for manoeuvre.

In other words, when the clemency decision is criticized for being untrammelled it is necessary to recognize the existence of a number of important constraints. While legal forces may not be at work there are certainly cultural, social, psychological, and institutional factors that place some parameters around the exercise of discretion. Shared values and perspectives, processes of informal socialization, and bureaucratic regimes, all worked in the direction of generally predictable outcomes.

The minister summarized the case for his government colleagues and conveyed the judge's view so it is interesting to look at the extent to which the different personalities were required to discharge this function and the pattern of outcomes for each of them. Table 6.1 shows the number of cases dealt with by each Minister for Justice prior to the abolition of capital punishment in 1990. Not too much can be read into these figures given that they held office for widely different periods (Boland was in charge the longest), had no control over the number of cases that came before them, and there were other significant factors in play, especially the view of the judge and the gender of the condemned person. But, given the weight attached to the minister's oral report, and the absence of competing sources of information, there was scope for the minister to decide which aspects of the case should be emphasized, thereby allowing his predilections to come into play. O'Higgins was in post for one capricious case (Boylan) and Boland for two (MacCurtain and Stevenson) so their ratios of executions to commutations would have been even less favourable had circumstances not intervened.

The secretary of the Department of Justice was a powerful figure behind the scenes, especially as his tenure likely exceeded that of several consecutive ministers and he may previously have occupied a more junior role in the department, so would have been intimately familiar with the workings of its administrative machinery. While they did not have any formal decision-making

Table 6.1 Merciful ministers?

Listed chronologically	Executed	Commuted
Kevin O'Higgins	12	14
W.T. Cosgrave	0	0
James FitzGerald-Kenney	4	8
James Geoghegan	1	1
Patrick J. Ruttledge	3	8
Gerald Boland	14	12
Seán MacEoin	1	4
Daniel Morrissey	0	1
James Everett	0	1
Oscar Traynor	0	4
Charles Haughey	0	2
Seán Lemass	0	0
Brian Lenihan	0	0
Michael Moran	0	0
Desmond O'Malley	0	0
Patrick Cooney	0	0
Gerard Collins	0	2
Jim Mitchell	0	1
Seán Doherty	0	0
Michael Noonan	0	2
Alan Dukes	0	3
All	35	63

Note: All twelve of the men sentenced to death by non-jury courts prior to 1964—six of whom were executed—were dealt with by Gerald Boland. One case (Michael Conway) arose during P.J. Ruttledge's tenure as minister but at a time when he was indisposed and Boland had taken charge of the portfolio on an interim basis. Charles Haughey was Minister for Justice when the last murderer convicted by a jury and sentenced to death had his sentence commuted to penal servitude for life. The table is based on the identity of the minister on the day the government decided whether or not the law should take its course.

power with regard to the disposal of death penalty cases, it is difficult to imagine that their years of experience, knowledge of precedent and past cases, and skilful construction of memoranda would not have shaped their minister's approach to a case.

They acted as a filter (removing what they believed to be irrelevant dross) and a still (repeatedly purifying the narrative until it settled).

There were six secretaries between independence and the imposition of the last mandatory death sentence for murder. Two were in post for a matter of months: Daniel Browne, from March 1933 to January 1934, who oversaw a single execution (John Fleming) and John Duff, from January 1949 to August 1949, who oversaw a single commutation (Mary Daly). After Peter Berry took charge in February 1961, there were only two cases to consider (David Galvin and James Kelly, both commuted). The other three secretaries (H.J. O'Friel, S.A. Roche, and T.J. Coyne) dealt with the remaining eighty-six cases.[2] This allowed them to develop a repertoire of case-handling skills that enabled the materials required for this most grave of decisions to be collated quickly, systematically, and dispassionately. They established effective decision routines. (Andrew Ward was secretary when consideration was given to capital murder cases in the 1980s, by which time execution was never seriously contemplated.)

Bresler (1965: 64) recited a mantra that guided Home Secretaries in the United Kingdom from the 1880s to the 1960s: 'The exercise of the Prerogative of Mercy does not depend on principles of strict law or justice, still less does it depend on sentiment in any way. It is a question of policy and judgment in each case.' This mantra is relevant to the matters under consideration here in that they were more muddled than Bresler allowed. Justice was often involved and so too was sentiment, but the decision to spare a life still had an element of art about it.

Public Opinion

Politicians were never deaf to the cries of their constituents and stood ready to add to the clamour for clemency should they be asked to do so. Strange (1995: 602) remarked that, when it came to cabinet consideration in Canada, the outcome for condemned persons 'was equally determined by the weight not of judicial opinion but of the political ramifications of execution or

[2] Their periods in office were as follows: H.J. O'Friel, 20 September 1922 to 6 March 1933; S.A. Roche, 6 March 1934 to 21 January 1949; T.J. Coyne, 6 September 1949 to 21 February 1961 (O'Donnell et al. 2005: 398).

commutation'. The balance was different in Ireland, where the judicial view weighed heavily—only once was the judge's plea for mercy ignored—and governments proved themselves capable of resisting tidal waves of public pressure. Sometimes they were almost reckless as to the consequences, especially when it came to IRA members. Bitter experience made them wary of leniency for fear of facilitating further violence. But they were also resolute in non-political cases where the level of public dissatisfaction with the proposed execution was palpable.

Irish governments were not unduly concerned by the need to reflect—or indeed to co-opt—public opinion. They comprised men who had been hardened by war and they took a long and wide view. They were guided by their consciences and the preferences of their peers rather than fear of an adverse public reaction. Sometimes they may have spared a life not because they feared public opprobrium but because they felt that to allow the law to take its course might transform public indignation at the crime into sympathy for the criminal. Such a sentiment probably motivated de Valera's attempts to prevent the execution of IRA men in Britain in the 1940s, while sanctioning the same practice at home (Doyle 2015). There was the additional pragmatic consideration, of course, that the immediate threat to the state was less acute when IRA operations took place outside its borders.

There were executions that went ahead despite strong, widespread, and well-coordinated opposition. Large numbers of petitions were submitted in favour of Henry Gleeson and Bernard Kirwan, but the Minister for Justice of the day—Boland in each case—was not for turning. If he was disturbed by public sentiment there is no evidence of this in the extensive available records. Six folders full of petitions accompany Gleeson's prisoner file. The first batch contains more than 4,300 signatures according to an accompanying letter from his solicitor. Subsequent batches contain in the region of an additional 3,400 signatures, by my estimation. Petitions with around 1,300 signatures arrived at the Department of Justice on the day that Gleeson was executed. To generate so much support over such a short period of time indicates the degree of national uneasiness that existed about the conviction, but the government remained unmoved.

There was a similar campaign in favour of Kirwan, which attracted thousands of signatures, many people completing and returning a slip that was published in national newspapers to indicate their desire to see the condemned man live. Again the government was not deflected from its course. The fact that Kirwan had served a previous seven-year sentence of penal servitude and was a 'ticket of leave' man at the time he was convicted of his brother's murder no doubt counted against him in the eyes of the state (and in the eyes of the jury to whom this fact was disclosed during the trial). Public disquiet seems to have copper-fastened the government's resolve. (It is possible that notwithstanding the existence of a nationwide campaign, Garda soundings in the local area suggested that carrying out the execution in the case in question was an appropriate and proportionate response that would not offend against community sentiment.)

The electoral costs of ignoring the public were not high. Executions were relatively rare events—most counties generated a capital case no more than once every couple of decades (Table 2.2)—and when it came to general elections there were many more pressing issues upon which the electorate was keen to focus. Given that a TD [Teachta Dála; Member of Parliament] was sure to make representations if constituents wished him (or, rarely, her) to do so, it is by no means certain that they would have borne the brunt of any residual local anger in the event that the government did not listen. Nor would much have been achieved by making the Minister for Justice the lightning rod for public dissatisfaction, as the decision was not for him alone.

Only if an execution caused nationwide revulsion and the public was persuaded that a different government would have acted differently would there have been possible adverse consequences at the polls during a subsequent election. This was never likely to be the case as the two main parties oversaw similar numbers of executions.[3] While the electorate may have derived comfort from the idea that they could vote out the politicians who ignored them, there was no guarantee that the replacements would be any more responsive.

[3] Sixteen executions occurred under the Cumann na nGaedheal government of 1923–32; seventeen under Fianna Fáil, 1932–48; one under the first inter-party government, 1948–51; and one under Fianna Fáil, 1951–4. The number of commutations during each of these government's lifetimes were twenty-two, twenty, five, and one respectively. The execution rate was lowest for the inter-party government.

Governments could ignore petitions without facing major consequences in terms of re-electability. This, in combination with the phenomenon of groupthink, explains the depth of their intransigence. Other sources of outside influence, or organized opposition, such as that of an abolitionist movement, were of no great consequence. The state did not bend to the public will. In a pungent comment on one of the adverse impacts of a capital punishment regime, Koestler (1956: 163) wrote that: 'When the vision of the gibbet appears on the nation's horizon, opinion swings and twists like the body suspended from it; eyes bulge and reason is strangled.' The penal landscape in Ireland was not characterized by such distortions.

Groupthink

'Groupthink' refers to the tendency among some groups to arrive at a swift consensus at the cost of fully evaluating alternative courses of action (Janis 1972). It is most common in tightly knit, highly prestigious groups where membership is prized, leadership is strong, and there is a shared belief in the group's inherent morality. When a high level of stress is introduced to the mix, the group faces a moral dilemma, and external opponents are viewed disparagingly and in a stereotypical fashion, the stage is set for groupthink. Group members look to each other for support and find confirmation of that in arriving quickly at an agreed view. This phenomenon is likely when the decision-making body is cohesive, operates in isolation, evinces esprit de corps, and possesses high mutual regard, shared values, and a sense of moral righteousness.

Groupthink is a way of dealing with the stress caused by difficult decisions; the group serves as an emotional crutch for its members. There are strong pressures towards uniformity at the expense of thoughtful and morally appropriate decision-making. Allowing executions where the evidence was circumstantial and less than compelling, or mitigating factors were present and had been identified, are examples of groupthink. They exemplify poor decision-making processes leading to unfortunate outcomes. The pressure towards groupthink was probably greater in the absence of a judicial recommendation to mercy because now the government had a decision to make rather than a recommendation to follow. It was probably greatest in the single case where the judge's recommendation to mercy was ignored (see Chapter 4).

If the group does not have to explain its decisions, groupthink is further promoted. Irish governments in the 1920s and 1940s—when execution rates peaked and the subversive threat met with a fierce response from men who, in their day, were no strangers to subversion—shared these salient characteristics. They comprised small groups of men whose political formations had much in common. They were closer to the exercise of violence than their successors would ever be, and their commitment to the preservation of the state was unswerving. Their approach was consensual and the agenda of government meetings tended to be full, limiting the time available for discussion and consideration of divergent views. These conditions promoted conformity and poor decision-making. In an early comment on this issue, Alexander Hamilton (1788), in one of a series of essays written in support of the proposed US Constitution, posited that the pardoning power should be placed within the hands of an individual rather than a group, because, 'as men generally derive confidence from their numbers, they might often encourage each other in an act of obduracy'.

The governments that met when murder attracted a mandatory death sentence made their decisions in secret. They were not subject to external oversight or review. A non-compliant minister could be relieved of his duties. These factors militated against diverse views, dissenting voices, and robust discussions. P.J. Ruttledge was replaced as justice minister by Gerald Boland because he lacked the steel to see the job through to its neck-breaking conclusion. Bowyer Bell (1997: 168) described Ruttledge as 'assumed by some to be too gentle to grasp the nettle of coercion'. He was moved from Justice to Local Government and Public Health in 1939, the justice portfolio being assigned to Boland 'who had proved himself a suitably hard man when he took over briefly from Ruttledge three years before when Ruttledge was ill' (p. 168).

As Table 6.1 shows, the proportion of death-eligible cases that resulted in execution was much higher for Boland (a majority; fourteen out of twenty-six) than for Ruttledge (around one-quarter; three out of eleven). Interestingly, and perhaps relatedly, Ruttledge resigned from government on health grounds in August 1941, within a week of the execution of Richard Goss, in the wake of the executions of two other IRA members the previous year, and with every indication that more would follow as an inevitable consequence of the government's 'exhausting struggle against militant republicanism' (MacEoin 1997: 542). MacEoin's view was that Ruttledge 'may not have wished to continue to be a party in that struggle' (p. 542). Boland had no such qualms and *all* of the IRA men sentenced to death prior to 1964 were dealt with on his watch.

External pressure reinforced the tendency towards groupthink, creating a siege mentality and a state of us versus them. This explains why governments remained implacable in the face of well-subscribed petitions, even when members of the victim's family were among the signatories. Conversely, however, when the intervention was more direct (e.g. personal representations by a judge) or there was prolonged internal division, groupthink was less likely to follow. Under these conditions, group members could not avoid giving due consideration to alternative approaches or thinking of the object of their deliberations in more rounded, less stereotypical, terms. Sometimes what was required was a pause in the action to allow the injection of a contrary position. In some cases the decision was delayed and the interval allowed reconsideration and reversal. In others a confident and respected oppositional voice was given an opportunity to be heard (see Chapter 7).

Even when a decision had been made and recorded in the minutes it could be revisited and revised during the short interval that existed between the confirmation of a sentence and its execution. This explains why some unsavoury characters were spared while others—who generated at least as much public anxiety—were not. It required someone as influential as a judge (who appeared in person) or a bishop (whose appeal was forceful) to challenge this closed mindedness and to cause the group to rethink its inherent morality. Governments managed to maintain emotional distance from their legislative colleagues and their electorates but they were prone, on occasion, to subservience. Why bishops or judges occasionally strove to unsettle settled minds is not clear at this remove but it cannot have been on account of a principled objection to capital punishment as on other occasions the same individuals chose to remain silent.

A great deal of reliance was placed on the report from the Minister for Justice at the meeting when clemency came up for consideration. In only six cases between 1932 and 1952 was a transcript of the judge's charge to the jury made available to the government and in one further case a ten-line summary of the judge's charge was provided. Copying such documents posed a challenge requiring the allocation of scarce secretarial and administrative resources; unnecessary duplication constituted wasteful (and unpatriotic) expenditure. Judges' summations could be lengthy and were not the kind of material that busy politicians would have welcomed seeing among their cabinet papers.

These cases attracted a high level of publicity and it is likely that ministers would have been aware of the key facts, even in the absence of a detailed verbatim note. Sometimes the confidential Garda report prepared for the Department of Justice referred to the prisoner's suspected involvement in other crimes. While the rules of evidence would have precluded the jury from knowing about such matters, the minister was aware of them and they may have affected the tenor of his report to government, or even his view about the desirability of allowing the condemned person to live. Coupled with time constraints, pressure to conform, and membership of an in-group, the lack of information and an absence of guidelines contributed to groupthink.

The concept of groupthink helps us to understand both the government's apparent immunity to external pressure (the group becomes even more cohesive and committed to the rectitude of its position) as well as its vulnerability to the injection of an outside view (someone of unquestionable integrity can disrupt the decision-making process, prompt a rethink, and initiate a reversal; the government is no less resolute afterwards but the object of its resolution has changed).

Groupthink is less likely in coalition governments where cohesion is imperfect. Seán MacBride was Minister for External Affairs in the first inter-party government. The variety of political parties constituting this government militated against quick and easy consensus.[4] When William Gambon's case came up for consideration it was decided not to recommend clemency. As MacBride's government colleague and fellow opponent of the death penalty Noël Browne (1986: 128–9) recalled in his memoir, their opposition was easily overcome:

> ... on a number of occasions both of us argued for clemency for men under sentence of death ... Because of what I had heard about General Mulcahy [Minister for Education] and the 'seventy-seven', I watched his reaction. In

[4] The 5th Government of Ireland (18 February 1948 to 13 June 1951) comprised Fine Gael, the Labour Party, Clann na Poblachta, Clann na Talmhan, the National Labour Party, and one Independent TD.

his usual style on such 'simple issues', he was curt, brash and uncomplicated: 'They must hang.' The deeply religious [Joseph] Blowick's [Minister for Lands] comment, in his high-pitched squeak, was, 'Hang them, hang them.' There was no attempt to argue or to rationalize their positions. With their majority they had no need to.

Browne's assessment seems excessively bleak as Gambon was the only person hanged by this government while five were spared.[5] When introducing his own Bill to abolish capital punishment in 1981, Browne told the Dáil that: 'I had the distasteful experience in the fifties of being in a minority of two in a government which hanged two men, one of whom I firmly believe was mentally defective'.[6] It is interesting that his recall was erroneous given the apparent importance of the issue to him, and it is not clear who the mentally defective person was, although it is unlikely to have been Gambon.[7] Again he was wrong to say that he was in a minority of two on two occasions as there must have been a majority, if not unanimity, in all but one case if the condemned person was, in fact, spared. Finally, he misremembered the decade. Gambon was hanged in the 1940s not the 1950s.

The views espoused by MacBride and Browne would have been easy to dismiss given their divisive personalities and controversial political pedigrees but, all the same, a decision to allow a man to die demanded a high level of agreement.[8] Had Gambon appealed, introducing a pause, and had the judge managed to obtain the audience he sought (see Chapter 7), things might have ended differently. Interestingly, while MacBride was part of the government that did not advise President Seán T. O'Kelly to commute Gambon's sentence, O'Kelly had kept open a line of communication from the government to MacBride when the latter was Tomás MacCurtain's barrister, and this had created the context

[5] The General Mulcahy to whom Browne refers played a key role in the executions of eighty-one opponents during the civil war (see Chapter 1).

[6] Dáil Debates, 5 May 1981, Noël Browne, vol. 328, col. 2151.

[7] Perhaps he thought that John Fanning had been hanged when in fact the government of which he was part had commuted the sentence? Browne's incomplete grasp of the facts may be explained by his reluctance to attend cabinet meetings (MacBride 2005: 224).

[8] Mulcahy and MacBride were adversaries of old, the former having authorized the latter's detention in 1927 on suspicion of involvement in the murder of Justice Minister Kevin O'Higgins (Nic Dháibhéid 2011: 83).

where the decision to allow MacCurtain hang was reversed (see Chapter 7).

Arbitrary or Principled Decisions?

It was legitimate for the executive to take account of extra-legal factors. Indeed this was precisely why the clemency power resided with it rather than being vested in a judicial body. The government could bring a community perspective to bear, it could individualize decision-making and balance law enforcement against other priorities. This was entirely appropriate, even if it evoked consternation on a variety of levels (see Chapter 3). In addition, the fact that the clemency decision was made by elected representatives enhanced its legitimacy, as the public could always replace their representatives should they become dissatisfied with their decision-making.

Some of the debate in this area concerns the impropriety of a judge allowing personal or community values to intrude on the selection of an appropriate sentence. But it might be argued that the government encapsulated the public's view or, at the very least, it was reasonable for it to take such a view into account. This was, of course, the whole point of petitions begging for mercy which implored the minister, president, or Taoiseach to do the right thing. A government could achieve a morally correct outcome where the judge was limited to a legally correct one; and the government could take a further step—denied to the judge under a mandatory sentencing scheme—and show clemency.

Albert Pierrepoint (1974: 208) claimed on the final page of his autobiography that 'the reason for a reprieve was always fundamentally political ... The trouble with the death sentence has always been that nobody wanted it for everybody, but everybody differed about who should get off.' In a sense this was true because these decisions were made by politicians. But it suggests that party politics may have played a role and Ireland offers no evidence to support this contention.

The key question is the extent to which clemency was exercised in a principled manner. Were the decisions random or patterned? If a pattern can be discerned, what does it look like? What was the mix of legal and extra-legal factors that inclined a government one way or the other? Were there clusters of identifiable characteristics that made mercy more likely? According to Acker and Lanier (2000: 201): 'An element of caprice inevitably accompanies executive clemency decisions.' It was certainly true that some of those condemned benefited from the operation of chance but, generally speaking, the variation in the Irish cases was predictable. Unexpected turns of events could shape outcomes profoundly but it would be going too far to suggest that the process was arbitrary, that it was akin to a game of chance (see Chapters 8 and 9).

There is no record setting out why the government took the decision it took in any particular case. But, by studying the pattern of decisions in death-eligible cases, it was possible to arrive at some general conclusions about the most influential factors. The first, and most important, filter was whether the judge recommended mercy. If he did, the odds of clemency increased significantly. As discussed in Chapter 4, there was just one case where the judge's call for clemency was ignored. But there were ten cases where the judge felt that the law should take its course and it did not. What swayed the government in these cases?

The first factor was gender. Three involved women (Kate Owens, Frances Cox, and Mary Cadden) and the government had set itself against hanging any more women after Annie Walsh met Thomas Pierrepoint on 5 August 1925. The greater the number of women shown clemency, the more difficult it became to deviate from this path without raising major questions of consistency and fairness. Precedent offered a refuge to decision-makers; it could be called upon to insulate them from criticism in the unlikely event of a view emerging that a particular woman should not be spared. It is fair to say that a firm precedent had been established that women would not be hanged, however awful their crimes. Sixteen women had been sentenced to death and reprieved between Annie Walsh and Frances Cox, a trend that was unlikely to be reversed even though neither judge nor jury called for Cox to be spared.

This leaves seven cases where the judge did not call for the 'prerogative' to be exercised. In six of these the jury recommended mercy (Patrick Aylward, John Ryan, Denis Leen, Leo O'Brien, James Tierney, and Martin Griffin). This leaves just one case of a man who was recommended to mercy by neither judge nor jury but who was spared. This was Robert Stevenson, a British able seaman convicted of strangling a prostitute, whose petition for clemency was supported by the Holy See.[9] Lobbying from the Vatican must have been particularly difficult to resist in the kind of self-consciously confessional state that Ireland had become. (Had Michael Manning's solicitors thought of enlisting papal support, Manning—who, unlike Stevenson, was Catholic—might have been spared.[10])

If the government ignored a judge's call for clemency it was accepting that someone should die despite advice to the contrary from the person best-placed to advise it on the matter. They could do this, but it would require a degree of determination that was rarely present. Also it would be somewhat akin to a high-stakes retrial, an activity that governments were reluctant to become involved in. It was different when judges did not call for mercy but governments spared the prisoner. This was for two reasons. First, the judge never lobbied for death, but simply remained silent on the question or stated that there was no reason for the law to be deflected from its course. Secondly, there was a qualitative difference between allowing someone to live in the absence of calls for their death and allowing someone to die in the presence of calls for them to be spared. While both involved the executive taking a view opposed to the one offered by the judge, the consequences for the condemned party could not have been more different.

[9] As the Department of Justice noted, this communication was 'in accordance with the Holy See's practice of supporting such petitions when requested to do so, but the Minister has been advised that the intervention of the Holy See in this case need not be taken as showing that, in the view of the Vatican Authorities, this particular case has exceptional features'. Memorandum for government—question of reprieve for Robert James Stevenson, 2 July 1954, NAI, JUS/2005/171/3615.

[10] The Vatican also intervened on behalf of husband and wife Noel and Marie Murray, anarchists with links to the republican movement, who were sentenced to death in 1976 for the murder of a member of An Garda Síochána (see Postscript). The papal nuncio visited President Ó Dálaigh on 8 July 1976 with a letter that the president transmitted to the Taoiseach the same evening, along with a covering note stating that he had drawn His Excellency's attention to Article 13, sections 6 and 9 of Bunreacht na hÉireann and pointed out that no action would be taken until the appeal process had run its course, NAI, PRES/2007/125/83. It is not clear what weight was given to this intervention or who had requested it, although its impact may have been diluted by the fact that the nuncio, Gaetano Alibrandi, was 'a figure whose sympathy for Irish republicanism was a constant source of friction' in government circles (Moloney 2002: 236). The irony of the Bishop of Rome being pressed into service on behalf of a pair of violent anarchists was not commented upon at the time.

The government's clemency decision was the outcome of a deliberative process which proceeded along clearly delineated tracks. There was evidence of gender discrimination which accrued to the consistent advantage of women. Significant weight was accorded to the recommendations of the judge and jury who were familiar with all of the facts of the case and may have called for clemency to prevent what they perceived as potential injustice. It may be, of course, that when judges and juries recommended mercy they did so having taken account of extra-legal factors (e.g. the perpetrator's age, relationship with victim, or socioeconomic status) and that there was an element of arbitrariness at this level of analysis.

In some cases where there was a consensus that the person deserved to die, they were spared. In other words, mercy tempered justice on a small number of occasions (see Appendices I and III). The men who made these decisions took the judicial recommendation very seriously; they had appointed the judges so why would they not hold them in high regard? Beyond this, they were swayed by the gender of the condemned person (regardless of their crime), community sentiment (as expressed by the presence or absence of a jury rider), and, rarely, extraneous factors. It seems reasonable to conclude that government decisions regarding clemency were seldom arbitrary (except where mercy intruded as an autonomous virtue or there was evidence of caprice) but that they were often unfair (in that they discriminated in favour of women). Sometimes, influential figures from outside government attempted to exercise some sway and their efforts are the subject of the next chapter.

7

Blurring the Separation of Powers

There is a tripartite division of powers in Ireland and no organ of state may interfere with the functions exclusively ascribed to another. One branch of government—the legislature—sets the parameters of punishment through the enactment of laws. Another—the judiciary—imposes punishment. A third—the executive—becomes involved in exercising clemency. The boundaries may seem clear but they are porous. When capital punishment was under consideration judges, legislators, governors general, and even the president, attempted to influence the executive in ways that ranged from the dubiously acceptable to the constitutionally impermissible. There was no evidence of the executive or legislative branches attempting to influence the judiciary; when judicial advice was sought it was with circumspection, patience, and deference.

The independence of the judiciary was compromised because the executive retained the power to alter the sentence imposed on a criminal who had been dealt with by due process of law. The competency of the executive came into question when judges intervened in its deliberative processes. The fact that, in their correspondence with the Department of Justice, judges often made unambiguous recommendations regarding the desirability—or otherwise—of commutation shows that there was not perfect functional separation. That their representations were made at the invitation of the government shows that their contribution was not seen to be repugnant to the Constitution.

But sometimes their involvement went further than the written communication of a view. Judges attended meetings of government; they lobbied for a particular outcome. This was a clear incursion by one branch of government into another branch's sphere of competence. The fact that their attendance was not recorded on the minutes of government meetings suggests that it

Justice, Mercy, and Caprice: Clemency and the Death Penalty in Ireland. First Edition. Ian O'Donnell. © Ian O'Donnell 2017. Published 2017 by Oxford University Press.

was seen as unorthodox at the time and that there was a desire to ensure it remained behind the scenes. The lack of formal acknowledgement must indicate, at the very least, some concern about the propriety of their presence. The fact that judicial attendance was elsewhere noted on the files suggests that its significance was not unappreciated. In three cases—Patrick Boylan, Patrick Heffernan, and William Wall—judges spoke directly to governments in the interval between the confirmation of the sentence and the date set for its execution. In two others—Agnes McAdam and Mary Daly—the judicial intervention came later and was effective in prompting release.

Interfering Judges

When a judge attempted to persuade the executive to exercise its lawful authority to forestall the implementation of a properly imposed sentence, this could be viewed as an implicit criticism of the legislative branch. If legislators did not want every murder to attract a mandatory penalty of death then it was for them to change the law and not for the judiciary to find ways to deflect it from its course. Legislative tardiness caused huge distress, especially in cases where a death sentence was announced but there was little chance it would be carried out. It also cost lives in that as long as the statutory arrangements persisted, use being made of them remained a possibility. Writing about the prerogative of mercy, Bresler (1965: 58) observed that: 'Muddling through is a characteristic of the incompetent and the English'. The incoherent approach to law reform in Ireland suggests that this characteristic was more widely shared.

When sitting in Dáil Éireann, members of the government were acting as legislators whose duty it was to make laws that would apply equally to every citizen. But, when sitting around the cabinet table, the same men were charged with weighing each case on its merits and deciding whether it would be appropriate to resentence. They were responsible for making the law and for negating its effects. These should have been difficult roles to reconcile but there is no evidence to suggest that those involved felt unduly burdened doing what was expected of them.[1]

[1] This may be explained by the fact that, in large part, the body of law taken over at independence—including the mandatory death sentence for murder—had been created at Westminster.

Alcohol, jealousy, and a cut throat

Patrick Boylan, a 23-year-old single man who worked as an electric welder, lived in Dublin with his parents. He had no previous convictions. On 5 December 1936 he spent the afternoon drinking before returning home for an evening of music and dancing. On the way, he collected his 18-year-old girlfriend, Norah Whelan, together with her sister and brother-in-law. At the party he quarrelled with two men (uninvited guests) who were taking what he considered to be an improper interest in Miss Whelan. Blows were exchanged. Whelan told Boylan that she was finished with him. He asked to speak to her in private in the yard whereupon he attacked her with a razor and she ran screaming into the house.

Boylan attempted to pursue her indoors, declaring that: 'I have cut her throat, and I want to kiss her before she dies.' Denied access to the house he stated: 'I know I done it, I will swing for it', before clambering over the garden wall and quitting the scene.[2] Shortly afterwards, when an ambulance arrived to collect Whelan, who succumbed to her injuries within hours, he returned to the house and resumed fighting one of the men he had been squabbling with earlier in the evening. The fight was broken up and he disappeared. Late the following night he called to his uncle's house where he was arrested and charged with murder.

Boylan claimed he could remember nothing that transpired after Whelan told him their relationship was over. At trial, he claimed that a head injury received at work several years earlier, in combination with the alcohol he had consumed on the evening in question and the stress of learning that his girlfriend had tired of him, had impaired his mind and rendered him incapable of controlling his actions. The jury did not accept the insanity defence and, having retired for fifty-five minutes, returned a verdict of guilty of murder but with a strong recommendation to mercy. Mr Justice O'Byrne donned the black cap and imposed the mandatory death sentence. Boylan appealed but the conviction was upheld.

The Executive Council was not persuaded that there were grounds for commuting the sentence. They disregarded the jury's

[2] Memorandum prepared by An Garda Síochána—Metropolitan Division, 16 March 1937, NAI, JUS/18/2093A & B.

call for mercy and the many petitions received in Boylan's support. They rejected the judge's argument that the prerogative of mercy should be exercised because although Boylan was not insane his crime was unpremeditated and had resulted from a toxic combination of 'drink, wounded vanity, jealousy and bad temper'.[3] On 30 April 1937, the Executive Council confirmed the execution date for 7 May.

But, two days before the execution was scheduled to take place—and too late to contact the executioner before he left home—the Executive Council reconsidered the case and reversed its decision.[4] The recorded attendance was identical on each occasion, comprising its president, all ministers, attorney general, secretary to the Executive Council, and parliamentary secretary to the president. What caused this change of mind?

No explanation can be discerned from the minutes of the Executive Council meetings or the contemporaneous records. However, a memorandum prepared some years later, and written in the Irish language, noted that Mr Justice O'Byrne was present at the meeting on 5 May. He was dissatisfied with the decision to allow the hanging to go ahead and felt that the sentence should be commuted. Clearly, his view prevailed and he prevented an otherwise inevitable execution. The memorandum stated: 'It was thought at the time that it would be preferable not to make any reference to this business on the file'.[5] The same memorandum revealed that a judge was present when the government changed its mind about the execution of Patrick Heffernan in 1951; on this occasion it was Cahir Davitt, who had the added distinction of not having been the trial judge in the case (see next section).

[3] Letter from John O'Byrne to Minister for Justice, 23 April 1937, NAI, TSCH/3/S9849A.

[4] The executioner and his assistant were paid their fees and expenses for a wasted journey to Dublin.

[5] Untitled memorandum, 11 March 1953, NAI, TSCH/3/S7788B (my translation). O'Byrne's determination was noted in his obituary which stated that he had a 'restless, consuming passion for justice' and that he went to great lengths to prevent a hanging that he did not believe should go ahead 'once at least, battering successfully upon the doors of the Executive Council' (*Irish Times*, 15 January 1954). According to Deale (2007: 83), O'Byrne 'had a fatal defect for a judge. He was too strong minded, and once he had made up his mind found it difficult to entertain anything which might change it.' This 'fatal defect' proved to be life saving for Patrick Boylan.

The disposal of Boylan's case was interesting also in that the Executive Council issued the commutation order itself rather than making a recommendation to the governor general. This was because the decision was made in the interval between the abolition of the office of governor general and the installation of the first president of Ireland.[6]

O'Brien (2006: 234) argued with reference to the Boylan case that:

> Had O'Byrne J simply accepted the government's original rejection of his advice it would have created a precedent and marked a serious departure from established procedure, one which might conceivably have seen the decision-making process with regard to reprieves pass from the professional hands of the judiciary into the relatively amateurish grasp of politicians.

But the politicians already had this deliberative process firmly within their 'amateurish grasp' in that the judge's recommendation was not taken in a number of previous cases—Patrick Aylward, John Ryan, Denis Leen, and Leo O'Brien—in all of which the judge said 'No' to mercy but the government said 'Yes'. The same pattern of decision-making is found in the cases that followed Boylan. O'Brien overestimated the supposedly unprecedented nature of Boylan's case.

A bicycle, a shotgun, and a dead teenager

Patrick Heffernan, a 27-year-old casual labourer and former soldier from Lumcloon in County Offaly, was found guilty of murdering Rose Hand, a 16-year-old typist whom he knew slightly. Rose left home to cycle to work on 12 May 1950 but did not arrive at her intended destination. Her body was found the next day under a bush at the side of the road. Her underwear, stained with blood and mud, were concealed nearby. There were no signs of sexual interference.

[6] The office of governor general was abolished on 11 December 1936 and Douglas Hyde was inaugurated as president on 25 June 1938. Thomas Kelly and James Tierney were similarly dealt with. Mary Somerville was the first person whose death sentence was commuted by the president. John Hornick was the only person executed during this hiatus. (For pertinent dates see Appendices I and II.)

Heffernan claimed that he had overtaken Rose on his bicycle when he was returning home from his job as a night watchman. He used to hunt rabbits in the morning and the shotgun that he used for this purpose was resting on his handlebars. He maintained that he hit a bump in the road, and the shotgun was accidentally discharged, killing Rose. In panic, he hid her body. The gun was defective and Heffernan was habitually careless with it. During the trial he demonstrated how the 'accident' had occurred, sitting on the bicycle with the gun across the handlebars. There was no evidence of premeditation but the fact that he hid the body and quit the scene counted heavily against him. So too did his reputation as a man of immoral habits.

Heffernan's conviction was overturned and a retrial ordered because the jury had been allowed to separate. Accompanied by their keepers (members of An Garda Síochána) they took a break from their deliberations to go on a Sunday outing to a hotel in Glendalough, County Wicklow. At the hotel they socialized with members of the public and shared their bus back to Dublin with them, circumstances deemed by the court to constitute a 'grave irregularity'.[7] Heffernan was retried and reconvicted. On neither occasion did the jury add a rider. The judge on the second occasion, Mr Justice Kingsmill Moore, did not agree with the jury, feeling that manslaughter would have been a proper verdict.

On 9 March 1951, the first occasion that Heffernan's case was considered by the government, it was decided to allow the law to take its course, despite the reservations expressed in writing by the sentencing judge. The government meeting began at three o'clock and ended two hours later. Daniel Morrissey, Minister for Justice, was present. Seán MacBride, Minister for External Affairs, was absent. Given the duration of the meeting and the fact that there was other business to transact, the decision in Heffernan's case could not have taken long to agree.

Following this decision, and having previously indicated that he would not be appealing but rather hoping that his clemency petition would be favourably received, Heffernan's legal team submitted an application for leave to appeal. This was considered and dismissed on 1 May 1951. Cahir Davitt was a member of the Court of Criminal Appeal and he subsequently approached

[7] *People (AG) v Heffernan* [1951] IR 206.

the attorney general to inform him that he believed there were grounds for sparing Heffernan. The attorney general asked him to consult with the other judges (George Murnaghan and Martin Maguire) to see if they shared his view. He did as requested and reported back that they did not. The attorney general asked him if he would be prepared to address a meeting of the government. He said he would. He did.[8]

On the second occasion that Heffernan's case was considered, the scenario was very different. The meeting extended over two days, from 11.30 a.m. to 3 p.m. and from 6 p.m. to 8 p.m. on Friday 11 May, resuming on Saturday 12 May between 1 p.m. and 3 p.m. Morrissey was absent (he had informed the Taoiseach in advance that he believed the law should take its course). MacBride was present. Davitt was present, although this is not recorded. The secretary of the Department of Justice wrote in 1958 that he was heard at this government meeting 'and did my best to get him hanged'.[9] His attendance was not noted on the minutes so either he was there and, like Davitt, this was not recorded for posterity, or his recollection was flawed. In any event the decision to allow Heffernan's execution to proceed was reversed. (The duration of this marathon meeting is unlikely to have been prolonged greatly by any of the other matters under consideration which were relatively minor, namely agreement to change the name of a townland in County Cork from Kingwilliamstown to Ballydesmond and the dismissal of a clerical officer, a shorthand typist, and a postman.)

For Heffernan, the breach of the separation of powers seems obvious. The judge who attempted to sway the government had no role in either of his trials, was in a minority on the Court of Criminal Appeal, and orchestrated an audience with the government so that he could attempt to reverse a lawful decision of which he did not approve. That he managed to do so speaks volumes about his persuasive powers but raises difficult questions about the respective roles of the judiciary and the executive.

[8] No written record of Davitt's argument exists. Memorandum prepared for Minister for Justice, 7 January [sic] 1951, NAI, JUS/2005/170/8695.

[9] Note from T.J. Coyne to Minister for Justice, 26 February 1958, NAI, JUS/2005/170/8695. In this note the secretary observed that: 'This man owes his life to Judge Davitt who was given an opportunity of being heard at a Government meeting.'

If other condemned men had had the services of such a champion the rate of executions would surely have been lower.[10] Given that Davitt's view was shared neither by his appeal court colleagues nor by the government at its first meeting (nor, indeed, by the local community who felt that Heffernan should have been hanged), his arguments must have been forceful indeed.[11]

Heffernan will never have known the debt he owed to one of the judges who turned down his appeal. Had Davitt not intervened, Heffernan would have been executed despite the trial judge's plea to spare him.[12] Kingsmill Moore expressed relief when he learned Heffernan was to live, indicating in his letter to the minister that had the jury convicted of manslaughter he would have felt an eight-year sentence to be appropriate. This was Kingsmill Moore's only capital case.

A born criminal?

William Wall, aged 28, was convicted in 1959 of the murder of Bridget Farrell, an elderly widow, in her home on a small farm in Hugginstown, County Kilkenny. He repeatedly beat her about the head with a stick, searched the house for money, and left her for dead. Departing the house he met the victim's brother and enquired of him whether it would be acceptable to answer a call

[10] Davitt must have impressed the government with his oratory (or at least not alienated himself from them completely) as, at its meeting on 12 June 1951, the government appointed him President of the High Court, with effect from the following day.

[11] This lack of sympathy seems to have endured, the prison chaplain writing after Heffernan had served a considerable period behind bars that, 'after the lapse of seven years, people are still indignant that justice and law did not take their due course'. Report of interview with Patrick Heffernan by Thomas Browne, 28 March 1958, NAI, JUS/2005/170/8695.

[12] Heffernan benefited from another reversal of decision-making when his release came up for consideration. In April 1962 he was informed that there could be no mitigation of his sentence, yet five months later he was living in Birmingham with a brother who had undertaken to find him employment and accommodation. In 1965 he was questioned by the English police at the request of An Garda Síochána who needed to establish his whereabouts on a particular date in the context of an ongoing inquiry. Heffernan was indignant and wrote to his local TD who, as requested, intervened on his behalf with the Department of Justice. Letter from O.J. Flanagan to Peter [Berry], 8 February 1965, NAI, JUS/2005/170/8695.

of nature at that spot on the roadside, or more prosaically as he put it: 'Is it any harm to shit in here?'[13] The brother, who had paused at the gate to urinate before calling in to his sister, said that would be fine and Wall made his away along the road and out of sight.

The brother found the door unlocked and Bridget on the floor in a pool of blood with her spectacles and false teeth on the ground beside her. Drawers had been pulled open and rifled through and the contents of the house were disturbed. She died around three hours later in an ambulance that had been summoned to bring her to hospital for emergency treatment. Three weeks after the attack Wall handed himself over to the police, made a full confession, and brought them to the field where he had discarded the murder weapon.

An illegitimate child, Wall had been boarded out from the county home to a family in Kilkenny with whom he had lived for a number of years and where he returned on occasion afterwards. At the time of the murder he was staying with them and helping out around the farm in return for bed and board and a small amount of pocket money that he used for 'amusements and cigarettes'.[14] He was a man who had come into conflict with the law before, having spent time in reformatory school for theft and having been sentenced to six years penal servitude for wounding and shooting with intent to murder.

Wall was tried at the Central Criminal Court before Mr Justice Davitt. Concerns about his sanity were raised during the trial, but the jury was not persuaded by them and found him guilty without any recommendation to mercy. He initiated, but later abandoned, an appeal and his case came up for the government's consideration on Friday 29 May 1959. Davitt was invited to attend part of this meeting but an unsigned memorandum reveals that his presence was not recorded in the minutes.[15] Nor did the minutes record that Wall's case had been debated, implying that a decision was not made on this occasion. At its meeting on Tuesday 2 June

[13] Transcript of trial, examination of Thomas O'Keeffe, 11 May 1959, NAI, CCA 24/59.

[14] Transcript of trial, examination of Mary Cuddihy, 11 May 1959, NAI, CCA 24/59.

[15] Unsigned note, 30 May 1959, NAI, TSCH/3/S7788C/94.

the government decided to advise the president to commute Wall's sentence to penal servitude for life; he did so the same day.

We know nothing of the nature of Davitt's intervention but it seems reasonable to assume that serious thought was being given to allowing the execution go ahead if he was invited to brief the government and if consideration of the case straddled two meetings separated by a bank holiday weekend. It seems likely that he was invited because the government was unsure how to proceed given the rarity of executions by this time, and that his view was influential in causing at least some of the waverers to incline towards leniency.[16] If the jury had made a recommendation to mercy, the way forward may have been more obvious to the government. Another aggravating factor was Wall's history of violence. In any event, he was spared and on 12 June he was moved to Portlaoise Prison to serve his sentence. At the end of the following month he was certified insane and on 5 August 1959 he was transferred to the Central Mental Hospital.[17]

As discussed above, eight years previously Davitt had won the day for Heffernan when he engineered an invitation to the government meeting when his case was decided for a second time. Key differences on this occasion were that he had been the trial judge and that he was invited to attend the first meeting when Wall's case came up for consideration.[18] There is a difference between a judge manoeuvering to get a hearing in a case that he did not try when the government has made up its mind and

[16] Davitt had used a variety of legal ruses to save the lives of several men who appeared before military courts during the civil war and faced the death penalty (see Bureau of Military History, witness statement 1751, The Hon. Justice Cahir Davitt, at pp. 18–21, 43, 53–5, 68–70). As he summarized his position: 'I was not in favour of executing anyone if it could be avoided' (p. 83).

[17] It has not been possible to discover how long Wall stayed at the Central Mental Hospital (CMH) in Dundrum, County Dublin. However, a search of death registrations from 1960 to 2016 yielded one possible match by name and year of birth. William Wall, a 48-year-old single man who lived close to the CMH and worked as a lorry driver, took his own life by carbon monoxide poisoning in December 1978. This may be a false positive as it is possible that Wall was still alive in 2016 or had emigrated with the result that his death was recorded in another country. But it is plausible that he was discharged from Dundrum and remained in the area until his suicide.

[18] Similarly, in Boylan's case the judge engineered an appearance before the government after it had decided to allow the law to take its course and formally recorded that decision.

he wants to change it, and a judge being invited along when the matter is initially considered, perhaps to elaborate on the view expressed in his letter to the Minister for Justice or to give the government a sense of his position, in toto.

The first scenario would seem to constitute a clear interference with the separation of powers. The second is less clear as the judge was always invited to express a view and, while this was usually in writing to the minister who, in turn, gave a verbal report to the government, it was perhaps only a matter of degree if the judge's view was communicated in person to the government rather than mediated by the minister. Indeed, it could be argued that the latter position had something to recommend it, although for judges routinely to attend government meetings to discuss the implementation of sentences they had imposed would clearly breach the separation of powers doctrine.

For Boylan and Wall it might be argued that the judge was simply extending his role, taking an opportunity to elaborate more fully the view he was invited to give regarding the possibility of clemency. A case could be made that what was at issue here was simply a restatement and elaboration of the judicial view. But this is not wholly persuasive. The judge's involvement should have ended when his letter was written, if the invitation to write one was accepted. He did not have a role in the deliberative process which ensued, and nor should he have attempted to fashion one for himself. His view was one of the factors, albeit a very significant one, that the government weighed during its decision-making process. He was invited to give a view and, when he gave it, his input should have concluded. It was inappropriate for a judge to intervene to ensure that his view, above the other considerations, became the determinative one. The fact that judicial attendance at meetings of government was rare—I have found only three cases—and that it was hidden at the time, indicates that the practice was viewed with some unease by those who were aware of it.

Davitt's oath of office required him to 'uphold the Constitution and the laws' and to do so 'without fear or favour, affection or ill-will towards any man'.[19] It is arguable that he breached this in two respects. First, by favouring certain condemned persons for special treatment he was acting in an unfairly discriminatory

[19] Article 34.5.1 of Bunreacht na hÉireann.

fashion. Secondly, by allowing the judicial branch to intrude on territory that should have remained beyond its purview he was acting unconstitutionally. The popular sense would probably be that he was a humane man attempting to insert the virtue of mercy where he saw space to do so, or to create space if none was apparent, but his behaviour certainly suggests that he was not acting 'without fear or favour, affection or ill-will'.

A lesson learned?

Davitt had been the judge for William Gambon, the penultimate man to be hanged, whom he sentenced to death on 3 November 1948. This was the only one of five capital sentences imposed by Davitt that was carried out and the only one where he had not clearly expressed a view in favour of clemency. When passing sentence, Davitt said he was in complete agreement with the jury's verdict, which was guilty with no recommendation to mercy. In his letter to the minister the following week he stated he was 'not aware of any circumstances of mitigation in the case' (word underlined twice in handwritten original).[20] But, curiously, he advised 'for reasons which I think adequate' that the decision be deferred from the following day (Friday 12 November) until Tuesday. The reasons were not stated.

Did he believe that, legally speaking, there were no grounds for mitigation, but that Gambon might be spared anyway and that the first step was to inject a pause into the proceedings so that he could attempt to intervene? Did he try to exercise his influence behind the scenes? If so, this approach proved ineffective, and he may have learned that if such an occasion arose subsequently he would have to address the government in its entirety and in person.[21] Gambon's death may have been a factor in Davitt's subsequent behaviour regarding Heffernan and Wall.

[20] Letter from Cahir Davitt to Minister for Justice, 11 November 1948, NAI, JUS/18/11223A.

[21] The minutes of government meetings show that a decision was made regarding Gambon on 19 November (this was the next meeting after 12 November). It was based on a memorandum from the Minister for Justice dated 13 November, suggesting that the reason for the deferral was that the government was not ready to proceed on 12 November, rather than they were acceding to the judge's request.

Gambon did not appeal his conviction. Having killed his good friend, John Long, it was thought that he wanted to die. He committed the crime on 22 August 1948, was convicted on 3 November, and hanged on 24 November. It would have been very difficult for any judge to save the life of a man who seemed to welcome death. Further complicating matters, there was evidence of indirect legal pressure on the executive in his case. While Gambon was awaiting his fate in the condemned cell in Mountjoy Prison, Cearbhall Ó Dálaigh (former attorney general and later to be chief justice and then president of Ireland) wrote to the national newspapers justifying capital punishment (*Irish Times* and *Irish Independent*, 10 November 1948). This may have further stiffened the government's resolve.

Ó Dálaigh's letter was in response to a speech made by Seán MacBride condemning Gambon's forthcoming hanging and describing judicial execution as uncivilized and an ineffective deterrent (*Irish Times*, 25 October 1948). This speech sparked a row as MacBride was a government minister expressing a personal view about a decision made by government, in contravention of the principle of collective responsibility. In a parliamentary debate on the day that Gambon was hanged the Taoiseach was asked with biting humour if, to reduce the potential for future confusion, it might be possible 'to have some signal given, such as the flying of a flag over Government Buildings, whenever a Minister is speaking in a manner in which he is expected to be taken seriously?'[22]

When David Galvin's case came up for consideration in 1961 the Taoiseach (Seán Lemass) asked the Minister for Justice (Charles Haughey) to put the judge (Thomas Teevan) on standby in case the government wished to be addressed by him. The government minutes do not indicate that he was in attendance, but given that they were silent on his predecessors' presence they are not an entirely reliable guide to who was there. Lemass knew that judges sometimes made covert representations of this kind, having been Tánaiste and Minister for Industry and Commerce when Davitt addressed a meeting of government, at which he was present, regarding Wall's case.[23]

[22] Dáil Debates, 24 November 1948, Seán Lemass, vol. 113, col. 312.

[23] In a newspaper article written within days of the Court of Criminal Appeal upholding the death sentences on Noel and Marie Murray, James

A Belt of the Crozier

Judges were not the only elite group to attempt to have their voices heard when a decision was made with which they begged to differ. Bishops sometimes intervened, but with mixed results. A letter from a bishop was not always influential, but sometimes it was not intended to be; a tepid and equivocal missive could be sent to satisfy a parishioner but not to sway a government. The view of James Downey, Coadjutor Bishop of Ossory, prevailed in Aylward's case. The intervention came late in the day—there was no time to inform Pierrepoint of the change of plan before he left home—but it was decisive and Aylward lived (see Chapter 9).

On the other hand, Patrick O'Neill, Bishop of Limerick and a former professor of moral theology, had no success in Manning's case. His letter to the president was to the effect that he had been visited by Manning's heavily pregnant wife and her mother who implored him to write to the president to beg for mercy. The bishop agreed to write the letter and did so. He went no further than to state that he was acceding to this request, declining to express a personal view about whether the execution should go ahead. It was, at best, a perfunctory entreaty. There was an apologetic tone to the brief letter, which was penned in the Irish language, and concluded: 'I do not wish to interfere, in any manner, in matters of law and court but I do according to as I have been asked'.[24]

A letter from William Codd, Catholic Bishop of Ferns, on behalf of John Hornick was a half-hearted effort by any standard; the reader gains the impression that he was trying to assuage his conscience having not signed a petition in the case rather than to use any ecclesiastical muscle to save a man's life.[25] A Church of Ireland Bishop, the Most Revd Dr John Godfrey Fitzmaurice Day,

Downey observed (probably in relation to David Galvin) that, 'in one instance, it was said that a reprieve was decided only on the casting vote of the then Taoiseach, Mr. Lemass. Certainly the Lemass Government [23 June 1959 to 10 November 1966] was divided on the general question of capital punishment' (*Irish Times*, 3 August 1976).

[24] Translation by Dr Meidhbhín Ní Úrdail, UCD School of Irish, Celtic Studies and Folklore.

[25] Letter from W. Codd to Minister for Justice, 22 April 1937, NAI, JUS/18/2149.

met with de Valera the day before Hornick's execution, but it was too late and to no avail; the government had made up its mind the previous week. This rare display of interdenominational solidarity was not enough to save Hornick, a Protestant, from the gallows.

There were other episcopal interventions in cases where the likelihood of execution was remote. The Archbishop of Dublin intervened in Jane O'Brien's case out of concern that were she to be executed this would cast 'a sinister shadow' over the 'glorious celebrations' of the Eucharistic Congress that was taking place in the city at the time.[26] As a woman there was no realistic chance that she would ever stand on a scaffold.

Another Bishop of Ossory, Patrick Collier, wrote to the Taoiseach in response to the death sentence imposed on Michael Walsh for his part in the murder of Michael Devereux (see Chapter 5). He noted that he had refused to sign a public petition calling for Walsh's reprieve, preferring to send a private letter in which he could discharge his 'conscientious duty to recommend the exercise of mercy'. The bishop drew attention to the 'degrees of guilt among the condemned men' offering the view that 'Walsh was the least guilty. He is regarded more as a dupe and tool than as a murderer.' He signed off with the following plea: 'I do not think the Cause of Justice, or Public Order, would suffer by the reprieve of Walsh, and I earnestly recommend the exercise of mercy in his case to the Executive Council.'[27] He was silent as to the fate he believed should await Patrick Davern and George Plant, the other men sentenced to death in this case.

This intervention was successful but Davern was spared as well and it seems that the government's intention was to execute Plant and that the ultimate sanction was unlikely to be exacted in the other cases. This was not a case where a cabinet was resolute and then changed direction; it was not an example of caprice. This was a relatively easy request to accede to. Had the bishop asked for Plant to be spared this would have been quite a different matter.

[26] Letter from Edward J. Byrne to James Geoghegan, 25 June 1932, NAI, TSCH/3/S8653.

[27] Letter from Patrick Collier to Éamon de Valera, 27 February 1942, NAI, TSCH/3/S12741.

Lineage, leaks, and the bishop's palace

On 13 June 1940, Tomás MacCurtain was condemned to death for the murder of Garda John Roche in January of the same year. This sentence precipitated an outpouring of public emotion. MacCurtain evoked particular sympathy given how much his family had already suffered in the cause of Ireland. His father (also Tomás), Sinn Féin Lord Mayor of Cork, was assassinated in front of his family in March 1920 during the War of Independence. As one petitioner put it:

> I am sure you will appreciate the feelings of men like myself who through all the vicissitudes of political life have cherished memories of our fallen comrade as we wait in anticipation of the evil hour when an English hangman is to be employed by an Irish government to choke the breath of life in our comrade's son.[28]

Despite many such pleas the government decided to let MacCurtain hang and to brace itself for the storm of outrage that would ensue. Thomas Pierrepoint had arrived at Mountjoy Prison with his assistant and all of the necessary arrangements were in place. According to MacEoin (1997: 823) Pierrepoint had observed MacCurtain through the spy hole in his cell door. This would have enabled him to estimate the required drop and to prepare the ropes accordingly. It was also reported that a pine coffin had arrived in the prison to receive MacCurtain's remains.[29]

MacCurtain survived after some opportune litigation by his defence counsel, Seán MacBride, who exploited the legal order that his client was attempting to overthrow in order to vindicate his rights. MacBride (2005: 127) described how Tánaiste and Minister for Finance, Seán T. O'Kelly, with whom he was friendly, kept him 'fully informed' of developments within the cabinet, advising him to take any sort of delaying action he could in the courts. O'Kelly told him that a majority of the government was

[28] Letter from Patrick Brady to Éamon de Valera, 3 July 1940, NAI, TSCH/3/S11974.

[29] When the execution was cancelled the coffin was put back in storage only to be retrieved several months later to receive the body of another IRA man, Patrick McGrath (MacEoin 1997: 813) who stood before a firing party in Mountjoy Prison on 6 September 1940. Another coffin was required for Thomas Green who was executed in the same prison on the same day, also by the army's Eastern Command.

opposed to showing clemency and that 'if you could, some way or another, succeed in postponing the execution ... I will be able to swing things back in favour of a reprieve' (MacBride 2005: 127). That the second most senior government office holder was surreptitiously advising the lawyer for a condemned man whom the government of which he was part wished to hang was a flagrant breach of cabinet confidentiality.

MacBride followed this advice, seeking an order of habeas corpus late in the afternoon the day before the execution was scheduled to take place and, when it was refused, lodging an appeal moments before the court offices closed. This ploy had been anticipated and arrangements had been put in place to convene the Supreme Court that evening if it proved necessary to do so. However, when efforts were made to bring the court together it was impossible to make contact with Mr Justice Murnaghan who had gone for an extended walk with his dog. As a result the chief justice made an order postponing the execution (MacBride 2005: 129). In the interval that ensued, further pressure was brought to bear. By the time the Supreme Court dismissed the case a few days later the government's firmness of resolve had weakened and MacCurtain was spared.

It is not clear from the archival materials why the government had such a sudden and dramatic change of mind. MacEoin (1997: 823) shed some light on the matter, arguing that the day before MacCurtain was scheduled to hang, a parliamentary delegation consisting of five TDs and one senator, all from the condemned man's constituency of Cork, entered the office of the Minister for Justice, Gerald Boland, and informed him that they would resign from the Fianna Fáil party in the event that the execution went ahead. While elected members routinely made representations to ministers regarding matters of concern to their constituents, this differed in that it was a concerted attempt—underpinned by a credible threat—to influence the functioning of the executive in an area where the Oireachtas was precluded from having a say, namely the decision about clemency.

Cardinal Joseph MacRory, Archbishop of Armagh, Primate of All Ireland and a staunch republican, added his voice to the chorus of calls for MacCurtain to be spared. By MacEoin's (1997: 823) assessment this was the crucial intervention: 'While De Valera was skilled in brushing off representations, the one coming from Ara Coeili [sic; residence of Archbishop of Armagh] may have helped to save MacCurtain.'[30]

Examination of the minutes of government meetings gives a sense of how close MacCurtain came to losing his life. The first decision regarding his death sentence was taken on 4 July 1940, the day before his planned execution, and this was to grant a reprieve of a little more than one week.[31] The government met again on 5 July and 9 July. At its meeting on 10 July it decided—without explanation—to advise the president to commute the sentence. Had the decision to defer the execution not been made, MacCurtain's death sentence might not have been the subject of a government decision before it was carried out (unless it was intended to confirm it at the meeting on 4 July, although this would have been very late in the day). The government met ten times between MacCurtain's conviction and the decision to postpone his execution but his predicament was not formally considered at any of these meetings.

MacCurtain's invisibility in the minutes of government meetings sets him apart from other political prisoners whose fate was considered, minuted, and sealed promptly.[32] He was shown clemency through gritted teeth. This was a merciful act that did not emanate from a merciful disposition, thus satisfying the criteria for 'caprice' (see Chapter 2).

[30] MacRory was an influential churchman who was held in high regard, and viewed with great affection, by the Irish public. When he died, the *Irish Independent* observed that the country had lost 'a great shepherd, a far-seeing statesman, a patriotic Irishman, and a devoted Ulsterman' (15 October 1945). The *Irish Times* acknowledged him as 'one of the great Irishmen of our time' (15 October 1945).

[31] Schedule B to the minutes contains the Order, signed by de Valera as Taoiseach and bearing the official seal of the government.

[32] Peter Pringle was interned with MacCurtain in 1957. He recalled the latter telling him that he was not informed his sentence had been commuted until shortly after 8 a.m. on the morning he thought he was to be hanged, by which time he had written his final letters and prepared himself for the gallows (Pringle 2012: 162–3). If true—and allowances must, of course, be made for memories fading over time and a certain amount of dramatic licence—this implies that the authorities delayed passing on the news of the commutation when it was made on 10 July until the rescheduled execution date of 13 July. It seems unlikely that MacCurtain's legal team would not have got word to him more swiftly—when his execution was postponed on the evening of 4 July his barrister visited him in the prison 'immediately afterwards' (MacBride 2005: 129).

MacCurtain was fortunate to be convicted two months before military courts were introduced (see Chapter 5). Had he been dealt with under their auspices it is unlikely that he would have survived as there was no right of appeal and the government met quickly post-conviction to commute the sentence or to advise the adjutant general to put the necessary arrangements in place regarding the empanelling of a firing party. Under such a scenario he would almost certainly have received the soldier's death that seemed to be his destiny and that would have consolidated his family's status as heroes of republicanism.

Entreaties from His Excellency

There was one case where the president lobbied the government. Michael Manning's file contains a handwritten letter, in Irish, from Seán T. O'Kelly, to the Taoiseach, Éamon de Valera.[33] This communication was prompted by the letter to the president from the Bishop of Limerick, referred to in the previous section. The president did more than simply forward the bishop's letter, he called for Manning to be spared: 'I would greatly wish to save the life of this person young Manning who has been sentenced to death if at all possible.'[34] He expressed his understanding of how difficult it must be for the Taoiseach making a judgement in cases like this but left him in no doubt as to his personal preference, which was that he be advised to commute the sentence.

At worst, this was a violation of the separation of powers doctrine as it involved the president attempting to influence the executive. At best, it indicated a lack of clarity around the respective roles of president and government as the former was bound to accept the decision of the latter and had no input into the deliberative process. This unprecedented intervention cannot be attributed to a lack of familiarity with the procedures as O'Kelly had been president since 1945 and had previously commuted several death sentences to penal servitude for life. He would have been well aware of the constitutional limits to his powers and the fact that when it came to matters of clemency he was a mere cipher. O'Kelly went beyond what the Constitution permitted. Had it

[33] 10 April 1954, NAI, TSCH/3/S15641.

[34] Translation by Dr Meidhbhín Ní Úrdail, UCD School of Irish, Celtic Studies and Folklore.

come to public attention at the time, such interference might have precipitated a political brouhaha. (President O'Kelly was incautious in committing his views to paper and one wonders whether on previous occasions he, or other presidents, had expressed similar sentiments in person or over the telephone.)

The government considered Manning's case on 3 March 1954. The meeting lasted only thirty-five minutes (12.30 p.m. to 1.05 p.m.) which would suggest that a consensus was arrived at without too much difficulty. The case was reconsidered on 13 April 1954, possibly as a result of the letter from the president the previous day enclosing the correspondence from Bishop O'Neill and making his own view clear. The government affirmed its original decision not to cancel the execution. Clearly, judges were more persuasive than bishops. Or a personal appearance was necessary to persuade waverers. Or, when it came to temporal matters, less weight was accorded to clerical interventions.[35]

A note accompanied the government decision for the Taoiseach to telephone the president as soon as possible in light of his letter and the outcome of the meeting. The Taoiseach did so on the afternoon of 13 April, after the government had concluded its deliberations. One wonders whether the Taoiseach's urgent telephone call to the president was to upbraid him for overstepping the mark and to remind him of the limits to his powers or to explain why, despite his sincere entreaties, he was not going to be asked to commute the sentence to penal servitude for life. (It was probably the latter given how close the two men were and how long their political careers had been intertwined.)

[35] As Manning's fate shows, not every case that received further consideration resulted in a different outcome. Neither was reconsideration invariably prompted by an intervention from a judge or a bishop. In Dermot Smyth's case the government decided on 3 January 1939 not to recommend that the sentence be commuted. The condemned man made a statement on 4 January implicating others in the killing of Cornelius Dennehy and stating that he was not the actual gunman. This was investigated by An Garda Síochána and the judge's opinion was sought. He felt that the claim did not 'throw any doubt on the verdict of the jury' and that he saw no reason to modify his view which was that this was a callous and calculated murder that lacked extenuating circumstances. Report prepared by John O'Byrne, 5 January 1939, NAI, JUS/18/3138A & B. After consultation with the attorney general and Taoiseach, the minister brought the matter back to the Executive Council and the decision was affirmed on 6 January. Smyth was hanged the following day.

There is no evidence that clemency decisions were related to the electoral cycle in that they were not more likely when a general election was imminent. But Manning may be an exception to this rule. He was hanged on 20 April 1954, four days before the dissolution of the 14th Dáil. The general election took place on 18 May. Was de Valera attempting to flex his muscles in the hope that this might enhance his party's prospects in the polls? Did he believe that it would be electorally advantageous to appear resolute on matters of law and order? Did he have to advise the president in the same telephone conversation that, contrary to his wishes, Manning would be hanged, and that he would be going to the people and the president would have to dissolve the Dáil? This may explain why Manning was executed, even though he was young, drunk, pitiful, the crime was obviously unpremeditated, his 22-year-old wife was pregnant, and the president wanted him spared.

Had the country not been about to vote, Manning's chances of surviving might have been greater. So too was he unfortunate that the key officeholders—de Valera was Taoiseach and Boland was Minister for Justice—were well used to executions. Robert Stevenson's application for leave to appeal was refused on 24 June 1954, a little more than three weeks after a new government had been formed, and the president was advised to commute his sentence. Had Manning's execution been delayed, he might have been spared. Had Stevenson been convicted a month earlier, he might have been hanged. If the hanging was in any way calculated to curry favour with voters the plan backfired as Fianna Fáil was not returned to power.

O'Kelly's attempt to influence a government decision may have been an unprecedented act for a president but, when he was governor general, Domhnall ua Buachalla made representations to the Minister for Justice, P.J. Ruttledge, in John Fleming's case. Acknowledging that this was a matter in which he had no influence and that he was acting in a personal capacity at the behest of relatives of the condemned man, he noted that there was no direct evidence of Fleming's guilt and that this might provide a loophole.[36] This (somewhat guarded) exhortation was unsuccessful. Similarly, in Denis Leen's case the governor general, Timothy Healy, when forwarding correspondence passed to him by the

[36] Letter from Domhnall ua Buachalla to Pádraig [Patrick Ruttledge], 1 January 1934, NAI, JUS/H234/6221B.

Colonial Office in London, asked that the plea for mercy from the condemned man's wife be given consideration, but this seemed more of a formality than a full-blooded request for the former soldier's life to be spared (see Chapter 9).

Judges Again, Now Expediting Release

Two years after Agnes McAdam's trial, the judge (George Gavan Duffy) took it upon himself to write to the minister recommending reduction of the life sentence to a term of five or seven years. This letter triggered the decision to release her early. Interestingly, Gavan Duffy wrote his letter on 15 April 1948, two months after Seán MacEoin took office as minister. The incumbent for the previous eight-and-a-half years, Fianna Fáil's Gerald Boland, might have been less open to special pleading from a former political adversary.

Mary Daly's release on 22 December 1953 was prompted by a long letter from Mr Justice McLoughlin who acted as her counsel and had, the previous year, been appointed to the High Court. This was an early intervention after his elevation to the bench. Again the separation of powers was blurred in that a decision that should be reserved to the executive was influenced by a member of the judiciary. Counsel did not write until he had assumed judicial office; was this intended to shroud his lobbying in a cloak of supposed impartiality?[37]

When considering the extent to which judges involved themselves in executive functions and vice versa, it is worth noting that s. 23 of the Criminal Justice Act, 1951 allowed the government to commute or remit any punishment except a capital one and to delegate this power to the Minister for Justice. This practice had been common prior to being placed on a statutory footing. In 1995 the High Court found that the power was being used

[37] In Mary Kiernan's case, by contrast, the Minister for Justice took the initiative, asking the department's secretary to write to the judge less than four months post-conviction, to enquire 'whether there are any mitigating circumstances in this case which would now render the prisoner a proper object of mercy'. Letter from H.J. O'Friel to Mr Justice O'Byrne, 3 February 1927, NAI, JUS/H234/1491. The following day the judge advised that she be released 'after a few months from now' and, accordingly, she regained her freedom on 1 May 1927.

routinely—around 5,000 petitions were being sent to the minister each year for remission of fines and commutation or remission of prison sentences—and had become 'a parallel or alternative system of justice'. The court concluded that henceforth it must be exercised 'sparingly and for special reasons with proper maintenance of records'. In reaching its decision, the court recognized that the minister was not required to exercise the power in public, but that 'for the exercise of any power, whether constitutional, statutory or otherwise, some accountability is essential'.[38]

It could be argued that the correlation between the penalty awarded by the court and paid by the offender was more imperfect in Ireland than elsewhere given widespread petitioning. Politicians have long been comfortable lobbying ministers for the early release of their constituents.[39] If citizens felt it was appropriate for their elected representative to endeavour to get the minister to mitigate the consequences of a criminal conviction or to speed a relative's release, perhaps they would not have been troubled by the thought that judges and bishops were occasionally making similar efforts on behalf of condemned persons.

So who were the beneficiaries of the clemency decision? A categorization of these fortunate murderers is offered in the next two chapters.

[38] *Brennan v Minister for Justice* [1995] 1 IR 612.

[39] This practice has endured. In January 2007, a junior minister wrote to the Minister for Justice, Equality and Law Reform on behalf of two constituents who were seeking early release from prison. One was a child rapist, the other a murderer. In the ensuing controversy it emerged that, since entering parliament in 1992, he had sent more than 200,000 letters from his constituency office dealing with a wide range of voter concerns (O'Donnell 2011: 496).

8

Undoing Death I

When the law has run its course and a clear direction appears to have been set, the executive can always intervene to ensure arrival at an alternative destination. It cannot make the legal consequences fiercer but it can do a great deal to soften them. Morris characterized clemency decisions in capital cases as 'often fortuitous and discriminatory' (cited in Lavinsky 1965: 39). The argument presented throughout this book is less emphatic. There is a discernible pattern to these decisions in Ireland, the key independent variables can be identified, but occasionally caprice plays a role. They are not both fortuitous *and* discriminatory, but a few are the former and many are the latter; there is a trend but it can be bucked.

Certain characteristics predictably accrued to the prisoner's advantage and these are reviewed in this chapter and the next. But, even when taken into account, there remained cases where the outcome was wayward, where the sentence would have been carried out had it not been for unexpected events. It cannot be denied that there was an element of luck involved. While one could not predict with complete confidence how the government would deal with a particular case, the most pertinent factors emerge from an examination of case disposal in the aggregate. When justice considerations were raised by the trial judge, they generally prevailed (cabinets were in no hurry to retry cases). Whether mercy would be exercised was more difficult to anticipate, especially where IRA members were concerned. Caprice, by definition, was unpredictable.

A Cruel Lottery?

Strange (1995) described capital punishment in Canada as a 'lottery'. Similarly, in a study of the Australian State of Victoria,

Justice, Mercy, and Caprice: Clemency and the Death Penalty in Ireland. First Edition. Ian O'Donnell. © Ian O'Donnell 2017. Published 2017 by Oxford University Press.

Douglas and Laster (1991: 155) held the practice to be 'the most lawless of sentences. It is indeed death by lottery'. The situation in Ireland cannot be represented thus. The defining feature of a lottery is that every outcome has the same odds of occurring; it is a random process. If the process is random then every person sentenced to death has the same chance of having their sentence executed. But whether clemency was granted was not a matter of chance; it was structured in clear ways, usually by justice considerations and then by gender. If every woman was a winner, as in Ireland after 1925, the process cannot be described as akin to lottery.

Scrutinizing the Canadian case, Strange (1995: 596) observed that, 'cabinets conducted case reviews like primitive lotteries—as if they drew lots to determine whether or not to execute'. She elaborated that the results were not random because the range of legal and extra-legal factors considered in each case influenced the decision in predictable ways. But surely this is the opposite of a lottery? Strange (1995: 596) acknowledged that there were 'patterns of severity' but expressed surprise at the way individual cases were resolved which went against the trend. However, the general pattern can still be valid even if it does not apply in particular cases and to argue otherwise is to risk committing the ecological fallacy. Strange (1995: 600) argued that: 'In spite of governmental assurances of fair and impartial reviews, patterns of mercy and severity were nevertheless discernible'. But is there necessarily a contradiction here? Fair reviews could lead to patterned outcomes if similar factors were accorded similar weight. Also, if there were discernible outcomes, how could this be described as a lottery?

In clemency cases in Ireland the parameters were clearly set: women were never hanged (with one exception); judicial recommendations to mercy were always accepted (with one exception); infant lives were not greatly valued; political offenders met with a bifurcated response in that if they were not put to death swiftly they were released swiftly; and the clemency process was seen as a way of adjusting trial outcomes so that they were better aligned with popular notions of deserved punishment. The government had the freedom to decide what to do in each case but the results were predictable most of the time. A pattern of structured decision-making culminated in a binary outcome that remained vulnerable to unexpected influences. What Strange described was akin to a multivariate analysis where the weights associated with the different variables could, cumulatively, predict the outcome with a reasonable degree of confidence. This is another way of conceptualizing the repeated drawing of lots that she recounted.

It was unusual for women to kill outside the family circle and, when they did, it was sometimes to clear the way for a new relationship. Their murders tended to be intimate and in accordance with what were considered to be appropriate gender roles at a time when divorce was impossible and illegitimacy was scandalous. It was understandable that a woman would wish to create a situation where she was a widow so that she could marry again (or that her intended was a widower so that he was free to take her hand), or where it did not enter into public knowledge that she had become a mother outside wedlock.

It was exceptional for the perpetrator and victim not to have been personally acquainted. Often they were friends, family members, work colleagues, or neighbours. Excluding the political murders, there were only seven cases where there was no history of prior contact and even in these cases there was a contractual relationship of kinds between the parties. One involved a prostitute and her client (Robert Stevenson), another an abortionist (Mary Cadden) and her client, and a third a taxi driver and his passenger (James Tierney). Two others involved soldiers whose defence was that they had been following orders (Denis Leen and James Murray). One involved a soldier (Patrick Fagan) who shot an officer who had denied him somewhere to stay overnight and demanded the surrender of his rifle. There was only one case where the perpetrator and victim had nothing in common. This was Mary Daly's hammer attack on a pensioner at prayer in church.

Murderers who avoided the noose fell into one of six categories with a clear gradient in how sympathetically they were viewed, as indicated by the duration of their coercive confinement and the likelihood that the judge and jury would recommend mercy. At one end of the scale were those who destroyed an unwanted child, 92 per cent of whom aroused the sympathy of judge and jury and who were denied their liberty for forty-four months, on average. At the other end of the scale were those whose treatment was capricious, only 20 per cent of whom received a joint recommendation to mercy and whose average period of confinement was 115 months. These trends are summarized in Table 8.1 and

Table 8.1 Avoiding a date with the hangman

	Number	Months coercively confined (median)	Judge and jury recommend mercy (per cent)
Burden of unwanted child	13	44	92
Sex and jealousy	11	88	60
Dreadful deeds, turbulent times	7	72	60
Legally sane, strikingly odd	7	134	57
Chivalry	5	88	50
Caprice	5	115	20

Note: Forty-nine persons were tried by jury and spared. Thomas Kelly's case could not be categorized.

the categories are dealt with in descending order of importance in this chapter and the next.[1]

Thomas Kelly was the only person who could not be categorized. He was convicted of the murder of Patrick Henry, whose battered and burned body was found in the cottage they shared. The conviction was overturned on appeal and the jury failed to agree at a retrial. Tried a third time, he was convicted again and sentenced to death. There was doubt about the safety of the conviction as several witnesses claimed to have seen the dead man the day after his murder was believed to have taken place, by which time Kelly was known to be some distance away from the crime scene. The jury made a recommendation to mercy and the judge endorsed this call.

The Burden of an Unwanted Child

The jury recommended mercy every time an unwanted child was murdered and the judge endorsed this recommendation in all but one case (Kate Owens). The perpetrator was usually, but

[1] The vignettes that follow are based on the individual case files listed in the bibliography. Direct quotations, which are used sparingly for the reasons set out in Chapter 1, are attributed to the relevant primary source.

not always, the mother.[2] On one occasion a newborn was killed by his father. When Edward O'Connor's girlfriend, Margaret Steele, discovered she was pregnant she asked him to marry her but he refused, possibly because she had a child four years previously with another man. When her son, Paul, was born she told O'Connor to find someone to adopt him, and on the night of his christening O'Connor called to her house on his bicycle. An argument ensued about whether a bicycle was a suitable mode of transportation and father and son departed after midnight in a taxi paid for by Miss Steele. By this stage it was too late to bring the baby to the house where he hoped the child might be taken in and, in his panicked wanderings, O'Connor, who was anxious that his family would not learn of his predicament as an unmarried father, found himself near the banks of the River Tolka in which he drowned Paul. His plight attracted sympathy and he spent only three years in prison.

On another occasion the perpetrator was a grandmother. Mary Somerville took her daughter Mary Anne's child from her immediately after birth, placed her in a shopping bag with three heavy stones and dropped her into a well near the house they shared. Perhaps from bitter personal experience she knew the hardships that an illegitimate child would face and wished to spare another generation the same rejection; the stain of illegitimacy was remarkably durable. The jury deliberated for a little over half an hour and returned a verdict of guilty with a strong recommendation to mercy. Mr Justice O'Byrne observed that while he believed there were no grounds for mercy he also believed that it should be exercised. As he explained this peculiar logic:

> If the life of a newly-born baby is as sacred as the life of an adult person (a fact which seems to me to be incapable of denial), there seems to be no valid reason for the exercise of the prerogative of mercy in this case. On the other hand, the accused is a woman and, however illogical it may be, this is a matter which cannot be overlooked. In addition, the date of the execution has, I understand, been fixed for the 23rd day

[2] Maguire (2016: 63) found that only eighteen of more than 600 defendants in infanticide and related cases from the 1920s to the 1950s were spouses or sexual partners of the woman whose child was killed. Like the women, they were treated leniently by the criminal justice system, indicating that victim age, as well as perpetrator gender, was a pertinent consideration.

of December—two days before Christmas. These two circumstances would incline me to exercise the prerogative in this case.[3]

The government accepted the judge's recommendation and, for the first time, the president (who had replaced the governor general) was advised to commute a sentence to penal servitude for life. On the second anniversary of her scheduled execution Somerville was released on licence to the Bethany Home in the Dublin suburb of Rathgar where she stayed for less than two months before taking up residence with a son of hers in Northern Ireland.[4]

On the third occasion where the killer of an infant was not the mother, it was an aunt. Rose Edwards acted in concert with her sister Elizabeth to kill the latter's two-week old daughter after her discharge from the county home to which she had admitted herself under a false name. Before leaving the county home she was warned to look after the child properly and not to abandon her but when the police visited her a fortnight later there was no baby to be found. Her parents expressed ignorance of any pregnancy stating that they thought she was in hospital on account of appendicitis. The fact that they did not question her as to the purpose of the Garda visit, had not enquired as to why she had been in hospital or visited her there, suggests a desire to remain blind to the facts.

While a body was never discovered it was believed that the child had been thrown into the River Suck. Rose spent twenty months in prison after her conviction before being discharged to the care of her parents. Elizabeth spent longer in prison (twenty-nine months) and a further fifteen months with the nuns before she too rejoined her parents. There was some reluctance to release Elizabeth for fear that she lacked the moral fortitude to prevent herself being preyed upon by unscrupulous men with the obvious attendant risks.

Response

All of those who killed infants received lenient treatment. While these were shocking killings, they resulted from the perpetrators

[3] Note re: Mary Somerville by John O'Byrne, 10 December 1938, NAI, JUS/18/3110.

[4] The Bethany Home was a residential institution run by evangelical Protestants for unmarried mothers and their children, and for female ex-prisoners.

following the rules of an intolerant and stigmatizing society. If anything, their actions indicated a profound allegiance to norms that were contrary to their own, and more particularly their children's, interests. What saved these murderers was not so much their gender or relationship with the victim, but an unspoken acknowledgement that their predicament was a result of society's moral strictures and a low value placed on infant life.

The mother who brutally erased the life of her newborn child was the object of clemency as a matter of routine. Echoing Kant's view that infanticide merited lenient treatment on account of the social circumstances that fostered it (see Chapter 3), an editorial in the newspaper of record, published two days after the commutation of the death sentences imposed on the Edwards sisters, noted that:

> We do not advocate leniency towards infanticide. We hold, however, that one of its chief causes is the cruel and often hypocritical attitude of Irish public opinion—especially in the rural areas and small towns—towards moral lapses, and we hold that such intolerance is the chief of all crimes. The fact that an Irishwoman who has sinned should be less frightened of the guilt of infanticide than of the opinion of her neighbourhood is an awful indictment of our civilisation. (*Irish Times*, 20 May 1935)

The same editorial noted the ambivalent public attitude towards 'political' murderers and the comparatively lenient treatment extended to them. (The six IRA members whose sentences were commuted prior to 1964 served less time coercively confined—collectively—than Elizabeth Hannon, a simple-minded domestic servant, who killed her hours-old son in August 1927.)

On occasion the child was believed to be the product of rape as in the case of Deborah Sullivan who delivered a baby boy early one February morning on the side of a mountain in Killorglin, County Kerry as she made her way to the county home. When the child was born she left him on the mountain and he was found in a stream two days later. Sullivan returned home where she had another son to care for, said nothing about what had happened, and carried on with her daily chores. She recounted feeling weak and frightened and having put the baby in a bush but could not explain the drowning.

The jury returned a verdict of guilty with a strong recommendation to mercy. The judge advocated that early effect be given to the recommendation of the jury. The government accepted these proposals and Sullivan was transferred on 2 November 1929 to Our Lady's Home for Discharged Female Prisoners run by the Sisters of Charity of St Vincent De Paul on Dublin's Henrietta Street. She was released in June 1932 with Mary Moynihan (see later under 'Sex and Jealousy') in honour of the Eucharistic Congress. Anxious about the reaction she might face from neighbours if she was reunited with her family, Sullivan chose to take up a paid situation in another of the Sisters' houses.

Repeat offenders

Sometimes the women sentenced to death for murdering their offspring had given birth before and the children had not survived. Elizabeth Hannon returned from ten o'clock Mass in Mullingar to the house where she was employed as a domestic servant. Feeling sick in the stomach she went to the lavatory where she delivered a male child. She buried the child alive in a sandpit at the rear of the house, fracturing his skull with the stones placed on top of him. Two previous children had each, she claimed, been stillborn. Hannon spent less than three years in prison but another thirty in the convent to which she was discharged.[5]

Mary Kiernan left the county home in Mullingar with a healthy 12-day-old daughter named Bridget whom she threw into a canal on account of what she described in her petition for early release as a sense of 'shame and disgrace'.[6] There was scepticism about the extent to which her actions could be attributed to a fear of being

[5] This period of confinement contrasted dramatically with the judge's observation that: 'If she had been found not guilty of the murder, but guilty of concealment of birth, I would have imposed a sentence on her of six months imprisonment'. Letter from W.J. Johnston to Minister for Justice, 12 December 1927, NAI, JUS/H234/2016. It was also a marked departure from the view expressed by the Minister for Justice that: 'It should be made clear to the girl that while she must be kept in the home for a substantial period of time, she will be released in a few years, the number being dependant [sic] on her own conduct' File note by James FitzGerald-Kenney, 27 June 1930, NAI, JUS/H234/2016.

[6] Petition of Mary Kiernan to Minister for Home Affairs [sic], 31 January 1927, NAI, JUS/H234/1491. These were frugal times and the printed form upon which the petition was written was still made out to the 'Minister for Home Affairs' even though this office had been replaced by that of the Minister for Justice in 1924. New stationery required stronger justification than an out-of-date addressee!

socially ostracized as: 'It is against the prisoner to some extent that she had an illegitimate child in 1919. It cannot be argued that she was overcome by the overwhelming shame of a first lapse.'[7] This first child died. (By my estimation the mother was around fifteen at this time.) The jury was not clear about the relationship between moral culpability and legal responsibility, initially returning a verdict of 'guilty but not responsible for her actions', which the judge refused to accept. She was released from prison after six months.

Kate Owens was a serial killer of her children. On 10 May 1943 she was charged with the murders of three infants whose corpses were found buried in her garden. Nine years earlier she had been convicted of concealment of birth, bringing the total number of dead babies to four; a brutal form of family planning. The judge did not lend his support to the jury's call for mercy, writing to the secretary of the Department of Justice in the following terms:

> ... the evidence clearly pointed to a calculated and premeditated killing of this child—the fate suffered by three or four illegitimate children previously born to this defendant—no other verdict was reasonably possible on the evidence. I have no comments to make on the Jury's recommendation to mercy, as I deem this to be the sole prerogative of the Minister and the Government.[8]

The tenor of Mr Justice Haugh's letter is clear. He believes that the jury came to the correct conclusion and he does not add his voice to their call for lenient treatment. The judge donned the black cap when passing sentence, a practice that had been discontinued some years earlier by a number of his colleagues (see Chapter 4). This may be a further indication that he was not averse to the law taking its course. Owens' release was delayed until she had passed the menopause. It was felt that if she was released while still fertile this might place another child in danger:

> ... the prisoner's history tends to show that she has not the will power to resist her physical impulses and her release now might only result in a second conviction for child murder. I think the question of her release should be deferred for another two years: she is now about forty-one years of age and perhaps by that time she may have passed the child-bearing stage.[9]

[7] Note to Minister, 7 February 1927, NAI, JUS/H234/1491.

[8] Letter from Kevin Haugh to Mr Roche, 22 November 1943, NAI, JUS/18/6678A & B.

[9] Note on file, 10 November 1947, NAI, JUS/18/6678A & B.

The minister agreed with this sentiment and in due course, two years later, with evidence from the prison doctor that the menopause was approaching, she was released to a situation that had been found for her by the Sisters of Charity.

Catherine Ahearne was unusual in that she was married and it was her husband's child she disposed of. But the child had been conceived out of wedlock and the marriage was solemnized the month before the birth. It was not a successful union and she continued to live with her parents and siblings after she was wed, with her new husband staying occasionally in the short period between marriage, murder, and imprisonment. The husband, described as 'a rather lazy and worthless man',[10] left for Australia soon after the trial and some half-hearted efforts to reunite the pair came to naught. Ahearne was discharged from prison to the care of her parents four years after her conviction and the last word on her husband was that he was tramping the roads in his adopted country where he had succumbed to the effects of drink. Perhaps she avoided transfer to a religious institution because her child was legitimate so there was no moral stain to be removed?

Mary Anne Keane was married but her husband had sent her to the county home when he discovered she was pregnant with another man's child. She drowned her 3-week-old son, Patrick, in a bog hole on her way back to her husband's house when her lying-in ended. She spent seventeen months in prison after her conviction before being discharged to the Sisters of Charity Magdalen Asylum in Donnybrook on 4 November 1930. There were concerns about her low mentality and 'loose moral character' which, together with a lack of resettlement options, meant she remained coercively confined until at least 1939 (and perhaps as late as 1963).[11] She would have been discharged earlier had it been possible to effect a reconciliation with her husband.

[10] Petition—Catherine Aherne [sic], 27 November 1930, NAI, JUS/H234/2603A.

[11] She was still with the nuns in Donnybrook in May 1939, her husband was refusing to accept her and, given her limited capacity and a family history of psychiatric disorder, there was little prospect of securing her a position as a domestic servant. Her file was next accessed, and formally 'put away' by the Department of Justice, in November 1963. It is not known why her situation came to attention again and whether she had remained with the Sisters of Charity during the intervening period. The calculation of her time in coercive confinement (Table 10.3) is based on the minimum duration of stay.

Five of these births took place in hospitals and, as a consequence, the babies were older and more robust when they were killed and there could be no pretence that they had been stillborn. This indicates the desperate straits that these women thought themselves in—they had given birth in an institution, the birth was registered, the possibility of successfully covering their traces was slim, but they destroyed the child anyway. Typically, they were admitted under an assumed name and may have felt that this would have prevented detection. Given that some of them used the putative father's name it is unlikely that this was ever going to be a foolproof strategy. Sometimes the staff expressed concern about the prospects for the child. While in hospital there was some chance that they could conceal their true status as single and shamed; if they returned to their families with a surprise baby any prospect of successful subterfuge evaporated. None of those who gave birth in the county home actually arrived home with the baby.

Margaret Finn provides a good example of the tragic circumstances in which women destroyed their babies. She lived with her mother, illegitimate brother, and cousin, Brigid Crowe, in a dilapidated hut in Ruan, County Clare. The three women shared a bed. Informing Brigid that she had a pain in her stomach, the pair hurried to a field behind the house so that the baby could be delivered and done away with before the mother's attention was drawn to their absence. Margaret went down on her knees for ten minutes, the child arrived, and she asked for a bootlace which she tied around his neck. The dead child was placed under stones in the field. Brigid raised concern about the baby not being baptized and that 'it would be in darkness all its life time' to which Margaret replied 'Let it the bastard'. She rounded up the goats and the two young women went in for breakfast with the apparently unsuspecting mother.[12]

Both were charged with murder. Tried separately, Crowe was acquitted. What is shocking is how sordid the whole event was, and yet in some respects it was so mundane. Also notable was the shroud of silence. The mother who shared her bed did not know she was pregnant. The two accused did not talk about the

[12] Statement of Bridget [sic] Crowe, 30 June 1930, NAI, JUS/H234/3118A & B.

baby afterwards, except on one occasion when it was suggested they would go to the body. When convicted and invited to say why the sentence of death should not be imposed, 'the prisoner made no reply, but gripped the dock rail with one hand and wept bitterly'.[13]

Elizabeth Doran had been widowed for seven years when she gave birth to a son in the Rathdrum County Home on 3 March 1926. Twelve days later, on her way home, she strangled the child and buried his remains at the side of the road. Two explanations were offered for her conduct: that she wished 'to conceal her fall from her neighbours' or that she wanted 'to rid herself of the burden of the child's maintenance'.[14] The post-mortem examination found milk in the baby's stomach indicating that he had been fed within two hours of his death. This captures the curious combination of care and callousness that characterized the case. Was he fed to stop him mewling, to settle him before he was dispatched? A woman of low intelligence, Doran was certified insane shortly after her conviction and transferred to the Central Mental Hospital.

Reform

Murderous mothers were pitied but understood. They were seen as vulnerable women who had already suffered greatly and who did not deserve to die. Further downplaying the harm they had caused, their crimes were usually referred to as infanticide rather than murder. Even in the decades before infanticide legislation was introduced this conduct was viewed as less than a capital offence. Often they moved from prison to another form of institutional care and these transfers were motivated by the same kind of paternalism that saved them from the noose: it was to protect the poor creatures from themselves. Women were seen as not fully rational adults, as persons who should not be held to the same standards as men for their behaviour.

The more reflective government members must have appreciated that these women's conduct resulted from profound shame

[13] *Irish Times*, 4 March 1931.

[14] Department of Justice memorandum, 19 June 1926, NAI, JUS/H234/1297.

at their failure to live up to the social and sexual mores that were privileged by the new nation. By reacting as they did, they showed a deep awareness of what constituted acceptable conduct in the austere, doctrinaire Ireland that was emerging, and for this it would have been hypocritical—to say nothing of being disproportionately severe—to make them suffer further. The religious sensibilities of the Catholic men who were government members may have been troubled by the fact that babies who had not been baptized would spend eternity in Limbo. This was another burden that their mothers would have to bear, which allowed of no temporal relief.

Women who killed their babies seldom initiated appeals. It seems to have been generally understood that if they threw themselves on the mercy of the government they would be spared and that there was no need to cause the state the additional expense (preparing transcripts, allocating court time, paying lawyers) and inconvenience of an appeal. The Edwards sisters' case was appealed because there was an important legal issue at stake, namely the absence of a victim's body, and Christina Russell's appeal—heard, unusually, after the sentence had been commuted—was on the grounds that the dead child was not hers and that the cause of death had not been established. Russell drowned her 20-day-old son Thomas on her way home from the South Dublin Union hospital. She has the distinction of the shortest interval between conviction and commutation: sentenced to death on 27 November 1930 after the jury deliberated for a quarter of an hour, the death sentence was commuted the following day.

O'Brien (2006: 258) observed that: 'In Ireland each reprieve represented at best a postponement and at worst a refusal to deal intelligently with the whole issue of capital punishment; each execution reflected yet another failure by the Irish people to face their own shortcomings.' The first part of this statement applies with particular force to the tardiness with which the problem of infanticide was addressed; indeed by the time legislation was introduced the problem had largely disappeared (Table 1.1). When the Infanticide Act, 1949 came into force it was more a belated attempt to bring the law into alignment with the long-established practice than a humanitarian response to the plight of distressed women for whom there was a wide gulf between what was morally and legally deemed to be an appropriate punishment. It may have been easier to deal with the 'problem' once it was no longer pressing.[15]

Perhaps the government was slow to move on infanticide because a view persisted that there were deserving and undeserving cases and that it might be necessary on some occasion to discriminate between them? An argument along these lines is not entirely persuasive as even a multiple baby killer like Kate Owens was spared and did not have an overly long stay in custody (she was discharged to a convent after sixty-five months).

The Infanticide Act, 1949 was intended, in the words of the Minister for Justice:

> ... to eliminate all the terrible ritual of the black cap and the solemn words of the judge pronouncing sentence of death in those cases ... where it is clear to the Court and to everybody, except perhaps the unfortunate accused, that the sentence will never be carried out.[16]

That it took so long for the legislation to be introduced says a great deal about the stigma associated with the crime and the reluctance to discuss the problem let alone to deal with it.

Perhaps there was a view, not made explicit, that any weakening of the legal regime might promote illegitimacy, something that the young state, with its emphasis on piety and celibacy, would have wished to forestall. The middle-aged men who attended meetings of the government between 1922 and 1949 would doubtless have had little enthusiasm for discussing a taboo issue such as sex outside marriage which they may have found morally repugnant. While there was sympathy for the perpetrators, especially in the minority of cases where a murder conviction ensued and the death sentence was imposed, this was not enough to prompt them to take action.

Sigler (2016: 242) noted that: 'Where justice itself is fundamentally misconceived, the fitting response is not a plea for charity, but the full-throated roar of moral indignation.' The absence of such a 'full-throated roar', on account of the strict moral code of

[15] Given that the statute eventually enacted drew heavily on the laws introduced in England and Wales in 1922 and 1938, and that the need for it had been identified soon after independence, it is difficult to understand why it was delayed for so long other than a reluctance to accept that if legislation of this kind was required, the moral strictures of independent Ireland were being ignored, with lethal consequences.

[16] Seanad Éireann debates, 7 July 1949, General MacEoin, vol. 36, col. 1472.

the day, meant that mothers who killed their babies continued to hear the sentence of death pronounced in circumstances where no one believed that the macabre ritual would continue to its stated conclusion. Because their plight roused insufficient indignation they were required to undergo the ordeal of receiving a death sentence and begging for mercy even though the chances of an execution were non-existent. The unfortunate women could not have been expected to know this; by and large they were poorly educated, socially unsophisticated, of limited intelligence, and untutored in the ways of the law.

The destruction of unwanted babies was smothered under blankets of shame, silence, and secrecy. Killings were furtive and rushed, and the murderer went back to her routine activities with barely an interruption. Given the cramped conditions in which many of these women lived, the pressure they must have been under to conceal their condition from those close to them was intense; so too managing the bitter mixture of regret, disappointment, and relief that must have accompanied their actions. One wonders how successfully they truly hid their predicament. If a sister or mother—who may have shared their bed—suspected, it is plausible that they would have said nothing during the pregnancy and made no comment later on the lack of issue.

The likelihood that a woman, particularly if delivering her first child, would do so in silence is slim. It must have taken some effort to ignore the tell-tale signs of pregnancy (the morning sickness, weight gain, cravings) and delivery (the contractions, waters breaking, fear, pain, unassisted delivery of a child and its afterbirth). This is all, of course, assuming that there were no complications. Then to perpetrate the crime and destroy the evidence before attempting a return to normality without displaying any obvious emotional turmoil. Were the mother's cries or the gasps and first faltering breaths of her child really not audible to anyone? It is inconceivable that some mothers or some sisters did not suspect. Better to say nothing and hope that the problem disappeared than to give voice to suspicion and then have to acknowledge a profound failure to live up to a strict moral code.

Sex and Jealousy

Another group of condemned persons who avoided a date with the hangman involved romantic entanglements that had soured, and coercive sex. There was a degree of empathy for drunken husbands killing wives with whom they could not live amicably, or lovers dispatching rivals so that they could call upon the exclusive attention of their paramour. Sometimes the victim and perpetrator were intimates and the death was certain to diminish the perpetrator's future life. These were crimes of passion and jealousy, furious killings carried out by men who were labouring under a variety of burdens (social inadequacy, debt, heavy alcohol consumption, occasionally self-harm). When the relationship that they relied upon as a source of constancy was shown to be without solid foundations they believed that their lives were about to collapse around them. By lashing out they ensured that the object of their affections could not transfer her attachment elsewhere; this was pyrrhic consolation for the slight they felt. These impulsive acts were sometimes sorely regretted. Why punish any more a man who has already suffered so much by killing the one he loves (or someone else close to him which results in the termination of the relationship anyway)?

In the following three cases the perpetrator acted suddenly and viciously but the jury was sympathetic, adding a recommendation to mercy. Leo O'Brien's wife accused him of being unfaithful on the basis of intelligence received from her sister's husband, John Stokes. The same informant also revealed that O'Brien was heavily in debt. A commandant in the National Army who was under severe financial pressure and had been asked to resign from his position, O'Brien took two revolvers from his quarters, cycled to Stokes' house, declared: 'You have finished my life with Leonie and now I am going to finish yours', before firing three shots at close range.[17] He then stepped over the body of the deceased and left the house. The murder occurred about ten minutes after his wife had levelled the accusation of infidelity. The first jury could not agree but he was convicted after a second trial when the jury made a strong recommendation to mercy and he became the last person to have their sentence commuted by a governor general.

There was sympathy for O'Brien among the public on account of the part he played in the struggle for Irish freedom. His patriotism was offered in mitigation and so too was the fact that he had been brutalized by war: 'his experiences while on active service

[17] *Attorney General v Leo O'Brien* [1936] IR 263.

during the 1919–21 period, when he was still under twenty-one years of age, had inculcated in him a disregard for the sacredness of human life'.[18] After more than a decade in custody O'Brien was released on licence but reimprisoned for a short time when he attacked his wife's new partner. He was a jealous man who was quick to anger.

John Fanning was infatuated with Kathleen Boyne, a widow with two young children, with whom he had been keeping company for eighteen months. They quarrelled regularly and while Fanning was keen to get married this desire was not reciprocated. When told that the relationship was at an end Fanning kicked and choked Boyne, leaving her body in a field and maintaining for several days the lie that they had gone out together for the evening but had travelled home separately. He cut a forlorn figure. An only child who had few friends growing up, there was no evidence of insanity but a doctor who examined him as a teenager reported that he had, 'a fish mouthed expression usually associated with stupidity'.[19] This assessment was a bit harsh given the photographic evidence: he was short, weak-chinned, and bespectacled but not fish-faced.[20]

The jury recommended mercy and the judge echoed this call. Fanning was a docile and industrious prisoner who gave no cause for concern that he would reoffend and he was released after six years to the care of a priest in England who was a boyhood friend. Fanning had himself studied for the priesthood for several years.

Vincent McGrath struck Patrick White on the head with a gimlet when he saw him talking to his ex-girlfriend, Noreen Clune. The tool penetrated White's temple and entered the brain to a depth of two-and-a-half inches. White died in hospital a few days later having received the last rites at the roadside. The men were neighbours and close friends and on the day of the killing they had cycled to Mass together and shared some drinks. McGrath had previously attacked another man he found cycling with Clune after a dance.

[18] Memorandum for Government in connection with petition from Leo O'Brien for mitigation of commuted sentence of penal servitude for life, 12 February 1946, NAI, JUS/18/8626A.

[19] Memorandum from An Garda Síochána, Superintendent's Office, Howth to governor, Mountjoy Prison, 6 November 1948, NAI, JUS/10979A & B.

[20] Description of the convict, photographs on reception and on discharge, NAI, JUS/10979A & B.

He handed himself in to the police and made a full admission. The jury found him guilty but added a strong recommendation to mercy. The judge exhorted the government to be merciful on the basis that the killing was not premeditated and that White was unlucky to die from the wound sustained.

It was argued at the trial that the brain injury was not sufficient to cause death and that White had choked on his blood when he was put into a car, seated in an upright position, and transported to hospital. McGrath served a little under seven years after conviction. He was well-received in his home community including by his victim's family.

In other cases motivated by sex and jealousy the killing was a vicious rape where there was little in the way of previous affection. Patrick Monaghan inflicted a fierce sexual assault on a 56-year-old spinster who lived close to him before choking her to death. The pair had argued that morning as Monaghan was on his way to Mass and the row continued the same evening when he was returning home, drunk. He had been heard to announce that he would have sex with her. When her body was found it was clear that she had sustained severe injuries.

Monaghan was married with four children and had been in court on one prior occasion when he was bound over for stealing a magneto from a car. He was a heavy drinker and considered by the prison doctor to be intellectually dull. There was an element of victim blame at work here and derogatory comments about the victim's character served to downplay the harm caused. In a detailed commentary the trial judge suggested the case was not at the most serious end of the scale, noting that: 'The medical evidence was that the deceased was not virgo intacto, but had been an unmarried mother. Probably this was known locally. It would be no palliation of the crime; but might indicate that the accused did not anticipate as violent resistance as was offered.'[21] Such casual misogyny says a great deal about the mores of the time. Another report described the victim as 'a woman of cantankerous disposition', as if this was somehow a relevant consideration.[22]

[21] Memorandum on the case of Patrick Monaghan by William Black, 19 June 1939, NAI, JUS/18/3406A & B.

[22] Proposal to release on licence Patrick Monaghan, November 1950, NAI, JUS/18/3406A & B.

Thomas O'Rourke was jealous of his wife, Joan, who was twenty years his junior. There was no evidence of infidelity on her part but the marriage had been an unhappy one for some time and he had been violent to her in public on a number of occasions. After a day of heavy drinking at the hotel they ran together he began a sustained and savage assault, beating her to death and violently raping her with 'a twisted or hooked pointed instrument'.[23] The instrument was not found but it 'could have been a corkscrew'.[24] This would have been symbolically appropriate given that the husband was paranoid about her supposed infidelity and angry at her drinking. Newspaper reports mention these severe stab wounds but are silent as to their location. Perhaps this aspect of the proceedings would have been too offensive to bring to the public's attention? The jury was, of course, made aware of them and they are dealt with in the judge's summation during which Mr Justice Davitt observed that: 'This whole case reeks of alcohol; it stinks of alcohol'.[25]

O'Rourke fought in the War of Independence and served two periods in the National Army, retiring at the rank of lieutenant; these matters were stated in the memorandum to government regarding whether or not to recommend commutation to the president.[26] O'Rourke also referred to his war record in his clemency petition, adverting to the fact that he was involved in the shooting of a member of the Royal Irish Constabulary.[27] It seems that, even at a remove of forty years, participation in the independence struggle was deemed worthy of extensive mention, accounting for most of the content of this brief petition. Also, it was more than a little ironic that part of the plea for clemency by a man convicted of murder was his attempt on the life of another. Could this be because the petition was addressed to Minister for Justice Oscar Traynor who may have been thought sympathetic

[23] Memorandum for government, question of reprieve of Thomas O'Rourke, 7 May 1959, NAI, JUS/2005/170/5610.

[24] *Irish Independent*, 28 April 1959.

[25] Charge to jury, 1 May 1959, NAI, JUS/2005/170/5610.

[26] Memorandum for government, question of reprieve of Thomas O'Rourke, 7 May 1959, NAI, JUS/2005/170/5610.

[27] Petition of Thomas Tobin O'Rourke, late of the Central Hotel Kilmallock, County Limerick, and now a prisoner in Mountjoy jail Dublin, retired army officer and hotel keeper, to Oscar Traynor, 6 May 1959, NAI, JUS/2005/170/5610.

to such tales of derring-do, given his own involvement in the independence struggle?

David Galvin battered Elizabeth Gould's skull to a pulp in a frenzied assault with a stone before throwing her over a wall into a field. He admitted the killing but could not say why he had done it. It was suspected that he might have launched the attack to prevent her telling his girlfriend that they had been together. A letter from the prison chaplain described Galvin based on the impressions of those who had been taking an interest in his spiritual welfare as he awaited execution:

> The prisoner appears to be of low mental capacity. His conversation is very limited and his reading consists almost exclusively of comic papers. Neither before nor since the day of his sentence to death has he shown any sign of emotional reaction to his position. He is not bitter against anyone nor, on the other hand does he appear concerned about himself or the distress he has caused to his family. This lack of sensitivity is very unusual, in our opinion, in the circumstances.[28]

The governor concurred with this view.

James Kelly subjected Kate Connolly to a brutal rape and lethal assault at her two-room cottage in Carraroe, County Galway. Knowing that there was a warrant out for his arrest in England where he had acquired convictions for a range of offences including larceny and grievous bodily harm, he travelled to Connemara, a place he detested, at his wife's instigation. Connolly was found on the roadside 300 yards from home with severe head injuries, extensive bruising and scarcely able to speak. The living room and bedroom of her cottage were in disarray and there were spatters of blood on the walls and bed. She died on the way to hospital. Kelly went to Galway after the murder and bought new clothes. He was arrested the following day in Dublin when he disembarked from a bus. Six years after his sentence was commuted he was released to his wife and children in Oxford.

Sometimes the murder was a doomed attempt to clear the way for a new relationship. Mary Moynihan, a domestic servant, felled her mistress, Nora Horgan, with a slasher, in the vain hope of being able to marry her master. She was found guilty but the jury and judge were sympathetic. As in many such cases the

[28] Letter from Joseph A. Carroll to governor, Mountjoy Prison, 8 February 1962, NAI, JUS/2005/170/5710.

evidence was circumstantial and there were some concerns that Moynihan may have been protecting the true assailant, or, that if she carried out the attack she may have been in thrall to someone else. She spent sixty-seven months in prison after her conviction before being released on licence to Our Lady's Home. The probation officer involved in her case was aware that there was an offer of a place from the Sisters of Charity in Donnybrook but did not want Moynihan to mix with the 'women of evil life' who were housed there.[29] She preferred Our Lady's Home because it was not a Magdalen Asylum, so had a better class of resident. This is an illuminating comment on the priorities of the day, namely that a convicted murderer might be damaged by association with women of loose morals.[30]

Annie Walsh and Martin Joyce also committed murder in furtherance of their relationship. The victim was Daniel (Sonny Dan) Walsh, Annie's husband, a simple, slow-witted man who drank heavily and slept alone in a small room in his house while Joyce slept there with his wife. Sonny Dan was found face down in a shallow stream with an almost empty bottle of poitín [illegally distilled alcohol] in his pocket. There were no signs of a struggle but the money that had been in his possession when he left the house that evening was gone. The location of the body and its position in the water suggested foul play although it was some time before any arrests were made. It was alleged during the trial that there had been previous attempts to poison Sonny Dan by putting guano in his tea. He had commented on the strange taste but drank it without ill effect. There was no evidence that a splash of excrement in a man's tea could prove lethal but at the very least it indicated a degree of pre-existing animosity. Walsh's first husband had died in the United States and there was innuendo at the time about the circumstances of this death and the

[29] Letter from Kathleen Sullivan to secretary, Department of Justice, 21 June 1930, NAI, JUS/H234/1744.

[30] When offering Elizabeth Edwards a place at Our Lady's Home, the reverend mother asked if she could come under an assumed name, 'which would make matters easier for her and for us also'. Letter from Marie MacDonnell to governor, Mountjoy Prison, 24 August 1937, NAI, JUS/18/885A & B. This was a continuation of the pattern of secrecy and lies that began when Elizabeth admitted herself to the county home under a false name (Mrs Mannion) having told her parents she required treatment for appendicitis.

fact that a woman who had been widowed twice by the age of 42 had led a younger man astray.

Finally, Denis Foy had been drinking the afternoon he met 6-year-old James McGrath and took him to a nearby wood where he strangled him before placing his naked body near a stream. The conclusion reached by a psychiatrist for the defence at his trial was that the unpremeditated and alcohol-fuelled killing 'was the result of a disease of the mind either of an epileptic or schizophrenic nature'.[31] The psychiatrists for the state gave evidence that while of low intelligence there was no sign of insanity or any mental deficiency.[32]

[31] Case report, unsigned and undated, NAI, JUS/2005/170/6124.

[32] Memorandum for government, question of reprieve of Denis Foy, 21 February 1959, NAI, JUS/2005/170/6124.

9

Undoing Death II

The previous chapter dealt with murderers who escaped the noose for crimes that were broadly associated with love, loss, and coercive sex. The remainder—described next—had distinctively different motivating factors. They were viewed less sympathetically by judges and juries and spent longer in custody (Table 8.1).

Dreadful Deeds Done in Turbulent Times

Seven cases involved men who were in possession of arms which they used to devastating effect for a miscellany of reasons. These killings occurred between August 1922 and December 1923, when the country was embroiled in, and then emerging from, a period of civil war. The convictions were recorded after hostilities had ended.

John Hogan, of Ennis, County Clare, was convicted the day after William Downes (the first man to be hanged after the civil war) for shooting dead a neighbour with whom his family had a dispute regarding a turf bank. He sought medical and spiritual attention for his victim before making his getaway. The victim was a pugnacious man who had been undeterred by a warning shot and it was believed that had Hogan not fired again there would have been an altercation in which the eventual killer would have ended up being the injured party. Both judge and jury recommended him to mercy.

The dispute was personal but Hogan was armed and on active service and release petitions stressed his political involvement. He was a former IRA captain who had taken the anti-treaty side during the civil war. At the time of the killing he 'was illegally in possession of firearms to be used against the state as then constituted'.[1] During his prison sentence he was non-compliant, going

[1] Petition from Michael Moran to governor general, 6 July 1928, NAI, JUS/H234/2024A.

Justice, Mercy, and Caprice: Clemency and the Death Penalty in Ireland. First Edition. Ian O'Donnell. © Ian O'Donnell 2017. Published 2017 by Oxford University Press.

on hunger strike, attempting to escape, and refusing to wear a uniform or carry out prison work. Hogan served eight-and-a-half years before he was unconditionally released. He remained politically involved afterwards.

John Ryan was a sergeant in the National Army who had recently developed an alcohol problem. Drunk on poitín he met Michael Caudy, a man who was well-known to him and with whom he was on friendly terms. The pair went to a public house together and, walking along the road afterwards, they had a quarrel that ended when Ryan produced his revolver and fired two shots; the first missed, the second struck home. This was a spontaneous act, the spark for which was never established. Ryan tried to stem the blood coming from his victim's face, handed his revolver to another soldier who had witnessed the shooting, and said he had not meant to shoot him. He served a little under five years after his conviction before being released on licence.

Joseph Butler was a soldier in the National Army who was drinking in a bar with military colleagues in uniform and with their weapons. His childhood friend Michael McSweeney bought them a drink and an argument ensued that became more heated on the road outside. An officer told McSweeney to go home to prevent matters escalating further and he began to walk away across the fields in the company of a friend. Butler followed with his rifle, called on the pair to halt and shouted 'scatter' to his soon-to-be victim's companion.[2] The men separated and he took aim, resting his gun barrel on a wall, and firing three shots.

The officer who had sent McSweeney home took charge and Butler went to fetch the doctor. Butler's defence was that the gun had gone off accidentally. He was arrested by the military on 21 August 1922, handed over to the civic guard on 22 February 1923, and eventually convicted on 18 July 1924. Following an unsuccessful appeal his sentence was commuted to penal servitude for life, later remitted to ten years to be reckoned from when he first entered custody in August 1922.

James Murray and Joseph Bergin were soldiers in the National Army. The former was a captain in the Intelligence Department, the latter a military policeman at Tintown Camp in County Kildare. Bergin was believed to be relaying information from

[2] Transcript of trial, examination of Henry Morgan, 18 July 1924, NAI, CCA 4/24.

internees in his custody to their supporters outside. He was abducted, interrogated and shot six times in the head. His body was recovered from the canal at Milltown Bridge, County Kildare. Murray left the country shortly afterwards travelling to Liverpool, then Glasgow, and on to Buenos Aries before returning to Dublin twelve months later. This was the unofficial execution of a spy which Murray claimed had been sanctioned by the military intelligence colonel to whom he reported. Murray believed he was carrying out his patriotic duty by arresting and interrogating Bergin before killing him. He was surprised, given the times, that he had to face trial for following orders, let alone the death penalty.

Numerous petitions were submitted in this case, whose signatories included TDs and senators. The view seemed to be that many other people had done the same or worse and that it was unjust to single out an otherwise honourable man for criminalization and punishment. This view was not shared by the Department of Justice which, in a memorandum to Kevin O'Higgins, spelled out clearly that—notwithstanding the context—this was a cruel, premeditated and 'appalling' crime.[3] Even when Murray's health went into terminal decline four years after his imprisonment the authorities were unyielding in their refusal to release him so that he could die at home rather than in a prison cell.

Charles Molloy was a teenager who took advantage of the turbulent times to supplement his income through armed robbery.[4] With two friends he stopped a delivery van on the road in Ballycumber, County Offaly with a view to robbing it. The driver, John Finlay, got out of the van to remonstrate with the attack party. All were from the area and they knew each other. A shot was fired and Finlay fell to the road, dead. Molloy was not arrested for more than two-and-a-half years, during which time he continued to live at home. The reason for the delay was that the man who had witnessed the killing did not come forward initially. No reason was offered for this tardiness. The jury was sympathetic and made a strong recommendation to mercy. Mr

[3] Memorandum from secretary, Department of Justice to Minister for Justice, 18 July 1925, NAI, JUS/H234/781.

[4] He was nineteen years old although in one of his mother's petitions for mitigation of sentence she gave his age as sixteen. Letter from Annie Molloy to Minister for Justice, August 1928, NAI, JUS/H234/1119A & B.

Justice Sullivan supported the jury's plea for mercy arguing that the crime was not premeditated, the perpetrator was young, and the country was lawless at the time. He was released after six-and-a-half years, in honour of the Eucharistic Congress.

Patrick Fagan also benefited from the Eucharistic Congress which triggered his release on licence after the same period in custody as Molloy. Fagan was another man with access to arms during troubled times who acted with lethal rashness. A private in the National Army looking for somewhere to stay overnight, he arrived in uniform with another soldier at the family home of Lieutenant Patrick Moran. They were refused admittance as the house was full. Moran (not in uniform) came to the door, identified the other soldier, and demanded he hand over his rifle, which he did. When Fagan was approached he fired and fled. He deserted the army and may have switched sides to join the anti-treaty forces. When arrested several years later he claimed the gun had discharged accidentally and that he did not know his victim's identity, although when his companion obeyed an order to surrender arms he must have at least suspected they were in an officer's presence.

When Fagan was at liberty in January 1933 and wished to come off his ticket of leave he claimed his killing was 'a military one committed in the civil war in August 1922'.[5] It did not have the hallmarks of a political crime but it took place during a volatile period and this strengthened the case for preferential treatment. The lapse of time between this cold-blooded killing and Fagan's trial may have redounded to his ultimate advantage. Had he been apprehended swiftly he may have been quickly executed; there would have been little sympathy for a soldier who deserted having shot an officer dead because a request for shelter was refused. But, by the time he was brought to justice the civil war was over, the public mood had changed, and there was no desire to open old wounds.

Antecedents

Raised regularly (if not always successfully) was a plea on behalf of someone who had fought for the establishment of the state that was now considering whether to do away with him. This emphasized a common tradition of sacrifice and the existence of shared

[5] Untitled memorandum, 6 January 1933, NAI, JUS/H234/1132A.

values. It carried the subliminal message that without what I and others like me did in the struggle for independence, you would not now be occupying a position of power. It was a debt being called in, an argument that I willingly risked my life to create a state where I would be subordinate to you, and for you to allow my life to be taken would be an abomination, a violation of everything that so many hold dear. This was a powerful bargaining counter. It was a deliberate attempt to narrow the empathy gap: we had each other's backs during the revolutionary period and now, for a final time, I am asking you to cover mine, a request that in other circumstances would be granted without demur.

On one occasion the plea invoked sacrifices made for King George V rather than in the struggle for national self-determination. Denis Leen's wife directed her entreaty to the War Office in London. This extraterritorial appeal was unique. She wrote that her husband was one of six brothers and six brothers-in-law who served in the British Army during the Great War, and that now he was facing execution for following an order given by his superior officer:

> Therefore Lords and Gentlemen, I now appeal to you to blot out that awful stain which my husband has to undergo from myself and my family, also his own family who so nobly went forward in the hour of need to assist the rights of their country for King and Empire.

Mrs Leen implored the War Office to intervene with the head of the Irish government so that her husband might be spared, remarking that 'no time can be wasted. The fatal day is not so far off.'

Leen's is the only death penalty case for which a file exists among the records of the Governor General's Office available in the National Archives of Ireland for the post-independence period. A file was created because the War Office forwarded Mrs Leen's letter to the Colonial Office which passed it on to Governor General Timothy Healy, who transmitted it to the President of the Executive Council with an additional handwritten comment on the despatch to the effect that: 'Some piteable [sic] appeals from Leen's wife have gone to the Minister for Justice. Please take same into consideration also.'[6]

[6] Letter from governor general to President of Executive Council, 4 July 1924, NAI, Governor General's Office, F. 318.

It is interesting that Mrs Leen should have thought it proper to communicate with London in order to influence events in Dublin; this was patriotism of an unusual hue. It is also interesting that the response to her desperate plea was to deem it outside the remit of the authority to which it had been sent and to request the governor general to confirm Leen's conviction so that he could be formally discharged as a reservist with the Royal Munster Fusiliers, the regiment he had joined in January 1915 and served with for seven years before joining the National Army.

An additional factor in Leen's case was that Lieutenant Jeremiah Gaffney was executed for his role in the same crime (which involved the shooting at the roadside of Thomas Brosnan, a young man who had been taken from his home by a party of Free State soldiers in what was thought to be a reprisal attack for the killing of a member of the civic guard a few nights earlier). It would have been disproportionate to hang Leen too, especially as he was a minor player whose actions were coerced. Leen's sentence was commuted on the day of Gaffney's execution.

Legally Sane but Strikingly Odd

Seven of those spared exhibited signs of mental instability by a clinical rather than a legal yardstick. Some behaved bizarrely and others seemed to lack insight into the harm they had caused. Sometimes chronic alcohol abuse was a factor.[7] Judge and jury recommended mercy in just over half of these cases (Table 8.1).

William Devereux almost decapitated his sister-in-law, Anne, with a hatchet after she threw a poker at him. There was a history of tense relations between the pair. Devereux had poor vision and did not notice that Anne had her 10-month-old daughter, Kathleen, in her arms. The child died also. The prison doctor was sympathetic, noting that 'nagging acts as a cumulative poison on certain temperaments ... drop by drop the reservoir of resentment is filled and one day the last drop causes the barriers of reason to be swept away in a flood of ungovernable anger'.[8] This

[7] It was not invariably the case that those who appeared unbalanced were spared. William O'Shea is a case in point and one wonders if he would have survived had his co-accused, Thomas White, who actually shot Maureen O'Shea, not been found insane and sent to the asylum rather than the gallows.

[8] Report on William Devereux's mental state prepared by B.J. Hackett, 27 November 1923, NAI, JUS/H234/3507A.

is an example of a case where mercy intruded as an autonomous moral virtue and the prisoner received less than he was thought to deserve (see Chapter 4). Mercy and justice were independent values jostling for supremacy and mercy won.

Hannah Flynn had worked for a short time as a domestic servant for Margaret O'Sullivan and her husband. When her services were dispensed with on account of disobedience and suspected dishonesty she directed a campaign of harassment and abuse at her former employers, claiming they owed her money. They denied underpayment but gave her much of what she demanded nonetheless. When Mr O'Sullivan returned from Mass one Sunday he found the house in chaos, blood everywhere, and his wife on floor with her face almost chopped off. Flynn had ransacked the premises, taking a considerable amount of money after she butchered Mrs O'Sullivan with a hatchet. She walked home wearing a shawl that belonged to her victim under which she carried a parcel of stolen goods. Her barrister argued that she was clearly insane by the popular understanding of the term if not by the narrow legal definition.

When the jury returned its guilty verdict, it made a strong recommendation to mercy on account of Flynn being mentally defective. The judge endorsed this view, which had been supported by evidence from the prison doctor, who stated that her 'intellect was of a very low type and that her responsibility was much below normal'.[9] She spent 224 months in prison—longer than anyone else who received the mandatory death penalty for murder—because her own family members were deemed to be abnormal, and unsuitable carers. She spent longer again in the Good Shepherd Convent in Limerick to which she was discharged (see Chapter 10).

James Tierney (aka O'Neill) hired a taxi in Cork city to take him approximately twelve miles to Carrigaline. He stopped near the house of a former employer to which he hoped to gain access in order to steal money. Denied admission he went away but returned early the next morning, this time driving the taxi himself. Later that morning the body of Thomas Vickers, the taxi driver, was found in a field near the house. He had been strangled with his own tie. It transpired that Vickers had insisted on

[9] Letter from Jonathan Pim to Minister for Home Affairs, 27 February 1924, NAI, JUS/18/2679A & B.

accompanying Tierney on foot across the field in the direction of the house, probably because he feared he would not be paid his fare, and that Tierney killed him to get rid of the hindrance he had become. Evidence was presented at trial of motorcycle accidents that may have caused neurological impairment and of times when he lost consciousness and had been hospitalized. His father, who had not known he was in Ireland at the time, described him as 'certainly not normal' and his probation officer in England wrote that: 'He gave the impression of being mentally abnormal and seemed to be living in a world of fantasy'.[10] There was a history of insanity on both sides of the family.

James Fennell was a serving soldier who shot two sergeants, one of whom died. He carried out his attack in the barracks. Other soldiers were woken by the sound of gunfire and saw him shooting. The insanity defence was raised—unsuccessfully—at his trial and one of the psychiatrists who examined him described him as a 'moral imbecile' who was incapable of comprehending what he had done.[11] The trial judge believed him to be insane.

Martin Griffin lived with his wife and mother-in-law on a small farm in Galway. In 1925 the latter drew up a will leaving the farm to a son in the United States. This was never changed and when she died eighteen years later Griffin started drinking heavily and kept drinking for a fortnight culminating one evening when he went to bed drunk at about ten o'clock, bringing alcohol with him. He woke around midnight, drank more whiskey and stout, and argued with his wife. A few hours later he got a lamp, left the house and fetched a large hatchet from the barn. With this implement he struck his half-asleep wife at least eight times.

The couple had been on 'friendly and affectionate terms'[12] since their marriage in 1923 and the motive was thought to be anger at his wife for not persuading her mother to change the terms of the will.[13] Having slaughtered his wife at around 4 a.m. Griffin gave himself up

[10] Report on James Edward O'Neill prepared by Mary L. Connor, Police Court Probation Officer for Newbury, Berks, 26 March 1937, NAI, JUS/18/9238A & B.

[11] Report by Chief R.M.S., Grangegorman Mental Hospital, 21 May 1940, NAI, JUS/18/4066A & B.

[12] An Garda Síochána, Galway, 8 June 1943, NAI, JUS/18/6470A & B.

[13] Memorandum from Department of Justice to governor, Portlaoise Prison, 28 January 1944, NAI, JUS/18/6470A & B.

to the police at 6:40 a.m. There was a family history of insanity but the medical officer in Mountjoy Prison could find no gross mental abnormality. For a man with no previous convictions and no history of marital disharmony this was a stunningly vicious response to a setback that must have been anticipated for some time.

Daniel Duff was a member of An Garda Síochána who had been working with a colleague, James Byrne, to provide armed protection to a landowner whose life was believed to be under threat as a result of a controversial land acquisition. On the night in question a heated exchange occured. Duff said he thought Byrne was reaching for his gun having said he would 'blow his brains out'[14] so he grabbed his own weapon and fired twice. There had been quarrels between the men before but they had always passed without enduring rancour. On a previous occasion Duff said that Byrne had produced his weapon and threatened to shoot; he had not reported this incident at the time. The murder was an impulsive act following provocation and no real motive could be established.

Duff had been on continuous night duty seven days a week for nine months and this was affecting his health and wellbeing. He was tired, irritable, losing weight, and breaking out in boils. He had been advised to report sick and a transfer to different duties was under active consideration. He had consumed seven pints of porter before going on duty that evening, but was not believed to be drunk. He whispered an act of contrition into his victim's ear and then ran directly to the house of the family he was protecting calling out that he had shot his colleague dead after 'a terrible row'.[15]

The newspapers reported that Duff dressed for court in a 'blue suit with a Fainne [lapel pin indicating a preference to speak the Irish language]' and that he 'stood erect'; the epitome of the Gael, proud even in his dishonour.[16] The governor of Portlaoise Prison wrote that he 'would not consider him to be in any way of the criminal type'.[17] A juror was excused from service because he

[14] Memorandum for government in connection with the case of Daniel Joseph Duff, sentenced to death for the murder of Garda James Byrne, 4 December 1946, NAI, TSCH/3/S13961A.

[15] *Irish Press*, 21 November 1946.

[16] *Irish Press*, 22 November 1946.

[17] Memorandum from governor, Portlaoise Prison to secretary, Department of Justice, 21 November 1949, NAI, JUS/18/9710A & B.

'had a conscientious objection to capital punishment'.[18] Once again, while not satisfying the legal criteria for madness this was a strikingly odd act carried out by a man who was clearly carrying a large burden of psychological stress.

In September 1945, Agnes McAdam put strychnine into a cake that she had baked for a social event to mark the departure of two priests for the missions. Several hundred guests were expected to attend. She delivered the cake to a neighbour's house where the food for the reception was being collected. The neighbouring couple sampled the wares and gave a slice to the dog. The husband and dog died and the wife became violently ill. McAdam could not have known who would eat her cake and her actions were portrayed as a misguided practical joke. She was described as 'mentally abnormal' and it was discovered that several family members were in local asylums. It was felt that she could not be held morally responsible for her actions and so the sentence of death was commuted to penal servitude for life.

The existence of family histories of insanity was not surprising given the high level of psychiatric confinement during the period. The rate of hospitalization for mental illness in the Free State was higher than in any other country for which statistics were available and the disproportionality was especially evident among the lower social classes. In 1963, the year before the abolition of the mandatory death penalty for murder, the rate of hospitalization per 100,000 for agricultural workers was 3,465 compared to 123 for employers and managers (O'Sullivan and O'Donnell 2012: 10, 271).

Chivalry

The Royal Commission on Capital Punishment (1949-53: 12) in the United Kingdom noted the existence of a 'natural reluctance' to hang a woman, observing that the prisoner's sex was sometimes identified as a pertinent consideration by the Home Secretary. This reluctance was not confined to one side of the Irish Sea. There were five women to whom clemency was granted solely on account of their gender. Otherwise they were unsympathetic characters. There was a squeamishness about allowing women to die, no matter how heinous their crimes.

[18] *Irish Press*, 20 November 1946.

Hannah O'Leary was involved in the murder of her brother Patrick who was beaten to death in his bed, decapitated, and dismembered. Evidence produced at trial suggested that the multiple injuries to Patrick's head were likely to have been caused by the blunt end of a hatchet or a hammer with something like a reaping hook or carving knife used to hack the corpse asunder. His head was found by a neighbour in a potato sack in a field, with other body parts widely scattered over the O'Leary farm and adjoining properties. While the search for his remains was underway a dog ran past with a well-gnawed arm in its mouth; when shouted at, it dropped the evidence.

Hannah's mother, brother (Con), and another sister (Mary Anne) were all initially charged with conspiracy to murder. This charge was later dropped and the children were charged with murder. A nolle prosequi was entered against the mother on the conspiracy charge. Mary Anne died in prison before the trial took place as a result of a cancerous growth near her eye. Con was hanged for his part in the atrocity. The prison doctor described Hannah as 'a dull, stupid-looking woman and from close personal observation and questioning of her, I would describe this prisoner as a person of more or less defective reasoning power'.[19] The jury found her guilty after an absence of twenty-two minutes with a majority recommending mercy. Her sentence was commuted to penal servitude for life on 25 July 1925 and she remained in prison until 18 September 1942 when she entered the Magdalen Asylum on St Mary's Road, Cork. She died there on 6 December 1963. She would have been released to the community had anyone been prepared to take responsibility for her.

The O'Leary case is a signal example of how intra-familial hostility—rooted in the fact that Patrick had inherited the farm with nothing left to his siblings—could have dreadful consequences. One family member was murdered, another died in prison awaiting trial, another was executed, and another was sentenced to penal servitude for life. The mother walked free, but to a homestead devoid of her children; those not implicated in the murder had moved away. The mother died four years later in the county home. According to a newspaper report entitled 'Lonely Funeral'—'The hearse containing the remains of Mrs O'Leary

[19] Letter from F. MacCormack to secretary, Department of Justice, 17 July 1925, NAI, JUS/18/2770A & B.

passed through Clonakilty, the only person in attendance being the undertaker' (*Irish Independent*, 1 February 1928).

Jane O'Brien would surely have been executed had she been male. She cut a hole in the hedge near the gate to the house at Killinick, County Wexford that she shared with her nephew John Cousins. When Cousins arrived home after a visit to his fiancée she shot him in the stomach from a range of four to six yards. O'Brien was hostile towards her nephew's fiancée to whom she had sent anonymous letters and postcards. She feared that when the pair wed she would be excluded from the house. It was the victim's house, in which his late father's sister (O'Brien) was also living with her only child (a son). There was no history of alcohol abuse or mental instability. Those who came into contact with O'Brien believed her to be an intelligent, hard, and calculating woman. It was rumoured that she had poisoned her brother the previous year and with the nephew out of the way the property would be hers. One local described her as 'a Devil' and the view from the Garda Commissioner's office was that the law should be permitted to take its course.

The position of the Department of Justice as expressed in the memorandum prepared for the consideration of the Executive Council was that: 'The Department cannot recollect any case in which there appears to have been so complete an absence of extenuating circumstances'.[20] Much was made of the murderer's gender in the petitions that were submitted on her behalf and it was argued that only one woman had been executed since independence and for a far more gruesome crime. As noted in Chapter 7, when the Executive Council was considering the question of commutation, its attention was drawn to a letter from the Archbishop of Dublin to the Minister for Justice adverting to the fact that an execution would cast 'a sinister shadow' across the city at a time when its residents were basking in the glory of one of the largest eucharistic congresses of the twentieth century.[21] O'Brien was discharged on licence to Our Lady's Home on 21 July 1941.[22]

Mary Daly was a 27-year-old woman in financial distress who bludgeoned 83-year-old Mary Gibbons to death. Daly said that

[20] Jane O'Brien, a prisoner under sentence of death, 13 July 1932, NAI, TSCH/3/S8653.

[21] Letter from Edward J. Byrne to James Geoghegan, 25 June 1932, NAI, TSCH/3/S8653.

[22] O'Brien's case excited the interest of a Scottish criminologist who, on 27 March 1935, wrote to the *Dublin Gazette* for further particulars. The letter was passed to the Department of Justice which responded asking him why he wanted

Gibbons had attempted to take her handbag and she struck out to protect herself with a hammer that she happened to have on her person. The victim, who expired a week later, swore in a dying declaration that she had been attacked while at prayer in her local church and was repeatedly struck on the head with the hammer as she attempted to escape, the exit door being blocked by Daly. A worshipper outside heard the cries for help, forced open the door with the assistance of some men who were working nearby, and found the two women struggling. The pathologist estimated there had been fifteen blows to the head. The perpetrator was frail and the victim was robust for her age which explains why she was not immediately overwhelmed by such a sustained assault.

Daly was in arrears with rent and had other bills to settle. It was surmised that she went to the church with a hammer in her shopping bag to break open offertory boxes and steal their contents but did not do so because children were present. Shortly afterwards she saw Gibbons deep in prayer, attempted to take her handbag and in panic hit her with the hammer when she thought she had been detected.

Tried and convicted, Daly's conviction was quashed by the Supreme Court. She was retried and reconvicted. The jury made a strong recommendation to mercy after each trial and the judge concurred. According to a petition prepared by her solicitor she had been eleven weeks in the condemned cell, had heard the death sentence passed upon her twice, and had five dates set for her execution.[23] In a letter to the minister the judge wrote that: 'Purely as a matter of personal impression, I want to let you know that I doubt if this woman will live six months. I think the strain of two trials has been terrible and quite beyond her powers'.[24] Four-and-a-half years later she was released on licence.[25]

the information. He explained that he was compiling a 'Biographical Dictionary of Criminology', expressed surprise that his letter had been forwarded to the authorities, and respectfully requested some details of the case. Letter from H.L.B. White to assistant secretary, Department of Justice, 19 June 1935, NAI, JUS/18/2737A & B. A decision was taken not to issue any reply.

23 Petition from P.J. Ruttledge to Minister for Justice, 2 May 1949, NAI, JUS/2005/170/7622.

24 Letter from George Gavan Duffy to Minister for Justice, 30 April 1949, NAI, JUS/2005/170/7622.

25 One of the pages in this closed prisoner file, relating to a petition seeking early release, has been defaced with the single word 'SHITE' written in pencil

Frances Cox was another unsympathetic character whose gender would appear to have been decisive in saving her life. She put strychnine in her brother Richard's orange squash or administered it as a powder on four occasions, the final of which resulted in a violent seizure and death. The siblings had seemed to get on well previously but Frances wanted Richard out of the way so that she could marry and inherit the farm. Her defence counsel submitted that her mental health was affected by the birth of a child a week earlier, which she had killed. She was charged with the murder of her child but her plea of guilty to manslaughter was acceptable to the court and she was bound over to keep the peace for two years on her own bond of £10. The day this sentence was handed down she was released and immediately rearrested for her brother's murder. The jury was not sympathetic and added no rider to the verdict. The judge did not erect any obstacles to the law taking its course, reporting a lack of extenuating circumstances in the evidence.

One of the facts that saved Cox was that she had killed her newborn child. The Minister for Justice was swayed by the argument that she may have been mentally deranged at the time she killed her brother on account of her recent experience of unassisted child birth together with 'suppressed lactation'.[26] It is an unusual turn of events when the deliberate killing of a child mitigates the murder of an adult. Cox sobbed quietly when the sentence of death was passed but had nothing to contribute when invited to say why she should not be hanged. About one thousand people gathered outside the courthouse to hear the verdict (*Irish Independent*, 22 November 1949). She served a little over seven years before being released.

Mary (Mamie) Cadden did not intend to kill her 'victim' but was regarded unsympathetically by jury and judge, neither

across two paragraphs. Mary Agnes Daly, petition for release, 29 February 1952, NAI, JUS/2005/170/7622. It is unlikely that this annotation can be attributed to one of the civil servants responsible for maintaining the file as legitimate comments tended to be inked. It is not known why a reader in the National Archives of Ireland would be moved to scrawl such an inarticulate expression of dissatisfaction on a national record.

[26] Death sentence, Frances Cox, Department of Justice, 21 December 1949, NAI, JUS/18/11757A & B. Cox disclosed that she had miscarried the previous year and delivered a stillborn child in 1944. Two of the TDs from her area made representations on her behalf, calling for mercy to be extended. One described her as a 'sex maniac'. File note, 21 December 1949, NAI, JUS/18/11757A & B.

of which called for mercy. An abortionist whose client, Helen O'Reilly, died as a result of a botched procedure, Cadden dragged the body from her rooms and left it on the street nearby. A former midwife, born in the United States, she had been in custody on two prior occasions (twelve months imprisonment for child abandonment and five years penal servitude for unlawfully procuring a miscarriage). She was seen as encouraging sexual promiscuity and immorality by offering a solution to its unfortunate consequences. Cadden had not intended to harm O'Reilly but was convicted of murder under the doctrine of constructive malice which held that an accidental death that occurred in the course of committing a felony was to be treated as murder.[27] The felony in this case was the attempt to procure a miscarriage.

Cadden was one of the few sentenced to death who uttered more than a sentence from the dock when invited to comment on her predicament. She was a truculent exception to the tendency for stunned or remorseful silence, her remarks indicating a mixture of defiance, madness, and anti-Catholicism.[28] Most of those who found themselves in this situation had become ciphers upon whom the law would work through to (or be diverted from) its neck-breaking conclusion. Even if they were not cowed by the proceedings (and, as marginalized and poorly educated men and women, they were unlikely to have the wit or the wherewithal to buck against the system) their contributions from the dock would seem inaudible against the magnitude of their impending annihilation. Less than two years after her conviction Cadden was certified insane and transferred from Mountjoy Prison to the Central Mental Hospital where she died on 20 April 1959.

Protective effects of gender

These were very fortunate women. They committed appalling crimes and, had they been men, it is likely that their rendezvous with the hangman would not have been cancelled. Cadden was something of an exception in that had the law been modernized

[27] This doctrine was abolished by s. 4 of the Criminal Justice Act, 1964.

[28] When the jury returned its verdict and the judge pronounced sentence Cadden exclaimed: 'You won't get the chance'. When the judge then exhorted the Lord to have mercy on her soul she declared: 'I am not a Catholic. Take that' (*Irish Times*, 2 November 1956).

she would not have faced the death penalty, no matter how defiantly she stood against society's mores. She was considered monstrous as much for her contrarian stance as her actions. A recidivist offender, she continued to transgress despite serving previous sentences. Her reckless disregard for the lives of children and the unborn was explicit; casual neglect of infants was common but it was hidden and shameful, not brazen like Cadden's. She was elderly and unmarried. She was operating in the heart of Dublin, close to parliament buildings, not in some anonymous backstreet. It is difficult to imagine a character who was so at odds with the society in which she lived and whose conduct raised so many uncomfortable questions. She served a function which was tacitly acknowledged and openly condemned. Had her 'patient' survived, both parties would have been liable to prosecution and, if convicted, to face a maximum sentence of penal servitude for life for the crime of procuring a miscarriage under s. 58 of the Offences Against the Person Act, 1861.

Cadden was responding to a problem that was exacerbated by the ban on contraceptives introduced in 1935. It says a great deal about the prevailing context that a state which stigmatized illegitimacy to such an extent that it was not uncommonly responded to with neglect, child abandonment, or deliberate harm would proscribe the kind of products that might have prevented the problem occurring in the first place. The real issue, it would appear, was sex outside marriage and one wonders if the subsequent pregnancy was a cause of schadenfreude for the men who made the laws and wanted to see the immoral suffer if they could not restrain themselves. They had no inclination to spare (female) citizens the repercussions of their actions.

Moore (1989: 208) described pardons granted on gender grounds as 'outrageous' and commented that discrimination of this kind was 'universally disparaged'. Such disparagement was far from universal in Ireland where successive governments had no difficulty sparing women simply because they were women. She listed a variety of other types of pardon that cannot be justified on retributive grounds including those granted to promote the public welfare, or to reward past actions, or for pity's sake, or based on the recommendation of the judge or jury, or based on the individual's family connections (p. 209). Most of these are found regularly in Ireland. It is interesting that granting clemency for reasons that retributivists would have found deeply unsatisfactory did not seem to cause any discomfort among the Irish politicians who bandied them about as perfectly reasonable grounds for sparing individuals from the otherwise inevitable consequences of their convictions.

Given that all of the key actors were men, one wonders whether they held indulgent views of the 'weaker sex' that assumed they, like children, could not be held fully responsible for their actions. When biological factors, such as childbirth and its aftermath, intervened the men were even more mystified and even more willing to accept that the women must have been incapable of understanding the magnitude or implications of what they had done. These patronizing and patriarchal views redounded hugely to the women's advantage. Even the most callous and remorseless woman benefited from these beliefs of inherent inferiority.

Calculating killers became pitiful creatures, at the mercy of biology or forces they could not be expected to control or comprehend. The perpetrator was recast as a victim. Their capacity and culpability were immediately brought to the fore. They were seen as not properly accountable for their actions, however murderous. Sometimes men also benefited from negative gender stereotypes (e.g. nagging as a 'cumulative poison' (Devereux); the victim not being 'virgo intacto' (Monaghan); and possibly some of the drunken killings of women by their husbands and lovers discussed in Chapter 8). The death sentence was abolished de facto for women in 1925. Whatever was said about formal equality before the law, governments exempted women from its rigours.

Annie Walsh must have felt that as a woman she was sure to be spared the noose like Hannah Flynn and Mary Moynihan whose crimes were, if anything, more savage and at least as calculating, but whose sentences had been commuted the previous year. Hannah O'Leary was convicted eleven days before Annie Walsh and her sentence was commuted on 27 July, as Annie Walsh awaited her fate in the condemned cell at Mountjoy Prison. It is not surprising against this background and given that a woman had not been executed since Mary Daly in 1903 that Walsh hoped for a commutation right up to the end. One interesting coda to Annie Walsh's case is that she was buried in the grounds of the Mountjoy men's prison; no gender discrimination was shown post-mortem.

Mr Justice Meredith, a Kantian scholar, believed that the death penalty should be executed only in exceptional cases but that a blanket exemption for women was wrong: 'To make the question turn simply on sex—to commute the sentences in all cases of women and to carry them out in all cases of men—is, I consider flagrantly unjust'.[29] When women are spared, as a category, this cannot be interpreted as a series of acts of mercy. It must be named for what it is, namely unfair discrimination. There is no just reason why all but one of the female murderers, but only around half of the male murderers, should have been spared.

Caprice

The final group—all men—would have died had not unforeseen, and unforeseeable, events intervened. (Patrick Boylan, Tomás MacCurtain, Patrick Heffernan, and William Wall were discussed in Chapter 7). Clemency was first denied and there was a late change of mind. These swings could be sudden, the reasons are difficult to unravel at this remove, and the consequences were—quite literally—life changing. This process could not operate in reverse as the president commuted the sentence within hours of receiving the recommendation from government, so there was no time for a change of heart. Boylan, Heffernan, and Wall benefited from a judge addressing a meeting of government. The remaining cases (including MacCurtain) benefited from ecclesiastical interventions.

Patrick Aylward was a 63-year-old farmer who had spent forty years working as a cutler in the United States, returning to his native area of Mullinavat, County Kilkenny eleven months before he was charged with murder. Shortly before 5 p.m. on 21 April 1923 he called to a neighbouring house and put 18-month-old Willie Holden on the fire, holding him there for a time. Aylward and the victim's mother had an antagonistic relationship. A local doctor who gave evidence at the trial described him as a member of 'a family of four "mental defectives" who lived like a colony of badgers' in a house that was filthy and unfit for human habitation and that he was a 'degenerate' who was 'mentally abnormal' and

[29] Letter from James C. Meredith to Minister for Justice, 30 December 1933, NAI, JUS/H234/6221B. Some years later, the Royal Commission on Capital Punishment (1949-53: 65) arrived at a similar position: 'although the idea of executing a woman is naturally repugnant, there are no rational grounds on which discrimination between men and women in this matter could be justified'.

'subject to insane impulses'.[30] Nonetheless the doctor believed him to be responsible for his actions.

A majority of the jury recommended mercy but the judge felt that the evidence of guilt was clear and that no crime could be more 'atrocious' than roasting an infant on a fire.[31] In his letter to the Minister for Home Affairs, Lord Chief Justice Molony stated:

> Although the prisoner is a degenerate, I see no reason whatever to doubt but that he was fully conscious of the act he was doing, and that the act was wrong ... If the prisoner is responsible in law for his actions, I am afraid I am unable to see any mitigating circumstances which would make the prisoner an object of mercy.[32]

The Executive Council decided that the law should take its course, but reconsidered in light of further reports, including a letter from the Coadjutor Bishop of Ossory, and decided to recommend a commutation. Given the lateness of the decision there was insufficient time to contact the executioner before he left home so he arrived in Dublin to find there was no work, but received his usual fee and expenses.[33] Aylward's death sentence was commuted to penal servitude for life. He was released in June 1932, along with several other convicted murderers, in recognition of the Eucharistic Congress that took place in Dublin that month.

Robert Stevenson was a British able seaman whose ship, Pass of Ballater, had docked in Dublin. He met a prostitute, Mary Nolan, in a public house and arranged to have sex with her in a nearby lane. While embracing her he claimed to have noticed that she was trying to pick his pocket. He struck her, knocking her out. He took the £1 he had given her for her services back from her hand and strangled her. He spent the rest of the evening drinking before picking up another prostitute with whom he spent the night. He was arrested a week later at Limerick docks. Neither judge nor jury advocated mercy and his application for

[30] Letter from M.P. Coghlan to P. Buggy, 20 December 1923, NAI, JUS/H234/1865A.

[31] Letter from T.F. Molony to Minister for Home Affairs, 26 November 1923, NAI, JUS/H234/1865A.

[32] Letter from T.F. Molony to Minister for Home Affairs, 10 December 1923, NAI, JUS/H234/1865A.

[33] Pierrepoint was displeased by the delay in reimbursing him for this wasted journey. Letter from Thomas Pierrepoint to sheriff, 12 February 1924, NAI, JUS/2007/56/1.

leave to appeal was refused. The scene appeared to be set for an execution.

This murder was very similar to Michael Manning's the previous month. Both involved married men, aged 24, who had drink taken and killed vulnerable women without evidence of planning. A key difference was that one victim was a young prostitute and the other an elderly nurse. Manning was not referred to in Stevenson's file even though he was hanged only weeks before the latter was convicted. The fact that Stevenson was British, and non-resident in Ireland, may have helped his case as the government would surely have wished to avoid creating a diplomatic incident. This certainly worked to his advantage in terms of mobilizing some international support and placing the state at risk of embarrassment if the execution went ahead. Stevenson's parents enlisted the help of their local member of parliament, a British representative of the Council of Europe, who organized a petition to be sent from the Council's Consultative Assembly bearing the signatures of two of the Irish representatives.

The possible ramifications for international relations may have been a factor in this case; Ireland did not want to cause ripples at the Council of Europe, of which it had been a founder member in 1949. But it is not clear that this would have been sufficient (the fact that James Lehman had been born in the United States did not save him in 1945). However, there was an intervention from unexpected quarters. As noted in Chapter 6, Stevenson (a Presbyterian) submitted a petition for clemency that was supported by the Holy See. The communication from the Vatican, in combination with the petition from the Council of Europe, and the victim's far from ideal status, was sufficient to cancel his appointment with the executioner.

Having avoided the noose, condemned men and women remained in prison to serve the terms of penal servitude that had been substituted for their death sentences. For how long is the subject of Chapter 10.

10

Release

Executive clemency describes the power vested in the Executive Council (later, government) to advise the governor general (later, president) to commute a sentence of death to one of penal servitude for life. The decision about when to release those to whom clemency had been shown involved an analogous process in that politicians once again became involved in determining what constituted an appropriate quantum of punishment. Prior to 1944 this decision was reserved to the Minister for Justice, taking account of the advice provided by his officials. After that date the government was always informed in advance of potential release dates. Whether there was a role for the president was not entirely clear.

In the early years of the Free State an intermediate step was occasionally taken whereby penal servitude for life was remitted to a fixed number of years.[1] When this happened, women benefited disproportionately on account of the enhanced remission available to them under the prison rules. Martin Joyce and Annie Walsh each had their sentences reduced to ten years penal

[1] The attorney general's advice was that if a life sentence was considered 'excessive' and it was felt that a lesser period of penal servitude would suffice, this decision was not to be made public. Rather a note was placed on the prisoner's file directing that the case be reviewed after a specified number of years 'which virtually means that the prisoner will then be released'. Letter from Hugh Kennedy to Minister for Home Affairs, 19 November 1923, NAI, JUS/H234/2024A. For example, the governor general commuted Denis Leen's death sentence to penal servitude for life on 13 March 1924. On 5 December 1925 the Executive Council reduced this to the time equivalent to a three-year sentence, allowing for the prevailing rate of remission (one quarter). He was released on licence on 8 May 1926, having served twenty-seven months. Similarly, Christina Russell's death sentence was commuted to penal servitude for life on 28 November 1930 and further reduced—by the governor general—to five years penal servitude (less standard remission) on 18 November 1933.

Justice, Mercy, and Caprice: Clemency and the Death Penalty in Ireland. First Edition. Ian O'Donnell. © Ian O'Donnell 2017. Published 2017 by Oxford University Press.

servitude but he served seven years and 192 days (based on one-quarter remission) and she served six years and 236 days (based on one-third remission).[2] The release of a life-sentence prisoner could be unconditional or on licence. After 1964, in cases of capital murder, every death sentence was commuted to a term of forty years.[3]

The consideration of whether and when to grant release followed the same tripartite scheme as that involved in granting clemency (see Chapter 2). Some releases were capricious, such as when the government decided there would be no review until a specified period had elapsed, yet when the time came and the review was initiated, it transpired that the person was no longer in prison. The reason for this unexpected turn of events was not always clear. Some releases were rooted in considerations of justice in that they were based on a combination of a risk assessment, a comparison of how long the individual had served compared with other similarly situated offenders, and a judgement that continued detention would do more harm than good as far as avoiding reconviction was concerned; these prisoners had earned release.[4] Some releases were merciful in that the offender's circumstances inclined the government towards leniency but, as described in detail below, mercy could be double-edged because release from prison not infrequently involved transfer to a religious-run institution and, ultimately, an extended period of coercive confinement.

This chapter has two aims. First of all, to analyse elements of the decision-making process associated with the release from

[2] The gender bias in remission was eliminated by s. 59 of the Prison Rules 2007 which introduced a standard rate of one quarter (and an enhanced rate of up to one third for prisoners who, through their conduct, had reduced the risk of recidivism).

[3] This practice was placed on a statutory footing by the Criminal Justice Act, 1990 which specified that anyone convicted of certain aggravated murders must be sentenced to life imprisonment (s. 2) and ordered to serve at least forty years (s. 4) to which remission would apply (s. 5).

[4] There was a view that after ten years or so of a life sentence, prisoners tended to become 'jittery', 'morose', and 'less amenable to prison discipline', with adverse implications for their physical and mental health. If they were held much beyond this time they found resettlement more difficult and this was contrary to society's interests. Memorandum for government in connection with the petition of James Fennell for mitigation of commuted sentence of penal servitude for life, 17 December 1948, NAI, JUS/18/4066A & B.

prison of men and women who had originally been sentenced to death and, secondly, to explore the onward destinations of those so released.

Procedures

Individuals serving sentences of penal servitude for life were released on licence under the powers granted in the Penal Servitude Acts, 1853 to 1891 and the Executive Powers (Convicts' Licences) Order, 1937. Section 5 of the Prevention of Crimes Act, 1871 specified that licence holders must notify the police of their place of residence and any change of address and that males, but not females, must report monthly to the local chief of police.[5] Section 4 specified that if licence conditions other than those set out in statutory form were to be applied—such as residence in a home operated by a religious congregation—they had to be laid before both Houses of the Oireachtas. To obviate this requirement, an understanding was arrived at with the women concerned on the basis that they would be released without going through this rather cumbersome procedure, so that they could not be compelled to stay at the home, but in the event of an unauthorized departure their licence would be revoked.[6] However, there had been no revocations since 1881 and this step was unlikely to be taken.[7]

[5] The Minister for Justice could release the licence holder from these reporting obligations at a later date subject to good behaviour and satisfactory police reports.

[6] The written authorization for release stated that the prisoner was relieved of her obligations under s. 5 of the Prevention of Crimes Act, 1871, so long as she placed herself under the care and supervision of the mother superior of a specified home. It is unlikely that many of the women concerned, who were often characterized as barely literate and slow witted, would have understood that this meant simply that if they moved they were obliged to inform the police of their whereabouts.

[7] Minute sheet—Deborah Sullivan, 21 October 1929, NAI, JUS/H234/2590. Indeed, there was some uncertainty regarding whether a revocation on these grounds would be legally permissible given that it was open to the government to add a condition of residence to the licence by laying the special condition before the Houses of the Oireachtas. By choosing not to do so, any departure from a home did not constitute a breach of a licence condition. Memorandum from S.A. Roche to Minister for Justice, February 1930, NAI, JUS/H234/1744. Of course, a breach of other conditions—typically to preserve the licence and

In other words, the women who remained in these homes could have exited without any immediate legal impediment, the only statutory requirement being that they notify the police of their change of address (although where they would have gone and how they would have survived were significant considerations). Once a transfer to a home had been effected the emphasis was on moral suasion rather than legal remedy. The fact that Mary Somerville left the Bethany Home to which she had been transferred—and indeed the jurisdiction—after a brief stay shows that unimpeded onward movement was possible, and that at least some women may have been aware of the legal ambiguity associated with their continued detention (see Chapter 8).[8]

On 18 April 1944 the government directed that the Minister for Justice must henceforth inform it in advance of any action he proposed to take regarding prisoners who had been sentenced to death and whose release was being considered.[9] The first case to be dealt with under the revised arrangements was that of Leo O'Brien and the question arose as to whether the correct procedure was for the president to remit the sentence of penal servitude for life, because under Article 13.6 of the Constitution only he could commute or remit punishment in capital cases.[10] It was not clear whether a capital case ceased to be one when it was commuted to penal servitude. If it did not, there was a continuing role for the president. If it did, or if what was at issue was seen as an aspect of sentence administration rather than an act of commutation or remission, then there was no need to involve the president. Pending an overhaul of the law in

produce it when requested to do so, to live a law-abiding and productive life, and to not associate with disreputable characters—could result in revocation.

[8] In accordance with the conditions of her licence, Somerville informed An Garda Síochána (and, indeed, the governor of Mountjoy Prison) of her new address. Letter from governor, Mountjoy Prison to secretary, Department of Justice, 15 February 1941, NAI, JUS/18/3110.

[9] The decision that the Minister for Justice could no longer unilaterally trigger the release of a person whose death sentence had been commuted, was made in the context of a review of procedures for the release of persons who had been found guilty but insane at the time of their trial but who were later certified to be sane. Memorandum for government, 29 March 1944, NAI, TSCH/3/S13311A.

[10] Memorandum for government in connection with petition from Leo O'Brien for mitigation of commuted sentence of penal servitude for life, 7 February 1945, NAI, JUS/18/8626A.

this area, the practice continued as before, without the head of state's involvement.

Unusually, when the proposal to release Tomás MacCurtain came up for consideration in 1948, the government decided to advise the president to remit the sentence. The involvement of the president reflected the wider circumstances of MacCurtain's conviction and the commutation of his death sentence (see Chapter 7), the fact that he had been dealt with by the Special Criminal Court, and the desire to release him unconditionally.[11] This move renewed uncertainty about where the decision-making authority resided but it did not set a precedent and, in anticipation of a review of the law in the area, there was a reversion to the previous practice of the minister alerting the government to planned releases, without reference to the president.[12]

One effect of the Criminal Justice Act, 1951 was that the minister was no longer required to advise the government of his intentions in these cases.[13] Nevertheless, he continued to do so, in accordance with the long-established convention. In 1953, when Mary Daly's case came up for consideration, the attorney general advised that the current practice be adhered to until the 'long awaited tidying up … of this archaic code is accomplished'.[14] In light of this advice, the minister proposed Mrs Daly's release to the government in the customary fashion.[15] Until the release of the last person to receive a mandatory death sentence for murder the Minister for Justice continued to issue the licence having notified his government colleagues of his intention to do so. Whether a capital case remained a capital case post-commutation was never satisfactorily resolved but the question became less vexed in light of consistent practice over many years.

The Criminal Justice Act, 1960 introduced the possibility of temporary release for prisoners. The legislative intent was to provide a means of releasing prisoners for short periods but, as

[11] Commutation and remission of punishments, 10 April 1951, NAI, TSCH/3/S9485A.

[12] Explanatory note, 13 July 1962, NAI, TSCH/3/98/6/65.

[13] Letter from H. Ó D. to rúnaí cúnta [assistant secretary], 13 July 1962, NAI, TSCH/3/98/6/65.

[14] Letter from P.P. O'Donoghue to ard-aighne, 6 November 1953, and ard-aighne's reply, 12 December 1953, NAI, TSCH/3/S9476B.

[15] Letter from T.S. Ó Donnabháin to secretary, Department of the Taoiseach, 19 December 1953, NAI, TSCH/3/S7788B.

the number of life-sentence prisoners grew, and an appropriate sentence-review mechanism did not exist, they came to be granted 'temporary release' that could be renewed indefinitely.[16] While the term 'parole' was regularly employed to describe this practice it was something of a misnomer.

A body called the 'parole board' exists today but its function is simply to advise the minister on matters of sentence administration for prisoners serving life sentences or fixed terms of eight years or more; it has no power to order release (Griffin and O'Donnell 2012).[17] The parole board was preceded by a sentence review group set up in 1989, four years after the last two death sentences were imposed. All but the murderers of members of An Garda Síochána had been released at this stage and when they came up for consideration the decision, unusually, was not for the government. As discussed further under the 'Why?' section, they were released under the terms of the Good Friday Agreement or as a result of a Supreme Court case taken by Noel Callan.

When?

Vaughan (2009: 326) noted that, by the end of the nineteenth century, murderers whose death sentences had been commuted to penal servitude for life were not considered for release until they had served twenty years. In the ensuing decades the average time served fell and, by the late 1970s, it stood at seven-and-a-half years.[18] When one considers that a man sentenced to death but shown clemency in the late-nineteenth century spent longer in

[16] The Minister for Justice, when discussing the proposed legislation, stated: 'The intention is to apply the grant of parole to cases where a close relative of a prisoner has died or is in imminent danger of death or where the domestic circumstances are such as to make it desirable, for humanitarian reasons, to grant parole; additionally, parole leave may be granted at intervals to selected long-term prisoners to enable them to regain some experience of freedom and perhaps to arrange for employment' (Dáil Debates, 28 June 1960, Oscar Traynor, vol. 183, col. 559–60).

[17] At time of writing (March 2017), the legislation to create a parole board was still awaited and the decision whether (and when) to release a life sentence prisoner remained one for the Minister for Justice and Equality.

[18] It rose rapidly thereafter, averaging nineteen-and-a-half years between 2010 and 2014 (Griffin and O'Donnell 2016: 270). Those convicted of capital murder were a class apart, serving thirty of the forty years imposed after remission was applied, unless released as a result of the Good Friday Agreement.

custody, in harsher conditions, and against a background of limited life expectancy compared to his counterpart a century later, there is only one possible interpretation: the softening of punishment over time. For those convicted and sentenced to death by non-jury courts the contrast was striking: men dealt with by special courts in the 1980s served, on average, twenty years longer in prison than their counterparts from the 1940s (Table 10.1).[19]

When the issue of release came up for review, the first consideration was the time already served, vis-a-vis a corresponding sentence of penal servitude (e.g. six years in custody equated with an eight-year sentence for a man and a nine-year sentence for a woman), and how the case compared with other life sentence prisoners. A measure was taken of practice in neighbouring jurisdictions and efforts were made to ascertain how long murderers in Ireland served in relation to their counterparts in Northern Ireland and in England and Wales.[20] While there were no hard and fast guidelines, broad principles emerged to ensure that release would not take place until a period of incarceration had been completed that was not disproportionately lenient with regard to the gravity of the crime. For example, as a 'working rule', the prison term thought appropriate for a woman who had killed her baby was two years, followed by a more open-ended period of coercive confinement at a religious institution.[21]

These rules were deployed when petitions were received from TDs and others regarding early release. They could be used to justify continued detention—he has not done enough time compared to those who went before, or release—he has now served longer than anyone else. Even if governments deviated from the rule there was reassurance to be found in being able to point to, if not necessarily follow, an established template.

[19] Some women spent longer inside than convicted terrorists. Hannah O'Leary was coercively confined for 462 months after conviction and Hannah Flynn for more than 550 months.

[20] Excluding extreme cases, the average in England and Wales, between 1919 and 1937, was twelve years; in Northern Ireland it was seven years. Memorandum for government in connection with the petition for release of Leo O'Brien, a prisoner serving a commuted sentence of penal servitude for life, 21 March 1945, NAI, JUS/18/8626A.

[21] Memorandum by James FitzGerald-Kenney, 17 November 1929, NAI, JUS/H234/2603A.

Table 10.1 Months in prison

	Men				Women	
	Jury trial		Non-jury trial		Jury trial	
	Median	(range)	Median	(range)	Median	(range)
1923–9	77	(27–103)	—	—	40	(2–224)
1930–9	132	(127–48)	21	n/a	30	(20–109)
1940–9	73	(36–143)	49	(45–93)	63	(43–88)
1950–9	92	(3–142)	—	—	21	n/a
1960–4	83	(76–86)	—	—	—	—
1965–90	—	—	287	(165–392)	—	—
All	88	(3–148)	165	(21–392)	40	(2–224)

Note: Time in custody is reckoned from date of conviction. When there was just one conviction during a period, no range is stated. William Wall was transferred to the Central Mental Hospital after three months in prison. Three men died during their prison sentences: James Murray after forty-nine months (pulmonary TB), Thomas O'Rourke after thirty-eight months (cardiac disease), and Seán McCaughey after fifty-six months (hunger strike). They have been omitted from the calculations in this table.

While Department of Justice officials had a general sense of how long should be served, the release date depended more upon the belief that the individual had done all that they could to rehabilitate themselves, that further incarceration would be counterproductive, and that a persuasive resettlement plan existed. There was a readiness to vary licence conditions towards this end, when possible. Also taken into account were reports from close observers of the prisoner such as the prison governor, medical officer, and chaplain, who passed on their assessments to the Department of Justice. The age and physical condition of the prisoner were factors, although not determinative, as on rare occasions the individual was allowed to die in custody.[22] In later years, when a professional probation service came into existence, its reports were accorded significant weight.

[22] Severe illness did not prompt mercy. James Murray failed to persuade the authorities to sanction his release when he became critically ill and he spent his final days coughing and spluttering in prison custody. In Thomas O'Rourke's case, the lack of mercy was partly because he had not been in prison long before his health deteriorated and partly because the crime had caused such revulsion that lenient treatment could not be contemplated. More benignly, it was also

The trend in time served by men convicted after jury trial varied during the period under examination, with those convicted in the 1930s serving longest.[23] For non-jury cases the trajectory was emphatically upwards: twenty-one months for the single case in the 1930s compared with an average of 287 months for those convicted in the 1980s. Men whose sentences were commuted served more than twice as long as women—eighty-eight months compared with forty months—but the range was narrower. When cases of infanticide are put to one side, the gender difference narrows considerably. There was a gulf in time served between women who killed infants (median: twenty-seven months; broadly in accordance with the Department of Justice guideline of two years) and women who killed adults (median: eighty-four months). This difference carried across to the total duration of coercive confinement which averaged forty-six months and 112 months respectively.[24] Excluding Edward O'Connor, the only man convicted of murdering his own child, the median time served for men was ninety months.[25]

For women whose death sentences were commuted there was wide variation in the time spent in prison (Table 10.1). For example, Deborah Sullivan was released five months after her conviction for the murder of her illegitimate child in County Kerry while Hannah Flynn served eighteen years and eight months for

felt that he might be better off remaining in prison so that he could avail of free medical treatment. In Seán McCaughey's case, the intransigence he faced was because the government had learned to its cost the price of leniency towards IRA hunger strikers (see Chapter 5). Mary Cadden died of heart failure in the Central Mental Hospital (CMH).

[23] When discussing time served, this is post-conviction. In addition, there would have been a period of remand in custody averaging four to five months (somewhat longer when there was a retrial).

[24] Excluding Mary Cadden who died in the CMH eight months after she was certified insane and transferred there from prison. Given the wide variation in time served, medians are used rather than means. The figure differs from that in Table 8.1 which is based on all infant killers, including Edward O'Connor, the only father to be sentenced to death for the murder of his child.

[25] O'Connor served three years in prison, illustrating the lesser value placed on infant life and sympathy for the highly stressful predicament that any unmarried parent could find themselves in. Patrick Aylward and Denis Foy killed children who were not their own and served significantly longer (103 months and 112 months respectively).

murdering the wife of a Kerry farmer.[26] Although their time in prison differed greatly, Sullivan and Flynn had in common that neither returned to the community. Sullivan was sent to Our Lady's Home where she remained until the Eucharistic Congress of 1932 (see later under 'Why?'). The Good Shepherd Sisters agreed to take Flynn into their care as the Sisters of Charity had done several weeks earlier for another female lifer, Hannah O'Leary, who had served almost as long (seventeen years and three months). The two women's further detention was not motivated by any desire to exercise control over them. Quite simply, they were so institutionalized at this point that independent living would have been a step too far and no one else could be found to offer accommodation and support.[27]

Flynn and O'Leary were notable not only for the length of time they spent in prison but also for the duration of their coercive confinement. Flynn spent thirty years in the Good Shepherd Magdalen asylum in Limerick before being sent to the county hospital where she died. O'Leary died twenty-one years later in the Sisters of Charity Magdalen asylum in Cork. Between them they spent over eighty-four years incarcerated.

Thus, when the state intended to be lenient by discharging a woman to the care of the nuns, its actions sometimes had the opposite effect and the duration of institutionalization extended beyond what was ever envisaged or what any man had to endure. In a few cases these female murderers ended up serving the equivalent of whole-life sentences, the salient difference as regards the loss of liberty being that they did not take their final breaths in a prison.[28] In other words, it could happen that the jury made a

[26] Only Elizabeth Doran spent less time in prison. She was transferred to the CMH two months after her conviction, and spent almost five years there before being conditionally discharged to the care of her son.

[27] In a note regarding their continued imprisonment the secretary of the Department of Justice stated that: 'We would let them go any time if there was any place for them to go. I am told that they are not unhappy where they are'. Memorandum from S.A. Roche to Minister for Justice, 20 May 1940, NAI, JUS/18/2770A & B.

[28] The available files do not contain details of what happened to women after their discharge to a religious institution. These gaps were filled by studying the (anonymized) case histories in the report of the Inter-Departmental Committee to Establish the Facts of State Involvement with the Magdalen Laundries (2013) and matching them to the cases of interest; by examining the lists of names on

strong recommendation to mercy, the judge endorsed this call, the government was persuaded that it would be wrong to allow the sentence of the court to take effect, the time served in prison was short, but the woman remained confined until death.[29] This was the dark side of benevolence.[30]

Mary Kiernan benefited from the swiftest release to the community. Sentenced to death on 28 October 1926, her sentence was commuted on 8 November 1926, and on 1 May 1927 the unexpired portion of her sentence was remitted. For the murder of her 12-day-old daughter, Bridget, she spent only six months in prison under sentence and no time at all in any other institution.

Whither?

In petitioning for, or accepting, the terms of their release women typically agreed to go to the nuns and men typically offered to emigrate. If there was a family member in Britain, Canada, Australia, or the United States this was alluded to, and if the prisoner was prepared to enter a convent this too became part of the argument in favour of release. A significant proportion of the women were discharged from prison to some other form of coercive confinement, usually a convent but sometimes the Central Mental

the laundries' gravestones (www.magdalenelaundries.com; Magdalen Names Project; site accessed 8 May 2015); and by searching death registrations at the General Register Office for matches by name and date of birth. Only for Mary Anne Keane did it prove impossible to uncover any reliable information relating to the likely duration of her stay with the nuns.

[29] Elizabeth Hannon was 30 years old when she killed her child; she spent less than three years in prison, but the rest of her life (another thirty years) in Dublin's High Park convent. Margaret Finn was 25 on conviction, spent a little over two years in prison, but the rest of her life in the Magdalen Asylum in Donnybrook, on Dublin's southside. Agnes McAdam, aged 53, spent three years and seven months in prison after her conviction. She was escorted by a prison officer to the Good Shepherd Convent in New Ross, County Wexford, where she remained until transferred to a nursing home to die thirteen-and-a-half years later. Hannah Flynn and Hannah O'Leary never returned to the community either, but they spent much longer in prison before moving to convents.

[30] These religious institutions were not places of ease or of quiet, prayerful reflection. The work regime was gruelling, the conditions were austere, the dietary was basic, the degree of identity transformation was profound (inmates were assigned new names and their past lives were effaced), and confinement there carried an enduring stigma.

Hospital (CMH); only seven out of twenty-one were permitted to re-enter the community directly. For men, anything other than release to the community was exceptional (Table 10.2).

The gender politics of the release decision repays scrutiny. Paternalism may have saved women's necks but it also diverted some of them into lifetimes of compulsory penitence. They were both advantaged and disadvantaged on account of their gender. If the home to which the woman was transferred had an associated laundry she spent her days scrubbing away the criminal and moral stains that had led her there. These women were shown clemency in the name of justice or mercy but denied their liberty for extended periods. They were treated harshly for their own good, the stern hand of the state and the Sisters was required to prevent them from straying.

Some were pathetic and hopeless creatures for whom resettlement in a potentially hostile community was not a realistic prospect; the convent was a refuge for these women at a time when few other supports were available. Some, no doubt, felt that they deserved to suffer for what they had done and that they had earned a lifetime of prayer and forced labour. When we think of coercive confinement in general rather than penal servitude in particular it becomes clear that they experienced compassion's

Table 10.2 Post-prison destinations

	Men	Women
Community	24	7
Religious institution	0	12
Central Mental Hospital	1	2
Other hospital	1	0
Died in prison	2	0
All	28	21

Note: Of those convicted before non-jury courts who avoided execution (all male), twelve were released from prison custody to the community, one (Thomas Hunt) was transferred to an internment camp for five months, and one (Seán McCaughey) died on hunger strike. Eleven women were transferred to convents run by Catholic religious congregations and one (Mary Somerville) was discharged to the Church of Ireland Bethany Home in the Dublin suburb of Rathgar.

hard edge. Two of the women who were discharged to the community rather than to another form of institutional life stayed with religiously inspired carers. Annie Walsh was released to Catherine Lennon, the wife of a protestant clergyman, and Frances Cox was offered a home by another God-fearing woman, Major Acton of the Salvation Army.

Although clemency was shown in infanticide cases, the type of society that gave rise to these crimes also ensured that the perpetrators, while not imprisoned for long compared to male murderers, were coercively confined for extravagant periods. The shame and stigma of unmarried motherhood were widely understood and served to negate the risk of execution and to mitigate prison sentences. But the self-same factors ensured that pain and captivity continued in another guise. When coercive confinement rather than prison time is considered, the apparent gender difference in the duration of incarceration narrows. Indeed, for the 1920s and 1940s, it is reversed (Table 10.3).[31]

The duration of coercive confinement was calculated up to the point when a release date was fixed. If the woman left the home at this point but found a position in a convent somewhere else this subsequent period was not included on the basis that the woman's liberty had been restored but she chose to remain with the nuns, even if not subject to any conditions and in a different institution. This is probably best viewed as employment rather than coercive confinement, even though the two lifestyles probably had much in common (with the notable advantage that the woman was no longer residing with other convicted criminals).[32] In some cases the practical arrangements required to give effect to the unconditional release took time to put in place. In other words, life with the nuns may have continued for a while after the strictures of coercive confinement had formally been shaken off.

[31] The median is used rather than the mean in the tables that address time served because the existence of a few extreme values distorts the picture. For example, the mean for the 1920s is sixty-nine months—compared to a median of forty—on account of the 224 months spent in prison by Hannah Flynn and the 207 served by Hannah O'Leary.

[32] Kate Owens was a partial exception as her release was conditional on entering employment with the Sisters of Charity, where she felt she was 'held'; liberty was not fully restored for a couple of years. It is possible, of course, that had she not accepted the offer of employment, her period of coercive confinement would have been extended.

Table 10.3 Months in coercive confinement

	Men		Women	
	Jury trial	Non-jury trial	Jury trial	
	Median	Median	Median	(range)
1923–9	77	—	85	(6–551)
1930–9	132	21	42	(20–271)
1940–9	73	52	88	(61–204)
1950–9	92	—	30	n/a
1960–4	83	—	—	—
1965–90	—	287	—	—
All	88	165	79	(6–551)

Note: Not all of the women who were transferred from prison to another site of coercive confinement regained their liberty. Mary Cadden died in the Central Mental Hospital. Hannah Flynn died in the county home to which she was transferred from a convent. Agnes McAdam died in the nursing home to which she had been moved from a convent. Hannah O'Leary, Elizabeth Hannon, and Margaret Finn remained with the nuns until death. The period of coercive confinement is reckoned from date of conviction to date of release or death. Where the date is uncertain the most proximate one is used; in other words the figures in the table are based on minimum estimates. Where there was just one conviction during a period, no range is stated. It was not possible to discover how long William Wall spent in the Central Mental Hospital.

Paralleling the slow pace of law reform when it came to removing child killing from the net of death-eligible crimes was the lack of interest in what happened to women who were discharged to convents. There is a poignant note on Agnes McAdam's file where, in response to an enquiry as to her whereabouts in 1965, it was stated that she had been released to the care of a religious community and that it was not known if she was still alive.[33] She had died two years prior to the receipt of this letter. Given that I could discover her date of death relatively easily at a remove of more than half a century it seems implausible that an official in the Department of Justice could not have done so at the time, and callous that they did not deem this worth doing.

Mulryan et al. (2002) found that, between 1850 and 2000, women committed to the CMH on child murder or infanticide

[33] Letter from Department of Justice to James J. Smyth, 15 February 1965, NAI, JUS/18/9074A & B.

charges spent 9.3 years there on average. Like female prisoners, there was considerable variation in the time these patients were detained, ranging from three months to thirty-eight years. This was longer than women who had been jailed for the same acts, especially if convicted of manslaughter or concealment of birth.

In a study of women admitted to the same institution between 1910 and 1948, twenty-four of whom had been charged with killing (usually of their child), Kelly (2008: 318–19) found that the mean duration of detention was 5.6 years (range: less than one year to twenty-seven years). For those who arrived with a life sentence, the average time in the asylum was 13.5 years. The medical records, which were available for thirty-two cases, indicated that 22 per cent died in the CMH, 28 per cent were transferred to local asylums, 3 per cent went to prison, and 3 per cent were transferred to a convent.[34] The remainder were released 'cured', or to the care of family or friends, or the outcome was unknown.

Women who avoided a murder conviction because they were deemed unfit to plead or found guilty but insane spent long periods in the CMH before moving to other forms of coercive confinement (often the local asylum, on rare occasions prison or a convent; see Chapter 1). What appeared on the face of it to be a pattern of lenient treatment turned out to involve long-term institutionalization in any event; albeit with an orientation that was ostensibly therapeutic. The subtlety of this distinction was no doubt lost on the poorly educated women who faced many years in austere psychiatric institutions. The nature of the treatments available at the time would have added to their distress, and no doubt to their docility, especially if they found themselves subjected to insulin coma therapy, electroconvulsive therapy, or psychosurgery.

Thomas Kelly was one of only two men convicted by a jury not to be released from prison to the community. In November 1947, aged 68, he was in poor health and there were no relatives to take care of him. He had been in prison for more than eleven years and was sent to St Kevin's Hospital in Dublin for treatment. The following month he was released on licence from the hospital. William Wall was transferred to the CMH soon after his arrival

[34] Kate Moran, a 30-year-old servant charged with murdering her twin daughters, was found guilty but insane on 25 February 1932 and sent to the CMH (then known as the Central Criminal Lunatic Asylum). She was discharged to the care of the nuns after thirty-two months.

in Portlaoise Prison.[35] One political murderer (Thomas Hunt) was transferred from prison to the Curragh internment camp where he spent five months before being released. This explains the difference between Tables 10.1 and 10.3, where the median duration of coercive confinement for men convicted by non-jury courts in the 1940s is slightly longer than the median prison term. For all other periods the median terms served by men after jury and non-jury trials are identical.

The twenty-eight men whose death sentences were commuted to penal servitude for life after jury trials served an aggregate of one month's additional confinement after leaving prison (this was Thomas Kelly's brief stay in St Kevin's Hospital). This averages out at around one day each.[36] The fourteen men convicted by non-jury courts served an aggregate of five months after release (this was Thomas Hunt in the Curragh camp); an average of under two weeks each. The total number of additional months of coercive confinement for the twenty-one women who avoided the noose was 1,621 (minimum estimate), with a median of twenty-two months.

Moral differences matter

The Magdalen asylums at High Park (Drumcondra) and Gloucester Street were run by the Sisters of Our Lady of Charity of Refuge. A different congregation, the Sisters of Charity, operated St Mary Magdalen's Asylum in Donnybrook. The Sisters of Charity of St Vincent de Paul ran Our Lady's Home on Henrietta Street. All of these institutions were in Dublin and received female murderers on their release from the city's Mountjoy Prison.

[35] Accommodation was found for Martin Griffin in a night shelter run by the Society of St Vincent de Paul but there was nothing compulsory about the arrangement. This was motivated partly by a desire to do right by an old man who would otherwise struggle to survive in a strange city (Griffin was 65 years old when released) and partly out of concern to prevent adverse media comment should he attempt to commit suicide having been released without the proper supports: 'This is the kind of case on which the British Sunday Papers would go to town in showing up our inhuman attitude'. Note re: Martin Griffin by Peter Berry, 14 March 1955, NAI, JUS/18/6470A & B.

[36] This is a minimum estimate as it has not been possible to establish how long William Wall spent in the CMH (see Chapter 7).

The homes operated by the different religious congregations served very different purposes and housed very different populations. A Department of Justice memorandum on Our Lady's Home set this out unambiguously:

> Most of the cases assigned to Our Lady's Home are girls convicted of petty pilfering but there are also some infanticide cases. The cases assigned to the Good Shepherd Convents are, for the most part, 'street walkers', and women of loose morals. The aim of the Good Shepherd Nuns is to retain these women who are generally known as Penitents in the convent in the hope that they may elect to stay permanently as Magdalens. The Good Shepherd Nuns belong to an enclosed Order and never leave the precincts of their convent. The women and girls committed to them are not allowed outside the Institution. It is important to bear these facts in mind when considering the work of the various Homes.[37]

According to Evelyn Carroll (1941: 4), a probation officer who was familiar with the institutional provision available for women and girls who came before the courts on serious charges, Our Lady's Home accepted 'first offenders provided they are not of immoral character' and 'the "better types" among girls charged with infanticide and kindred crimes'. The home catered chiefly for those aged between eighteen and twenty-four years. There was a preference for referrals from the courts and most inmates were committed under the Probation of Offenders Act, 1907 to spend a fixed period there (often twelve months) instead of going to prison. Some young women were sent on a voluntary basis by parents or social workers. When leaving the care of the Sisters who ran the home, women who were not returning to their families were found positions as domestic servants or as maids in one of the city's hospitals or in another institution operated by a religious body.

Our Lady's Home compared favourably with the Magdalen asylums where the regime was strict and the religious training imparted to the inmates was directed at leading them to renounce the world and its temptations and to enter upon a life of penitence at the institution.

Carroll felt that these arrangements worked well: 'On the whole, results from this home are fairly satisfactory. The girls

[37] Our Lady's Home, 13 January 1944, NAI, JUS/90/16/77.

are given the advantage of a fresh start without the stigma of a prison sentence and many of them definitely make good' (p. 4).[38] A detailed report on the home prepared by an inspector from the Department of Industry and Commerce, at the behest of the Department of Justice, described it as suitable for 'discharged female Catholic prisoners; also for girls whose faith or morals are in danger'.[39]

Those who were sent to Our Lady's Home (including released life sentence prisoners) were received with a view to preparing them for employment, isolating them from potentially corrupting peers, and holding them for a relatively brief period of time. There was a simmering anxiety that if they were sent elsewhere this might cause further moral slippage which could spread to the outside community when the woman was eventually set free, thereby undermining the project for national purity. There was a footnote to Carroll's memorandum to the effect that: 'We have also to consider that the women charged with such offences as infanticide are far less guilty than the larger numbers in the more exalted walks of life who have recourse to the use of contraceptives and abortifacients' (p. 2). This says a great deal about the moral environment of the day, when to use contraception was considered more heinous than to murder a child.

Women knew that convents were punitive places. In 1924, Richard Devane, a Jesuit priest, noted that a magistrate had informed him that women offenders often 'expressed to me in Court a desire to go, in *some* cases they have begged to be sent, to prison rather than a Home' (cited in O'Sullivan and O'Donnell 2012: 56; emphasis in original). Devane was baffled at this intelligence and found the women's attitude to be odd and unreasonable, given what he saw as the loving care extended to them by the nuns. He acknowledged that some easing of the penitent's life might be appropriate but could not explain the disinclination on the part of wayward women to avail of what the Sisters offered.

[38] In 1944, for example, there were twenty-eight admissions to Our Lady's Home, of which eighteen resulted from court cases and ten were voluntary. During the same year, nineteen inmates were returned to their parents, situations were found for six, and four were transferred to other homes. Report—1944, NAI, JUS/90/16/77.

[39] Our Lady's Home, 13 January 1944, NAI, JUS/90/16/77.

We know enough now about the degrading and harsh life of the penitent to understand their reluctance.

Senator Connolly O'Brien's comments in a parliamentary debate in 1960 show that this sentiment endured over time:

> If I were asked to advise girl delinquents, no matter what offences they were charged with, whether to go to prison on remand, or to go to St Mary Magdalen's Asylum on remand, I would advise them wholeheartedly to choose prison, because I think having a record of having been in prison as a juvenile delinquent would not be so detrimental to the after life of the girl as to have it legally recorded that she was an inmate of St Mary Magdalen's Asylum.[40]

The use of convents as an adjunct to the criminal justice system was rare before independence. According to Rattigan (2012: 208–11), of fifty-one women convicted of the murder or manslaughter of an infant, or of concealment of birth, between 1900 and 1921, one was sent to a convent (in Dublin) and another to a Salvation Army home (in Belfast). Matters changed dramatically thereafter. Between 1922 and 1950, of 151 women convicted of the same range of crimes, half were sent to religious institutions (seventy-four to convents and four to the Bethany Home). The new Irish state was characterized by a prurient penality. Chastity for the unmarried became integral to the maintenance of social and moral order.

Embarrassing oversights

The record in the government minutes of 9 February 1962 of the decision to spare David Galvin's life was a little more detailed than usual. After the standard statement to the effect that the president was to be advised to commute the sentence to penal servitude for life in exercise of the power vested in him by the Constitution, the following paragraph appeared:

> The foregoing decision was arrived at on the understanding that the reprieve in this case would be followed by a long term of imprisonment, and it was decided that this understanding should be brought to the notice of the Government in the event of the question of Mr Galvin's release from custody being submitted to them.

The fact that the government took such an unusual step reinforces the suggestion made in Chapter 7 that Galvin came close

[40] Seanad Debates, 13 July 1960, Nora Connolly O'Brien, vol. 52, col. 2006.

to the gallows. The same language is found in the minutes of the government meeting that took place on 10 August 1962 when the decision to advise the president to commute James Kelly's death sentence was recorded. In neither case did the man serve as long as the government intended. Galvin was out of prison seven years after his conviction and Kelly after six.

Similar recommendations had been made in the past and not honoured. For example, the releases of Patrick Fagan and Charles Molloy, each of whom had served less than six-and-a-half years, in honour of the Eucharistic Congress in 1932 conflicted with the stipulation by the Executive Council that their cases should not be reviewed before ten years had elapsed. This decision was not well communicated. As Molloy's and Fagan's ten-year deadlines approached, the Department of Justice was alerted so that the minister might be prompted to take 'any action he may consider desirable'.[41] The news that the men had been released some years previously must have come as quite a surprise.

These releases were not based on criminal justice considerations and we cannot know if they were merciful (Molloy's and Fagan's certainly were as they coincided with a major religious celebration) but we can say they were capricious.

Why?

There were six releases in honour of the thirty-first Eucharistic Congress which took place in Dublin between 21 and 26 June 1932 amid scenes described by the pontiff himself as of 'stupendous magnificence'.[42] For one-quarter of the country's population to be on its knees simultaneously in the Phoenix Park was

[41] Letters from secretary, Department of President of Executive Council to secretary, Department of Justice, 12 February 1936, NAI, JUS/H234/1119A & B and NAI, JUS/H234/1132A.

[42] The pope's words were recalled in a newspaper editorial lamenting the death of Cardinal MacRory (*Irish Independent*, 15 October 1945). Four men were released directly from Portlaoise Prison: Charles Molloy and Patrick Fagan on 21 June, each having served seventy-seven months; William Devereux and Patrick Aylward on 30 June, each having served 103 months. On 22 June, two women were released from Our Lady's Home: Mary Moynihan (ninety months after conviction and twenty-three months after entering the home) and Deborah Sullivan (thirty-six months after conviction and thirty-one months after entering the home).

something truly remarkable. It would perhaps have been surprising had there been no gesture towards prisoners during such a huge event in a country where Catholicism was so dominant.

The fact that the women released to acclaim the Eucharistic Congress—Mary Moynihan and Deborah Sullivan—were discharged from convents indicates that their continued confinement was acknowledged as coercive and excessive. Yet, both remained with the nuns on a voluntary basis afterwards. Sullivan's actual (unconditional) release did not take effect for a further six months at which point she took up a 'paid situation' in one of the congregation's homes. Her desire to stay with the Sisters of Charity of St Vincent De Paul was explained as follows by her probation officer: 'She does not want to face the neighbours around her home.'[43] Moynihan was similarly adrift, returning to the reverend mother after a visit home so that a position could be found for her in one of the congregation's houses, which it was, two months after her release, at St Philomena's orphanage in Stillorgan, a suburb of Dublin.

The release of women from homes run by Catholic religious congregations to mark a major ecclesiastical event says a great deal about the shared priorities of church and state in relation to acceptable moral standards and social order. The fact that the women found it impossible to resettle afterwards indicates that these priorities were shared by the community more generally. (The Eucharistic Congress releases did not meet with universal approval. A note on Deborah Sullivan's file expressed some doubt about the wisdom of releasing her as she seemed happy in the convent and 'there is something a little silly about the proposal to release these women "in honour of the Eucharistic Congress" '.[44])

Hannah Flynn and Hannah O'Leary might have benefited from leniency at the time of the Eucharistic Congress having been in custody for 100 months and 84 months respectively. But they were passed over and, having missed this opportunity, would each spend another decade in prison before being discharged to the care of the nuns. The other capital prisoners at the time of the Eucharistic Congress had been convicted relatively recently

[43] Letter from Kathleen Sullivan to secretary, Department of Justice, 27 June 1932, NAI, JUS/H234/2590.

[44] Minute sheet—Deborah Sullivan, 21 October 1929, NAI, JUS/H234/2590.

(Martin Joyce, Annie Walsh, and Catherine Ahearne in June 1929, Christina Russell in November 1930, and Margaret Finn in March 1931) and so had not spent long enough inside to merit serious consideration.[45]

The Holy Year of 1950 was another occasion when prisoners benefited from Catholic celebrations. The government decided that anyone serving a sentence of imprisonment with less than one month unexpired on 1 January 1950 would be released at once; those with more than one month remaining would receive remission of 50 per cent, up to a maximum of three months. For those serving fixed terms of penal servitude, six months remission was to be granted in each case. Those serving commuted death sentences were not obliged on this occasion.

There were two interesting aspects to the Holy Year amnesty. First of all, it was prompted by the Vatican, which suggested (via the Ambassador in Rome) that the government should grant:

> ... an amnesty to a certain number of ordinary prisoners whose offences are of the less serious kind and should publicly declare that this action was in accordance with the principles of charity and mercy imposed upon all by the spirit of the Holy Year and in harmony with the Holy Father's desire that the special clemency should be shown by those in authority'.[46]

Secondly, the scheme finally adopted was more modest than originally proposed by the Minister for Justice, Seán MacEoin, which was for a 25 per cent discount across the board, to acknowledge that the Vatican had asked for a 'significant gesture'.[47]

Another example of prisoner releases coinciding with a church occasion took place on 25 February 1965 to mark the elevation of the Most Revd Dr Conway, Archbishop of Armagh and Primate of All Ireland, to the Sacred College of Cardinals. On the day that Dr Conway accepted the red hat from Pope Paul, forty-five prisoners

[45] All prisoners due for release within one month of the date of the congress were reviewed and thirty-nine were released. Memorandum for government: amnesty for Holy Year, 17 October 1949, NAI, TSCH/3/S14620. The daily average prison population in 1932 was 627 (O'Donnell et al. 2005: 145.) A petition for the release of all first offenders to mark the congress was considered by the Executive Council on 17 June 1932, but not granted. Extract from cabinet minutes, 18 June 1932, NAI, TSCH/3/S6005/19A.

[46] Memorandum for Government, 17 October 1949, NAI, TSCH/3/S14620.

[47] Memorandum for Government, 17 October 1949, NAI, TSCH/3/S14620.

had the balance of their sentences remitted and walked free from prison.[48] There was another wave of releases to mark the visit to Ireland in 1979 of Pope John Paul II. Since then, the trajectory has been for prisoner release initiatives based on Catholic celebrations, including the traditional Easter and Christmas releases, to diminish in significance (O'Donnell and Jewkes 2011) and it is difficult to imagine that they could be revived. As fewer shared values can be taken for granted, and transparency is emphasized, and victims' voices are raised, the degree of daring that such a venture would require increases and its likely public acceptability decreases. No longer can it be assumed that the divine origins of mercy will resonate with a devout public.

Statecraft

Tomás MacCurtain was released from his sentence of penal servitude for life on 9 March 1948, alongside Henry (Harry) White (aka Anderson) and James Smith, the only other political prisoners in the country at the time. The following day, *The New York Times* reported the Taoiseach's rationale with these words: 'This action, Mr. Costello said, had been taken to remove any source of irritation or resentment among a small section of the populace at a time when so much good-will was being manifested toward the new government'. He was quoted in the *Irish Press*, also on 10 March, as saying that, after careful examination, he had concluded that continued 'detention of these men would only result in perpetuation of resentment and unrest and that the public interest would be best served by releasing them'.

Costello's actions were intended to quell any lingering sense of rancour that might be stoked into something more oppositional should the period of detention be unnecessarily prolonged. This was a more eloquent statement that the conflict had ended and that the state desired the restoration of harmonious relations with former enemies, than any formal legal arrangement or treaty could have made.[49] It was also the act of a state that was

[48] Official news item, Department of Justice, 25 February 1965, NAI, JUS/2002/2/97.

[49] MacCurtain did not repay the trust shown in him with loyalty to the state. He was jailed by the Dublin District Court in January 1957 for membership of an unlawful organization and possession of incriminating documents.

growing in confidence that it could exercise power benevolently without appearing incautious. Six months after the last IRA prisoners were released, Costello declared that Ireland was a republic and would be leaving the Commonwealth. Legislative effect was given to this declaration in the Republic of Ireland Act, 1948, which came into force the following year.

Costello's words echoed those of Hamilton (1788) that the principal argument in favour of a pardoning power was that, 'in seasons of insurrection or rebellion, there are often critical moments, when a well-timed offer of pardon to the insurgents or rebels may restore the tranquillity of the commonwealth; and which, if suffered to pass unimproved, it may never be possible afterwards to recall'. Hamilton was describing a scenario where swift action was required and, if it was necessary to obtain the sanction of the legislature, the opportunity might be lost. Costello's actions were not tightly constrained by time but the sentiment remained the same.[50]

Prior to the abolition of the mandatory death sentence for murder in 1964, political prisoners had either suffered a swift death or been granted quick—and unconditional—release; there was to be no convict's licence for the IRA man.[51] The release had to be unconditional in these cases as there would not have been an admission of guilt, an expression of remorse, or even an acknowledgement that the conviction and sentence were legitimate. For other prisoners, early release depended on contrition, reformation, and a clear plan for the future. IRA men were treated differently at every point in the proceedings. They were no more likely to be executed than other murderers (see Chapter 4) and if spared prior to the 1980s they served less time in prison than other men whose death sentences were commuted (Table 10.1).

Capital murder

Those sentenced to death post-1964, all of whom had been convicted of murdering on-duty members of An Garda Síochána, were

[50] For this reason, Hamilton felt that 'the benign prerogative of pardoning should be as little as possible fettered or embarrassed'.

[51] Memorandum for government in connection with petition for the release of Michael Walsh and Patrick Davern who are serving commuted sentences of penal servitude for life for the murder of Michael Devereux, 7 November 1945, NAI, TSCH/3/S7788B.

released either under the terms of the Good Friday Agreement (if they were affiliated to a group that supported the ceasefire in Northern Ireland), or having served three-quarters of their forty-year commuted sentences (if they were not politically aligned but benefited from the successful Supreme Court case taken by Noel Callan, referred to in Chapter 5). It was clear that the government's intention in Michael McHugh's case was that he would serve the prescribed term in full. The minutes of the cabinet meeting held on 19 December 1985 were unambiguous:

> Following consideration of a memorandum dated 18 December, 1985, submitted by the Minister for Justice, it was decided to advise the President, to commute to penal servitude for forty years, the sentence of death imposed by the Special Criminal Court on 3 December, 1985, on Michael McHugh on his conviction of the capital murder of Garda Sergeant Patrick Morrissey, on the understanding that the full sentence of forty years would be served without remission.

The language used in Noel Callan's case did not contain any reference to an 'understanding' that the full forty years would be served, suggesting perhaps that the government of the day distinguished between the culpability of the two killers of Garda Morrissey. There are faint echoes here of Minister for Justice Gerald Boland's comment in Hunt's case that he was an easily led young man who had not realized the full extent of what he was involved with (see Chapter 5). The difference was that Callan served thirty years as opposed to Hunt's five and, had he not persisted with a legal action—which was strenuously resisted by the state—he would have remained in prison for another decade; judges, rather than politicians, were the ultimate arbiters of his release date.

Callan's action had a more immediate effect for Colm O'Shea and Patrick McCann, each of whom had served thirty-two years and eight months when the case was decided, and were released within weeks as a result, thereby benefiting from an unexpected—and substantial—discount on their sentences.[52] Had it not been

[52] In 2016, McCann was re-imprisoned for ten months at Tullamore District Court following charges of trespass, theft, criminal damage, arson, and interfering with property (*Irish Independent*, 30 April 2016). He was a shambling figure, institutionalized and ill-equipped to contend with life at liberty. He expressed a desire to return to prison where he would be relieved of the responsibility of self care. Soon after he finished this sentence he was in court again on

for these events it is almost certain that the men would have served the full forty-year terms in light of the lack of any ambiguity regarding the government's intentions when their death sentences were commuted.[53] O'Shea and McCann were 'quietly released from jail' in August 2013 (*Irish Independent*, 14 October 2013). Indeed, their release was so quiet that the newspapers did not find out about it until several months later.

Had any of these men been members of the IRA they would have been released much earlier, alongside the capital murderers whose membership of a 'qualifying organisation' allowed them to avail of the terms of the Criminal Justice (Release of Prisoners) Act, 1998 which gave effect to the terms of the Good Friday Agreement. This legislation permitted the government or the Minister for Justice to commute or remit sentences or to order release. A commission was established to advise the minister on the question of sequencing with a view to releasing all eligible prisoners over a two-year period. As noted in Chapter 5, the four IRA men who had been convicted of capital murder (Peter Rogers, Patrick McPhillips, Brian McShane, and Thomas Eccles) were early beneficiaries of this process, regaining their liberty on 22 December 1998.[54]

The terminology of pardon, clemency, or mercy was not used to describe this accelerated release programme, no doubt out

a criminal damage charge. Homeless, drunk and struggling with mental health problems, he continued to find it difficult to cope (*Irish Times*, 15 March 2017). McHugh came to attention again for his alleged role in a brawl at a public house; it is not known if criminal proceedings followed (*The Evening Herald*, 9 January 2016).

[53] The statement issued by Government Information Services read: 'The President, on the advice of the Government, in accordance with Article 13 of the Constitution, has today commuted the sentences of death passed on Patrick McCann, Colm O'Shea and Peter Pringle, to sentences of penal servitude for forty years. The Government's decision so to advise the President was taken on the basis that the full sentence of forty years will be served without remission in each case', 27 May 1981, NAI, PRES/2013/97/22.

[54] A total of forty-nine prisoners were released in the Republic of Ireland, twenty-five of whom had been repatriated. The majority (thirty-eight) were members of the Provisional IRA, six claimed membership of the INLA, and five were unaligned (Release of Prisoners Commission 2000: para. 13). For McShane, Phillips, and Eccles, the cabinet said nothing at its meeting on 20 February 1986 about understanding that the term was to be served in full without remission, again perhaps reflecting their level of involvement in the crime for which they had been convicted.

of deference to the sensibilities of the victims of the Troubles in Northern Ireland and the political sensitivities around releasing men who many thought should languish behind bars for the full duration of the terms substituted by the government for the death sentences imposed by the Special Criminal Court. Nonetheless, what they received was in the nature of a conditional pardon; they were not relieved of culpability for what they had done but the legal consequences that followed their acts were ameliorated.

The releases were subject to a variety of conditions relating to future conduct.[55] One of these prisoners explained that, for what remained of his forty-year term, he was required to be of sober habits and not to make any public utterances that could distress the family of the Garda for whose murder he had been sentenced to death. Unlike other released life sentence prisoners there was no reporting requirement.[56] The release decision was in each case took account of the seriousness of the offence committed and the need to protect the community. But, given that all qualifying prisoners were to be released within a fixed time frame, the commission's primary concern was choreography. As in the 1940s, murderers who could call on political motivation received swifter release than those who could not.

It is necessary to differentiate amnesties for particular classes (e.g. IRA prisoners) and amnesties where a selection is made (e.g. those accompanying the Eucharistic Congress), from other, more quotidian, uses of executive clemency. Mercy, by definition, requires individualization—one of its defining features is its singularity—so amnesties based on categorical decision-making cannot properly be seen as instances of mercy. Neither do amnesties necessarily exemplify justice because some eligible prisoners may have served much longer than others when released. Nor do they involve caprice because they are the outcome of a deliberative process.

The Eucharistic Congress releases were a manifestation of mercy in that individualized assessments resulted in the reduction of deserved punishment. The six individuals concerned had

[55] Release of Prisoners Commission (2000: para. 12). Of around 450 prisoners released on licence, ten were back in prison by July 2011 for alleged involvement in politically motivated offences with another thirteen re-imprisoned for 'ordinary' crimes (McEvoy and Mallinder 2013: 457).

[56] Interview with author, 1 June 2016.

got what the state stipulated their conduct merited, namely commuted sentences of penal servitude for life, and any further mitigation depended on the favourable disposition of the government. Also, as there was not a blanket release of lifers this 'amnesty' is probably better seen as multiple simultaneous instances of mercy.

The release of IRA men in the 1990s was different. This was motivated by a desire to consolidate the peace process in Northern Ireland, not out of sympathy for the prisoners' plight. While the releases were staggered, all qualifying prisoners exited prison within the two-year time frame.

The Good Friday Agreement was a hybrid affair. It had some of the qualities of an amnesty in that it was applied to a category of prisoner, was politically inspired, and aimed at the restoration of national harmony. But it was individualized in that the beneficiaries were released in batches, based on an assessment of the harm caused and the risk posed.

These releases emphasized the importance of clemency as a means of promoting the interests of peace and security; of reinforcing the authority of the state; of being able to release prisoners without returning to the vexed question of culpability; of forgetting without forgiving; of exacting less than what is due in the interests of national tranquillity; of sacrificing considerations of justice on the altar of pragmatism.

Postscript

Ireland ceased being a killing state by degrees. The final execution took place on 20 April 1954 when Michael Manning felt Albert Pierrepoint place a noose around his neck.[1] A carter from Limerick, Manning had ambushed and suffocated Catherine Cooper, a nurse forty years his senior. This was a brutal crime involving a vulnerable victim who was badly beaten and sexually assaulted. By Manning's own account he was making his way home after a day's drinking when he saw a woman he did not recognize walking alone. As he put it afterwards: 'I suddenly lost my head and jumped on the woman and remember no more until the lights of a car shone on me.'[2] Manning took flight at this point but was arrested within hours.

He apologized for what he had done and blamed his appalling conduct on the effects of the large quantity of alcohol he had consumed. He also argued that while guilty, he was insane. The jury was not persuaded and convicted him of murder. In accordance with the law the judge imposed the mandatory sentence of death. Manning wrote to the Minister for Justice from his prison cell seeking mercy but his supplications were to no avail. Similarly, a petition for clemency signed by members of the Cooper family failed to deflect justice from its dismal course. Adding to the poignancy of the occasion, Manning's young wife was heavily pregnant with their first child. She wrote to the governor of the prison the week after her husband had been executed to thank him and his staff for their kindness, and to request a death certificate so that she could claim the widow's pension to which she had prematurely become entitled.

[1] Manning was the only person to be executed by the Republic of Ireland, which replaced the Free State in 1949.

[2] Petition from a person under death sentence for mitigation of sentence, 26 February 1954, NAI, TSCH/3/S15641.

Justice, Mercy, and Caprice: Clemency and the Death Penalty in Ireland. First Edition. Ian O'Donnell. © Ian O'Donnell 2017. Published 2017 by Oxford University Press.

It appears that Manning bore his sentence well, passing his time smoking Players cigarettes and reading the *Irish Independent*. On the morning of his execution he attended Mass. The prison's Catholic chaplains reported afterwards that he faced death with 'fortitude and resignation'.[3] Just before 8 a.m. on 20 April 1954, Albert Pierrepoint and his assistant Robert Stewart entered the condemned man's cell and pinioned his wrists. Together they made the short journey to the hang house. Upon arrival Manning was positioned on the oak trap doors. His legs were strapped, a linen cap was pulled over his head, and the rope was fixed in place. The officials stood aside, the lever was pulled, and Manning fell to his death. Pierrepoint prided himself on his skill calculating the drop required to break a prisoner's neck swiftly; having carried out several hundred hangings he had unrivalled expertise in this regard. For Manning, who stood five feet three inches in his socks and weighed ten stone, the length of the drop was set at eight feet and two inches. Death was said to be instantaneous.[4]

In the aftermath of the execution Pierrepoint is reputed to have observed that: 'I love hanging Irishmen. They always go quietly and without trouble. They're Christian men and they believe they're going to a better place.'[5] The prison officers involved on the day were less sanguine. For them, dealing with a broken body was a rare and unpleasant duty. To help alleviate their distress, the medical officer requisitioned two bottles of whiskey.[6] The horror of hanging was never to be repeated.

If a law remains on the statute book there is a chance that it will be enforced however slender the base of public and political support. It could be argued that Michael Manning was a victim of legislative tardiness (the Infanticide Act, 1949 had removed

[3] Extract from Catholic chaplain's journal of 20 April 1954, NAI, JUS/2005/171/4073.

[4] This differs from the length specified in the 1892 Table of Drops (six feet) and the revised 1913 version (seven feet and two inches). A former Mountjoy governor, Sean Kavanagh, who worked closely with Pierrepoint, recalled that he tended to opt for a slightly longer drop than the table indicated. Memories of Mountjoy jail as told by former governor Sean Kavanagh to Liam MacGabhann, Mountjoy Prison Museum.

[5] *Irish Post*, 26 July 2006; echoing his uncle's comments twenty-five years earlier, after he hanged John Cox (see Chapter 1, note 1).

[6] Letter from W. Kennedy to secretary, Department of Justice, 22 June 1954, NAI, JUS/2005/171/4073.

the threat of execution from one category of killers but progress was slow for others) and political opportunism (a general election was imminent). The previous hanging had taken place almost six years earlier and this was of William Gambon, a man who had no desire to escape the noose.

Over time, execution came to be seen as a brutal anomaly in a system guided by ideas of parsimony and rehabilitation. While several years elapsed between each of the last executions this was not because there was an increase in the number of commutations, but rather because there were fewer potentially death-eligible cases coming before the courts. It is arguable that if there had been more murders during the 1950s there would have been more executions. As we saw in Chapter 7, the government seemed to have seriously contemplated hanging William Wall in 1959 and David Galvin in 1962.[7]

James Kelly was the last person to be sentenced to death whose conviction was not overturned on appeal.[8] On 25 May 1962, he was tried at the Central Criminal Court for the murder of a 58-year-old widow who had been found, severely injured, on the road near her home in County Galway (see Chapter 8). Medical evidence suggested that Kelly—who had been treated for alcoholism in England—had been insane for at least four years, that he was an 'aggressive psychopath'.[9] The jury concluded that he was sane and convicted him of murder.

The first persons convicted of the offence of capital murder created by the Criminal Justice Act, 1964 were husband and wife Noel and Marie Murray who killed Garda Michael Reynolds in St Anne's Park, Raheny in September 1975 and

[7] William Hopkins was also lucky to live. The government decided on 10 March 1953 not to advise the president to commute his sentence. His conviction was overturned on appeal and at his retrial on 14 May 1953 he was found unfit to plead and committed to the CMH. Death sentences reviewed by government in period since 1st January 1944, NAI, TSCH/3/S7788B.

[8] Shan Mohangi was the last person sentenced to death before the Criminal Justice Act, 1964 came into force, but his conviction was overturned by the Court of Criminal Appeal (*The People (Attorney General) v Shan Mohangi*, CCA, unreported, 14 May 1964).

[9] Memorandum prepared by counsel and solicitor assigned by Central Criminal Court to defend James Kelly, 1 August 1962, NAI, JUS/2005/170/6339. Seán MacBride was part of Kelly's legal team, continuing his unparalleled involvement in capital punishment cases.

were sentenced to death the following year. As the gunwoman, Mrs Murray was more culpable, meaning that it would have been impossible to execute her husband while sparing her, without highlighting the discriminatory nature of the practice. Hanging a man and a woman for the same crime would have been a step too far, even for the most hardened politician. Gerald Boland may have had the stomach for it, given his track record of executing subversives (Table 6.1) but he had died in 1973.

A report in the *Irish Independent* on 10 June 1976, the day after the Murrays were sentenced to death, noted that:

> A major talking point in legal circles last night centred on the availability of an official hangman should the death sentences not be commuted ... since Britain abolished hanging there is no official hangman in these islands. However, there have been reports that a British executioner has recently carried out hangings in Rhodesia and it is possible that he may be available here if necessary. A Garda source last night intimated that an English hangman would be available if required.

On 30 July 1976 the Murrays' appeals against their death sentences were dismissed and the Court of Criminal Appeal fixed the execution date for 17 August 1976.[10]

Was it thought likely that Albert Pierrepoint could be cajoled out of retirement for a final trip across the Irish Sea? He was 71 years old at the time, three years younger than his uncle Thomas was when he came to Ireland to hang Charles Kerins in 1944. Given that the arrangement with the Pierrepoints was a private one and that Thomas kept working in Ireland even when there were growing doubts about his physical capabilities (O'Donnell and Doyle 2014: 109–10) it is possible that someone in An Garda Síochána could have thought of tempting Albert back into action from the comfort of his position behind the bar in his aptly named public house, Help the Poor Struggler, in Oldham. But there could hardly have been much confidence that such an approach would have succeeded. Pierrepoint's autobiography had appeared a

[10] This news excited a great deal of interest internationally and there were two applications for the (non-existent) post of executioner, one from Germany (letter from Ralph Weymers to Taoiseach, 19 June 1976) and the other from Northern Ireland (letter from W.H.K. Cuthbert to Republic of Ireland Government, 10 June 1976), NAI, DFA/2006/133/700.

couple of years previously and showed his (belated) ambivalence regarding capital punishment.[11]

Another horrific incident took place in the interval between the Murrays' convictions and the confirmation of their death sentences. On 21 July 1976, the British ambassador to Ireland, Christopher Ewart-Biggs, was blown up in his car by the IRA. Another passenger (Judith Cooke) died also, and the driver (Brian O'Driscoll) and fourth occupant of the car (Brian Cubbon) were severely injured. Like the murder of a police officer, the murder of a diplomat was a capital offence. This was an audacious attack for which no one was ever convicted. Liam Cosgrave, not known as an opponent of capital punishment, was Taoiseach at the time. After an emergency meeting of the cabinet he stated that, if the ambassador's killers were caught, they would 'face the full rigours of the law' (*Irish Times*, 3 August 1976). Former justice minister Desmond O'Malley told the media that the death penalty could not be ruled out as the ultimate deterrent given the prevailing security situation (*Irish Times*, 26 July 1976).

Executioner Wanted—in 1976

It was during this torrid time that an unusual message was transmitted from Dublin to London, namely a request for the services of an executioner.[12] The file associated with this request was not available at the National Archives of the UK having been retained by the Home Office. Intrigued, I applied to have sight of it under the Freedom of Information Act, 2000 but my application was denied on two grounds: that disclosure of the file's contents would be detrimental to the relationship between Ireland and the UK, and that it would have adverse implications for effective police operations.[13] I sought an independent review of this decision and

[11] Pierrepoint was not yet in the nursing home where in 1992, shortly before his death and suffering from dementia, the matron denied newspaper reports that he was obsessed with knots (Seal 2016: 94).

[12] Request from the Garda (Republic of Ireland police) to the Metropolitan Police Special Branch (instead of through Government channels) for the services of an executioner: Home Office not in favour and drafted suggested reply for Metropolitan Police to Garda, 1 Jan. 1976–31 Dec. 1976, NAUK, HO 325/84.

[13] Personal communication, Home Office Information Rights Team, 7 October 2015. The relevant sections of the legislation were 27(1) (international relations) and 31(1) (law enforcement).

this was partially successful with the result that some newspaper clippings and three redacted documents were eventually released. I was told that the file was small, containing fewer than fifteen items, but that 'despite its size, and the passage of time that has elapsed ... some of the material ... remains particularly sensitive and could still have a considerable impact on Anglo-Irish relations'.[14] The finding of the Information Rights Team at the Home Office was that the public interest in disclosing did not outweigh the public interest in withholding.

Surprised at the reluctance to release forty-year-old information regarding a punishment that had been abolished in Ireland, de facto, since 1954, I appealed this decision to the Information Commissioner's Office. My complaint was deemed valid and it was found that the tardiness of the Home Office response was in breach of the legislation but the Information Commissioner's Office upheld the decision not to release the majority of the file's contents. The decision letter revealed that the withheld information related to exchanges within the UK government that were not intended for wider dissemination. It noted that 'this information is sensitive, as a result both of relating to the continued possibility for capital punishment at that time in Ireland and of what it reveals about the UK authorities' opinion of this approach by the Garda to the Metropolitan Police'. The letter stated that if these few papers were released, the disclosure 'would necessitate a diplomatic damage limitation exercise', notwithstanding the historical nature of the events in question.[15]

The implication that the draft reply was never issued by the Metropolitan Police was supported by my research in Ireland as there was no trace of this correspondence—or, indeed, anything related to it—in the Garda Museum and Archives.[16] This means either that it was sent without the proper authority or that the Garda archives are incomplete. The former would seem a more likely explanation and this may account for the reluctance to release the file, even at such a remove. If the request had

[14] Personal communication, Home Office Information Rights Team, 22 March 2016.

[15] Personal communication, Information Commissioner's Office, 10 August 2016.

[16] Personal communications, various dates, October and November 2015, January 2016.

originated with someone acting in an official capacity they could have expected that it would become public at some stage, but not if it was sent by an angry member of the force at his or her own initiative.[17] The contents of this unauthorized letter must have been highly inflammatory given that arguments in favour of its release proved unpersuasive so long afterwards.

In any case, as events unfolded the request for an executioner proved to be wishful thinking. On 9 December 1976 the Supreme Court substituted a conviction for murder for Noel Murray's capital murder conviction. Marie Murray was retried by the Special Criminal Court and found guilty of murder. The capital murder convictions did not stand because it could not be shown that the Murrays knew their victim, who was off-duty and not in uniform when he pursued them after a bank robbery, was a member of An Garda Síochána.

The request for an executioner shows two important things. First, that there was a minority who believed that necks should be broken for some crimes. Secondly, that it was deeply ingrained that the breaker of such necks would come from England (even though no one had been sentenced to death there since 1965).[18] There were pockets of support in An Garda Síochána for the retention of the death penalty as late as 1990 when the Criminal Justice Bill that proposed total abolition was being debated in the Dáil. An excerpt from a particularly forthright article published in the *Garda Review* in February of that year was read into the proceedings of the House. It argued that:

> We have to accept that in every society there lives a small percentage of human vermin, incurably evil and sadistic thugs for whom prison is not a deterrent. Justice demands that the ultimate deterrent must be kept at the ready to deal with them when they snuff out an innocent life in a cruel, calculating and premeditated manner. They are a cancer in our society and like a cancer feeding off the human body which must be removed, they too must be removed from the body politic.[19]

[17] Also, a formal communication would have emanated from the Department of Justice, not An Garda Síochána.

[18] An approach to France might have been more fruitful as the guillotine was still in use at the time. The last man to hear the swoosh of a descending blade was Hamida Djandoubi, who was decapitated in September 1977.

[19] Dáil Debates, 1 June 1990, Pat McCartan, vol. 399, cols. 1224–5.

These comments were considered to be reprehensible by the deputies who contributed to the debate for whom the arguments in favour of retention were entirely unconvincing.

Posthumous Pardon

As discussed in Chapter 3, justifications for clemency often focus on its desirability as a fail-safe, a final way to correct injustices for which there is no legal remedy. Sometimes the injustice results from human error, which can never be eradicated. Sometimes it results from the inability of even the most comprehensive set of rules to deal with the specific requirements of every particular case. But, like all human processes, it is fallible and the possibility of executive clemency is not a guarantee against miscarriages of justice.

Henry (Harry) Gleeson, a farmhand, was hanged on 23 April 1941 for the murder of Mary (Moll) McCarthy. The victim, who lived in straitened circumstances in the small community of New Inn, County Tipperary, had seven illegitimate children. The final child died after three weeks and was the only one whose father's identity McCarthy did not disclose. She never associated with more than one man at a time and was said to have laboured under the delusion that each of her 'seducers' would marry her. While shunned somewhat by her neighbours for her immorality, McCarthy generally maintained cordial relations with them and was seen as a quiet and inoffensive woman. On the night of her death she told her children she was going to get potatoes from Gleeson but never returned. Her body was discovered the next morning, with gunshot wounds to the neck and face.

Speculation was rife about the identity of the likely perpetrator. Clearly, someone had to be called to account and Gleeson, who reported finding the body, and who was believed to have fathered the seventh child—something he denied—fitted the bill. He was thought to have carried out the murder for fear that McCarthy would tell his uncle, upon whose farm he worked and from whom he hoped to inherit, that they were in a relationship and that his uncle would dismiss him as a result; this would have rendered him destitute. He had already given her potatoes without the uncle's knowledge.

There was disquiet at the time about whether Gleeson could have committed this awful crime and, while the people of New

Inn remained tight-lipped about the events that thrust them into the national spotlight, concerns about the possibility of a wrongful conviction did not dissipate. Seán MacBride was junior counsel for Gleeson. It was his first non-political capital case and it affected him deeply. He visited his client in the condemned cell and was convinced of his innocence. At their final meeting Gleeson stated that he was prepared to die and that he would depend upon MacBride to clear his name posthumously (Nic Dháibhéid 2011: 163–4). When MacBride was in government he arranged for the remains of executed republicans to be released to their next of kin; Gleeson, an innocent man, remained where he had been laid to rest inside the prison.

This execution continued to play on MacBride's mind. In a debate on the abolition of capital punishment, he told the Dáil how: 'I know from my own experience that certainly in one case, not a political case, in which I was involved as a lawyer, I had grave doubts as to the accused man's guilt. These doubts have been greatly intensified since, but nothing can be done. It is too late'.[20] In 1963 when MacBride spoke on television of his view that Gleeson was innocent the late prisoner's file was produced for the minister's attention with a strong, but unsubstantiated, rebuttal attached.[21]

In a book published more than half a century after the execution Bourke (1993: 77) made a strong case for Gleeson's innocence, arguing that, 'by his handling of the trial, the trial judge, mainly (but by no means exclusively) through his address to the jury after the evidence had concluded, behaved so partially that he effectively denied Gleeson a fair trial' and further that 'the person charged by law with ensuring an impartial hearing played a major part in sending Gleeson to the gallows' (p. 79). His charge to the jury, according to Bourke, 'read, and must have sounded, like one long selective attack on Gleeson. By the time it was over, the jury's verdict was predictable. What was surprising was its recommendation that Harry Gleeson should not hang' (p. 80). Finally, the judge told the jury that he agreed with their verdict

[20] Dáil Debates, 21 November 1951, Vol. 127, Col. 1165; MacBride does not identify Gleeson in his remarks.

[21] A note from the secretary of the Department of Justice to the minister stated that the government had '<u>the best of reasons</u>' for knowing he was guilty,

(*Irish Times*, 28 February 1941). Fagan (2015: 209–10) went further and, drawing on Bourke's files, named the local men believed to have been the true culprits.

On 19 December 2015, following the government's advice, President Michael D. Higgins exercised his right of pardon under Article 13.6 of the Constitution in respect of Gleeson's conviction. This was an acknowledgement that the state sometimes got it wrong, with profound and irreversible consequences.[22] On 13 January 2016, the Minister for Justice, Frances Fitzgerald, issued a statement of regret, apology, and exoneration observing that:

> The exercise, on the advice of the Government, by the President of his constitutional power of pardon is the highest remedy available in Irish law in these circumstances. It is an exceptional course of action, never before called upon in a posthumous case, nor after such a passage of time, but it is entirely warranted. The pardon wholly remits the sentence imposed as if Mr. Gleeson had not been charged or convicted. It has the effect of completely clearing Mr. Gleeson's name and is intended to make clear that no residual suspicion remains in the eyes of the State. It is our hope that this will be a fitting tribute to his memory, and that by placing this matter on the record of both Houses of the Oireachtas, that this will be publicly and formally recognised for posterity.

This was an enhanced pardon. It obliterated the stain on Gleeson's character with an emphatic declaration that he was not guilty as charged. It was more than a statement that he was wrongfully convicted; it was a declaration of his innocence. Pardons of this kind are an admission of failure, an acknowledgement that a person was wrongfully put to death, a belated effort to make good, to do justice where it should have been done before. While the sentiment expressed is laudable, the language used is somewhat unfortunate. Although it is clear that the effect of the action is to wipe the slate clean, it is nevertheless the case that one cannot be pardoned for what one has not done. A pardon implies

but these reasons were not given (underlined in original). 30 January 1963, NAI, JUS/18/4517A & B.

[22] Thomas Quinn was the first person whose wrongful conviction was acknowledged by the state. Found guilty of armed robbery at the Circuit Court on 4 March 1940, he was sentenced to five years penal servitude. So that there would be no ambiguity about what was intended, Quinn personally received a signed copy of the instrument of pardon with the presidential seal affixed, 23 December 1940, NAI, PRES/1/P1889.

guilt, it simply frees the guilty from the legal consequences of their crimes. It is anomalous to pardon someone for being innocent. A pardon is an expression of forgiveness, the excusing of a fault; when the person is innocent the state should be seeking his or her forgiveness. When the innocent person has been put to death at the hands of the state, and their forgiveness cannot be sought, words fail.

Kathleen Dean Moore (1989: 228) ended her book on the pardon with the following four sentences:

> In many ways, a history of pardons is a history of the moral development of nations. Superstitious and arbitrary pardons marked societies just beginning to develop governments. The capricious use of pardons as acts of grace marked a time when power, in all its manifestations, was used arbitrarily and not always benevolently. If America reforms the institution of pardon to be responsive to considerations of justice above all others, then it will have taken a further step toward a more just nation.

The first and fourth of Moore's concluding sentences apply directly to the analysis in this book, which charts a similar arc towards rational punishment in Ireland. I hope that I have shown how the gradual disappearance of 'justice' (in that clemency was no longer required to counteract deficiencies in the criminal law) and 'caprice' (because it was no longer acceptable) indicate the growing confidence and maturity of the Irish state, as does the courage to retain a small space for 'mercy', however problematic it might prove to be in its implementation. When capital punishment was abolished for all crimes in 1990 the penultimate step towards maturity was taken. The final one was the amendment to the Constitution in 2001 which removed all references to the death penalty and prohibited its reintroduction. At last Ireland had become the kind of country some of its founders hoped it would be when it won its independence.

Appendix I
Convicted of Murder after Trial by Jury, and Spared

Name	Age	Offence	Victim	Method	Conviction	Commutation	Rationale
John Hogan	21	31/10/22	James Cullinan	Shot	30/10/23	22/11/23	Justice
* William Devereux	57	15/2/23	Anne Devereux	Stabbed / hacked	22/11/23	17/12/23	Mercy
* Patrick Aylward	63	21/4/23	William Holden	Burned	26/11/23	24/12/23	Caprice
John Ryan	24	16/5/23	Michael Caudy	Shot	12/2/24	5/3/24	Justice
Denis Leen	27	6/12/23	Thomas Brosnan	Shot	21/2/24	13/3/24	Justice
Hannah Flynn	27	1/4/23	Margaret O'Sullivan	Stabbed / hacked	27/2/24	4/3/24	Justice
Joseph Butler	29	21/8/22	Michael McSweeney	Shot	18/7/24	7/8/24	Justice
* Mary Moynihan	19	9/9/22	Nora Horgan	Stabbed / hacked	12/12/24	27/12/24	Justice
James Murray	26	13/12/23	Joseph Bergin	Shot	12/6/25	18/7/25	Mercy
Hannah O'Leary	36	26/2/24	Patrick O'Leary	Stabbed / hacked	30/6/25	25/7/25	Justice
* Charles Molloy	19	12/2/23	John Finlay	Shot	25/1/26	17/2/26	Justice
* Patrick Fagan	32	11/8/22	Patrick Moran	Shot	4/2/26	17/2/26	Justice
Elizabeth Doran	40	15/3/26	Infant son (unnamed)	Choked	3/6/26	22/6/26	Justice
Mary Kiernan	22	26/9/26	Infant daughter (Bridget)	Drowned	28/10/26	8/11/26	Justice
Elizabeth Hannon	30	21/8/27	Infant son (unnamed)	Buried alive	12/12/27	17/12/27	Justice
Mary Anne Keane	23	2/3/29	Infant son (Patrick)	Drowned	10/6/29	12/6/29	Justice

Name	Age	Offence	Victim	Method	Conviction	Commutation	Rationale
* Deborah Sullivan	21	12/2/29	Infant son (unnamed)	Drowned	13/6/29	18/6/29	Justice
Martin Joyce	33	30/5/28	Daniel Walsh	Drowned	21/6/29	31/7/29	Justice
Annie Walsh	42	30/5/28	Daniel Walsh	Drowned	21/6/29	31/7/29	Justice
Catherine Ahearne	26	30/3/29	Infant daughter (unnamed)	Choked	25/6/29	28/6/29	Justice
Christina Russell	28	6/9/30	Infant son (Thomas)	Drowned	27/11/30	28/11/30	Justice
Margaret Finn	25	17/6/30	Infant son (unnamed)	Choked	3/3/31	5/3/31	Justice
Jane O'Brien	51	26/3/32	John Cousins	Shot	8/6/32	15/7/32	Mercy
Elizabeth Edwards	28	16/10/34	Infant daughter (Mary Teresa)	Not known	28/3/35	18/5/35	Justice
Rose Edwards	22	16/10/34	Infant niece (Mary Teresa)	Not known	28/3/35	18/5/35	Justice
Leo O'Brien	33	3/11/34	John Stokes	Shot	27/6/35	9/8/35	Mercy
** Thomas Kelly	55	10/9/35	Patrick Henry	Beaten	14/11/36	21/12/37	Justice
Patrick Boylan	23	5/12/36	Norah Whelan	Stabbed / hacked	6/3/37	5/5/37	Caprice
James Tierney	27	24/11/36	Thomas Vickers	Choked	9/4/37	21/5/37	Mercy
Mary Somerville	53	11/7/38	Infant grand-daughter (unnamed)	Drowned	15/11/38	13/12/38	Justice
Patrick Monaghan	26	5/2/39	Lily McEvoy	Choked	19/5/39	27/6/39	Justice
James Fennell	21	11/2/40	Stephen Ryan	Shot	29/6/40	6/8/40	Justice
Martin Griffin	53	1/3/43	Bridget Griffin	Stabbed / hacked	5/6/43	25/6/43	Mercy
Kate Owens	36	7/4/43	Infant son (unnamed)	Choked	22/11/43	9/12/43	Mercy
Agnes McAdam	53	26/9/45	James Finnegan	Poisoned	15/2/46	9/4/46	Justice
Daniel Duff	22	25/9/46	James Byrne	Shot	21/11/46	6/12/46	Justice

Name	Age	Offence	Victim	Method	Conviction	Commutation	Rationale
John Fanning	28	27/5/48	Kathleen Boyne	Choked	22/10/48	29/10/48	Justice
Edward O'Connor	31	3/6/48	Infant son (Paul)	Drowned	26/10/48	29/10/48	Justice
** Mary A.B. Daly	27	10/8/48	Mary Gibbons	Beaten	12/11/48	3/5/49	Justice
Frances Cox	30	29/5/49	Richard Cox	Poisoned	21/11/49	23/12/49	Mercy
** Patrick Heffernan	27	12/5/50	Rose Hand	Shot	13/11/50	15/5/51	Caprice
Robert Stevenson	24	22/12/53	Mary Nolan	Choked	13/5/54	6/7/54	Caprice
Mary Cadden	62	17/4/56	Helen O'Reilly	Botched abortion	1/11/56	4/1/57	Mercy
Denis Foy	21	20/11/58	James McGrath	Choked	19/2/59	24/2/59	Mercy
Thomas O'Rourke	59	29/12/58	Joan O'Rourke	Beaten	1/5/59	12/5/59	Justice
William Wall	28	19/1/59	Bridget Farrell	Beaten	13/5/59	2/6/59	Caprice
Vincent McGrath	33	22/11/59	Patrick White	Stabbed / hacked	12/3/60	6/5/60	Justice
David Galvin	20	28/3/61	Elizabeth Gould	Beaten	25/10/61	9/2/62	Mercy
James Kelly	32	12/7/61	Kate Connolly	Beaten	24/5/62	10/8/62	Mercy

Notes

Ordered chronologically by date of conviction. William Devereux killed his sister-in-law, Anne, and her 10-month-old daughter, Kathleen; no proceedings were taken in the latter case. The body of Elizabeth Edwards' daughter, Mary Teresa, was never found so the cause of death is unknown.

* Eucharistic Congress releases: William Devereux, Patrick Aylward, Charles Molloy, and Patrick Fagan were discharged from Portlaoise Prison; Mary Moynihan and Deborah Sullivan left Our Lady's Home, Henrietta Street, Dublin.

** Cases where a retrial was ordered after a finding of guilt and the accused person was again sentenced to death. For these individuals the date of the initial conviction is listed.

Appendix II
Convicted of Murder after Trial by Jury, and Hanged

Name	Age	Offence	Victim	Method	Conviction	Execution	Executioner
William Downes	24	19/10/23	Thomas Fitzgerald	Shot	29/10/23	29/11/23	T. Pierrepoint
Thomas Delaney	38	27/6/23	Patrick Horan	Beaten	12/11/23	12/12/23	T. Pierrepoint
Thomas McDonagh	43	25/5/22	Ellen Rogers	Shot	12/11/23	12/12/23	T. Pierrepoint
Peter Hynes	40	15/1/22	Thomas Grimstone	Beaten	22/11/23	15/12/23	T. Pierrepoint
Jeremiah Gaffney	23	6/12/23	Thomas Brosnan	Shot	14/2/24	13/3/24	T. Pierrepoint
Felix McMullen	26	21/1/24	Patrick O'Halloran	Shot	10/7/24	1/8/24	T. Pierrepoint
Cornelius O'Leary	40	26/2/24	Patrick O'Leary	Stabbed/ hacked	30/6/25	28/7/25	T. Pierrepoint
Michael Talbot	23	24/10/24	Edward Walsh	Stabbed/ hacked	9/7/25	5/8/25	T. Pierrepoint
Annie Walsh	31	24/10/24	Edward Walsh	Stabbed/ hacked	10/7/25	5/8/25	T. Pierrepoint
James Myles	22	27/2/24	John Smyth	Shot	18/6/26	15/7/26	W. Willis
James McHugh	31	24/4/26	William Dollison	Beaten	27/10/26	24/11/26	T. Pierrepoint
Henry McCabe	48	31/3/26	Peter McDonnell	Beaten	13/11/26	9/12/26	T. Pierrepoint
William O'Neill	19	8/5/27	Margaret Farrell	Beaten	2/12/27	29/12/27	T. Pierrepoint
Gerard Toal	20	16/5/27	Mary Callan	Choked	26/7/28	29/8/28	T. Pierrepoint
John Cox	33	21/12/28	Jacob Kunz	Beaten	14/3/29	25/4/29	T. Pierrepoint

Name	Age	Offence	Victim	Method	Conviction	Execution	Executioner
David O'Shea	33	8/2/31	Ellen O'Sullivan	Beaten	12/6/31	4/8/31	T. Pierrepoint
Patrick McDermott	28	3/9/32	John McDermott	Shot	17/11/32	29/12/32	T. Pierrepoint
John Fleming	31	26/7/33	Ellen Fleming	Beaten	21/11/33	5/1/34	R. Baxter
John Hornick	36	25/1/37	James Redmond	Beaten	15/4/37	17/6/37	T. Pierrepoint
Dermot Smyth	33	17/8/38	Cornelius Dennehy	Shot	29/11/38	7/1/39	T. Pierrepoint
Daniel Doherty	29	19/9/40	Hannah Doherty	Choked	30/11/40	7/1/41	T. Pierrepoint
Henry Gleeson	38	20/11/40	Mary McCarthy	Shot	27/2/41	23/4/41	T. Pierrepoint
Patrick Kelly	31	17/4/41	Mary Breheny	Drowned	23/10/41	18/12/41	T. Pierrepoint
Bernard Kirwan	34	22/11/41	Laurence Kirwan	Not known	5/2/43	2/6/43	T. Pierrepoint
William O'Shea	23	15/3/43	Maureen O'Shea	Shot	16/6/43	12/8/43	T. Pierrepoint
James Lehman	40	19/3/44	Margaret Lehman	Poisoned	25/10/44	19/3/45	A. Pierrepoint
Joseph McManus	41	6/10/46	Alice Gerrard	Shot	25/1/47	31/3/47	A. Pierrepoint
William Gambon	28	22/8/48	John Long	Beaten	3/11/48	24/11/48	A. Pierrepoint
Michael Manning	24	18/11/53	Catherine Cooper	Choked	17/2/54	20/4/54	A. Pierrepoint

Notes

Ordered chronologically by date of conviction. James Myles was not tried for the murder of John Smyth's son; John Jr. Henry McCabe was not tried for the murders of the five other victims in his case. The cause of Laurence Kirwan's death could not be established because a badly decomposed torso was all that was ever recovered. James Lehman successfully appealed his conviction but was retried and again sentenced to death on 24 January 1945.

Appendix III Sentenced to Death by a Non-jury Court

Name	Age	Offence	Victim	Conviction	Commutation	Rationale	Execution
Michael Conway	25	26/4/36	John Egan	21/7/36	24/7/36	Mercy	—
Tomás MacCurtain	25	3/1/40	John Roche	13/6/40	10/7/40	Caprice	—
Patrick McGrath	46	16/8/40	Richard Hyland	20/8/40	—	—	6/9/40
Thomas Green	25	16/8/40	Richard Hyland	20/8/40	—	—	6/9/40
Thomas Hunt	21	16/8/40	Richard Hyland	23/9/40	25/9/40	Justice	—
* Richard Goss	26	18/7/41	—	1/8/41	—	—	9/8/41
* Seán McCaughey	26	2/9/41	—	18/9/41	25/9/41	Mercy	—
Patrick Davern	41	28/9/40	Michael Devereux	26/2/42	2/3/42	Justice	—
Michael Walsh	32	28/9/40	Michael Devereux	26/2/42	2/3/42	Justice	—
George Plant	38	28/9/40	Michael Devereux	26/2/42	—	—	5/3/42
* Maurice O'Neill	25	24/10/42	—	5/11/42	—	—	12/11/42
Charles Kerins	26	9/9/42	Denis O'Brien	9/10/44	—	—	1/12/44
Patrick McCann	33	7/7/80	Henry Byrne	27/11/80	27/5/81	Justice	—
Colm O'Shea	28	7/7/80	Henry Byrne	27/11/80	27/5/81	Justice	—
Peter Rogers	36	13/10/80	James Quaid	11/3/81	1/7/81	Justice	—
Patrick McPhillips	29	10/8/84	Frank Hand	28/3/85	20/2/86	Justice	—

Name	Age	Offence	Victim	Conviction	Commutation	Rationale	Execution
Brian McShane	20	10/8/84	Frank Hand	28/3/85	20/2/86	Justice	—
Thomas Eccles	25	10/8/84	Frank Hand	28/3/85	20/2/86	Justice	—
Michael McHugh	25	27/6/85	Patrick Morrissey	3/12/85	19/12/85	Justice	—
Noel Callan	23	27/6/85	Patrick Morrissey	3/12/85	29/5/86	Justice	—

Notes

Ordered chronologically by date of conviction. With the exception of Charles Kerins, who was hanged by Thomas Pierrepoint, IRA members were executed by firing party; their final sensation was the sound of a fusillade rather than the tightening of a noose. Patrick McKeown was killed with Richard Hyland and John Morley died with Henry Byrne; on both occasions convictions were obtained in the latter's name only.

* Convicted of offences other than murder: Seán McCaughey was convicted of the assault and false imprisonment of Stephen Hayes; Richard Goss and Maurice O'Neill were convicted of shooting with intent to resist arrest.

Bibliography

I. Primary Sources

National Archives of Ireland (NAI)

Closed Prisoner Files (Department of Justice)

Catherine Ahearne, JUS/H234/2603A.
Patrick Aylward, JUS/H234/1865A.
Patrick Boylan, JUS/18/2093A & B.
Joseph Butler, JUS/H8/491.
Mary A. Cadden, JUS/18/3562A & B.
Michael Conway, JUS/18/1760B.
Frances A. Cox, JUS/18/11757A & B.
John Joseph Cox, JUS/H234/2495.
Mary Agnes Daly, JUS/2005/170/7622.
Thomas Delaney, JUS/H8/912.
William Devereux, JUS/H234/3507A.
Daniel Doherty, JUS/18/4097A.
Elizabeth Doran, JUS/H234/1297.
William Downes, JUS/H8/893.
Daniel Duff, JUS/18/9710A & B.
Elizabeth and Rose Edwards, JUS/18/885A & B and JUS/18/886B.
Patrick Fagan, JUS/H234/1132A.
John Fanning, JUS/10979A & B.
James Fennell, JUS/18/4066A & B.
Margaret Finn, JUS/H234/3118A & B.
John Fleming, JUS/H234/6221B.
Hannah Flynn, JUS/18/2679A & B.
Denis Foy, JUS/2005/170/6124.
Jeremiah Gaffney, JUS/H8/1085.
David Galvin, JUS/2005/170/5710.
William Gambon, JUS/18/11223A.
Henry (Harry) Gleeson, JUS/18/4517A & B.
Martin Griffin, JUS/18/6470A & B.
Elizabeth Hannon, JUS/H234/2016.
Patrick Heffernan, JUS/2005/170/8695.
John Hogan, JUS/H234/2024A.
John Hornick, JUS/18/2149.

Thomas Hunt, JUS/18/4312B.
Peter Hynes, JUS/H8/206.
Martin Joyce, JUS/H234/2599 and JUS/H234/2599 (2).
Mary Anne Keane, JUS/18/3540A & B.
James Kelly, JUS/2005/170/6339.
Patrick Kelly, JUS/18/4780A & B.
Thomas Kelly, JUS/18/1767A & B.
Charles Kerins, JUS/18/7774A.
Mary Kiernan, JUS/H234/1491.
Bernard Kirwan, JUS/18/1474A & B.
James Lehman, JUS/18/7666A & B.
Denis Leen, JUS/H8/1093.
Michael Manning, JUS/2005/171/4073.
Agnes McAdam, JUS/18/9074A & B.
Henry McCabe, JUS/H234/1503.
Tomás MacCurtain, JUS/18/8625A.
Patrick McDermott, JUS/H234/4684A & B.
Thomas McDonagh, JUS/H8/510.
Vincent McGrath, JUS/2005/171/4697.
James McHugh, JUS/H234/1490.
Joseph McManus, JUS/18/9767A & B.
Felix McMullen, JUS/H234/209.
Charles Molloy, JUS/H234/1119A & B.
Patrick Monaghan, JUS/18/3406A & B.
Mary Moynihan, JUS/H234/1744.
James Murray, JUS/H234/781.
James Myles, JUS/H234/1316.
Jane O'Brien, JUS/18/2737A & B.
Leo O'Brien, JUS/18/8626A.
Edward O'Connor, JUS/18/11108A & B.
Cornelius and Hannah O'Leary, JUS/18/2770A & B.
William O'Neill, JUS/H234/2003.
Thomas O'Rourke, JUS/2005/170/5610.
David O'Shea, JUS/H234/3593A & B.
William O'Shea, JUS/18/6535A & B.
Kate Owens, JUS/18/6678A & B.
Christina Russell, JUS/H234/3332A & B.
John Ryan, JUS/H234/1784.
Dermot Smyth, JUS/18/3138A & B.
Mary Somerville, JUS/18/3110.
Robert James Stevenson, JUS/2005/171/3615.
Deborah Sullivan, JUS/H234/2590.
Michael Talbot, JUS/H234/831.
James Edward Tierney, JUS/18/9238A & B.

Gerard Toal, JUS/H234/2267.
Annie Walsh [sentence commuted], JUS/H234/2599 and JUS/H234/2599 (1).
Annie Walsh [sentence executed], JUS/H1004/275.

The file relating to William Wall is not held at the National Archives of Ireland and could not be located by the Department of Justice and Equality or the Irish Prison Service.

Department of the Taoiseach

Minutes of meetings of the Executive Council (1923–37) and Government (1937–86).
John Fleming: death sentence, 29 Dec. 1922–3 Jan. 1934, TSCH/3/S2343.
Cases of John Hogan and James Murray, serving life sentences at Port Laoise prison, 29 Oct. 1928–15 July 1929, TSCH/3/S3415.
William Devereux: commutation of sentence, 17 Dec. 1923–2 Jan. 1924, TSCH/3/S3505.
Private Denis Leen, sentenced to death: petition on his behalf, 1 Mar. 1924–9 Dec. 1925, TSCH/3/S3648.
Charles Molloy, Bernagon [sic], Ballycumber, Co. Offaly: death sentence, 16 Feb. 1926–28 Feb. 1936, TSCH/3/S4877.
Patrick Fagan, Coole, Co. Westmeath: death sentence, 17–28 Feb. 1936 [sic], TSCH/3/S4878.
James Myles: death sentence (Ardee Bog Murder), 14–15 July 1926, TSCH/3/S5079.
Prerogative of mercy: exercise by President, 28 Nov. 1944–13 Mar. 1951, TSCH/3/S5081.
Mary Kiernan: commutation of death sentence to penal servitude for life, 4–8 Nov. 1926, TSCH/3/S5195.
James McHugh, death sentence: consideration for clemency, 18–22 Nov. 1926, TSCH/3/S5211.
Elizabeth Hannon: death sentence, 15–19 Dec. 1927, TSCH/3/S5571.
William O'Neill: death sentence, 22 Dec. 1927–26 Jan. 1928, TSCH/3/S5573.
Gerard Toal: death sentence, 14–18 Aug. 1928, TSCH/3/S5725.
Mary Cole: discharge from Mountjoy Prison, 28 Aug.–10 Sept. 1928, TSCH/3/S5744.
John Ryan: commutation of life sentence, 16 Nov. 1927–6 Dec. 1928, TSCH/3/S5801.
Patrick Aylward: sentence to penal servitude for life, 19 Feb. 1926–9 Apr. 1929, TSCH/3/S5832.
John Joseph Cox: death sentence, 14 Mar.–23 Apr. 1929, TSCH/3/S5853.
Mary Anne Keane: death sentence, 11–13 June 1929, TSCH/3/S5884.

Deborah Sullivan: death sentence, 17–19 June 1929, TSCH/3/S5886.
Catherine Aherne [sic]: death sentence, 26 June–1 July 1929, TSCH/3/S5891.
Annie Walsh and Martin Joyce: death sentence, 25 July 1929–6 Feb. 1930, TSCH/3/S5904.
Eucharistic Congress, 1932: proposal for release of first offenders from prison, 17–20 June 1932, TSCH/3/S6005/19A.
Christina Russell: death sentence, 27 Nov.–4 Dec. 1930, TSCH/3/S6096.
Margaret Finn: death sentence, 4–6 Mar. 1931, TSCH/3/S6129.
David O'Shea: death sentence, 22–28 July 1931, TSCH/3/S6176.
Patrick McDermott: death sentence, 19 Nov.–24 Dec. 1932, TSCH/3/S6375.
Elizabeth and Rose Edwards: commutation of death sentence to penal servitude for life, 15–18 May 1935, TSCH/3/S7777.
Death sentence: abolition proposals and commutation of sentences, 6 Dec. 1922–20 Apr. 1944, TSCH/3/S7788A.
Capital punishment: general file, 21 Mar. 1945–19 Feb. 1958, TSCH/3/S7788B.
Death sentences procedure: abolition proposals; commutation of sentences, TSCH/3/S7788C/94.
Death sentence: procedure; abolition proposals; commutation of sentences, Feb. 1962–Mar. 1964, TSCH/3/98/6/49.
* Leo O'Brien: dismissal from the Army, death sentence and release, 6 Oct. 1924–1 Dec. 1938, TSCH/3/S8005A.
* Leo O'Brien: dismissal from the Army, death sentence and release, 7 Feb. 1945–23 Mar. 1949, TSCH/3/S8005B.
Michael Conway: conviction by Constitution (Special Powers) Tribunal, 24 Oct. 1935–4 Apr. 1946, TSCH/3/S8210.
Jane O'Brien: death sentence, 13–15 July 1932, TSCH/3/S8653.
John Egan: murdered, Dungarvan, 1936, 28 Apr. 1936–21 Apr. 1937, TSCH/3/S8980.
Constitution (Special Powers) Tribunal: Michael Conway (death sentence), 22 July–20 Aug. 1936, TSCH/3/S9094.
Convicts: release on licence, 7 Feb. 1945–22 Jan. 1954, TSCH/3/S9476A & B.
Pardons, commutations and remissions: procedures relating to prerogative of mercy, 16 July 1926–12 May 1951, TSCH/3/S9485A.
Pardons, commutations and remissions: procedure, 6 Sept. 1922–18 June 1954, TSCH/3/S9485B.
Pardons, commutations and remissions: procedure; questions as to 'prerogative of mercy', July 1962–May 1965, TSCH/3/98/6/65.
* Pardons, commutations and remissions: procedure; questions as to 'prerogative of mercy', Feb.–Sept. 1969, TSCH/3/S9485C.

James Edward Tierney (otherwise O'Neill): death sentence, 10 Apr.–27 May 1937, TSCH/3/S9825A.
James Edward Tierney (otherwise O'Neill): death sentence, 12–24 Sept. 1947, TSCH/3/S9825B.
James Edward Tierney (otherwise O'Neill): death sentence, 7–14 May 1948, TSCH/3/S9825C.
Patrick Boylan: death sentence, 23 Apr.–13 May 1937, TSCH/3/S9849A.
Patrick Boylan: death sentence, 26 June–29 Sept. 1947, TSCH/3/S9849B.
John Hornick: death sentence, 3 May–18 June 1937, TSCH/3/S9862.
Thomas Kelly: death sentence, 2 Dec. 1936–23 Dec. 1937, TSCH/3/S10370A.
Thomas Kelly: death sentence, 25 Nov. 1947, TSCH/3/S10370B.
Mary Somerville: death sentence, 17 Nov.–15 Dec. 1938, TSCH/3/S11040.
* Dermot Smyth: death sentence, 29 Nov. 1938–7 Jan. 1939, TSCH/3/S11062.
Seán McCaughey (alias Seán Dunlop): death sentence, representations for reprieve, 21 Sept.–2 Oct. 1941, TSCH/3/S11136.
* Patrick Monaghan: death sentence, 22 May 1939–11 Sept. 1951, TSCH/3/S11316A.
Political prisoners and internees (1939–49), alleged ill-treatment, petitions for release etc., TSCH/3/S11443.
Seán Dunlop (alias Seán McCaughey): Special Criminal Court (No. 28/1939), 27 Dec. 1939–19 Sept. 1941, TSCH/3/S11574.
Trial by courts martial of civilians: emergency powers orders, 15 July 1940–16 Nov. 1950, TSCH/3/S11905A.
Tomás MacCurtain: conviction by Special Criminal Court (No. 151/1940), 5 Jan.–11 July 1940, TSCH/3/S11931A.
Tomás MacCurtain: conviction by Special Criminal Court (No. 151/1940), 5 Mar. 1948, TSCH/3/S11931B.
Tomás MacCurtain: death sentence, petitions for reprieve, 18 June–10 July 1940, TSCH/3/S11974.
* James Fennell: death sentence and remission, 3 July–6 Aug. 1940, TSCH/3/S11996A.
* James Fennell: death sentence and remission, 17 Jan. 1948–4 Jan. 1949, TSCH/3/S11996B.
Patrick McGrath and Thomas Green alias Francis Harte: conviction by military court for murder of Detective Garda Richard Hyland, 17 Aug. 1940–20 Sept. 1948, TSCH/3/S12048A.
Patrick McGrath and Thomas Green alias Francis Harte: petitions for reprieve, 23 Aug.–6 Sept. 1940, TSCH/3/S12048B.
Thomas Hunt: trial by Military Court for murder of Detective Garda Richard Hyland, 6 Sept. 1940–7 July 1945, TSCH/3/S12065.

Emergency: immediate measures to be taken by Government and Ministers in event of attack (including Emergency Govt. Agenda), 19 Sept. 1940–1 Jan. 1942, TSCH/3/S12078.
Richard Goss: death sentence, petitions for reprieve, 3–7 Aug. 1941, TSCH/3/S12127.
* Daniel Doherty: death sentence, 30 Nov.–31 Dec. 1940, TSCH/3/S12227.
Special Criminal Court: George Plant (No. 258/1940), 23 Dec. 1940, TSCH/3/S12249.
Special Criminal Court: remissions of sentences and forfeitures, 23 May 1941–23 Jan. 1942, TSCH/3/S12433A.
Richard Goss and Joseph O'Callaghan: trial by Military Court, death sentence and re-interment of body of Goss, 18 July 1941–3 Sept. 1948, TSCH/3/S12540.
Seán McCaughey: trial by Military Court, 10 Sept. 1941–23 July 1942, TSCH/3/S12590.
Patrick Kelly: death sentence, 27 Oct.–15 Dec. 1941, TSCH/3/S12673.
George Plant, Joseph O'Connor, Patrick Davern and Michael Walsh: trial by military court, 10 Dec. 1941, TSCH/3/S12682.
Military Courts: admission of signed statements as evidence, 30 Dec. 1941–28 Oct. 1942, TSCH/3/S12683.
Patrick Davern, George Plant, Michael Walsh: death sentence by Military Court 1943 [sic], petitions for reprieve, 28 Jan. 1942–13 Feb. 1946, TSCH/3/S12741.
Maurice O'Neill: trial by Special Military Court, 27 Oct. 1942–16 Sept. 1948, TSCH/3/S12996.
Maurice O'Neill: death sentence, petitions for reprieve, 6–10 Nov. 1942, TSCH/3/S13004.
Bernard Kirwan: death sentence, 1–28 May 1943, TSCH/3/S13236.
Martin Griffin: death sentence, 10 June 1943–15 Apr. 1955, TSCH/3/S13265.
William O'Shea: death sentence, 26 June–10 Aug. 1943, TSCH/3/S13274.
Insanity as a defence in criminal cases: proposed legislation, 10 Aug. 1943–29 Apr. 1944, TSCH/3/S13311A.
Insanity as a defence in criminal cases: proposed legislation, 15 June 1944–8 Mar. 1955, TSCH/3/S13311B.
Special Criminal Court: death sentence imposed on Charles Kerins (No. 58/1944), 4 Oct. 1944–16 Sept. 1948, TSCH/3/S13567.
Charles Kerins: appeals and petitions for reprieve, 2 Nov. 1944–20 Jan. 1945, TSCH/3/S13567/1.
James Herbert Lehman: death sentence, 17 Oct. 1944–19 Mar. 1945, TSCH/3/S13600.

Cardinal MacRory, archbishop of Armagh: death, 13 Oct 1945–19 Jan. 1953, TSCH/3/S13742.
* Agnes McAdam: death sentence, conviction and sentence, 12 Feb.–10 Apr. 1946, TSCH/3/S13804A.
* Agnes McAdam: death sentence, release from prison, 8–20 Sept. 1949, TSCH/3/S13804B.
* Kate Owens: death sentence, conviction and sentence, 29 Nov.–10 Dec. 1943, TSCH/3/S13383A.
* Kate Owens: death sentence, release from prison, 12–22 Apr. 1949, TSCH/3/S13383B.
Daniel Joseph Duff (Garda Síochána): death sentence commutation to penal servitude for life, 20 Nov.–9 Dec. 1946, TSCH/3/S13961A.
Daniel Joseph Duff (Garda Síochána): death sentence, release, 4 Dec. 1946–5 Nov. 1951, TSCH/3/S13961B.
Joseph McManus: death sentence, 15 Jan.–1 Apr. 1947, TSCH/3/S14009.
John Fanning: death sentence, 19–29 Oct. 1948, TSCH/3/S14416.
* Edward O'Connor: death sentence, 27–29 Oct. 1948, TSCH/3/S14417A.
* Edward O'Connor: death sentence, 22–30 Oct. 1951, TSCH/3/S14417B.
William Gambon: death sentence, 4–19 Nov. 1948, TSCH/3/S14429.
* Mary Agnes Daly: death sentence, commutation to penal servitude for life, 13 Nov. 1948–3 May 1949, TSCH/3/S14430A.
* Mary Agnes Daly: death sentence, release, 6 Oct. 1953–22 Jan. 1954, TSCH/3/S14430B.
Infanticide: legislation; Infanticide Act, 1949, 10 Aug. 1943–26 Oct. 1954, TSCH/3/S14493.
Holy Year, 1950: proposed amnesty for prisoners, 25 Aug.–28 Oct. 1949, TSCH/3/S14620.
* Frances Cox: death sentence, 22 Nov.–22 Dec. 1949, TSCH/3/S14689A & B.
* Patrick Heffernan: death sentence, 7 Mar.–12 May 1951, TSCH/3/S14992A.
* Patrick Heffernan: death sentence, 2 Nov. 1956–4 Jan. 1957, TSCH/3/S14992B.
Michael Manning: death sentence, 18 Feb.–21 Apr. 1954, TSCH/3/S15641.
Mary Anne Cadden: death sentence, 2 Nov. 1956–4 Jan. 1957, TSCH/3/S16116.
David Galvin: death sentence, Nov. 1961, TSCH/3/S17186/61.
Death sentence: procedure; abolition proposals; commutation of sentences, Feb. 1962–Mar. 1964, TSCH/3/98/6/49.
Peter Rogers: death sentence, TSCH/3/2011/127/839.

Files indicated with an asterisk had not been transferred to the National Archives of Ireland pursuant to section 8(4) of the National Archives Act, 1986 and were examined on site at the Department of the Taoiseach. One file had been removed for conservation and was unavailable (Henry Gleeson: death sentence, 15–18 Apr. 1941, TSCH/3/S12368).

Office of the Secretary to the President

Patrick Monaghan: death sentence, 1939, June 1939, PRES/1/P972.
Mrs. Mary Somerville: death sentence, 1938, Dec. 1938, PRES/1/P1101.
Dermot Smyth: death sentence, 1938, Nov. 1938–Jan. 1939, PRES/1/P1105.
Abolition of death penalty: general, Dec. 1938–Feb. 1939, PRES/1/P1123.
Abolition of death penalty: miscellaneous requests, Dec. 1938–Jan. 1939, PRES/1/P1124.
Death sentence on Tomás MacCurtain: request for reprieve, June 1940–Mar. 1948, PRES/1/P1743.
James Fennell: death sentence, July 1940–Aug. 1940, PRES/1/P1784.
Thomas Quinn, free pardon, PRES/1/P1889.
Remission of punishment for crimes not committed, general file, PRES/1/P1899.
Richard Goss: death sentence, July 1941–Aug. 1941, PRES/1/P2030.
Kate Owens: remission of death sentence, Dec. 1943, PRES/1/P2332.
Charles Kerins: death sentence, Nov. 1944, PRES/1/P2457.
Agnes McAdam: death sentence, 1946, Apr. 1946, PRES/1/P2735.
Daniel J. Duff: death sentence, Dec. 1946, PRES/1/P2937.
Maurice O'Neill: death sentence, Nov. 1942, PRES/1/P3005.
Martin Griffin: remission of death sentence, June 1943, PRES/1/P3089.
Edward O'Connor: commutation of death sentence, Oct. 1948, PRES/1/P4184.
John Fanning: commutation of death sentence, Oct. 1948, PRES/1/P4185.
Mrs. Mary Agnes Bernadette Daly: commutation of death sentence, May 1949, PRES/1/P4283.
Miss Frances Cox: commutation of death sentence, Dec. 1949, PRES/1/P4402.
Mr. Patrick Heffernan: commutation of death sentence, May 1951, PRES/1/P4640.
Mr. Robert James Stevenson: commutation of death sentence, July 1954, PRES/1/P5106.
Commutation of death sentence: Denis Fay [sic], Feb. 1959, PRES/1/P5420.

Commutation of death sentence: Thomas O'Rourke, May 1959, PRES/1/P5438.
Commutation of death sentence: William Wall, June 1959, PRES/1/P5444.
Commutation of death sentence: general correspondence relating to persons sentenced to death, including letters from families and acquaintances, May 1960–Oct. 1962, PRES/96/8/25.
Intervention in maters sub judice, general file, PRES/98/1/35.
Noel and Marie Murray: Achaini a fuair an tUachtarán chuir bheith an bháis, PRES/2007/125/83.
Procedures for death sentence commutations and jail sentence remissions, gives list of persons who appealed their sentences 1938–59, PRES/2008/149/2.
Commutation of death sentence (Colm O'Shea, Peter Pringle, Patrick McCann, 1981), PRES/2013/97/22.

Court of Criminal Appeal

Joseph Butler, 1924, CCA 4/24.
Mary Moynihan, 1924–5, CCA 17/24.
James Murray, 1925, CCA 16/25.
Cornelius O'Leary, 1925, CCA 18/25.
Hannah O'Leary, 1925, CCA 19/25.
Charles Molloy, 1926, CCA 7/26.
Patrick Fagan, 1926, CCA 8/26.
James Myles, 1926, CCA 13/26.
James McHugh, 1926, CCA 27/26.
Henry McCabe, 1926, CCA 31/26.
William O'Neill, 1927, CCA 31/27.
Gerard Toal, 1928, CCA 20/28.
John Joseph Cox, 1929, CCA 9/29.
Martin Joyce, 1929, CCA 15/29.
Annie Walsh, 1929, CCA 16/29.
Christina Russell, 1930–1, CCA 24/30.
David O'Shea, 1931, CCA 16/31.
Jane O'Brien, 1932, CCA 9/32.
Patrick McDermott, 1932, CCA 20/32.
Elizabeth Edwards, 1935, CCA 13/35.
Rose Edwards, 1935, CCA 14/35.
Leo O'Brien, 1935, CCA 24/35.
Thomas J Kelly, 1936–7, CCA 41/36.
Patrick Boylan, 1937, CCA 9/37.
James Edward Tierney, 1937 (otherwise James Edward O'Neill), CCA 11/37.
John Hornick, 1937, CCA 12/37.

Mary Somerville, 1938, CCA 36/38.
Dermot Smyth, 1938, CCA 40/38.
Patrick Monaghan, 1939, CCA 23/39.
James Fennell, 1940, CCA 25/40.
Daniel Doherty, 1940, CCA 41/40.
Henry Gleeson, 1941, CCA 10/41.
Patrick Kelly, 1941, CCA 33/41.
Bernard Kirwan, 1943, CCA 03/43.
William O'Shea, 1943, CCA 20/43.
Charles Kerins, 1944, CCA 94/44.
James Herbert Lehman, 1944, CCA 96/44.
James Herbert Lehman, 1945, CCA 10/45.
Agnes McAdam, 1946, CCA 16/46.
Daniel Joseph Duff, 1946, CCA 72/46.
Joseph McManus, 1947, CCA 11/47.
Mary Agnes Bernadette Daly, 1948, CCA 68/48.
Frances Cox, 1949, CCA 72/49.
Patrick Heffernan, 1950–1, CCA 80/50.
Patrick Heffernan, 1951, CCA 22/51.
Michael Manning, 1954, CCA 15/54.
Robert James Stevenson, 1954, CCA 29/54.
Mary Ann Cadden, 1956, CCA 36/56.
William Wall, 1959, CCA 24/59.
Thomas O'Rourke, 1959, CCA 36/59.
Vincent McGrath, 1960, CCA 4/60.
David Galvin, 1961–2, CCA 25/61.
James Kelly, 1962, CCA 33/62.

Felix McMullen, 1924, CCA 1/24 and John Fleming, 1933, CCA 40/33 could not be located at either the National Archives of Ireland or the Department of Justice and Equality.

Central Criminal Court, Dublin, State Books

Trials Record Book, Oct. 1924–Apr. 1925.
Trials Record Book, June 1925–June 1927.
Trials Record Book (County), Nov. 1927–June 1933.
Trials Record Book (County), Nov. 1933–Apr. 1941.
Trials Record Book (County), 1941–1945.
Trials Record Book (City), Feb. 1928–Nov. 1943.
Trials Record Book, Feb. 1946–Dec. 1952.
Trials Record Book, Jan. 1953–Dec. 1956.
Trials Record Book, 1957–1961.
Trials Record Book, Jan. 1962–July 1964.
Trials Record Book, Change of Venue Cases, June 1925–Dec. 1926.
Trials Record Book, Change of Venue Cases, Nov. 1927–June 1933.

Department of Justice

Our Lady's House, Henrietta Street, Dublin: annual grant, JUS/90/16/77.

Graves of executed prisoners: visits and upkeep, 1921–1934, JUS/90/16/157.

Publications by the National Council for Abolition of the Death Penalty, JUS/90/16/445.

Release of prisoners on parole, JUS/90/16/491.

Offences against the State (Amendment) Act 1940, JUS/93/2/9.

Release of prisoners to mark the occasion of the elevation of the Most Reverend Dr Conway to the Sacred College of Cardinals, Rome, Feb. 1965, JUS/2002/2/97.

Capital punishment: proposed abolition of, 1962–1964, JUS/2004/32/20.

Thomas Brosnan, Scartaglen, County Kerry: murder of Sergeant Woods, JUS/2007/56/9.

Letters written to the High Sheriff appointed to the Irish Free State by Thomas Wm. Pierrepoint, Official Executioner to the British Government, JUS/2007/56/1.

Murder of Joseph Bergin, military policeman, 1923–1925, JUS/2007/56/15.

General Prisons Board

Death Book, GPB CN5.

Governor General's Office

Execution of Denis Leen, F.318.

Attorney General's Office

Correspondence re: amendment of law on infanticide cases, AG/2000/10/2922.

Department of Foreign Affairs

Noel and Marie Murray, and Ronan Stenson, murder charge, DFA/2006/133/700.

Bureau of Military History

Witness statement 268, Liam T. Cosgrave.

Witness statement 1716, General Seán MacEoin.

Witness statement 1751, The Hon. Justice Cahir Davitt.

General Register Office

Death indexes, various years.

Mountjoy Prison Museum

Death sentences and commutations ledger.

Mountjoy Prison registry of deaths 1846–1996.
Murder trials 1928–1955.
Memories of Mountjoy jail as told by former governor Sean Kavanagh to Liam MacGabhann, undated.
Memorandum of instructions for carrying out the details of an execution, undated.

University College Dublin Archives

George Gavan Duffy Papers, P152/58-63.

Home Office (UK)

Request by the Garda (Republic of Ireland police) to the Metropolitan Police Special Branch (instead of through Government channels) for the services of an executioner: Home Office not in favour and drafted suggested reply for Metropolitan Police to Garda, 1 Jan. 1976–31 Dec. 1976, NAUK, HO 325/84.

II. Secondary Sources

Acker, J.R. and Lanier, C.S. (2000) 'May God—or the governor—have mercy: Executive clemency and executions in modern death-penalty systems', *Criminal Law Bulletin*, 36: 200–37.
Ancel, M. (1962) *The Death Penalty in European Countries*. Strasbourg: Council of Europe.
Barkow, R.E. (2008) 'The ascent of the administrative state and the demise of mercy', *Harvard Law Review*, 121: 1332–65.
Barnett, J.D. (1927) 'The grounds of pardon', *Journal of the American Institute of Criminal Law and Criminology*', 17: 490–530.
Bedau, H.A. (1990–91) 'The decline of executive clemency in capital cases', *New York University Review of Law and Social Change*, 18: 255–72.
Black, L. (2016) *Gendering the Condemned? Women and Capital Punishment in Ireland Post-1922*. Unpublished PhD thesis, Trinity College Dublin.
Bonaparte, C.J. (1910) 'The pardoning power', *Yale Law Journal*, 19: 603–8.
Bourke, M. (1993) *Murder at Marlhill: Was Harry Gleeson Innocent?* Dublin: Geography Publications.
Bowyer Bell, J. (1997) *The Secret Army: The IRA*. Revised third edition. London: Transaction.
Brady, C. (1974) *Guardians of the Peace*. Dublin: Gill & Macmillan.
Brennan, K. (2013) 'Punishing infanticide in the Irish Free State', *Irish Journal of Legal Studies*, 3(1): 1–35.
Bresler, F. (1965) *Reprieve: A Study of a System*. London: Harrap.

Brien, A. (1995) 'Mercy, utilitarianism and retributivism', *Philosophia*, 24: 493–521.

Browne, N. (1986) *Against the Tide*. Dublin: Gill & Macmillan.

Card, C. (1972) 'On mercy', *The Philosophical Review*, 81: 182–207.

Carey, T. (2013) *Hanged for Murder: Irish State Executions*. Cork: Collins Press.

Carroll, E.M. (1941) 'Memorandum re: Women and girls who come before the Central Criminal Court on serious charges . . .' Reproduced as Appendix 5 of report of Inter-Departmental Committee to Establish the Facts of State Involvement with the Magdalen Laundries.

Chadwick, R. (1992) *Bureaucratic Mercy: The Home Office and the Treatment of Capital Cases in Victorian Britain*. London: Garland.

Coogan, T.P. (2002) *The IRA*. New York: Palgrave.

Davis, F. (2007) *The History and Development of the Special Criminal Court 1922–2005*. Dublin: Four Courts Press.

Deale, K.E.L. (2007) *Beyond Any Reasonable Doubt? Irish Murder Trials*. Dublin: Fitzbaggot Publications. (Originally published in 1971 by Gill & Macmillan.)

Digeser, P.E. (2003) 'Justice, forgiveness, mercy, and forgetting: The complex meaning of executive pardoning', *Capital University Law Review*, 31: 161–78.

Dooley, E. (1995) *Homicide in Ireland 1972–1991*. Dublin: Stationery Office.

Dooley, E. (2001) *Homicide in Ireland 1992–1996*. Dublin: Stationery Office.

Douglas, R. and Laster, K. (1991) 'A matter of life and death: The Victorian executive and the decision to execute 1842–1967', *Australian & New Zealand Journal of Criminology*, 24: 144–60.

Doyle, D.M. (2015) 'Republicans, martyrology and the death penalty in Britain and Ireland, 1939–1990', *Journal of British Studies*, 54: 703–22.

Doyle, D.M. and O'Donnell, I. (2012) 'The death penalty in post-Independence Ireland', *Journal of Legal History*, 33: 65–91.

Duff, R.A. (1990) 'Review essay/justice, mercy, and forgiveness', *Criminal Justice Ethics*, 9: 51–63.

Duff, R.A. (2007) 'The intrusion of mercy', *Ohio State Journal of Criminal Law*, 4: 361–87.

Evans, R.J. (1996) *Rituals of Retribution: Capital Punishment in Germany 1600–1987*. Oxford: Oxford University Press.

Fagan, K. (2015) *The Framing of Harry Gleeson*. Cork: The Collins Press.

Fielding, S. (2008) *The Executioner's Bible: The Story of Every British Hangman of the Twentieth Century*. London: John Blake.

Garland, D. (1990) *Punishment and Modern Society: A Study in Social Theory*. Oxford: Oxford University Press.

Garvin, T. (1996) *1922: The Birth of Irish Democracy*. Dublin: Gill & Macmillan.

Gibbons, P., Mulryan, N., and O'Connor, A. (1997) 'Guilty but insane: The insanity defence in Ireland, 1850–1995', *British Journal of Psychiatry*, 170: 467–72.

Gibbons, P., Mulryan, N., McAleer, A., and O'Connor, A. (1999) 'Criminal responsibility and mental illness in Ireland 1850–1995: Fitness to plead', *Irish Journal of Psychological Medicine*, 16: 51–6.

Greer, D. (2006) 'A security against illegality? The reservation of crown cases in nineteenth-century Ireland', in N. Dawson (ed.) *Reflections on Law and History: Irish Legal History Society Discourses and Other Papers*, 2000–2005. Dublin: Four Courts Press, 163–202.

Griffin, D. and O'Donnell, I. (2012) 'The life sentence and parole', *British Journal of Criminology*, 53: 611–29.

Griffin, D. and O'Donnell, I. (2016) 'Confusingly compliant with the European Convention on Human Rights: The release of life sentence prisoners in Ireland', in D. van Zyl Smit and C. Appleton (eds) *Life Imprisonment and Human Rights*. Oñati International Series in Law and Society. Oxford: Hart, 267–86.

Grupp, S. (1963) 'Some historical aspects of the pardon in England', *American Journal of Legal History*, 7: 51–62.

Hamilton, A. (1788) 'The command of the military and naval forces, and the pardoning power of the executive', *The Federalist*, No. 74.

Hanly, C. (2016) 'The 1916 proclamation and jury trial in the Irish Free State', *Dublin University Law Journal*, 39: 373–403.

Harris, B.V. (2003) 'Judicial review, justiciability and the prerogative of mercy', *Cambridge Law Journal*, 62: 631–60.

Harrison, R. (1992) 'The equality of mercy', in H. Gross and R. Harrison (eds) *Jurisprudence: Cambridge Essays*. Oxford: Oxford University Press, 107–25.

Haughton, S. (1866) 'On hanging, considered from a mechanical and physiological point of view', *Philosophical Magazine*, Series 4, 32 (213): 23–34.

Hawkins, K. (1992) 'The use of legal discretion: Perspectives from law and social science', in K. Hawkins (ed.) *The Uses of Discretion*. Oxford: Oxford University Press, 11–46.

Hestevold, H.S. (1987) 'On the moral status of punishment', *Law and Philosophy*, 6: 249–57.

Hood, R. and Hoyle, C. (2015) *The Death Penalty: A Worldwide Perspective*. Fifth edition. Oxford: Oxford University Press.

Hurd, H.M. (2007) 'The morality of mercy', *Ohio State Journal of Criminal Law*, 4: 389–421.

Hussain, N. and Sarat, A. (2007) 'Toward new theoretical perspectives on forgiveness, mercy, and clemency: An introduction', in A. Sarat and N. Hussain (eds) *Forgiveness, Mercy, and Clemency*. Stanford, CA: Stanford University Press, 1–15.

Inter-Departmental Committee to Establish the Facts of State Involvement with the Magdalen Laundries [McAleese Committee] (2013) *Report*. Dublin: Department of Justice and Equality.

Janis, I.L. (1972) *Victims of Groupthink: a Psychological Study of Foreign-Policy Decisions and Fiascoes*. Boston: Houghton Mifflin.

Johnson, D. (1996) 'Trial by jury in Ireland 1860–1914', *Journal of Legal History*, 17: 270–93.

Kant, I. (1797/1965) *The Metaphysical Elements of Justice: Part I of the Metaphysics of Morals* (translated, with an introduction, by J. Ladd). Indianapolis, IN: Bobbs-Merrill.

Kelly, B.D. (2008) 'Poverty, crime and mental illness: Female forensic psychiatric committal in Ireland, 1910–1948', *Social History of Medicine*, 21: 311–28.

Kelly, J.M. (1988) 'Hidden treasure and the Constitution', *Dublin University Law Journal*, 10: 5–23.

Kennedy, F. (2001) *Cottage to Crèche: Family Change in Ireland*. Dublin: Institute of Public Administration.

Kennedy, R. (2007) 'The media and the death penalty: The limits of sentimentality, the power of abjection', *Humanities Research*, 14(2): 29–48.

King, P. (2000) *Crime, Justice, and Discretion in England 1740–1820*. Oxford: Oxford University Press.

Kobil, D.T. (2007) 'Should mercy have a place in clemency decisions?', in A. Sarat and N. Hussain (eds) *Forgiveness, Mercy, and Clemency*. Stanford, CA: Stanford University Press, 36–63.

Koestler, A. (1956) *Reflections on Hanging*. London: Victor Gollancz.

Langbein, J.H. (2003) *The Origins of Adversary Criminal Trial*. Oxford: Oxford University Press.

Langhamer, C. (2012) '"The live dynamic whole of feeling and behavior": Capital punishment and the politics of emotion, 1945–1957', *Journal of British Studies*, 51: 416–41.

Lavinsky, M.B. (1965) 'Executive clemency: Study of a decisional problem arising in the terminal stages of the criminal process', *Chicago-Kent Law Review*, 42: 13–51.

Lee, J.J. (1989) *Ireland 1912–1985: Politics and Society*. Cambridge: Cambridge University Press.

Linebaugh, P. (2003) *The London Hanged: Crime and Civil Society in the Eighteenth Century*. Second edition. London: Verso.

Love, M.C. (2003) 'The pardon paradox: Lessons from Clinton's last pardons', *Capital University Law Review*, 31: 185–218.

Love, M.C. (2015) 'Justice Department administration of the president's pardon power: a case study in institutional conflict of interest', *University of Toledo Law Review*, 47: 89–107.

Macardle, D. (1937) *The Irish Republic: A Documented Chronicle of the Anglo-Irish Conflict and the Partitioning of Ireland, with a Detailed Account of the Period 1916–1923*. London: Victor Gollancz.

MacBride, S. (2005) *That Day's Struggle: A Memoir 1904–1951* (edited by Caitriona Lawlor). Dublin: Currach Press.

MacEoin, U. (1985) *Harry*. Dublin: Argenta Publications.

MacEoin, U. (1997) *The IRA in the Twilight Years: 1923–1948*. Dublin: Argenta Publications.

Maguire, M.J. (2016) 'Male defendants and infanticide in mid-twentieth-century Ireland', *New Hibernia Review*, 20(3): 62–80.

Markel, D. (2004) 'Against mercy', *Minnesota Law Review*, 88: 1421–80.

Marshall, O.R. (1948) 'The prerogative of mercy', *Current Legal Problems*, 1: 104–25.

McConville, S. (2014) *Irish Political Prisoners, 1920–1962: Pilgrimage of Desolation*. Oxford: Routledge.

McEvoy, K. and Mallinder, L. (2013) 'Amnesties, transitional justice and governing through mercy', in J. Simon and R. Sparks (eds) *The Sage Handbook of Punishment and Society*. London: Sage, 434–62.

Moloney, E. (2002) *A Secret History of the IRA*. London: Penguin.

Moore, K.D. (1989) *Pardons: Justice, Mercy, and the Public Interest*. New York: Oxford University Press.

Moroney, M. (1989) *George Plant and the Rule of Law: The Devereux Affair 1940–1942*. Tipperary Historical Society.

Morris, H. (1981) 'A paternalistic theory of punishment', *American Philosophical Quarterly*, 18: 263–71.

Moynihan, M. (1980) (ed.) *Speeches and Statements by Eamon de Valera 1917–73*. Dublin: Gill & Macmillan.

Muller, E.L. (1993) 'The virtue of mercy in criminal sentencing', *Seton Hall Law Review*, 24: 288–346.

Mulryan, N., Gibbons, P., and O'Connor, A. (2002) 'Infanticide and child murder: Admissions to the Central Mental Hospital 1850–2000', *Irish Journal of Psychological Medicine*, 19: 8–12.

Murphy, J.G. (1988) 'Mercy and legal justice', in J.G. Murphy and J. Hampton, *Forgiveness and Mercy*. Cambridge: Cambridge University Press, 162–86.

Nic Dháibhéid, C. (2011) *Seán MacBride: A Republican Life 1904–1946*. Liverpool: Liverpool University Press.

O'Brien, G. (2006) 'Capital punishment in Ireland, 1922–64', in N. Dawson (ed.) *Reflections on Law and History: Irish Legal History Society Discourses and Other Papers*, 2000–2005. Dublin: Four Courts Press, 223–58.

O'Donnell, I. (2005a) 'Violence and social change in the Republic of Ireland', *International Journal of the Sociology of Law*, 33: 101–17.

O'Donnell, I. (2005b) 'Lethal violence in Ireland, 1841 to 2003: Famine, celibacy and parental pacification', *British Journal of Criminology*, 45: 671–95.

O'Donnell, I. (2010) 'Killing in Ireland at the turn of the centuries: Contexts, consequences and civilizing processes', *Irish Economic and Social History*, 37: 53–74.

O'Donnell, I. (2011) 'Criminology, bureaucracy and unfinished business', in M. Bosworth and C. Hoyle (eds) *What is Criminology?* Oxford: Oxford University Press, 488–501.

O'Donnell, I. and Doyle, D.M. (2014) 'A family affair? English hangmen and a Dublin jail, 1923–54', *New Hibernia Review*, 18(4): 101–18.

O'Donnell, I. and Jewkes, Y. (2011) 'Going home for Christmas: Prisoners, a taste of freedom and the press,' *Howard Journal of Criminal Justice*, 50: 75–91.

O'Donnell, I., O'Sullivan, E., and Healy, D. (2005) (eds) *Crime and Punishment in Ireland 1922 to 2003: A Statistical Sourcebook*. Dublin: Institute of Public Administration.

O'Halpin, E. (2012) 'Counting terror: Bloody Sunday and *The Dead of the Irish Revolution*', in D. Fitzpatrick (ed.) *Terror in Ireland, 1916–1923*. Dublin: Lilliput Press, 141–57.

Ó Longaigh, S. (2006) *Emergency Law in Independent Ireland 1922–1948*. Dublin: Four Courts Press.

O'Reilly, G. (1947) *They Are Innocent! The Story of the Irish Republican Prisoners*. New York: Connolly Commemoration Committee.

O'Sullivan, D. (1940) *The Irish Free State and its Senate: A Study in Contemporary Politics*. London: Faber & Faber.

O'Sullivan, E. and O'Donnell, I. (2007) 'Coercive confinement in the Republic of Ireland: The waning of a culture of control', *Punishment & Society*, 9: 27–48.

O'Sullivan, E. and O'Donnell, I. (2012) (eds) *Coercive Confinement in Ireland: Patients, Prisoners and Penitents*. Manchester: Manchester University Press.

Palacios, V.J. (1996) 'Faith in fantasy: The Supreme Court's reliance on commutation to ensure justice in death penalty cases', *Vanderbilt Law Review*, 49: 310–72.

Pierrepoint, A. (1974) *Executioner: Pierrepoint*. London: George G. Harrap.

Potter, H. (1993) *Hanging in Judgment: Religion and the Death Penalty in England*. London: SCM Press.

Pringle, P. (2012) *About Time: Surviving Ireland's Death Row*. Dublin: The History Press Ireland.

Rainbolt, G. (1997) 'Mercy: In defence of caprice', *NOÛS*, 31: 226–41.

Rattigan, C. (2010) '"Half mad at the time": Unmarried mothers and infanticide in Ireland, 1922–1950', in C. Cox and M. Luddy (eds) *Cultures of Care in Irish Medical History, 1950–1970*. London: Palgrave Macmillan, 168–90.

Rattigan, C. (2012) *'What Else Could I Do?' Single Mothers and Infanticide, Ireland 1900–1950*. Dublin: Irish Academic Press.

Release of Prisoners Commission (2000) *Report on Activities*. Dublin: Stationery Office.

Roberts, H.R.T. (1971) 'Mercy', *Philosophy*, 46 (178): 352–3.

Rolph, C.H. (1978) *The Queen's Pardon*. London: Cassell.

Royal Commission on Capital Punishment (1949–1953) *Report*. Cmd 8932. London: HMSO.

Sarat, A. and Hussain, N. (2006) 'The literary life of clemency: Pardon tales in the contemporary United States', *TriQuarterly*, 124: 169–92.

Seal, L. (2016) 'Albert Pierrepoint and the cultural persona of the twentieth-century hangman', *Crime, Media, Culture*, 12: 83–100.

Sebba, L. (1977) 'Clemency in perspective', in S.F. Landau and L. Sebba (eds) *Criminology in Perspective: Essays in Honor of Israel Drapkin*. Lexington, MS: DC Heath and Co, 221–40.

Sigler, M. (2016) 'Equity, not mercy', in C. Flanders and Z. Hoskins (eds) *The New Philosophy of Criminal Law*. London: Rowman & Littlefield, 231–47.

Smart, A. (1968) 'Mercy', *Philosophy*, 43 (166): 345–59.

Smith, A.T.H. (1983) 'The prerogative of mercy, the power of pardon and criminal justice', *Public Law*, 398–439.

Smith, G.T. (1996) 'Civilized people don't want to see that kind of thing: The decline of public physical punishment in London, 1760–1840', in C. Strange (ed.) *Qualities of Mercy: Justice, Punishment, and Discretion*. Vancouver: UBC Press, 21–51.

Statman, D. (1994) 'Doing without mercy', *Southern Journal of Philosophy*, 32: 331–54.

Steiker, C.S. (2007) 'Tempering or tampering? Mercy and the administration of criminal justice', in A. Sarat and N. Hussain (eds) *Forgiveness, Mercy, and Clemency*. Stanford, CA: Stanford University Press, 16–35.

Strange, C. (1995) 'The lottery of death: Capital punishment, 1867–1976', *Manitoba Law Journal*, 23: 594–619.

Strange, C. (1996) 'Discretionary justice: Political culture and the death penalty in New South Wales and Ontario, 1890–1920', in

C. Strange (ed.) *Qualities of Mercy: Justice, Punishment, and Discretion*. Vancouver: UBC Press, 130–65.

Tasioulas, J. (2003) 'Mercy', *Proceedings of the Aristotelian Society*, 103: 101–32.

Thompson, J.G. (1899) *The Law of Criminal Procedure in Ireland*. Dublin: Hodges, Figgis.

Vaughan, W.E. (2009) *Murder Trials in Ireland, 1836–1914*. Dublin: Four Courts Press.

Walker, N. (1995) 'The quiddity of mercy', *Philosophy*, 70: 27–37.

Weber, M. (1922/1968) *Economy and Society: An Outline of Interpretive Sociology* (edited by G. Roth and C. Wittich), Vol. 3. New York: Bedminster Press.

Weihofen, H. (1939–1940) 'Pardon: An extraordinary remedy', *Rocky Mountain Law Review*, 12: 112–20.

Whelehan, N. (2014) 'The Irish revolution, 1912–23', in A. Jackson (ed.) *The Oxford Handbook of Modern Irish History*. Oxford: Oxford University Press, 621–45.

Index

abduction 206
abolitionism 1, 12–13, 82, 110–11, 133, 135, 145, 150, 213, 247, 258, 260
abortion 32, 34, 109, 184, 218, 241
Acker, J.R. 156
acquittal 21–2, 25, 56, 123–4, 192
act of contrition 11, 212
act of grace 52
age 26–7, 32, 158, 223
agricultural workers 213
Ahearne, Catherine 191, 245
alcohol 35, 161–3, 191, 197, 200, 202–3, 205, 211, 215, 220, 222–3, 252
Alibrandi, Gaetano 157n
Allen, Harry 15n
amnesty 40, 62, 136, 245, 250–1
An Garda Síochána 20, 21n, 47, 120, 133, 157n, 164, 166n, 212, 227n, 247, 255, 258
Ancel, M. 135
Anglo-Irish relations 256–7
Anglo-Irish Treaty 2, 204, 207
Anselm, Saint of Canterbury 81
appeal 28, 35, 171, 177, 194
appellate tribunals 83–84, 90
Ara Coeli (residence of Archbishop of Armagh) 176
arbitrariness 50, 64, 71, 103, 155–8
archives 14, 16, 19–20, 26, 105, 208, 256–7
  see also National Archives of Ireland
Armagh, Archbishop of 175, 245
armed robbery 2n
arraignment, without 22
arrest, resisting 116, 119, 121n
arson 24, 248n
assassination, political 3, 9–10, 123, 174
assault 24, 116, 125, 140
attorney general 19, 21n, 25n, 51n, 72n, 92–3, 162, 165, 171, 178n, 224n, 228
Attorney General v Leo O'Brien (1936) 197n
attrition 22, 25, 92
Australia 182–3, 191, 234
Aylward, Patrick 32, 86, 96, 156, 163, 172, 221–2, 232n, 243n

bank fraud 87n
bank robbery 137n, 258
Barkow, R.E. 62, 68–9, 75
Barry, Kevin 2n
Barnett, J.D. 77–8
Baxter, Robert 95n
beating 32, 34, 200
Beccaria, Cesare 62
Bedau, H.A. 66
Beggar's Bush barracks, Dublin 12n
bells tolling 16, 94
Bentham, Jeremy 61–2, 66
Bergin, Joseph 12, 205–6
Berry, Peter 147, 166n, 239n
Bethany Home, Dublin 187, 227, 235, 242
bias, judicial 162n
biographies, bloody 9–12
black cap 16, 74, 102-8, 161, 190, 195
black market offences 129
Black, L. 1
Black, William 104, 199n
blameworthiness 71, 77
blood sacrifice 139
Blowick, Joseph 154
Boland, Gerald 10–11, 117n, 119n, 125n, 128n, 131, 140–1, 145–8, 151–2, 175, 179–80, 248, 255
bombing 6, 119, 132, 256
Bonaparte, C.J. 62, 67, 73
'born' criminals 166–70

Bourke, M. 260–1
Bowyer Bell, J. 120, 131, 151
Boylan, Patrick 23n, 98n, 109n, 145, 160–3, 168n, 169, 221
Boyne, Kathleen 198
Brady, C. 131
Brennan v Minister for Justice (1995) 181n
Brennan, K. 25
Bresler, F. 49, 51–2, 81–2, 97, 109, 142n, 147, 160
Brien, A. 42, 62, 78
British Army 7n, 208
British police 131
Brosnan, Thomas 209
Browne, Daniel 110n, 147
Browne, Noël 153–4
Buachalla, Domhnall ua 51, 179
Budd, Gardner 53n, 104
Bunreacht na hÉireann 1, 50n, 157n, 169n,
  see also Constitution of Ireland (1937)
Bureau of Military History 10n, 11n, 19, 168n
bureaucracy 54, 75, 81, 145
  see also clemency
burglary 27
burial 38–9, 129
buried alive 19, 32, 34, 189
Burke, Luke 3n
burned bodies 185
burning 32, 34
Butler, Joseph 205
Byrne v Ireland (1972) 52n
Byrne, Henry 133
Byrne, James 212

Cadden, Mary 3n, 32, 80, 96, 99, 108n, 109, 156, 184, 217–19, 232n, 237
Callan, Noel 47, 117, 133, 136–7, 229, 248
Callan v Ireland (2013) 137n
Canada 147, 182–3, 234
capital murder 6, 21n, 147, 166, 225, 228, 229n, 256, 258
  capital sentences by county 32
  release 247–51
  state-sanctioned death 139–41
  see also extraordinary courts
capital punishment
  abolition of 1, 12–13, 82, 110–11, 133, 135, 145, 150, 213, 247, 258, 260
  colonial hangover 17
  history of 14–15
  referendum on 1–2
  retention of 9
  support for 5, 13, 133–4, 258
Capital Punishment Amendment Act (1868) 103n
caprice
  defined 43
  clemency 77–82
  undoing death 221–3
  release 225
carbon monoxide poisoning 168n
Card, C. 59
cardiac disease 231
Carey, T. 1
Carroll, Evelyn 240-1
Carroll, Mella 93n
Casement, Roger 2, 142n
categorical imperative 60n
categorization 43–5
Catholic Church/Catholicism 17, 37, 99, 142, 156–7, 172, 194, 218, 223, 235, 241–6, 253
  see also convents for women; papal intervention
Caudy, Michael 205
celebrations 40n, 77
religious 243, 245–6
celerity (speed of case processing) 36
  see also deterrence theory
Central Criminal Court 20, 26n, 89–90, 92, 101, 103n, 120, 130, 167, 254
Central Criminal Lunatic Asylum 23, 238n
Central Mental Hospital (CMH) 23, 24, 168, 192, 218, 231–9, 254n
certainty 36
  see also deterrence theory
Chadwick, R. 71, 75
chastity 242

child killings 203, 232n
  see also infanticide
child rape 181n
childbirth 220
  see also concealment of birth; infanticide; pregnancy
Childers, Erskine 12n
children 219
  see also child killings; child rape; childbirth; illegitimate children; infanticide; unwanted children
Children Act (1908) 27
Children Act (1941) 27n
chivalry 94, 185
  undoing death 213–21
choking 19, 32, 34, 199
Church of Ireland 129, 172, 235
Chuter-Ede, James 57
Cistercian Order 119n
civil war (1922–3) 2–4, 7n, 9–12, 122, 154n, 168n, 204, 207
civilian executions 13
Clann na Poblachta 153n
Clann na Talmhan 153n
clemency
  arguments for and against 54–84
  caprice 77–82
  celebrations 77
  classification of 30–9
  compromise of the jury 69
  condescending 70
  cons 63–71
  context 17–18
  definition 39–40
  differentiation of levels of culpability 76
  discretion and desert 56–63
  error correction 73–4
  executive 66–7, 71, 79, 81n, 91, 111, 224, 259
  extraordinary courts 128–9
  flexibility 71–2
  forward looking 76
  governments 156–7
  harshness, temperance of excessive 74
  irrationality of 65
  justice 77–82
  lack of standing 69
  leniency as firmness of purpose 77
  maintenance of standards 75–6
  to men after trial by jury 113
  mercy 77–82
  mode of conviction 113
  non-judicial actors 68–9
  personal aspects 74–5
  potential corruptness 66–7
  power 49
  precursor to law reform 72–3
  private virtue 64–5
  process 28–9
  promotion of inertia 67
  promotion of public confidence 73
  pros 71–7
  routine 70–1
  separation of powers doctrine 68
  space for intervening factors 76
  supererogation 41–2, 76–7
  trend in 46–7
  tripartite scheme 39–53
  undemocratic nature of 65–6
  unduly burdensome 70
  unfettered nature 66
  varieties of 44
clerical interventions 173, 178, 221
  see also papal intervention
Clinton, Bill 67
Clune, Thomas 91n
Codd, William 172
coercive confinement 191n, 225, 230, 232–3, 235–9, 244
  definition 24n
  time spent in 237
Cole, Mary 26–7
collateral damage 18, 67, 132
Collier, Patrick 173
Collins, Gerard 146
Collins, Michael 12n
Colonial Office, London 180
common law 71, 101n
Commonwealth 247
community, discharge to 24, 187, 191, 236–7
community sentiment 63, 66, 73, 78, 85, 101n, 118, 149, 158
commutation vs execution 5, 7–8, 147–8

compassion 30, 41–3, 45n, 46–7, 64, 73, 83, 128n, 132, 235
concealment of birth 25, 189n, 190, 238, 242
 see also abortion; infanticide
condescension 83
condign punishment 60n
confession 167
confessional state 157
confirmation of execution 35
Connolly, Kate 201
Connolly O'Brien, Nora 242
conspiracy to murder 214
Constitution (Amendment No. 17) Act (1931) 118
Constitution (Amendment No. 27) Act (1936) 51n
Constitution (Special Powers) Tribunal 118
Constitution of Ireland (1937) 1, 13, 49–53, 119, 159, 169, 177, 227, 242, 249n, 261–2
Constitutional amendment (2001) 1n, 262
contraceptives 19, 219, 241
 see also abortion; pregnancy
convents for women 189, 191, 195, 233–40
 see also Magdalen Asylums
convicted of murder after trial by jury
 hanged 267–8 (App II)
 spared 263–5 (App I)
Conway, Michael 116–19, 124, 139, 146
Coogan, T.P. 124
Cooney, Patrick 146
Cooper, Catherine 252
Cork Examiner 27
coroner's order for burial 38
corruptness
 clemency 66–7
Cosgrave, Liam 256
Cosgrave, W.T. 3, 10–11, 146
Costello, John A. 12, 246–7
Council of Europe 223
Court for Crown Cases Reserved 90n
Court of Criminal Appeal 20, 28, 90, 106, 107, 164–5, 171n, 254n, 255,
Court Officers Act (1926) 16n
Courts of Justice Act (1924) 89
Cousins, John 215
Cox, Frances 96, 99, 109, 156, 217, 236
Cox, John 36, 96, 253n
Coyne, T.J. 147, 165n
Criminal Appeal Act (1907) 90n
criminal damage 248n
Criminal Justice (Release of Prisoners) Act (1998) 40n, 136, 249
Criminal Justice Act (1951) 50, 180, 228
Criminal Justice Act (1960) 228
Criminal Justice Act (1964) 21n, 56, 132, 218n, 254
Criminal Justice Act (1984) 102n
Criminal Justice Act (1990) 21n, 225n
Criminal Law Amendment Act (1935) 19
Criminal Law (Suicide) Act (1993) 21n
criminal procedure 86n
criminology 215n, 216n
Crowe, Brigid 192
Crumlin Road Gaol 15n
culpability, levels of 34n, 76
Cumann na mBan 115n
Cumann na nGaedheal 149n
Curragh internment camp 239

Dáil Éireann 68, 93, 160, 179, 258
 debates 3n, 10n, 117n, 119n, 127–8, 140n, 154, 171n, 229n, 258, 260n
Daly, Mary (sentence commuted) 147, 160, 180, 184, 215–16, 228
Daly, Mary (sentence executed) 5n, 220
Darcy, Tony 127
data protection issues 19–20n
Davern, Patrick 44n, 47, 124–7, 130, 140, 173, 247n

Davis, F. 119n
Davitt, Cahir 103–4, 107, 162–71, 200
Day, John Godfrey Fitzmaurice 172–3
de Burca and Anderson v Attorney General (1976) 92n
de Freitas v Benny (1976) 42n
de Valera, Éamon 9, 12, 51, 116n, 127–8, 131, 148, 173, 174n, 175–9
Deale, K.E.L. 162n
death penalty
  abolition and/or restriction of 6, 7, 12–13, 133–6
  restrictions 46
  under sixteens 27n
  'volunteers' 35-6
death-eligibility, 46, 57, 100, 151, 156, 237, 254
  avoidance of 20–9
decapitation 209, 214, 258n
decision-making *see* government
Defence Forces 121
Delaney, Thomas 38–9, 86
dementia 256n
democratic principles 71
derangement 80
deterrence theory 36, 134n
Devane, Richard 241
Devereux, Michael 124–5, 130–1, 173, 247
Devereux, William 99, 209, 243n
Dictionary of Irish Biography 51, 125n
Digeser, P.E. 58n
Diplock, Kenneth 42
diplomacy 223
Director of Public Prosecutions 21n, 28
discount on sentences 248–9
discretion 54, 73, 79, 82, 95
  government 143–7
  see also clemency
discrimination 169–70, 220–1
  see also gender
disembowelling 95n
dismemberment 214
disparagement 219
dissolution of government 66
district asylums 24
Dixon, Beatrice 92
Dixon, Kevin 27, 104
Doherty, Seán 146
Donegal News 15n
Dooley, E. 24n
Doran, Elizabeth 108, 193, 233n
double hanging 38
double murder 27, 137n
Douglas, R. 183
Dowd, Michael 133
Downes, William 35, 39n, 204
Downey, James 172
Doyle v Wicklow County Council (1974) 23n
Doyle, Archie 131
Doyle, D.M. 1–2, 38n, 148
drowning 19, 26–7, 32, 34, 186, 188, 194
drugs 35
Dublin, Archbishop of 173, 215
Dublin City Commission 91n
Dublin Corporation 92
Dublin Gazette 215
duelling 60n
Duff, Daniel 212–13
Duff, John 147
Duff, R.A. 64, 82, 83n
Dukes, Alan 140, 146
duration of detention 238

Easter Rising (1916) 2, 4, 5, 7n, 8, 10–11, 51, 127, 137
Eccles, Thomas 47, 133, 136, 249
ecclesiastical intervention *see* clerical intervention; papal intervention
Edwards, Elizabeth 31–4, 92, 100n, 187–8, 194, 202n
Edwards, Rose 31–4, 92, 100n, 187–8, 194
Egan, John 117–18, 139
elections 3, 93n, 149–50, 179
electroconvulsive therapy 238
electrocution 108n
Ellis, Ruth 38
Emergency Powers (Amendment) (No. 2) Act (1940) 121

Emergency Powers (No. 41) Order (1940) 119n, 121, 123, 125n, 126n, 130n
emergency powers legislation 127
Emergency Powers Resolution 3
Emergency, the (1939–1945) 8–9, 13, 112, 128–31, 140
see also Second World War
emigration 234
empathy gap 55, 138, 141, 208
employers and managers 213
employment 229n, 236
England and Wales
execution for treason 95n
executioners 95
infanticide legislation 25, 195n
jury deliberations 87n
length of sentence 230
pardoning power 44
warrants for arrest 201
Enlightenment era 49
Ennis, James 108n
epilepsy 203
equality before the law 63–4
equitable treatment 79
error correction 73–4
see also clemency; pardon
Eucharistic Congress (1932) 77, 173, 189, 207, 222, 233, 243–5, 250–1
European Economic Community (EEC) 18
Evans, R.J. 15
Evening Herald 115n, 249n
Everett, James 11, 80n, 146
Ewart-Biggs, Christopher 256
executioner wanted (1976) 256–9
executioner, post of 93, 255n, 256
executive power
clemency 66–7
see also clemency: executive
Executive Powers (Consequential Provisions) Act (1937) 51n
Executive Powers (Convicts' Licences) Order (1937) 226
explosive substances 121n
expressive function (of capital cases) 75–6
extra-legal factors 155, 158
extraordinary courts 115–41
capital murder 132–41
legal manoeuvres 125–32
Special Powers Tribunal 117–20
Terror Court 120–5
extraterritorial appeal 208

Fagan, K. 261
Fagan, Patrick 107, 184, 207, 243, 261
false imprisonment 116, 140
Fanning, John 154n, 198
Farrell, Bridget 166
favouritism 64, 66, 82
fees and expenses (executioner) 162n, 222
female murderers 64, 94, 221, 233, 239
Fennell, James 41, 211
Ferns, Bishop of 172
Fianna Fáil 135, 149n, 175, 179–80
Fielding, S. 38n
final tally 28–9
Fine Gael 11, 135, 153n
Finlay, John 206
Finn, Margaret 27, 192, 234n, 237, 245
firearms 34n, 121n, 204
firing parties/squads 3, 12n, 16, 116n, 124–5, 174n
First World War 4, 7–8, 86, 208
FitzGerald-Kenney, James 11, 138n, 146, 189n, 230n,
Fleming, John 41n, 95n, 96, 99, 109–12, 147, 179
Flynn, Hannah 95, 210, 220, 232–7, 244
forced labour 235
forgiveness 39–40, 262
Four Courts, Dublin 2, 103
Foy, Denis 107, 203, 232n
France 258n
Franciscan order 125
fraud trials 87n
Free State Constitution (1922) 13, 52n, 118
Free State soldiers 209
Freedom of Information Act (2000) 256

frugality principle 61–2
  see also utilitarianism

Gaeltacht (Irish-speaking regions) 93n
Gaffney, Jeremiah 209
Galvin, David 92, 99, 132, 147, 171–2, 201, 242–3, 254
Gambon, William 35, 90, 153–4, 170–1, 254
Garda Museum and Archives 257
Garda Review 258
Garda Síochána Act (1958) 92n
Garland, D. 17
Garvin, T. 3
Gavan Duffy, George 103–4, 180, 216n
gender 37n, 156, 158, 186, 188, 213, 220, 230n, 235–6
  bias 96, 225n
  differences 45, 48, 64
  discrimination 64, 158
  equality 91n
  execution and commutation 30–1
  petitions referring to 215
  protective effects of 218–21
general elections 93n
  see also elections
Geoghegan, James 11, 146, 173n, 215n
geography of capital punishment 32–3, 101
George V, king of England 208
Germany 15, 132, 255n
Gibbons, Mary 215–6
Gibbons, P. 23–4
Gleeson, Henry 28–9, 40, 148, 259–61
Good Friday Agreement (1998) 40n, 136, 229, 248–9, 251
Good Shepherd Convent, Limerick 210
Good Shepherd Convent, New Ross 234n
Good Shepherd Sisters 233
Goss, Richard 116, 124, 151
Gould, Elizabeth 201
governments 142–58
  arbitrary vs principled decisions 155–8
  groupthink 150–5
  limits to discretion 143–7
  public opinion 147–50
Governor General's Office 163n, 208
Great War *see* First World War
Green, Thomas 36, 121–3, 131, 140, 174n
Greer, D. 90n
Greery, Michael 3n
grievous bodily harm 201
Griffin, D. 229
Griffin, Martin 97n, 156, 211, 239n
Groupthink 150–5
  see also government
Grupp, S. 72
guillotine 258n
guilt 71
guilty but insane 22–4, 56, 88, 227n, 238, 252
  see also insanity
guilty verdict 56, 86, 93, 210

habeas corpus 175
hacking, death by 32, 34
Hamilton, Alexander 81n, 151, 247
Hamilton, Liam 104n
hammer killing 110, 184, 214–16
Hand, Frank 47, 133
Hand, Rose 163
handcart 38–9
hanging judges 104, 107
hanging, trends in use 2n, 5, 8
hangman, avoidance of 185
Hanley, Mary 25n
Hanly, C. 91n
Hanna, Henry 103–4, 108
Hannon, Elizabeth 32, 188–9, 234n, 237
happiness theory 60n, 62
  see also utilitarianism
Hardiman, Adrian 137
Harris, B.V. 65n
Harrison, R. 65
harshness 74
  see also clemency

Haugh, Kevin 104, 190
Haughey, Charles 11, 13, 135, 146, 171
Haughton, S. 95
Hawkins, K. 143
Hayes, Stephen 32, 124, 130
health of prisoners 231
see also medical treatment
Healy, Timothy 179, 208
heart failure 32, 232n
Heffernan, Patrick 98–9, 107, 109n, 160–70, 221
Henry, Patrick 185
hereditary monarchy 50
Hestevold, H.S. 59
Higgins, Michael D. 261
'history by the neck' 14
Hogan, John 138n, 204–5
Holden, Willie 221
Holmes, Oliver Wendell 108
Holy See 99, 156–7, 223
Holy Year of 1950, 245
Home Office 256–7
Home Secretary 37n, 57, 69, 97, 142n, 143
homicide rates 5 7, 18, 24n
honour 60n
Hood, R, 77n
Hopkins, William 97n, 254n
Horan, Patrick 86
Horgan, Nora 201
Hornick, John 163n, 172–3
Houses of the Oireachtas, *see* Oireachtas
Hoyle, C. 77n
hunger strike 116, 120, 124–5, 127, 205, 231–2, 235
Hunt, Thomas 121, 124, 140–1, 235, 239, 248
Hurd, H.M. 59, 64
Hussain, N. 49, 143
Hyde, Douglas 163n
Hyland, Richard 36

identity transformation 234n
illegitimate children 25, 30–1, 167, 184, 186, 190, 195, 199, 219, 232
impartiality 180
impunity 63, 66
infant life 17
infant mortality rates 19
infanticide 5–6, 18–19, 22, 25–6, 30–2, 34, 41, 49, 60, 67, 71, 79–80, 90, 92–3, 100, 138, 187–8, 192, 217, 230, 232, 234, 236–8, 240–1
Infanticide Act (1949) 25n, 41, 71, 194–5, 253
infidelity 197, 200
see also marriage
Information Commissioner's Office 257
Information Rights Team, Home Office 257
inquest 16, 37–9, 94, 121, 125
inertia, promotion of 67
see also clemency
insanity 23–4, 88, 161, 192, 198, 203, 213, 209–13, 218, 222, 227, 232n, 238
see also guilty but insane
insulin coma therapy 238
integrity of the state 121n
interference with property 248n
interment 16, 38–9, 122n, 129
interrogation 124, 206
intimidation 129
Irish Army 8, 114, 123n, 131
Curragh Command 124
Eastern Command 174n
Irish Free State (Saorstát Éireann) 2–4, 8–9, 51–2, 64, 93n, 213, 224
Irish Independent 1n, 36, 91n, 107, 129, 171, 176n, 200n, 215, 217, 243n, 248n, 249, 253, 255
Irish language 51, 162, 172, 212
see also Gaeltacht; language
Irish National Liberation Army (INLA) 136n, 137n, 249n
Irish Pacifist Movement 13
Irish Post 253n
Irish Press 118n, 212n, 213n, 246
Irish Republican Army (IRA)
activities 116–17, 119–21
amnesties for prisoners 250
assassinations by 3

car bombings 256
civil war 204
crushing of 32
executions 36, 117, 122, 128–31, 134, 148, 151–2, 174n
first decades of independence 115
gunmen 47
informers 124
martyrs 125, 129, 139
members 7n, 10n, 13, 36, 148, 182, 188
proscription 118
Provisional 249n
releases 40n, 136–8, 247, 249, 251
response to 9, 112
risk posed by 115
Special Powers Tribunal 119
threat posed by 18, 127
see also hunger strike
Irish Republicanism 119, 131, 136n, 152, 157n, 177
Irish Times 3, 13, 27, 86, 87n, 92, 97n, 103, 105–7, 108n, 118n, 136n, 162n, 171, 172n, 176n, 188, 193n, 218n, 249n, 256, 261
irrationality *see* clemency
irresistible impulse 23n

Janis, I.L. 150
jealousy 80, 161–3
sex and 196–203
Johnson, D. 115
Johnston, William 104, 189n
Joyce, Martin 41, 99, 202, 224–5, 245
judges *see* juries and judges
judicial discretion *see* discretion
judicial observations 35
judicial review 68
Juries Act (1927) 88n, 92n, 101n
Juries Act (1976) 88n, 91n
Juries (Protection) Act (1929) 102
juries and judges 85–114
composition 91–5
donning the black cap 102–9
intimidation 102, 115, 123
jury deliberations, speed of 87
jury nullification 22, 57, 88
jury recommendation 35
jury room disquiet 100
jury service 91n
jury verdict 38
singular case 110–14
softening the verdict 95–102
weighing the evidence 85–91
Jurisdiction in Liberties Act 52n
justice
defined 41
clemency 55, 77–82
release 225

Kant, Immanuel 60, 82n, 111, 128n, 188, 220
Kavanagh, Sean 13n, 37n, 253
Keane, Mary Anne 191, 234
Kelly, B.D. 238
Kelly, J.M. 52n
Kelly, James 92, 101, 107, 108n, 147, 201, 243, 254
Kelly, John 80
Kelly, Patrick 108, 132
Kelly, Thomas 41, 103, 163n, 185, 238–9
Kennedy, Eileen 93n
Kennedy, F. 19
Kennedy, R. 37n
Kerins, Charles 116n, 122n, 123, 127–8, 131, 255
kidnapping 124
Kiernan, Mary 180n, 189, 234
Kilmainham Gaol 10
King, P. 87n
king of England 69, 108n
see also George V
King's Inns, Dublin 95
Kingsmill Moore, Theodore 104, 164–6
Kirwan, Bernard 32–4, 148–9
Kobil, D.T. 83
Koestler, A. 150

Labour Party 11, 135, 153n
Langbein, J.H. 87n
Langhamer, C. 12, 37n
language
of execution 94–5, 101, 249–50
see also Gaeltacht; Irish language
Lanier, C.S. 156

larceny 102, 201
Laster, K. 183
Lavinsky, M.B. 91
law reform
 clemency 72–3
Lee, J.J. 138
Leen, Denis 156, 163, 179, 184, 208–9, 224n
legal empathy 45
legal manoeuvres 125–32
 see also extraordinary courts
legal rights 42
legal sanity 185, 209–3
'legally sanctioned alegality' 49
Lehman, James 223
Lemass, Seán 12, 146, 171, 172n
leniency, as firmness of purpose 77
 see also clemency
Lenihan, Brian 146
lesser offence, conviction for 56, 88
lessons learned 170–1
lethal assault 201, 210
lethal violence
 trends in 5, 101
 victims of 6, 31
life expectancy 19, 230
life-sentence prisoners 229–30
Limerick, Bishop of 172, 177
Linebaugh, P. 7, 14
lobbying 14, 156–7, 159, 180–1
Locke, John 49
'lottery' of capital punishment 182–5
Love, M.C. 67

McAdam, Agnes 160, 180, 213, 234n, 237
McAleese Committee 233n
Macardle, D. 3
MacBride, John 10
MacBride, Seán 10n, 96n, 125, 153–4, 164–5, 171, 174–5, 254n, 260
McCabe, Henry 105–6
McCann, Patrick 28, 104, 117n, 133–7, 248–9
McCarthy, Mary 259
McCaughey, Seán 33–4, 116, 124–5, 130, 139–40, 231–2, 235
McConville, S. 125
MacCurtain, Tomás 44, 116, 120, 127–8, 139, 145, 154–5, 174–6, 221, 228, 246
McDermott, Patrick 102
McDonagh, Thomas 38–9, 96n
McEntee, Seán 118
MacEoin, Seán 11, 146, 180, 195n, 245
MacEoin, U. 124, 152, 174–5
McEvoy, James 25n
McEvoy, K. 250n
MacGabhann, Liam 13n, 37n
McGladdery, Robert 15n
McGrath, James 203
McGrath, Patrick 36, 119, 121–3, 127–8, 131, 140, 174n
McGrath, Vincent 23n, 53, 88, 92, 198–9
McHugh, James 38n, 105
McHugh, Michael 2, 29, 47, 117n, 133, 136–7, 248
McLoughlin, Richard 104, 107, 108n, 180
McManus, Joseph 87
McMullen, Felix 89–90
McNaghten Rules 23
McNeela, Jack 127
McPhillips, Patrick 47, 133, 136, 249
MacRory, Joseph 175–6, 243n
McShane, Brian 47, 133, 136, 249
McSweeney, Michael 205
madness 23–4, 218
Magdalen Asylum 24, 192, 202, 214, 233–5, 239–42
Maguire, Conor 104
Maguire, Martin 104, 108, 165
Maguire, M.J. 186n
Maher, Patrick 2n
maleficence 66
mandatory death penalty 21, 24n, 108n, 160n, 213, 247
 sentencing 56–7, 98, 155, 160
Manning, Michael 23n, 103, 106, 133, 157, 172, 177–9, 223, 252–3
Markel, D. 61, 66, 74
Markievicz, Constance 93n
marriage 23–6, 60n, 61, 76, 93, 184, 195, 197, 212
 see also infidelity

Marshall, O.R. 69
martyrology 125, 129–30, 139
medical inspection 37, 125
medical treatment 231–2, 238
memorandum for government 35, 72n, 90, 127n, 132n, 144, 157n, 162, 167, 170n, 198n, 200n, 212n, 225n, 227, 230n, 245n, 247n
mental illness 23–4, 154, 168, 217, 203
  hospitalization for 213
  mental abnormality 213, 221
  mental incapacity 201, 215
mercy
  defined 41–2
  clemency and 58
  justice 77–82
  merciful ministers 146
  motivation 45
  prerogative of 98, 99n, 147, 160, 162, 186–7
  pseudo 59
  recommendations to 97–8
  release 225
  relieves deserved suffering 80
Meredith, James Creed 104, 110–12, 220, 221n
Metropolitan Police, London 256–7
militant republicanism 119, 131, 139, 152
  see also Irish Republican Army (IRA)
military courts 3, 10, 119–26, 168n, 177
military intelligence 206
military personnel 7n
Ministers and Secretaries Act (1924) 3n
miscarriage 37n, 218–19
  see also abortion; pregnancy
miscarriage of justice 259–61
misogyny 199
  see also gender
Mitchell, Jim 146
mitigation of sentence 71, 166n, 170, 180n, 181, 206n
Mohangi, Shan 254n
Molloy, Charles 95, 206–7, 243
Molony, Thomas 86, 99n, 104, 108, 222
Moloney, E. 157n
Monaghan, Patrick 199
Moore, K.D. 60, 108n, 219, 262
moral theology 172
morality 150, 195–6, 202, 218
Moran, Kate 238n
Moran, Michael 146
Moran, Patrick 207
Morley, John 133
Moroney, M. 130
Morris, H. 70
Morrissey, Daniel 11, 146, 164–5
Morrissey, Patrick 47, 133
motivation 45–6
Mountjoy Prison 5n, 13n, 20, 27, 36–9, 96n, 122n, 134n, 139, 171, 174, 198n, 200n, 201n, 202n, 212, 218–20, 227n, 239, 253
Moynihan, M. 120
Moynihan, Mary 189, 201–2, 220, 243n, 244
Mulcahy, Richard 3, 12, 153–4
Muller, E.L. 45, 61
Mulryan, N. 237–8
multivariate analysis 184
murder
  attrition in trials 22
  capital, *see* capital murder
  methods of 34
  recorded 6
Murnaghan, George 103–6, 165, 175
Murphy, J.G. 58, 64
Murphy, Michael 3n
Murray, James 12, 85, 107–8, 184, 205–6, 231
Murray, Marie 157n, 171n, 254–8
Murray, Noel 157n, 171n, 254–8
Murtagh, Francis 108n
Murtagh, Rita 110
Myles, James 35, 95n

National Archives of Ireland 208, 217n, 256
  see also archives
National Army 12n, 197, 200, 205, 207, 209

National Labour Party 153n
national security 128
natural justice 122, 124
nervous breakdown 37n
New York Times 246
newspaper coverage 85–6, 171, 200, 212, 214–15, 239n, 243n
Nic Dháibhéid, C. 117, 129, 154n, 260
night shelters 239n
Nolan, Mary 222
nolle prosequi 28, 126, 214
non-jury court
  capital cases 116
  persons convicted by 28, 113, 130
  sentenced to death 269–70 (App III)
  Noonan, Michael 140, 146
Noone, Gerard 27
nooses 36–7
Northern Ireland 2, 15, 187, 255n
  abolition of the death penalty 133–4
  ceasefire 248
  length of sentence 230
  peace process 40n, 117, 136, 251
  Troubles, the 18, 133–4, 249–50
  see also Good Friday Agreement (1998)
notice posted on prison gates 16

Ó Dálaigh, Cearbhall 157n, 171
Ó Longaigh, S. 119–22
O'Brien, Denis 123, 130–1
O'Brien, G. 1, 4, 128, 163, 194
O'Brien, Jane 92, 107, 173, 215
O'Brien, Leo 23n, 156, 163, 197–8, 227, 230n
O'Byrne, John 104–6, 108, 112, 161–3, 178n, 180n, 186, 187n
O'Connor, Edward 186, 232
O'Connor, Joseph 124, 127
O'Connor, Rory 9–10
O'Donnell, I. 1–2, 5–7, 23, 24n, 25n, 34n, 38n, 45n, 117, 181n, 246, 255
Offences Against the Person Act (1861) 219
Offences Against the State Act (1939) 119n
O'Friel, H.J. 90n, 147, 180n
O'Halpin, E. 7n
O'Higgins, Kevin 3, 9–10, 86n, 90, 131, 138n, 145–6, 154n, 206
Oireachtas 20, 175, 226, 261
O'Kelly, Sean T. 154, 174, 177–9
O'Leary, Con 106, 214
O'Leary, Hannah 96, 107, 214, 220, 230n, 233–7, 244
O'Leary, Patrick 214
O'Malley, Desmond 146, 256
O'Neill, Maurice 36, 116, 124
O'Neill, Patrick 172, 178
O'Neill, William 27n
oratory 166n
O'Reilly, G. 125
O'Reilly, Helen 218
O'Rourke, Joan 200
O'Rourke, Joseph 3n
O'Rourke, Thomas 103, 200, 231
Ossory
  Coadjutor Bishop of 172, 222
  Bishop of 173
O'Shaughnessy, Thomas 89, 104
O'Shea, Colm 28, 104, 117n, 133–7, 248–9
O'Shea, William 209n
O'Sullivan, D. 102n
O'Sullivan, E. 24n, 213, 241
O'Sullivan, Margaret 210
Our Lady's Home for Discharged Female Prisoners 27, 189, 202, 215, 233, 239–41, 243n
Overend, Andrew 97n, 104, 108
Owens, Kate 41, 156, 185, 190, 195, 236n
Oxford University Press 111

pacifism 5
Palacios, V.J. 49, 67
papal intervention 109, 156–7, 223, 243n, 245–6
papal nuncio 157n
parameters of inquiry 12–20
pardon 39n, 40, 44, 66–7, 77, 118, 128n, 219, 247n, 249–50
  posthumous 259–62

parliamentary exchange 16
parole 229
parole board 69, 229
paternalism 99, 192, 235
pathology 216
payment rates for executioners 54
penal servitude 133, 141, 167, 218, 223–7, 230, 235, 248, 261n
  for life 10, 23–4, 48, 70, 119, 125, 138n, 146, 168, 177, 205, 213–14, 219, 222, 224–7, 230n, 242, 251
Penal Servitude Acts (1853 to 1891) 226
penology 78, 84
Pentonville Prison 2
People (AG) v Hayes (1967) 23n
People (AG) v Heffernan (1951) 164n
personal intervention 111
petitions 13, 35, 55, 63, 75, 92, 112, 150, 181, 227n
  antecedents 207–9
  Council of Europe 223
  defaced 216n
  to government 189n
  jury 54n, 89–90
  for mercy 70, 91, 155
  papal 156–7
  public 140, 148–9, 173–4
  solicitor 216
  TDs 230
  victims' families 20n, 152, 252
  war record references 200, 204
Pierrepoint, Albert 37, 73, 93n, 139, 155, 172, 252–6
Pierrepoint, Thomas 1n, 5n, 38, 156, 174, 222n, 255
Pim, Jonathan 104, 108, 111n, 210n
pinioning and masking 16
Plant, George 36, 124–5, 129–30, 173
plea *ad misericordiam* 99
poisoning 32, 34, 110, 168n, 202, 213, 217
poitín 202, 205
police and justice system 88
  police officers 7n
  police reports 63
political murder 17, 116, 123, 184, 188, 239
political prisoners 113–14, 116, 127, 129
political violence 2, 7n, 141
Pope John Paul II 246
Portlaoise Prison 124–5, 129, 136, 168, 211n, 212, 239
possession of incriminating documents 246n
posthumous pardon 259–62
  see also pardon
post-prison destinations 235
Potter, H. 37n
prayer 39n, 131, 184, 216, 235
precedent 99
pregnancy 93, 172, 187, 191–2, 196, 219
  see also abortion; infanticide; miscarriage
preparation for execution 36–7
prerogative 49–53, 105, 147, 247
  of mercy 1, 44, 65n, 69, 71, 98, 126, 160, 162, 186–7
Presbyterianism 223
President of Ireland 12n, 26n, 51, 93n, 107, 108n, 154, 163, 177–8, 227
President of the Executive Council 3, 11–12, 144, 208
Prevention of Crimes Act (1871) 226
Pringle, Peter 28, 132–5, 176n, 249n
prison chaplain 37n, 39, 166n, 201, 231, 253
prison governor 13n, 16, 37n, 93, 122n, 198n, 201–2, 211–12, 227n, 252
prison medical officer 38, 212, 231, 253
Prison Rules (2007) 225n
prison service 21n
prisoner purchases 55
prisoner of war 138n
private virtue, *see* clemency
Probation of Offenders Act (1907) 25, 240
procedural fairness 75n
property
  ownership 88, 92n
  requirement 91n

proportionality 47, 76, 80, 140
prostitution 109, 156, 222–3
Protestantism 173, 187n, 236
prudence 73
psychiatric disorder 191n, 203
  see also mental illness
psychological stress 213
psychopathic tendencies 254
psychosurgery 238
public confidence 73
  see also clemency
public debate 16
public duty 50
public opinion
  clemency 64, 110
  government 147–50
  hypocritical nature of 188
public safety 3, 121n
pulmonary TB 231

Quaid, James 133
Quakers 111
'quartering' 95n
Quille, Michael 123
Quinn, Máire Geoghegan 93n
Quinn, Thomas 261n

Rainbolt, G. 42n
rape 181n, 188, 199, 201
rapidity 35–9
Rattigan, C. 26, 242
recidivism 219, 225n
record keeping 16
recorded murder 6, 20,
reduction of sentence 180
Registry of Deaths (Mountjoy Prison) 122n
regret of being clement 128
rehabilitation 76, 231, 254
re-imprisonment 198, 248n
release 136, 166n, 224–51
  capital murder 247–51
  embarrassing oversights 242–3
  on licence 17
  moral differences 239–42
  procedures 226–9
  rationale 243–51
  statecraft 246–7
  temporary 229
  time 229–34
  whither 234–43
Release of Prisoners Commission 249n, 250n
religion 35
  religious celebrations 17
  see also Catholic Church/Catholicism; clerical intervention; convents for women; papal intervention; Protestantism
remand in custody 232n
remission 40, 48, 68, 118, 137, 224–7, 229n, 245, 248–9
  of fines 181
  of prison sentences 181
repatriation 249n
repeat offenders 189–93
reportage 16
reprieve 40, 155, 157n, 163, 172–6, 194, 242
reprisal attack 209
Republic of Ireland Act (1948) 247
republican convictions 115
research focus 15–17
respite 90n
retrial 28, 103, 164, 185, 232n, 254n
retributivism 79n, 59–60, 219–20
  retributive dilemma 58–61
  theory of punishment 65
revocation 226–7
revolutionary period 2–12, 141, 208
Reynolds, Michael 254
Rhodesia 255
rider attachment 96–8, 106–7
River Suck 187
River Tolka 186
robbery 71, 136n, 137n, 258
Roberts, H.R.T. 80
Robinson, Mary 93n
Roche, Stephen 72n, 123, 132, 147, 190n, 226n, 233n
Rogers, Peter 133, 249
Rolph, C.H. 52n
Royal Commission on Capital Punishment 37n, 73n, 93n, 97, 103n, 213, 221n
Royal Irish Constabulary (RIC) 11, 200

Royal Munster Fusiliers 209
Royal Navy 117
royal prerogative 52, 72n
Royal Ulster Constabulary (RUC) 131
rule of law 71
Russell, Christina 194, 224n, 245
Ruttledge, Patrick J. 11, 111n, 146, 151–2, 179, 216n
Ryan, John 156, 163, 205

Sabotage Campaign (S Plan) 119, 128
sacrifice 207–8
  see also blood sacrifice
St Kevin's Hospital, Dublin 238–9
Salvation Army 236, 242
sanity 41
  see also insanity; legal sanity
Saoirse–Irish Freedom 119n
Saor Éire 137n
Sarat, A. 49, 143
schizophrenia 203
Seal, L. 256n
Seanad Éireann 93
  debates 195n, 242n
Sebba, L. 62, 72, 77
Second World War 8, 128
  see also Emergency, the (1939–1945)
secularism 42n, 46–8
self-harm 197
sentenced to death: by non-jury court 269–70 (App III)
separation of powers 18, 112, 165, 180
  belt of the crozier 172–7
  bishop's palace 174–7
  blurring of 159–81
  breach of 68, 169
  entreaties from His Excellency 177–80
  interfering judges 160–71
  judges expediting release 180–1
  leaks 174–7
  lineage 174–7
serial killers 190, 195
'seventy-seven executions, the' 3, 153
severity (onerousness of sanction) 36
  see also deterrence theory
sex 217n, 218
  assault 199
  jealousy and 185, 195–203
  offences 24
  see also rape
Sex Disqualification (Removal) Act (1919) 91n
shared values 207–8
Sheehy-Skeffington, Hanna 92
sheriff's office 16, 222n
shooting 32, 34, 120
  death by 5, 116, 122, 164
  intent to murder 167
  murder by 204, 206, 209, 211–12
  of police officers 123
  shotgun crimes 163–6
Sigler, M. 195
Sinn Féin 174,
Sisters of Charity 191, 202, 233–4, 236n, 239
Sisters of Charity of St Vincent De Paul 189, 239, 244
Sisters of Our Lady of Charity of Refuge 239
Smart, A. 61, 78–9
Smith, A.T.H. 44
Smith, G.T. 5
Smith, James 246
Smyth, Dermot 178n
social class 213
social inadequacy 197
social science 143
social solidarity 77
Society for the Abolition of the Death Penalty 13
Society of St Vincent de Paul 239n
socioeconomic status 158
softening the verdict: trends 99–102
soldier's death 116, 133, 177
solitary confinement 125
Somerville, Henry Boyle Townshend 117
Somerville, Mary 93n, 163n, 186–7, 227, 235
sources 19–20
special branch 131, 256n
Special Criminal Court 105n, 228, 248, 250, 258

Special Powers Tribunal 117–20
see also extraordinary courts
stabbing 32, 34
statecraft 246–7
see also release
state-sanctioned death 2, 4, 12n
avoidance of 139–41
see also capital murder
Statistical and Social Inquiry Society of Ireland 111
Statman, D. 45n, 59
Steiker, C.S. 81
Stevenson, Robert 96, 99, 109, 145, 156–7, 179, 184, 222–3
stigma of confinement 234n
Stokes, John 197
Strange, C. 54, 147, 182–3
strangulation 37, 156, 192–3, 203, 222
suicide 21–2, 24, 26n, 37n, 168n, 239n
Sullivan, Deborah 96, 100n, 188, 226n, 232–3, 243n, 244
Sullivan, Timothy 104, 207
sunset clause 102
supererogation 41–2, 76–7
see also clemency
superstition 13n, 262
Supreme Court 20, 23, 36, 52n, 117, 122, 137, 175, 216, 229, 248, 258
Swanton, Kathleen 92
sympathy, lack of 166n

table of drops 95, 253n
taking down the body 37
Talbot, Michael 5n, 38, 86, 90, 106
Taoiseach, office of the 116n, 120, 144, 155, 165, 171, 172n, 177–9, 256
Tasioulas, J. 75n
TD (Teachta Dála; Member of Parliament) 149, 166n, 230
Independent TDs 153n
Teevan, Thomas 104, 171
temporary release 229
'terror court' 120–5, 128
hunger strike 124–5
see also extraordinary courts
terrorism 46, 122, 230n
thanatocracy 7–8
The Merchant of Venice 42n
The People (Attorney General) v Shan Mohangi (1964) 254n
theft 24, 167, 248n
theory of punishment 78–9
Thompson, Edith 37n
Thompson, J.G. 86n
Tierney, James 156, 163n, 184, 210–11
time in custody 35, 47, 117, 125, 229, 231
Toal, Gerard 106
translation 101
see also language
transportation of the body 38
Traynor, Oscar 11, 146, 200, 229n
treason 121n
trespass 248n
trial by jury (convicted of murder)
hanged 267–8 (App II)
spared 263–5 (App I)
Trial of Lunatics Act (1883) 23
tributes 43
Trinity College Dublin 95
Troubles, The *see* Northern Ireland

unanimity requirement 102n
unequal treatment 82
unfairness 82
unfettered *see* clemency
unfit to plead 22–3, 56, 88, 238, 254n
United Irishmen rebellion (1798) 129
United Kingdom
abolition of hanging 255
archives 256
British emigration 234
commutation 142–3, 147
death penalty debate 12–13
United States Constitution 81, 151
unlawful detention 125
unlawful imprisonment 121n
unlawful organizations 129, 246n

unwanted children
  burden of 185–96
  reform 193–6
  repeat offenders 189–93
  response 187–9
urban/rural divide 101
utilitarianism 58, 63, 79n
  utilitarian dilemma 61–3

Vatican, the 156–7, 223, 245
  see also papal intervention; Pope John Paul II
Vaughan, W.E. 5, 13, 34n, 229
vengeance 8, 55, 210
Vickers, Thomas 210
victims' families 20n, 69, 152, 252
violence 129, 157n, 168
  decline in 4–9
  violent crime 23
  violent death 5n, 24
volunteers 35–6

'walk to the gallows' 38
Walker, N. 59, 78, 84
Wall, William 19, 99, 107, 109n, 132, 160, 166–71, 221, 231, 237–9
Walsh, Annie (sentence commuted) 30–1, 41, 99, 101, 202, 224, 236, 245
Walsh, Annie (sentence executed) 5, 7, 30–1, 38–9, 64, 90, 106, 108, 156, 220
Walsh, Daniel 202
Walsh, Michael 44n, 47, 124–7, 130, 140, 173, 247n
War of Independence (1919–21) 2–4, 8, 11, 127, 198, 200
War Office, London 208
Ward, Andrew 147
Webb v Ireland (1988) 52n
Weber, M. 54
weighing and measuring 16
weighing the evidence
  procedures 89–91
Weihofen, H. 39n
Whelan, Máire 93n
Whelan, Norah 161
Whelehan, N. 7n
White, Harry 131, 246
White, Patrick 198
White, Thomas 209n
widow's pension 252
Willis, William 95n
women jurors 92
  see also gender
work regime 234
  see also convents for women; Magdalen Asylums
writing to the executioner 16
wrongful conviction 261
  see also posthumous pardon
Wyndham, George 102n

Yassin, Brenda 13n
yoga, practice of 125n

The manufacturer's authorised representative in the EU for product safety is Oxford University Press España S.A. of el Parque Empresarial San Fernando de Henares, Avenida de Castilla, 2 – 28830 Madrid (www.oup.es/en or product.safety@oup.com). OUP España S.A. also acts as importer into Spain of products made by the manufacturer.

www.ingramcontent.com/pod-product-compliance
Lightning Source LLC
LaVergne TN
LVHW011511200926
848484LV00001B/11
* 9 7 8 0 1 9 8 7 9 8 4 7 7 *